Crucial Elements of Police Firearms Training

BRIAN R. JOHNSON

43-08 162nd Street • Flushing, NY 11358
www.LooseleafLaw.com • 800-647-5547

Library of Congress Cataloging in Publication Data

Johnson, Brian R.
 Crucial elements of police firearms training / Brian R. Johnson.
      p. cm.
 Includes index.
 ISBN-13: 978-1-932777-30-7 (pbk.)
 ISBN-10: 1-932777-30-X (pbk.)
 1. Police training. 2. Firearms--Use in crime prevention--Study and teaching. 3. Police--Equipment and supplies. 4. Firearms. I. Title.
 HV7923.J64 2007
 363.2'32--dc22

                                                              2007011896

1st Printing - 2008
2nd Printing - 2009

Cover design by *Sans Serif, Inc.,* Saline Michigan

To some of the most committed and knowledgeable firearms instructors I have had the pleasure to work with over the years.

Deputy Chief Steve Dyke, Walker Police Department
Off. Dan Martinek, Walker Police Department
Off. Brad Williams, Walker Police Department
Off. Butch Redzinski, Walker Police Department
Special Agent Brian Luettke, ATF
John VanDyke, Kentwood Police Department
Sgt. Mike Geerlings, Kentwood Police Department
Sgt. Chris Yonkers, Barry County Sheriff's Department
Dep. Rob Horrmann, Barry County Sheriff's Department
Sgt. Tom Raymond, Kent County Sheriff's Department
Sgt. Mark Reminga, Kent County Sheriff's Department
Off. David Thompson III, Wyoming Police Department

B   rian Johnson is currently a Professor in Criminal Justice at Grand Valley State University, Grand Rapids, Michigan where he teaches police-related courses. His prior experiences include serving 6 years as the Assistant Director and 2 years as Interim Director of a regional police academy in the state of Michigan, where he was the use of force coordinator and taught Firearms, Defensive Tactics, and other skills to both pre and in-service police recruits. He also worked as a police officer in the state of Wisconsin. Brian is a graduate of several shooting schools, has served as a Subject Matter Expert on state-level use of force committees, and has authored several articles in the field of law enforcement. Johnson holds a Ph.D., an MS in Criminal Justice, and an MLIR in Labor Relations from Michigan State University. He also has a BA in criminal justice from the University of Wisconsin. At the time of this publication, he has trained approximately 1000 different police recruits, officers, and security personnel in firearms.

TABLE OF CONTENTS

This book is based on my years of service to the law enforcement profession as a trainer and an academician. The materials covered in this book will provide police recruits, officers, and firearms enthusiasts a great deal of information on building basic firearms skills. It also provides the reader with tactics to survive and win a gunfight. Unlike other firearm's books out on the market, this book will take a different approach to firearms training. It will not concentrate on war stories or embellish the career of the writer. It will provide useful, accurate, and detailed information on the legal, practical, and tactical components of using a firearm. In some parts, it will become quite detailed, while in other sections, it will refute some of the traditional methods associated with firearms training.

This book is broken into topical sections. The first section provides foundational-based materials related to the use of firearms. It begins by introducing the reader to the nature and extent of the use of force and firearms in the field of policing. This section of the book also provides an in-depth analysis of the laws associated with the use of force, particularly deadly force. Firearm's nomenclature is also reviewed in chapter three, while chapter four addresses firearms safety, a paramount concern for anyone who has contact with firearms.

The second part of this book examines the fundamentals of shooting. This section of the book provides the reader with an understanding of how the correct breathing, stance, grip, sight alignment, and trigger control all combine to create a stable shooting platform from which the shooter will be able to deliver accurate and controlled fire at the threat. The third section of the book, meanwhile, concentrates of winning a gunfight through better tactics. Put simply, gunfights are won through better skills and tactics than what the adversary has. Some of the issues covered in this section of the book include the use of the follow through, the draw, reloading techniques and clearing malfunctions. Special topics is the theme of the fourth section of this book. Chapters in this section will deal with off-duty carry, ballistics and shot/target analysis.

It has often been stated that a person cannot learn how to shoot by reading a book. This is true. Mastery of the movements and tactics are beyond the pages of this book. Mastery requires perfect practice on the part of the reader. It also requires a positive attitude and a winning mindset that never settles for a mediocre or average performance. In a nutshell, the term or belief "Good Enough" doesn't exist. The winning attitude requires going out on the range and settling for nothing but the best.

What this book will do is simple. It will improve the reader's decision-making skills, performance, and overall expertise in the field of firearms by increasing their knowledge in how to properly build firearm's skills and tactics. The reader must always remember the simple fact that knowledge is power. When combined with perfect practice and performance, this knowledge will serve to transform the officer into an excellent shooter.

The materials presented in this book are just a way. It is not the way. There are many techniques, tactics and books out on the market. Some are good while some are downright bad. What this book presents to the reader are those tactics and techniques that are academically sound, accepted, and used by practitioners. In fact, the information contained in this book originated from my classroom lesson plans and range outlines that have been used for several years to successfully train police recruits. In short, the information in this book works. It has served to build skills and win gunfights out on the streets.

A list of persons too long in length has assisted me in some manner in writing this book. Special appreciation goes to Jonathan White, Terry Fisk, and Cindy Breen from Grand Valley State University, George Zeeff and Gary Ebels from Grand Rapids Community College, and Mary Loughrey, Maria Felten and the staff at Looseleaf Law. I would also like to recognize all of my students -- the future of law enforcement. The profession is in good hands.

Be Safe,

Brian Johnson

Chapter 1

INTRODUCTION

T his is a book about winning a gunfight. The reader of this book must understand one simple fact. In a gunfight the goal is to stop the threat before the threat stops you or another person that you have a duty to protect. A gunfight is not like what you see on the television or in the movies. In some cases, it will unfortunately never be like anything that a police officer has adequately trained for. Consider, for example, this quote from Ed Morales, an FBI agent who survived and won the FBI's worst shoot-out to date that occurred in southern Miami on the morning of April 11, 1986.

> ....Keep in mind that the paper targets that you've been practicing on is no longer paper. The most dangerous animal in the world is an intelligent, experienced, well-armed adversary who is trying to avoid arrest or simply trying to kill you. That human target is not going to stand up straight like a paper target and let you shoot it. He's going to look for cover, move, maneuver, and shoot back. Having shots fired at you has an adverse impact on your ability to make good shot placement.... (Anderson, 1996, p. 123).

Tragically, two of Morales' fellow FBI agents did not survive the gunfight. Only one of the eight agents involved came out of it uninjured. The two suspects were killed. This entire gunfight lasted a little over four minutes. During this time period, the suspects fired 49 rounds while the agents fired 70 more. A more recent incident that gained national attention was the Amadou Diallo shooting that occurred in New York City on February 4, 1999. In a four to five second period, 41 rounds were fired by four different police officers who shot and killed Diallo. In the dark the officers thought Diallo had pointed a small caliber black handgun at them. However, it was simply his wallet that he pointed at the officers (Messina, 2000).

The above example reveals that a gunfight is a dynamic event that is won or lost in seconds. It is not a static event where the suspect is standing still. Officers need to move, shoot and gather information all at the same time. They need to multitask. They need to give verbal commands, communicate with other officers, look for cover and concealment and shoot while moving. Since this is a dynamic event, police officers need to develop those skills geared toward winning a gunfight in a dynamic perspective. You do not want to be that person that is shot. At the same time, it is also your responsibility as a police officer to protect your fellow officers and the public from such threats.

The Nature & Extent of Force in Police Work

BOX 1-1
THE NATURE & EXTENT OF FORCE

Type of force	Frequency of Use
Threats & Shouts	4 percent
Pursuit of a fleeing suspect	7 percent
Handcuff/restrain suspect	77 percent
Weaponless tactic	17 percent
Threaten to use weapon	3.7 percent
Used weapon	2 percent

Garner, J., Buchanan, J., Schade, J., & J. Hepburn. (November, 1996).
Understanding the use of force by and against the police.

The International Association of Chiefs of Police (IACP) study: *Police Use of Force in America* (2001) defines force as "that amount of effort required by police to compel compliance from an unwilling subject" (p.1). Force can range from simply an officer's presence that could compel an individual to do something that they would not have otherwise done. In other cases, it may be a verbal command, using the hands to control a suspect, or a combination of force-related activities. In the most extreme (and relatively rare) instances, it will involve the use of a firearm and deadly force to stop the threat.

Force is always something that a police officer will use to some degree over the course of their daily activities and their career. Research on the frequency of the use of force by the police in suspect encounters range from 0.8% to 58.1% (Garner, Maxwell & Heraux, 2002). In the IACP's study of force incidents, of the 1787 reported cases of physical force, only 0.167% or three cases resulted in the death of the suspect.

Garner et al. (1996) also conducted research on the use of force by Phoenix, Arizona police officers. The nature and frequency of these 1,777 force encounters are shown in Box 1-1. The researchers concluded that the use of force was infrequent and when used, it was at the lower end of the force continuum (such as verbal control of the suspect). Alpert and Dunham's (1999) research on the use of force in Eugene and Springfield,

Oregon in 1995 that analyzed 546 incidents also concluded that the most common types of force used were not serious or extreme. They included verbal commands (96%), handcuffing (94%), and searches (95%). As with the IACP study, the use of a firearm to control a situation was a relatively rare incident, making up a total of only six incidents or a little over one percent of all cases in the study.

Deadly Force Encounters

Research by the federal government on police-related shootings from 1976 to 1998 provides an overview of the use of deadly force by police officers in the entire United States. Data shows that on average there were 373 lawful police-related shootings per year, averaging about 2 persons per one million over the age of 13, while those that were lawfully killed under the age of 13 was about 1 person per one million residents. According to national data, from 1976 to 1998 (Brown & Langan, 2001):

- About 98 % of those killed by police were male;
- The majority killed (55%) were white;
- In about 65% of the cases, the officer and felons were the same race;
- Most of the suspects killed were in their teens or older; and,
- Felons in their twenties accounted for the majority of offenders who were killed.

A twenty-year review of deadly force incidents by Brubaker (2002) of 80 police-related shootings in the state of Minnesota from 1981 to 2000 found the following:

- The majority of shootings involved uniformed patrol officers.
- The average experience level of police officers involved in shootings was just under 10 years.
- The age of those killed ranged from 13 to 65. The average age of the suspect was 32.8 years of age.
- In the majority of incidents police officers were confronted primarily with firearms (handguns and long guns) while 20 more suspects had some type of edged weapon. Other weapons included vehicles.
- Just over 50% involved one officer firing their weapon. The remainder involved two or more officers.
- The majority of officers involved in shootings reported that they were tactically prepared. However, the majority of officers also reported that they were not prepared for the psychological impact the shooting had on them and their families.

Deadly Force Assaults Against Officers

According to national data, from 1976 to 1998, 1,820 police officers were murdered, averaging 79 officers per year or an average of 1 officer murdered for every 6,500 officers. The risk of a police officer being murdered has dropped since the 1970's. In 1978 the rate was 1 per 4,000; in 1988 it was 1 in 6,000, and in 1998, the rate was 1 in 11,000 officers. This drop can be attributed to several factors including better training, better police practices, and wearing body armor.

Of those 1,820 officers killed between 1976 and 1998:

- 39% were in arrest situations
- 16% were on disturbance calls
- 14% were investigating suspicious persons or circumstances
- 14% were enforcing traffic laws
- 11% were in ambush situations
- 6% were in other situations

Murdered officers also had an average of 9 years of service. Killers meanwhile, were predominately male (97%), and 54% were between the ages of 18-30 (Brown & Langan, 2001).

In another study that examined officers killed from 1993 to 2002 in the U.S., the FBI found that most police officers are killed by firearms, with handguns as the primary type of firearm used. Box 1-2 also shows that police officers are also in danger of attacks from other types of weapons, including longarms, knives, and other personal weapons. Box 1-2 also breaks down officers killed by region. While not controlling for population trends, the main point of this data is that officers are at risk regardless of where they work.

BOX 1-2
LAW ENFORCEMENT OFFICERS FELONIOUSLY KILLED
Region by Type of Weapon, 1991 – 2000

Type of Weapon	Total	Northeast	Midwest	South	West	U.S. Territories
Total	**636**	**63**	**116**	**278**	**130**	**49**
Handgun	443	48	80	187	85	43
Rifle	112	7	20	48	32	5
Shotgun	36	3	6	20	7	0
Total Firearms	**591**	**58**	**106**	**255**	**124**	**48**
Knife or cutting instrument	8	2	2	2	2	0
Bomb	9	0	0	9	0	0
Personal Weapons	3	0	0	1	2	0
Other	25	3	8	11	2	1

Law Enforcement Officers Killed and Assaulted (2002). This table does not include the 72 law enforcement officers killed in the World Trade Center Attack

The distance from the offender to police officer are shown in Box 1-3. The data in this table shows that the majority of police officers were killed in encounters in distances less than 5 feet. In addition, the data also shows that the vast majority of police officers from 1993 to 2002 were killed in relatively short distances of less than 20 feet. This table shows that *a gunfight is a close combat situation.*

BOX 1-3
LAW ENFORCEMENT OFFICERS FELONIOUSLY KILLED BY FIREARMS
Distance Between Victim Officer and Offender, 1993 – 2002

Distance in Feet	Total	Cum. Percent
Total	**591**	---
0-5	296	50.1
6-10	124	66.5
11-20	64	81.9
21-50	50	90.3
Over 50	47	98.3
Not Reported	10	100.0

Law Enforcement Officers Killed and Assaulted (2002). This table does not include the 72 law enforcement officers killed in the World Trade Center Attack

The FBI also maintains statistics on the types of calls that officers were responding to when they were attacked and killed. Of the 636 officers killed from 1993 to 2003:

- 32.2% were in arrest situations
- 15.4% were on disturbance calls
- 16.5% were investigating suspicious persons/circumstances
- 15.3% involved traffic stops or pursuits
- 15.1% were in ambush situations
  - 9.7% were unprovoked attacks
  - 5.3% were premeditated
- 2.4% occurred when dealing with mentally deranged suspects
- 3.1% involved handling, transporting, and the custody of prisoners

Box 1-4 provides additional information regarding the officer's response to the deadly force attack. In the majority of incidents, police officers were murdered without using or attempting to use their firearms to stop the threat. The data also shows that in less than 25% of the incidents the police used their firearm against the offender. In another 16% of the cases, police officers attempted to use their firearm to defend themselves and stop the threat, even though the attacker later killed them.

BOX 1-4
LAW ENFORCEMENT OFFICERS FELONIOUSLY KILLED
USE OF WEAPON DURING INCIDENT
1993-2002

Distance in Feet	Total	Percent
Total	**636**	----
Fired Own Weapon	136	21.4
Attempted to Use Weapon	103	16.2
Did not Use or Attempt to Use Own Weapon	346	54.4
Not Reported	51	8.0

Law Enforcement Officers Killed and Assaulted (2002). This table does not include the 72 law enforcement officers killed in the World Trade Center Attack

What is not included in this table is that from 1993 to 2002, an average of five officers per year were killed by or with their own weapon. Additional research has also shown this disturbing but decreasing trend. In 1978, 15.1% were slain with their own weapon: In 1988 15% were, while in

1998, 9.8% of the officers murdered were killed with their own weapon (Brown & Langan, 2001).

A myth in policing is that an officer is only in danger during the evening and early morning hours. While the statistics show that an officer may be at a greater risk during the evening and early morning hours, the data in Box 1-5 shows that police officers are at risk at all times of the day or night. Police officers must assume that on any given day, regardless of the time, they are at risk of being attacked and killed.

BOX 1-5
LAW ENFORCEMENT OFFICERS FELONIOUSLY KILLED (N=636)
TIME OF DAY
1993-2002

Time	Total	Percent		Total	Percent
A.M.			**P.M.**		
12:01 - 2	77	12.1	12:01 - 2	51	8.0
2:01 - 4	46	7.2	2:01 - 4	53	8.3
4:01 – 6	29	4.6	4:01 – 6	48	7.5
6:01 - 8	24	3.8	6:01 - 8	48	7.5
8:01 - 10	46	7.2	8:01 - 10	92	14.5
10:01 - 12	39	6.1	10:01 - 12	80	12.6

Not reported = 3

Law Enforcement Officers Killed and Assaulted (2002). This table does not include the 72 law enforcement officers killed in the World Trade Center Attack

The Motives of Police Killers

Information collected from the killers of police officers provides insight into the mind of a killer. In their interviews of police killers, FBI researchers concluded that there is no single personality type of a police killer. This psychological assessment of 50 offenders concluded that an antisocial personality disorder (i.e. lack of remorse, a sense of entitlement, lack of conscience, feeling for others and disregard for social obligations) was the most common personality disorder of the killer, comprising 56% of the cases. While this type of personality would be expected to be involved in violent crimes, 23% of the offenders were diagnosed as having a dependent personality type that is associated with being docile, passive and submissive. The researchers concluded that at all times officers should exercise caution when dealing with any individual, regardless of their level of compliance and demeanor (Pinizzotto & Davis, 1992).

Other research has looked at the criminal histories of offenders. Self-reported criminal activities of individuals who seriously assaulted and/or killed police officers revealed that the suspect's criminal histories involved weapons offenses. Other commonly reported criminal activities included larceny-theft, drug law violations, assaults and robberies. These individuals also indicated that their weapon of choice was a firearm, while more than 50% of them also indicated that they were involved in a shooting incident (doing the shooting or being shot at) prior to the assault on the police officer. The majority of offenders also revealed that they were using drugs or alcohol at the time of the assault. They also revealed that possessing firearms was part of their lifestyle. They carried them while involved in criminal activities, traveling, socializing, at home, and at work (Pinizzotto, Davis & Miller, 1997). Basically, these offenders were never without a firearm.

Research has also examined the behavioral descriptors of police officers who were killed. Some of the statements from individuals who knew these officers well included that they were: friendly, well liked, easy going, and hard working. In the context of tactics, these same officers were described as conservative in their use of force. They used force only as a last resort. Slain officers were also described as not as tactically sound as they should have been. Slain officers especially did not follow safe practices regarding arrests, traffic stops, waiting for backup, and dealing with prisoners. Some examples included failing to call for backup, acting alone prior to the arrival of backup, failing to completely search suspects, not using handcuffs properly, and positioning their vehicles incorrectly on traffic stops. In fact, it was determined that only two percent of the officers killed in this study did not make procedural errors. The rest made mistakes that cost them their lives (Pinizzotto & Davis, 1992).

Perceptual Shorthand

An officer's actions that an offender exploits have been coined perceptual shorthand. Perceptual shorthand can be considered those messages that an officer sends or displays to a would-be offender. For example, an attacker will pay close attention to the actions of an officer before they attack. Basically the offender "sizes up" the officer's actions. For example, if a police officer is tactically unsound, the offender may pick up on these errors and exploit them. Not maintaining tactical distance (the reactionary gap) between the officer and offender, keeping the hands in the pockets (decreasing effective response time to the threat), approaching a vehicle incorrectly on a traffic stop, and being inattentive to their surroundings are just some examples of poor tactics. Perceptual shorthand also applies to the officer's appearance. An officer who is physically unkept (i.e. dirty uniform, unshaven) and perhaps overweight and out of shape will project a message to the would-be offender that they could be easily overwhelmed. Other cues an officer may project to an offender is through their body language. Body language can be considered to be an expression of a person's inner thoughts and feelings. This non-verbal language may constitute up to 70% of what is "said." It includes facial and eye movements, body and hand movements, gestures, and posture (Chambers, 1996). Displaying a passive demeanor through body language could provide the motivated offender "perceptual shorthand" information to attack.

At the same time, officers also engage in perceptual shorthand on "what behaviors they observe on the part of the individuals and what meaning or attributes they give to these behaviors" (Pinizzotto, Davis & Miller, 2000, p. 87). How an officer perceives the totality of the circumstances determines how they will act or respond. An officer may let their guard down and not think tactically in "normal" or minor traffic stops, drunk driving stops, or other calls that they have gone to repeatedly (Pinizzotto, Davis & Miller, 2000). In other cases, they may become complacent in transporting prisoners; and, when dealing with females or juveniles because of cultural stereotypes that these groups of individuals are not as dangerous as others.

Summary of Findings on Deadly Force

The following points can be summarized from the research conducted on police shootings and officers killed in the line of duty. First, the use of some level or type of force is common in law enforcement. However, the use of deadly force is relatively rare. Second, in deadly force encounters the majority of officers involved are patrol officers who have less than 10 years experience. The majority of deadly force encounters involved male suspects in their 20's. Data regarding officer's killed also provides insight that others can learn from. First, officers are exposed to the threat of an attack in a variety of situations or calls. In the majority of cases, the distance between the offender and the officer was less than 5 feet, while in several incidents officers were killed with their own firearm. The time of day is not a factor. Officers are at risk at any given time. Self-report studies of police killers have also shown that carrying a firearm is a way of life for offenders. Basically, the underlying theme of the above statistics is that police officers must be prepared for deadly force encounters at all times. This preparation begins and ends with proper training.

Action vs. Reaction Situations & Deadly Force

Consider the fact that police officers are always responding to incidents or situations. In the majority of situations, as outlined by the statistics in this chapter, police officers were responding to some type of incident or call. If they were not responding to a call per se, they were reacting to the actions of an offender. A great deal of traditional police work is reactive in nature. For example, when an officer receives a call, they are reacting to something that has already occurred. In deadly force situations, the same concepts can apply: the officer is reacting to someone else's actions. Unfortunately, action is always faster than reaction. This point can be seen in Box 1-4 that shows that in the majority of situations where officers were killed, they did not have a chance to fire their weapon at their killer because they were too slow in reacting to the threat.

Research has also supported this point that action is faster than reaction. Tobin and Fackler (2001b; 2001c) refer to the delay in time it takes in perceiving and then reacting to that specific offender's action as the reaction-response time. Based on their research involving police recruits, the authors determined that the average reaction-response time for a police recruit to react to and fire their weapon at the threat was 0.677 seconds (Tobin & Fackler, 2001a). This is simply due to the fact that the human body relies upon different types of sensory input in order to make decisions. The environment and threat are three-dimensional, where the brain has to use multiple sources of sensory information including the eyes, sounds and touch to make proper decisions.

In many cases, however, the brain must determine a solution and the body acts accordingly, without complete sensory information. This is because reconstructing these events from an ambiguous and inaccurate environment takes time. This is often the situation faced in a gunfight. Ernst and Bulthoff (2004) point out that knowledge is often required or important to interpret sensory signals. Without his knowledge, poor actions could result.

This reaction time can be further broken down into three different components. According to Green (2000) these components include:

1. Mental Processing Time;
2. Movement Time; and,
3. Device Response Time.

Mental processing time is the time it takes for a person to perceive and respond to a threat. This is further broken into three substages that include:

    a.   Sensation (interpreting the sensory input [i.e. is that a gun?]);
    b.   Perception (yes, that is a gun); and,
    c.   Response Selection (the time it takes to make the response and mentally program the action or movement).

The second stage of reaction time is *Movement Time* (i.e. drawing the weapon from the holster, pointing and firing it at the threat). As a general rule of thumb, the more complex the response, the longer it will take to complete the task.

Last is *Device Response Time*. This deals with how long it takes for the activity or device to act upon the person or target. A bullet, for example, may not immediately stop a person.

There are also several factors that affect reaction time. These are shown in Box 1-6. In addition to these issues, there are a variety of other environmental and personal factors that will slow a person's response time in reacting to an offender's action(s). These may include multiple threats, lighting conditions, the training the officer has received related to the issue, and the stress tolerance levels of the officer.

BOX 1-6
FACTORS THAT AFFECT REACTION TIME

State of Attention – Being too relaxed or too tense increases response time. Intermediate states of arousal are best for response times
Age – Reaction times increase from the late 20's and beyond
Direct Vision- The fastest response time is when a person is looking directly at the object (not peripherally)
Practice – The more practice, the faster and less errors in the action
Fatigue – Reaction time slows when a person is fatigued
Distractions – The more the distractions, the slower the response time
Warnings of Impending Stimuli – If a person is warned of an impending action, their response time is faster
Exercise – Physically fit subjects have faster response times

---

Becoming a Proficient Shooter

Becoming a proficient shooter takes time and commitment. While individuals often assume that the development of proficient firearms skills only requires the mastery of the movements, this is a narrow perspective on becoming a good shooter. There are three elements involved in being a good shooter. First, individuals must have the proper mindset or philosophy. Primarily, this philosophy rests on the premise that "we fight the way we train." Another underlying component of "we fight the way we train" is the practice. The philosophy of practice requires that individuals acknowledge and accept that practice is essential to becoming a proficient shooter. The second component of the proficient shooter is the development of their cognitive abilities related to decision making and shooting. Last, are the actual physical skills associated with firearms. It goes without saying that police officers must have the physical skills and abilities to adequately perform in their profession. Police work and the use of firearms are physical activities. Since it is a physical activity, individuals must be physically fit at all times to carry out their duties at peak performance. Professional athletes need to be physically fit to perform effectively and so do police officers. Like professional athletes, part of the physical training process requires the acquisition of skills through the building of muscle memory and economy of motion.

The Shooter's Philosophy - "We Fight the Way We Train"

There are many individuals who can shoot quite well in controlled settings. They can make the right decisions in academic and/or non-dynamic situations where they are free from stress and physical harm. The term "we fight the way we train" means that individuals will revert back to their training when confronted with any task that they encounter. In the context of the preceding sentence, perhaps these individuals are really unprepared for a gunfight.

The key to effective training in law enforcement is that it must be comprehensive in the context of recognized and accepted tactics in the field. Unfortunately, there are several examples of how poor training can lead to deadly consequences. Perhaps one of the best-known examples of training officers incorrectly, also known as contra-training, was the Newhall Incident that occurred on April 5, 1970 in California. In this encounter, four California Highway Patrolmen (CHP's) were killed by two armed assailants in a gunfight. One of the officers was found dead with spent cartridges in his pocket. An investigation on why the officer had placed spent brass in his pocket was traced back to his range training. Officers at that time were taught to place their spent brass in their pockets, instead of letting them fall to the ground. In a high stress situation, however, the officers reverted back to the way they were trained. This is just one example of contra-training, which is learning tactically unsound activities on the range or during practice. Under high stress situations, individuals will fight the way they train. They will inadvertently revert back to what they were taught, regardless of whether the tactics learned were good or bad.

Too many times, as a trainer, I have seen police recruits come into the academy that have trained themselves in the basics of marksmanship and firearms handling. While some are very good shooters as they can accurately place their rounds on the target, they have not taught themselves to think and shoot tactically. On the other hand, some police recruits have taught themselves to be bad shots. These bad habits have often accumulated through years of training themselves incorrectly. It has a negative impact on that person's ability to think and perform tactically under high stress situations. What is even worse and unfortunate is that there are police officers who have not been properly trained in firearms and who are not tactically proficient in their use. They have become victims of contra-training.

Fighting the way we are trained also deals with one's equipment worn and used. Consider the fact that football players wear their full gear when practicing. Why? For protection, and so they know how to perform with their gear that is required for their success in next week's game. The same applies to firearms training. Police officers should wear what they wear when on duty. This includes body armor to prevent any serious injury and so they can learn how to function wearing their body armor. If an officer shows up on the range wearing Bermuda shorts and a lightened gun belt because it's "too heavy" with all of their equipment on it, this is not a realistic training environment at all. Furthermore, take for example those police officers that show up for range training in the cooler winter months. In many cases, the first thing they do is take off their hat, jacket and gloves to qualify. A police officer will not have the opportunity to take off their hat, gloves and jacket in a gunfight. Train in a safe and realistic environment!

It is also the individual's responsibility to develop the mental and physical skills necessary to win and survive a gunfight. In several cases, officers become complacent and "expect" their agency to properly train them. While several agencies do provide very good training for their officers, this mindset of expecting someone else to care about your personal safety and well-being is wrong. Training for a deadly force encounter begins with the individual officer. It requires that officers develop those requisite skills that will make them an effective gunfighter through training, perhaps paid for out of their own pocket.

Practice, Practice , Practice

Practice alone does not lead to perfection. What leads to perfection is perfect practice. Practice requires repetition until the shooter can perfectly execute the movements and tactics associated with winning a gunfight. Like other sporting activities, the skills learned in firearms are perishable. If the activity is not engaged in on a regular and consistent basis, skill levels will erode. Just like any other physical activity, such as golf or baseball, a person may be "rusty" at the beginning of the season. Unlike these sports, however, police officers do not have the luxury of being rusty. Their life, their partner's, and the citizenry could be endangered because of "rusty" skills.

The above points show the need for training. What may surprise some individuals is that the most in-depth and concentrated training that they will receive during their police career is the training they received in the police academy. In many situations, a person cannot assume or readily rely upon their agency to train them. Agencies may lack the expertise, time, and/or finances to train an officer. What training they will receive, meanwhile could be best described as minimal. It may occur at best during their range qualification on a quarterly or bi-annual basis where they might receive some one-on-one training so they can pass the course of fire. In another common training situation, the officer is pulled off the road for a short period of time, they shoot their allocated amount of rounds in a non-dynamic setting, and then return to the street. However, little training actually occurs in both these situations. Instead they are perfunctory sessions designed as a liability shield for the agency. In those agencies that do train, meanwhile, instructors may be pressed for time, or the agency may not have enough training time allocated because of budgetary issues.

Perhaps the best example of how practice and training leads to better performance can be seen with who the best shooters are in a police agencies. In several police agencies, for example, the best shooters are the range instructors. Why? Because they have the opportunity to practice more than other officers in their agency. Likewise, ask any good shooter where they learned to shoot and you will soon see that these individuals dedicated some of their own personal time and money to improve their skill levels.

Cognitive Abilities

Individuals often do not realize that an essential component of becoming a proficient shooter is acquiring the cognitive or "thinking" skills associated with firearms. Before a person can proficiently use a firearm, they must learn about all of the components of firearms and the legal issues associated with the use of force. A person may have very good practical skills in using a firearm. However, they may not have an understanding of when they can legally use deadly force. The lack of understanding of laws and tactics could lead to an officer to make poor decisions and get involved in a "bad shoot" situation. For example, while they knew how to handle the gun, they did not know when they could use it. This is especially apparent in understanding case law related to the use of force. Lacking the legal knowledge of when an officer can use deadly force could actually lead to that officer being hesitant in a deadly force situation. Even though they had the legal authority to stop the threat by using deadly force, they did not. While they had the skills to do so, they lacked the intelligence to make a correct decision. In other instances, because an officer did not know what to do, their reaction time was also decreased, giving the offender the tactical edge. The lack of knowledge related to firearms and the use of force will decrease response times in threat situations.

A Winning Mindset

At the same time, police officers must also have a winning mindset. A police officer should never give up. The winning mindset is established by acquiring as much information as possible regarding the legal, tactical and ethical components of force. A winning mindset and the power from that mindset is enhanced through perfect practice. Through perfect practice, an officer's confidence levels, critical thinking, and problem solving skills will also increase. Because of their acquired knowledge, the officer will outsmart the adversary though their intelligence. They will also have developed the mental attitude to never give up.

Mental Imagery

In other situations, a shooter assumes that all that is needed to become a proficient shooter is mastery of movements. Mastery of movement is just one component to becoming a good shooter. Shooters must also develop mental imagery. Mental imagery is mentally practicing an event. The person watches, remembers, and recites an action or activity without actually physically engaging in that activity. Studies have found that through mental imagery, neural motor pathways to specific muscles become more stimulated in those "imagined" areas, while in other cases, heart rates actually increase when imagining a physical activity (such as leg exercises). This shows that mental rehearsing is part of the learning process as the brain "shapes" motor output, leading to improved motor perform-ance (Jeannerod & Decety, 1995).

Shooters must visualize what they will do. Training requires visuali-zation on what the person will do in a real event – not what is occurring on the range during normal training. Visualizing helps maintain intensity in a low-stress training environment. It increases the level of stress and anxiety that a person experiences. In "normal" training, the motivated officer will not train in the context that it is simply "training." Instead, they will treat it as an actual event, visualizing the entire event from start to finish. Even if the actual training is static and not dynamic, the shooter is nevertheless psychologically constructing a dynamic and real event in their mind.

Part of mental imagery is maintaining a mental mindset. In any athletic event the person challenges the body as well as the mind. Mental break-downs and inattentiveness could cost points in any type of game. In a gunfight, a mental breakdown could lead to severe problems for the police officer. Since we fight the way we train, this means that shooters on the range must stay attentive at all times, and treat the training as serious. The mental mindset comes from within a person. They cannot be forced to think and concentrate. Personal dedication and motivation commits them to maintain a mental mindset, focusing on the task at hand.

The Physical Aspects - Muscle Memory

Shooting any type of firearm, especially under stressful combat condi-tions, requires the coordination of many muscles and the enactment of complex muscle movements to carry out a specific movement. Through perfect practice and repetition, shooters will soon find themselves com-fortable in going through the motions, doing the same exact movements every time. When a person reaches this stage, they have developed muscle memory.

Muscle memory is basically training the body to act in a reflective manner. Over time and through perfect practice, shooting will become instinctual. Shooters will be able to react and deliver rounds downrange without thinking of all of the minute processes involved. It will become effortless where actions will no longer be executed on a conscious level. The shooter will not realize what they have done until after the fact. The actions taken will be unconscious, but yet thorough, accurate, and controlled. For example, a proficient shooter's actions will look effortless and smooth. They are "in the zone" or "groove" where it appears that they are extremely focused. They are reacting without thinking, and perhaps when they are done shooting, they will not be able to explain their actions in detail to their coaches or fellow officers.

Training specific muscles to function in a way that ensures a smooth, automatic performance is necessary to master the use of the firearm. Muscle memory does not develop rapidly. In fact, it could take thousands of perfect repetitions. Nevertheless, developing muscle memory is the key to becoming an effective combat shooter. Muscle memory will lead to the shooter performing the same movements under high-stress situations. Consider, for example, a former student who was involved in a gunfight. In this particular incident, the deputy was in pursuit of a suspect vehicle whose occupants were involved in a series of bank robberies. The vehicle suddenly stopped, and the two suspects leapt out of the vehicle and charged the deputy's vehicle, shooting at the deputy with a rifle and handgun. While instinctively shooting back at the suspects, the deputy's firearm jammed. He did a tack-rack-assess (that he learned in the academy) and immediately reengaged the suspects who were later apprehended. During this gunfight the deputy was shot three times – in the hand, neck and thigh. Recovering from his wounds the deputy told the author that he never even realized that he did a tap-rack drill during the gunfight: It became an instinctive response to a malfunction. In this case muscle memory perhaps saved his life, as the suspects were never able to get close enough to his squad car because he continued to return fire.

Economy of Motion

Economy of motion and muscle memory are two interrelated, but independent concepts. Muscle memory deals with "training" the body to move in a certain manner. Economy of motion is minimizing body movements and reducing unnecessary and counterproductive muscle movements that take time and exert energy. Economy of motion basically means that a person is not using any more or less movements than what is absolutely required to successfully complete that movement. Instead of a series of sloppy and unnecessary movements, through economy of motion, the movements are synchronized, smooth and precise.

There are several benefits to economy of motion. They include:

- The reduction and/or prevention of fatigue and exhaustion — economy of motion limits the number of muscles that are being used, while also limiting the movement of those muscles that are being used.
- Increases Speed — It avoids erroneous angles and moves the body with the least amount of effort in the shortest possible time. Economy of motion promotes continuity, flow, and rhythm that will also lead to increased speed. By concentrating on economy of motion and muscle memory, a person will soon see that their reaction times are faster in responding to a threat.
- Combination techniques are the most prevalent area where economy of motion is useful. By restricting movement only to essential motions, techniques become faster and more fluid, while not wasting vital energy at times when the shooter may need every bit of energy s/he can acquire.
- It is the natural execution of a specific technique.
- It uses movements that follow direct angles and paths to further conserve one's movements.

To successfully win and survive in a gunfight, shooters need to move efficiently and effectively. This means that they must always move in a coordinated effort. Economy of motion relies upon muscle memory. As this book will point out, under stressful conditions a person needs to rely upon reflexive actions. Using reflective actions, the shooter does not have time to think about what they are going to do - they simply do it. This is one of the keys to tactical shooting - to instinctively react and shoot when the situation warrants the use of this type and level of force.

Conclusion

Force, as defined by the IACP is "that amount of effort required by police to compel compliance from an unwilling subject." (p.1). In the course of a police officer's duties, some level of forced is always used, ranging from their presence to deadly force. As this chapter has shown, the use of deadly force is a relatively uncommon event. Current statistics on deadly force encounters show that on average there were 373 police shootings per year between 1976 and 1998. The research shows that the majority of deadly force situations involved male suspects in their twenties who were armed with firearms. The data also shows that the majority of deadly force encounters are at close distances.

The research on officers killed in the line of duty was another topic in this chapter. According to national data an average of 79 officers per year are killed. The majority of these officers were killed by firearms in arrest or disturbance calls at distances of less than 10 feet in the late evening and early morning hours. Some of the reasons why these officers were killed vary. Their deaths could be attributed to perceptual shorthand, where through their actions or inactions, the offender exploited the officer's vulnerabilities. Other deaths, meanwhile, could be attributed to the fact that the officer did not have time to react to the actions of the offender in a timely manner.

This chapter also examined the three key points in becoming a proficient shooter. First, individuals must have the proper mindset. A proper mindset should be based in the context of "we fight the way we train". Using accepted and proven tactics in the field, combined with perfect practice and the correct equipment, proficiency can be achieved. Besides perfect practice, shooters must also expand their cognitive domain. Understanding firearms-related laws, the legalities of using force is critical. Additionally, in-depth knowledge of the functions and types of firearms, in combination with incorporating mental imagery when training, is crucial to success. This chapter has also pointed out that one of the most important aspects of becoming a proficient shooter is developing one's physical abilities. In this context, the body must be taught to act in a reflexive manner. This is achieved through perfect practice that requires repetition and economizing every move to ensure that each movement is synchronized, smooth and precise.

References

Alpert, G.P. & Dunham, R.G. (October, 1999). The force factor: Measuring and assessing police use of force and suspect resistance (pp. 25-44). In: Travis, J & Chaiken, J.M. (October, 1999). Use of force by police: Overview of national and local data: Washington, D.C.: National Institute of Justice.

Anderson, J. & Marsh, C. (1999). The Newhall incident: America's worst uniformed cop massacre. Clovis, CA: Quill Driver Books.

Anderson, W.F. (1996). Forensic Analysis of the April 11, 1986, FBI Firefight. W. French Anderson, M.D.

Brown, J.M. & Langan, P.A. (2001). Police and homicide: Justifiable homicide by police, police officers murdered by felons. Washington D.C.: U.S. Department of Justice.

Brubaker, L.C. (April, 2002). Deadly force: A 20-yesr study of fatal encounters. FBI law enforcement bulletin, 71(4), 6-13.

Chambers, D. (Feb/Mar, 1996). Police-defendants: Surviving a civil suit. FBI law enforcement bulletin, 65(2/3), 34-39.

Ernst, M.O. & Bulthof, H.H. (April, 2004). Merging the sense into a robust percept. Trends in cognitive science, 8(2), 162-169.

Garner, J.H.; Maxwell, C.D. & Heraux, C.G. (December, 2002). Characteristics associated with the prevalence and severity of force used by the police. Justice quarterly, 19(4), 705-746.

Garner, J., Buchanan, J., Schade, J., & J. Hepburn. (November, 1996). Understanding the use of force by and against the police. Washington, D.C.: National Institute of Justice.

Green, M. (2000). "How long does it take to stop?" Methodological analysis of driver perception-brake times. Transportation human factors, 2(3), 195-216.

Jeannerod, M. & Decety, J. (1995). Mental motor imagery: A window into the representational stages action. Current opinion in neurobiology, 5, 727-732.

Law enforcement officers killed and assaulted, 2002. Washington, D.C. Federal Bureau of Investigation.

Messina, P. (July-August, 2000). Dissecting the Diallo shooting: Four seconds to Hell. Law enforcement trainer.

Pinnizzotto, A.J. & Davis, E.F. (September, 1992). Killed in the line of duty: A study of selected felonious killings of law enforcement officers. Washington, D.C. Federal Bureau of Investigation.

Pinnizzotto, A.J.; Davis, E.F. & C.E. Miller III (October, 1997). In the line of fire: A study of selected felonious assaults on law enforcement officers. Washington, D.C. Federal Bureau of Investigation.

Pinnizzotto, A.J.; Davis, E.F. & C.E. Miller (July, 2000). Officers' perceptual shorthand. FBI law enforcement journal, 69(7), 86-89.

Police Use of Force in America (2001). Washington D.C.: International Association of Chiefs of Police.

Tobin, E.J. & Fackler, M.L. (Fall, 2001a). Officer reaction-response times in firing a handgun. Wound ballistic review, 3(1), 6-9.

Tobin, E.J. & Fackler, M.L. (Fall, 2001b). Officer decision time in firing a handgun. Wound ballistic review, 5(2), 8-10..

Tobin, E.J. & Fackler, M.L. (Fall, 2001c). Officer reaction-response time delay at the end of a shot series. Wound ballistic review, 5(2), 11-12.

T here is essentially no profession other than law enforcement (besides an executioner's assistant or related field in Corrections) in the United States where a civilian has the legal right to take another's life. When considering deadly force in this perspective, the use of force is an immense responsibility for law enforcement officers to handle. It requires in-depth knowledge of the use of force that can be divided into three primary areas. They include the tactical, moral, and legal responsibilities of force and deadly force.

Consider first, the officer's tactical responsibility. In order to possibly avoid violent confrontations and keep force at its lowest possible level, police officers must be tactically sound in all of their activities at all times (preceding chapters will cover this issue in-depth). In some cases, however, a police officer could actually create a situation that would warrant the use of deadly force. An example of an inadvertent or unintentional escalation of the use of deadly force would be where the officer is tactically unsound and inattentive to their surroundings. By displaying these tendencies, the officer would inadvertently "allow" the motivated offender to possibly engage in a deadly force attack on the officer or others. While the offender had the motive or intention to commit the activity, the officer's actions or inactions allowed this suspect to take advantage of the opportunity. While the officer may not be held civilly responsible for his/her actions, the failure to use appropriate tactics unfortunately escalated the situation to the level of deadly force.

What often makes this tactical responsibility difficult at times is the fact that officers are reacting to the actions of offenders as discussed in Chapter 1. This reactive position inadvertently always puts officers at a disadvantage. In order to overcome this disadvantage, officers must be properly trained, tactically alert, and mentally prepared for all encounters on the street. For now, however, remember that police officers have a tactical responsibility to prevent exposing themselves and citizens to the risk of injury or death.

Police officers must also make sound moral decisions regarding force. Poor moral decisions by police officers are readily reported on television and in the newspapers. The use of force is serious and officers must be cognizant that their actions or behaviors can easily deescalate a situation.

Conversely, in other situations an officer could purposefully escalate a situation to where the legal use of deadly force was warranted. Take for example a situation where a police officer could taunt or encourage a suspect to "reach for the knife" or encourage the suspect to fight with them. Proper de-escalation techniques (i.e. ordering the suspect to drop the knife) would have served to reduce the amount of force that was used. Instead, the officer, by his or her own motive and actions encouraged the suspect to engage in a deadly force assault. While these examples may be extreme (and it is hoped that an officer would never do such a thing), it does illustrate the point that an officer's actions or response to a force situation dictates the outcome. Hence, officers have a duty to protect the sanctity of life at all times through their ethical actions. At the same time, officers also have a moral and ethical duty to stop those offenders who are endangering the lives of others.

Last, officers have a legal duty to make sure that the level of force they use falls within the legal parameters as set forth through various court cases and their agency's policies and procedures. As this chapter will point out, case law has shaped and established acceptable minimum standards for the use of force in situations up to and including deadly force. Police agencies have also developed policies and procedures that conform to and often exceed those standards established by the courts to protect the citizenry and the sanctity of life. Agencies also have rigid training standards in order to further ensure that their officers will respond appropriately in force and deadly force situations.

Terms Related to Force & Excessive Force

Before getting into specific court cases and the appropriate use of deadly force when the situation warrants, some of the basic terms that will be used in this chapter will be reviewed. These terms include: Force, Deadly Force, Less - Lethal Force, Great Bodily Harm, and Excessive Force. Many other terms related to the use of force will be reviewed in this chapter.

Force

The International Association of Chiefs of Police (IACP) *Police Use of Force in America* (2001) defines force as "that amount of effort required by police to compel compliance from an unwilling subject" (p.1). Based on this definition, force includes non-verbal, verbal, and physical means of gaining the compliance of the suspect.

Deadly Force

The Model Penal Code (3.11[2], 1962) defines deadly force as "force which the actor uses with the purpose of causing or which he knows to create a substantial risk of causing death or serious bodily harm." It can also be defined as the use of any force that is likely to cause death or serious physical injury. Deadly force also includes force that is not likely to cause death or serious physical injury, but nevertheless unexpectedly results in death or injury.

Less-Lethal Force

Less-lethal force is that force which is unlikely, when properly used, to result in serious bodily injury or harm. Currently, there are a variety of less-lethal weapons and munitions on the market. Examples include beanbag rounds that are fired out of shotguns and the Taser®, an electrical incapacitation device that disables suspects through the use of a high voltage electrical current. When using these less-lethal systems to stop or apprehend individuals, police officers must realize that they could cause great bodily harm up to an including death if these devices are not properly used or applied against suspects.

Great Bodily Harm

The term great bodily harm lacks precise definition. It implies some type of injury that involves a substantial risk of death, serious permanent disfigurement, or protracted loss or impairment of the function of any bodily member or organ or other serious bodily injury (Wisconsin Statute §939.22 (14)). In Florida, great bodily harm is distinguished from slight, trivial, minor, or moderate harm, and does not include mere bruises that are likely to be inflicted in a simple assault and battery (*Key v. State*, 2003).

Michigan law (Sect 750.204) refers to great bodily harm as "serious impairment of a body function." This includes, but is not limited to, one or more of the following:

1. Loss of a limb or use of a limb
2. Loss of a hand, foot, finger, or thumb or use of a hand, foot, finger or thumb
3. Loss of an eye or ear or use of an eye or ear
4. Loss or substantial impairment of a bodily function
5. Serious visible disfigurement

6. A comatose state that lasts for more than 3 days
7. Measurable brain damage or mental impairment
8. A skull fracture or other serious bone fracture
9. Subdural hemorrhage or subdural hematoma

Excessive Force

Excessive force "is any force that is unreasonable or unnecessary to accomplish a legal objective" (Kappeler, 2001, p. 66). Excessive force can range from a simple push or shove of a person to a situation involving deadly force. Unlike deadly force that has clearer definition, excessive force claims are open to judicial interpretation (the legal bases for determining excessive force will be discussed later in this chapter). As a result, the elements or particulars of each case will need to be examined to determine if the actions of the officer(s) were considered to be excessive in nature. The only exception to this is when an officer commits an illegal activity. Case law has determined that in illegal arrests, even if an officer used a necessary and reasonable level of force, *any level* of force used against an individual constitutes excessive force (see for example, *Atkins v. New York* (1998)).

Supreme Court Decisions & the Use of Force by Police

The two most important cases that addressed the use of force by state agents or governmental officials were *Tennessee v. Garner* (1985) and *Graham v. Connor* (1989).

Tennessee v. Garner
& Deadly Force Standards

The existing minimum standard for the legal use of deadly force was established in the Supreme Court case of *Tennessee v. Garner* (1985). In this 1974 incident, Elton Hymon and his partner Leslie Wright, officers with the Memphis Police Department, responded to a "prowler inside" burglary call. The suspect, 15-year-old Edward Garner, fled from officer Hymon. Although Hymon saw no sign of a weapon, and though not certain, was "reasonably sure" and "figured" that Garner was unarmed, he shot Garner to prevent his escape. The bullet hit Garner in the back of his head. Garner later died as a result of the gunshot wound. Under the existing Tennessee statute and departmental policy, Hymon was legally justified in using deadly force to enact the arrest of Garner. This was based on the Common Law's "any fleeing felon rule" that existed at this time. Therefore, Hymon had the legal authority to use deadly force. Garner had committed a felony and he refused to stop for the police.

Garner's father brought action under USC 42 § 1983 in the Federal District Court for the Western District of Tennessee against the Memphis Police Department and its Director, the City of Memphis, the Chief, and Mayor of the City for violating his son's rights under the 4th, 5th, 6th 8th and 14th Amendments to the U.S. Constitution. The Federal District Court of Tennessee upheld the Tennessee law and concluded that the officer's actions did not violate Garner's constitutional rights. On appeal, the U.S. Court of Appeals for the 6th Circuit reversed and remanded the lower District Courts decision on the basis that the killing of a fleeing suspect constituted a seizure and was therefore constitutional only if "reasonable." However, the Tennessee statute, as applied to this case, failed because it did not adequately limit the use of deadly force by distinguishing between felonies of different magnitudes. The Court of Appeals concluded that "Officers cannot resort to deadly force unless they have probable cause.... to believe that a suspect [has committed a felony and] poses a threat to the safety of the officers or a danger to the community if left at large." To defend the existing state statute, the state of Tennessee appealed the Court of Appeals decision to the U.S. Supreme Court.

On appeal to the U.S. Supreme Court, the Court found that the existing Tennessee statute regarding deadly force was unconstitutional. It was determined that as the Tennessee statute currently existed, it was too broad because it authorized the use of deadly force against non-dangerous fleeing felons. The Court also determined that the use of deadly force is a seizure that is subject to the U.S. Constitution's 4th Amendment's reasonableness standard. In their discussion on what constitutes reasonableness, the Court established a balancing test where it was determined that:

> "[w]e must balance the nature and quality of the intrusion on the individual's Fourth Amendment interests against the importance of governmental interests alleged to justify the intrusion.... notwithstanding probable cause to seize a suspect, an officer may not always do so by killing him. The intrusiveness of a seizure by means of deadly force is unmatched. The suspect's fundamental interest in his own life need not be elaborated upon. The use of deadly force also frustrates the interest of the individual, and of society, in judicial determination of guilt and punishment. Against these interests are ranged governmental interests in law enforcement..."

The Court also found that deadly force is reasonable under limited circumstances:

"Where the officer has probable cause to believe that the suspect poses a threat of serious bodily harm, either to the officer or others, it is not constitutionally unreasonable to prevent escape by using deadly force. Thus, if the suspect threatens the officer with a weapon or there is probable cause to believe that he has committed a crime involving the infliction or threatened infliction of serious physical harm, deadly force may be used if necessary to prevent escape, and if, where feasible, some warning has been given"

The Court also supported the Court of Appeals decision that the rules set out in the Model Penal Code "accurately states Fourth Amendment limitations on the use of deadly force against fleeing felons." This code states:

The use of deadly force is not justifiable ... unless (i) the arrest is for a felony, and (ii) the person effecting the arrest is authorized to act as a peace officer or is assisting a person whom he believes to be authorized to act as a peace officer; and (iii) the actor believes that the force employed creates no substantial risk of injury to innocent persons; and (iv) the actor believes that (1) the crime for which the arrest is made involved conduct including the use or threatened use of deadly force; or (2) there is a substantial risk that the person to be arrested will cause death or serious bodily harm if his apprehension is delayed (Model Penal Code § 3.07(2)(b), Proposed Official Draft, 1962).

Graham v. Connor
& Excessive Force Standards

The standard used by the courts in determining if the level of force used in an incident is appropriate or excessive was established in the Supreme Court case of *Graham v. Connor* (1989). In this case Graham, a diabetic, felt the onset of an insulin reaction and had a friend drive him to a convenience store to purchase some orange juice to counteract the reaction. Upon entering the store, Graham saw a number of people ahead of him in the checkout line. Concerned about the delay, he hurried out of the store and asked his friend to drive him to a friend's house instead. Officer Connor of the Charlotte, North Carolina Police Department, saw Graham hurriedly leave the store and became suspicious of his actions. He stopped the vehicle and called for backup. In the ensuing confusion, Graham was handcuffed and thrown headfirst into a police car by four police officers. He also sustained various injures from the incident, including a broken ankle, cuts on his wrists, a bruised forehead, an injured shoulder, and a loud ringing in his right ear.

Graham brought action against the officers under a claim of excessive force under 42 USC § 1983, alleging that the officers had used excessive force in making the investigatory stop, in violation of his rights that were secured to him under the 14th Amendment to the U.S. Constitution. The federal district court found that the amount of force that was used by the officers was "appropriate under the circumstances," that there was "no discernible injury inflicted," and that the force used "was not applied maliciously or sadistically for the very purpose of causing harm," but in "a good faith effort to maintain or restore order in the face of potentially explosive situation." On Appeal, the 4th Circuit Court upheld the District Court's decision.

On Appeal to the U.S. Supreme Court, however, the Supreme Court determined that the lower courts had applied the wrong standard and remanded the case in order for the Court of Appeals to consider the claim under the reasonableness standard of the 4th Amendment. The Court concluded that claims involving the use of excessive force (deadly or non-deadly) in the course of an arrest, investigative stop, or other police activity involving a seizure of the citizen should be analyzed under the 4th Amendment's " reasonableness" standard rather than a "substantive due process" approach. Their logic was based on the premise that the 4th Amendment guarantees the citizens the right "to be secure in their persons… against unreasonable seizures." Hence, all force cases must be judged by reference to the 4th Amendment's "reasonableness" standard rather than a substantive due process claim, under the 14th Amendment.

The Concept of Reasonableness

The Court in *Graham* noted that determining whether a seizure is "reasonable" requires a careful balance "of the nature and quality of the intrusion on the individuals 4th Amendment interests against the counter-vailing governmental interests at stake." Recognizing that there is no precise definition or mechanical application of "reasonableness", the Court concluded that the proper application of force requires careful attention to the facts and circumstances of each particular case, including the severity of the crime at issue, whether the suspect poses an immediate threat to the safety of the officers and others, and whether the suspect is actively resisting or attempting to evade arrest by flight.

The decision noted that "reasonableness" must be judged from the perspective of a reasonable officer on the scene rather than 20/20 vision or hindsight. Furthermore, "... Not every push or shove, even if it might later seem unnecessary in the peace of a judge's chamber, violates the Fourth Amendment." The Court further determined that reasonableness must also embody allowance for the fact that police officers often have to make split second decisions in circumstances that are tense, uncertain, and rapidly evolving about the amount of force that is necessary in a particular situation. Based on these conditions or factors (the totality of circumstances), the concept of reasonableness in an excessive force case is "an objective one: the question is whether the officers actions are "objectively reasonable" in light of the facts and circumstances confronting them, without regard to their underlying intent or motivation." This is now known as the objective reasonableness test.

Making Effective Force Decisions

Time constraints and stress are just two of the many factors that influence decisions regarding the appropriate level of force to be used in a situation. From the above cases (and several more that have addressed the use of force), police administrators and planners have also created training models and guidelines to assist officers in making appropriate legal and ethical force decision(s).

The Use of Force Continuum

To assist law enforcement officers in making reasonable force decisions, agencies, states, and their respective Police Officer Standards and Training (POST) Commissions have created use of force decision models to provide guidance or assistance to officers in making better force decisions. These decision models provide guidance on what level of force may be appropriate, depending upon the actions of the offender. They range from the simplest non-aggressive behaviors and appropriate responses all the way to deadly force assaults committed by suspects. These models are called a variety of names. They can be called decision models, force continuums, or in the case of Michigan, it is called the Subject Control Continuum.

The key to all continuums is that they are based on two criteria: the suspect's level of resistance and the officer's level of control. Regardless of the specific terms used, continuums provide officers guidance on what level of control they can use, based on the suspect's level of resistance, all the way to the use of deadly force. These continuums are basically guidelines. They are not step-by-step procedures that must be followed. For example, if a police officer is confronted with an armed subject that is threatening their life, they can immediately engage in a deadly force response to stop the threat. They do not have to begin on the lower end of the continuum and try to attempt to stop the subject with some type of empty hand control technique or a baton strike. A response to a threat of this nature with a lower level of control would put the officer at a tremendous disadvantage.

Continuums prescribe what level of force can be used, based on the concept of reasonableness and the totality of the circumstances. When determining what level of force should be used, some of the factors that the California Police Officers Association states an officer should consider (but is not limited to), include:

- If the suspect is under the influence of drugs or alcohol
- If the subject is an Emotionally Disturbed Person (EDP)
- The proximity of weapons to the suspect(s)
- Other options available to the officer
- The seriousness of the crime
- The officer's level of training and experience
- The suspect's conduct
- The potential of injury to the officer and/or citizens
- Other exigent circumstances

The main point of all continuums is that they are decision models. These models are not set in stone, nor do they dictate exactly what an officer should do. Rather, they provide guidance on what would be reasonable in light of, or in totality of all circumstances of that particular incident. Thus, these continuums, regardless of design, incorporate the concept of reasonableness and the totality of the circumstances approach as determined by *Graham*. Continuums, such as Michigan's Subject Control Continuum, also follow the Graham decision in the context that it is the officer's decision in light of all circumstances that they encounter at that specific incident which dictates the appropriate level of force. Appropriate force decisions are based on the totality of the circumstances or on what the officer personally observed during the actual altercation or contact with the suspect — not on 20/20 hindsight.

One commonly used subject control continuum is from the Pressure Point Control Techniques (PPCT) program that was developed by Bruce Siddle. Under the PPCT system, Siddle advocates the conservative "One Plus One" theory in applying or using an appropriate level of force. This program proposes that officers can morally, legally and tactically use one level of force or control higher than that level of resistance displayed or used by the suspect, based on the concept of reasonableness and the totality of the circumstances. This continuum is based on the review of case law and Siddle's conceptualization that levels of resistance need to be controlled by different techniques, depending upon the level of resistance displayed by the offender.

The Deadly Force Triangle/Decision Model

To further assist police officers in making proper deadly force decisions, other models have also been created. Figure 2-1 illustrates the deadly force triangle decision model (Olson, 1998). The key to this model is that all three elements of deadly force must be present to justify the use of deadly force: Ability, Opportunity & Jeopardy.

Figure 2-1
The Deadly Force Triangle

Ability

Opportunity   Jeopardy

Ability

Ability means "the physical capacity to harm an officer or another innocent person" (Olson, 1998, p. 2). Ability asks the question: Does the perpetrator have the ability to cause death or great bodily harm? Usually ability is associated with a person who has a weapon, such as a firearm or knife. However, *it is not* limited to weapons. Ability can also include the suspect's personal capacity. For example, a very large and powerful person, an Emotionally Disturbed Person (EDP), or someone under the influence of a controlled substance may have the ability to inflict death or great bodily harm on an officer, exclusive of some type of weapon.

Opportunity

Opportunity asks the question: Does the perpetrator have the opportunity to use his ability to cause death or great bodily harm? Opportunity deals with the suspect's potential to inflict death or great bodily harm (Olson, 1998). For example, a suspect with a knife who is 10 feet from a police officer has the opportunity to attack a police

Training Tip: On your own or in a formal training setting, review some recent police-related shootings. Be sure to tie into the review the moral, legal and tactical elements of the case. Also reflect upon the aversion to killing and how to deal with this issue. Training of this nature will serve to assist in making better, effective force decisions.

officer. This same person who is 75 feet away lacks the immediate opportunity to inflict death or great bodily harm.

Jeopardy

Jeopardy asks the question: Once the perpetrator has the ability and the opportunity, do they then make substantial steps towards using them and actually place a person in jeopardy of death or great bodily harm? Jeopardy deals with taking advantage of one's ability and opportunity to inflict death or great bodily harm (Olson, 1998). An example of jeopardy would be when a suspect is armed with a firearm, and points that firearm at a police officer.

Jeopardy & The Concept of Necessity

In some situations, a suspect has the potential to cause death or great bodily harm. However, they do not pose the immediate threat. Under these situations, according to the U.S. Department of Justice's deadly force policy, deadly force can be used under the necessity criterion.

Necessity consists of two components: imminent danger and the absence of safe alternatives. Imminent danger means pending action. It does not mean instant or immediate. This means that a suspect *can* pose an immediate danger "even if at the precise moment [the subject] is not pointing a weapon at the officer" (Olson, 1998, p.3). Olson (1998) writes that the absence of safe alternatives includes "a suspect's response to commands, availability of cover, time constraints imposed by the action/reaction gap, and the lack of a reliable way to stop a threatening action instantly" (p. 3). In effect, the issue of absence of safe alternatives deals with the question of if the officer has time to react in a different manner to the threat. For example, in some situations an officer can avoid or disengage from a deadly force encounter. They can create distance, find cover, or retreat. While perhaps tactically correct to do so, in other instances they do not possess that option. Because they had no safe alternatives, deadly force is both legally and morally acceptable.

The Ethics and Morality of Using Deadly Force

As already mentioned in this chapter, deadly force includes both an ethical and legal component. The legal component of deadly force is relatively easy to understand. On the ethical side of deadly force, however, there are often some deep-seated moral issues. Police officers may feel uncomfortable and wrestle with the notion that they may at some time in their career be required to use deadly force against a suspect to protect another's life. This aversion to killing is natural, and is, perhaps, human nature. To be an effective police officer, however, this aversion must be overcome.

As a police officer, the sanctity of human life is paramount. At its basic core, the role of a police officer is to protect life at all costs to one degree or another. However, the issue of taking another's life may cause personal conflict and contemplation. This contemplation is natural, and it would be safe to assume that all officers, regardless of the bravado they express externally, have seriously contemplated the fact that they at some point in their career they may have to shoot someone to stop them from committing a serious crime. This shooting, of course, may result in the suspect's death.

Perhaps one of the best examples of the aversion to kill is seen in the classroom and discussions between citizens and police officers when there are questions related to deadly force. One of the most common questions is: Why not shoot them in the arm or leg? This is an inappropriate response to a deadly force situation. Police officers need to properly respond to threats and control those threats. This requires that the officer be in control of the situation by using one level of force higher than that displayed by the offender. This means that the officer must immediately stop the threat from committing a deadly force assault. Shooting a person in the arm or leg will not ensure that they are no longer a threat. When an officer has made the decision to use deadly force, based on legal and moral facts and issues, they must apply that level of force required to effectively stop the threat as fast as possible. This means that the officer must aim and place their shots in regions of the body where critical life processes occur — the chest and head.

Often this thought is unsettling. However, remember this point: police shoot to immediately stop a threat. They do not kill. Because the officer had to stop this threat at all costs, the suspect unfortunately died as a result of their wounds. Looking at the issue in this context, the officer killed this person, but in effect, their motive was to stop them — not kill them. The threat dying as a result of gunshot wounds was a consequence of their own fault in placing others in harm, for failing to obey the lawful commands of a police officer, and not being a responsible citizen. It is an unfortunate consequence that the suspect lost his or her life because of their actions. However, the suspect made a rational and free decision to engage in those actions that led to his or her own death. At the same time, the officer fulfilled their duty and oath when hired — they protected the sanctity of life.

As pointed out in the preceding paragraph, police do not kill. They stop threats. Police officers do not have an evil intent or malice. Police officers do not murder. To further support this point, murder is based on evil intent or malice aforethought (think of a murderer and a typical street crime involving a shooting). An officer's motives or intentions are just the opposite—to preserve life at all costs. In some situations this requires the officer to stop a threat, taking the suspect's life to preserve the life of others. Furthermore, an officer's intent is not to kill, even when an officer stops the threat by shooting. Once the person is stopped, the police officer needs to apply appropriate aftercare to that suspect in the form of first aid, etc. (this point will be discussed in depth in the Post Shooting chapter). The officer's duty has now changed. Before, their primary duty was to stop the threat, which they did. Now, their duty is to preserve life. In this case, the officer must now save the life of the suspect that perhaps seconds ago tried to kill them or someone else.

The Natural Aversion to Killing

Dave Grossman (1996) in his book, *On Killing*, provides an historical review and discussion on the intimacy and psychological impact on killing and man's aversion to killing other human beings. Grossman writes that throughout history, humans have been reluctant to kill other human beings, even in times of war. Some of the anecdotal evidence he provides in his book includes the battle of Gettysburg. After the battle, muskets were found on the battlefield with their barrels packed full of lead balls because solders would "fake" shooting, while still continuing to reload their musket with another ball in order to prevent being accused of being cowardly. Other wars, such as WWII and Vietnam, had similar situations where soldiers refused to shoot the enemy, but yet fired in the direction of the enemy or engaged in some other activity to reveal to their peers and leaders that they were adequately performing their duties. Grossman also writes that the aversion to killing becomes more difficult as the proximity to the threat decreases to the point where one can readily identify the threat or enemy. For example, it is easier for a pilot or bombardier at 20,000 feet to justify and reconcile their actions than a soldier in the field because of physical proximity. As pointed out in Chapter 1, most deadly force encounters are close range — they are intimate in nature, often involving physical contact with the aggressor. Statistically, this is the situation a police officer will most likely encounter, and according to Grossman, this is the most difficult type of killing.

In order to overcome this hesitancy or aversion to shooting suspects, several interrelated issues must be considered **prior** to becoming a police officer. Coming to terms with this issue is critical. Without coming to terms with one's duty, these subconscious issues will cloud and impede one's ability to respond appropriately in a deadly force situation. This could mean that the officer, their partner, and citizens will all be put in danger because of their reluctance to act. In addition to this natural aversion, other issues that need to be considered include cultural and religious factors.

Consider, for example, how cultural issues can affect force decisions. In some instances, a police officer would be hesitant to use force against certain individuals. They may include females or children, or perhaps an elderly person. This may be attributed to respect, or a socially constructed cultural expectation that the young, well-dressed female or older individual needs to be given greater respect (and hence less force). When it comes to the application of deadly force, however, none of these social expectations or social constructs should be considered. The use of deadly force is not based on the suspect's gender, age, socioeconomic status, or position in society. It is based solely on the actions of the offender. The only issue that should be considered is the fact that the suspect is engaging in a deadly force assault against you, a fellow police officer, or a citizen, and they must be stopped. For example, in scenario training at an entry school the author was partnered up with a police officer from a nation in the Pacific Rim area of the world. The author and this officer executed an entry into a room where a potential threat was located. Upon contact with the suspect, this particular officer would not secure the female (or even touch her) because in his culture it was not proper to be aggressive toward a female. Actions of this nature in the "real world" will lead to serious issues.

Often, the apprehension toward shooting a suspect and killing them is based on religious principles. Primarily, this is based on the Christian belief that killing is mortal sin, based on the 6th Commandment of the Old Testament and Exodus 20:13 in the New American Bible (St. Joseph Edition) that states "You shall not kill." In other Bibles, the wording may be a little different (e.g. Thou shall not kill). This commandment, combined with other religious thoughts, often creates moral dilemmas for officers. As pointed out by Dave Grossman, early Biblical translations interpreted this Commandment out of context. The Hebrew word that was originally used referred to a person killing for their own personal gain. It had nothing to do with killing under the authority to do so. Of course, there is a tremendous difference between killing or murdering someone for personal gain and killing to protect others. In the case of the police, police do not kill for personal gain. They stop the threat and subsequently kill to protect others. A more in depth review of the New and Old Testaments of the Bible also provides additional evidence that killing was just under certain situations (i.e. David and Goliath).

All of the above issues will cloud an officer's judgment to one degree or another. Consciously and subconsciously dealing with these issues during a high stress deadly force encounter will make an individual hesitate, exposing themselves and citizens that they swore an oath to protect to some type of deadly threat. In order to prevent this from occurring, the officer must adequately address these issues far in advance, as they prepare for their career in law enforcement. Through careful reflection, reading, and inquiry with other officers, people the officer intimately trusts, and experts in the field (such as the clergy), a greater understanding of the true role and necessity of killing can be achieved. While the aversion to killing may not be totally overcome, the officer will come to accept their role and responsibility as a protector in society and the burdens that come with that responsibility.

Deadly Force Policies — Examples

There are several deadly force policies that exist. Regardless of what agency or organization created these policies, they all follow the Garner decision. For example, the Michigan Commission on Law Enforcement Standards (MCOLES) states that a firearm can be discharged only under the following conditions.

These conditions include:

- In self defense;
- In defense of another when the officer has reason to believe there is imminent danger of death or great bodily harm; and
- On other occasions covered by departmental policy (e.g. shooting injured animals).

Discharging a firearm, meanwhile, is not allowed under the following conditions:

- Mere suspicion that a fleeing subject committed a life threatening felony;
- In non-life threatening felonies and misdemeanor offenses; and
- When an arrest may be affected using less than deadly force.

The U.S. Department of Treasury's policy is similar. This policy is shown in Box 2-1.

BOX 2-1
U.S. DEPARTMENT OF TREASURY
POLICY ON THE USE OF FORCE

Use of Deadly Force Policy

Deadly Force. Treasury Law Enforcement Officers may use deadly force only when necessary, that is, when the officer has a reasonable belief that the subject of such force poses an imminent danger of death or serious physical injury to the officer or to another person.

Fleeing Felons. Deadly force may be used to prevent the escape of a fleeing subject if there is probable cause to believe:

1. The subject has committed a felony involving the infliction or threatened infliction of serious physical injury or death; and

2. The escape of the subject would pose an imminent danger of death or serious physical injury to the officer or to another person.

Dated: October 17, 1995

The Use of Warning Shots

Often the question arises if a police officer can use a warning shot to "stop" a fleeing felon. Department policy, POST organizations and common sense prevents the use of warning shots to stop fleeing felons for the following reasons:

- The role of a police officer is to protect and ensure the sanctity of human life. The only time that deadly force is warranted is based on the criteria discussed earlier. Deadly force can be considered in the context of a traffic light. A warning shot can be considered a yellow light where the officer "cautions" the suspect that they may use deadly force. There is, however, no yellow light in a deadly force situation. If all of the elements of a deadly force assault are present and the officer has no other options (i.e. retreat) the officer must stop the threat (green light = go). If the elements are not present, they cannot morally and legally use deadly force (red light = stop).

- Case law has determined that purposefully discharging a firearm in the direction of another person or at a vehicle in which another person is believed to be constitutes deadly force (*Mattis v. Schnarr*, (1976)). A warning shot is a purposeful or intentional act that could endanger innocent bystanders and civilians.
- Police officers **must** be accountable for all rounds that are fired from their weapon. Firing a warning shot (in the air or ground for example) exposes innocent parties to potential injury or death. This could also expose the agency and officer to civil liability.
- If deadly force is legally and morally warranted, it is justified. If all of the legal and moral elements for deadly force are met, then deadly force must be used to protect oneself and/or others from harm.

Shooting at Moving Vehicles

It is very difficult to hit and stop a moving object, including motorized vehicles. As mentioned earlier in this section, purposefully firing a firearm in the direction of another person or at a vehicle in which another person is believed to be, constitutes deadly force (*Mattis v. Schnarr*, (1976)). Hence, firearms should not be discharged solely to disable moving vehicles. Policies related to shooting at motor vehicles vary from agency to agency. For example, the U.S. Department of Justice's policy on shooting at suspects in moving vehicles states that weapons may not be fired solely to disable moving vehicles. In other jurisdictions, and depending upon departmental policy, if an officer or another is "attacked" with a motor vehicle, deadly force may be used against the driver of the vehicle. Other agencies are more restrictive, stating that officers can only shoot at moving vehicles if they are being fired at from that particular vehicle.

Deadly Force Against Animals

During the course of one's career, a police officer will respond to vehicular and other types of accidents involving injured wildlife. There is also a high probability that they will also respond to other calls where there will be sick or injured animals that need to be "destroyed," "put down," or euthanized. Depending upon departmental policy, officers will often be tasked with the responsibility of using deadly force to humanely put the animal to death and end its suffering. While the use of a firearm may not always be warranted (depending upon the size of the animal, location, bystanders, etc.), it is the officer's responsibility to end this animal's suffering in a professional and safe manner, and in compliance with all departmental policies. If the agency has a policy, and there is a need to destroy the animal, officers should pay particular attention to safety issues (which will be discussed in the Safety Chapter). Officers should also pay particular attention to the impact that destroying this animal will have on the public's perception of the police and firearms use in general.

Consider the following case that happened at a one police department: A police officer shot a deer that was struck by a vehicle to put an end to its suffering. This officer practiced the safe handling of his firearm and made sure that the public and other officers were not at risk. He also made sure that no members of the public were present to see him shoot the deer. However, across the street two small boys watched the officer shoot the deer from a window of their house. This was a few days before Christmas. The children were traumatized because the police officer had just shot one of Santa's Reindeer. While the parents were sympathetic and accepting of what the officer had done, the boys did not "buy into" their parent's explanation of the event. In an effort to calm down their children, the mother called the agency and asked that the officer stop by and talk to her children to explain what he had done and that it was not one of Santa's Reindeer. The following day, this officer went to the house to convince the children that it was not one of Santa's Reindeer that he had shot, and that Santa and his Reindeer would still be stopping by Christmas Eve.

In other instances, domesticated or wild animals may threaten a police officer or citizen. Depending upon departmental policy, deadly force can be directed against dogs or other vicious animals when necessary in self-defense or defense of others (as is the case with the U.S. Dept of Justice's policy). When determining if deadly force is justifiable under these situations, the same conditions that warrant the use of deadly force against an individual should be used as the basis to justify the use of deadly force.

Drawing Firearms

The drawing of an officer's firearm is based on objective reasonableness and the totality of the circumstances of each particular circumstance the officer encounters. Depending upon departmental policy, officers may draw or display their firearm when they have reason to fear for their own safety or the safety of others, based on the concept of reasonableness and the totality of circumstances. Take for example, a traffic stop in a remote location where the officer does not have backup and the vehicle and suspect match the description of a recent armed robbery in the area. The suspect is also belligerent toward the officer. In this instance, drawing a weapon would be justified.

Civil Liability & Force

While police officers enjoy a certain degree of statutory immunity for activities they engage in over the course of their duties, in some instances they may exceed their legal authority and expose themselves and their agency to a civil liability lawsuit from those who are injured (i.e. physically, economically, psychologically). The injured party (known as the plaintiff) can include the actual person injured, or if dead, their dependants or estate can file a civil suit in the state or federal court system, depending upon the issue. Officers must also be aware that the inappropriate use of force will lead to disciplinary measures against them. These can include criminal charges at the state or federal level if force was used in an inappropriate manner (which will be addressed in greater detail in the Post-Shooting Chapter). It will also surely lead to a civil action.

Civil wrongs are called torts. In order for a plaintiff to successfully win a civil liability claim, Kappeler (2001) points out that they must prove the following four points or elements. These four elements include:

1. Duty
2. Breech of Duty
3. Proximate Cause
4. Damage, Injury or Harm

At the state level, claims can be filed against officers and the agencies they work for under the allegation that they breached a legal duty owed to the plaintiff. These claims can be based on an intentional act, such as a false arrest or any other incident where a reasonable and prudent officer should have known that their actions could lead to damage, injury or harm. They can also be based on negligence theory, which is based on the premise that the officer and their respective agency committed some activity that led to harm, such as a traffic accident, where the officer did not intentionally commit the act. Nevertheless, some type of harm resulted because of their action(s) or inaction(s). Take, for example, a situation where a police officer and his department are named as defendants in a force-related incident, where the injured person was truly an innocent citizen. The first element, duty, deals with the police officer's responsibility: the officer had a legal duty not to injure or harm the innocent party. Therefore, they breached that duty (#2). Next, the plaintiff needs to prove, based on the preponderance of evidence standard (not the standard of beyond a reasonable doubt which is the standard of proof in a criminal case) that the majority of the evidence presented shows that the officer's actions were the proximate cause (#3) and lead to the plaintiff's (#4) damage injury or harm, whether it be physical or psychological in nature.

Unlike state torts, the basis for suits under the U.S. Constitution (called constitutional torts) is more narrowly defined. In the federal court system, the most common way to file a claim is through the Civil Rights Act of 1871 codified as USC 42 §1983. The key element that must be proved in this type of case is that the officer's action(s) violated a constitutionally protected right. For example, if a police officer uses deadly force in an inappropriate manner, the injured party can file under USC 42 § 1983 claiming that the officer violated their 4th Amendment's protection against unlawful searches and seizures. Subsequent interpretations and case law have also determined that the municipality the officer works for (see the 1978 case of *Monell vs. New York Department of Social Services*, (436 U.S. 658)) is also liable for the actions of their employees.

According to Kappeler (2001) to successfully win or hold a municipality liable under 1983, the plaintiff(s) must prove the following:

1. That the plaintiff had a constitutionally protected right and they were deprived of those rights
2. The municipality had a policy or custom that was unconstitutional
3. This municipal policy or custom amounted to deliberate indifference to the plaintiff's protected right(s)
4. The municipality's custom or policy was the proximate cause of the violations of the plaintiff's constitutional rights

The recognized standard to prove a municipality's indifference to one's constitutional rights is known as Deliberate Indifference. This standard requires that a municipal official must have been aware of facts from which the inference of a substantial risk of serious harm could have been drawn. They must also have drawn the inference and then have acted with deliberate indifference to the risk. Consider the following example: A police department is being sued under 1983 for excessive force against an arrestee. The plaintiff presents evidence that there were numerous prior incidents with the agency where a reasonable and prudent police administrator should have recognized that there was a problem with their officers using force. Nevertheless, the administrator(s) did nothing or limited their actions to correct this problem, whereas similar events still occurred. Failing to address this problem (through better training, for example) therefore, constitutes deliberate indifference, since the administration should have known that the failure to adequately correct the problem could or would result in damage, injury or harm to citizens by the agency's officers.

Deliberate indifference can also be based on policy or custom. The department may have a defective written policy that led to the damage, injury or harm. In other cases, there is no policy or a policy that the officers do not follow. Take for example a police agency that knows that its officers are mistreating arrestees in the booking area (i.e. "excessive force"). Administrators know it is going on (based on personal observations, complaints, medical records, etc.) but they do nothing to address it. At the same time, there is a policy that prohibits these types of activities that the officers and administrators did not follow and disregarded. Even though there was a policy preventing conduct of this nature, the officers nevertheless violated the plaintiff's rights. In effect, the agency had an unwritten custom that violated a constitutionally protected right.

In a vast majority of cases, agencies are sued under 1983 in the context of the failure to train. The failure to train issue is often considered to be a deliberately indifferent activity. Under the concept of the failure to train, the agency should have known they needed to train in that specific area, as a prudent and reasonable police administrator should have been able to foresee that the failure to train in certain areas (such as firearms use) could lead to a constitutional deprivation. The case *City of Canton v. Harris* (1989), addressed the issue of a municipality's failure to train where the U.S. Supreme Court set forth the standards for deliberate indifference. Kappeler (2001) points out five elements that must be present for a plaintiff to win a failure to train suit under 1983. They include:

1. The training was in fact inadequate;
2. The officer's actions exceeded constitutional limitations;
3. The officer's actions arose in a typical situation that the officer deals with (traffic stops, force situations, arrests, etc.);
4. The training demonstrates a deliberate indifferent attitude toward persons with whom the police come into contact; and
5. There is a direct causal link between the constitutional deprivation and the inadequate training.

Case law interpretations based on the elements of a failure to train lawsuit do not require a pattern of constitutional violations to put a municipality on notice that its training program is inadequate. In those cases where policy itself is not unconstitutional, a single incident can establish the basis of an inadequate training program, especially if this evidence is coupled or combined with other evidence that shows that the training program is inadequate (Kappeler, 2001).

State & Federal Efforts in Controlling Firearms-Related Crimes

It is the responsibility of local, state, and federal law enforcement agencies to work independently and collaboratively to combat firearms-related crimes. In many instances, agencies acting independently of one another can be effective in addressing firearms-related crime. However, they often overlook how their shared resources and collaborative efforts can reduce firearms-related crimes. Often the failure to work collaboratively is based on the simple fact that local police agencies are unaware of federal firearms laws and the relevance or importance of these laws, particularly in how these laws can assist local police agencies in combating firearms-related crime. In other instances, it is based on the fact that agencies are simply reluctant to share information and perhaps the "glory" of solving the crime. Two issues, however, call for better relationships between local and federal agencies.

First, the federal government has at its disposal a variety of laws, enforcement techniques and sources of information to assist state and local police agencies in combating firearms-related crimes. The Bureau of Alcohol Tobacco, Firearms and Explosives (ATF) is the federal agency that is tasked primarily with the investigation of firearm-related crimes. Establishing a relationship with the federal government and ATF will serve to improve criminal investigations and reduce unlawful firearms activities at the local, state and federal levels. The information that local law enforcement obtains is instrumental in assisting federal agencies, including the ATF. The sharing of information is essential for effective crime control and making a community safer.

In many situations, federal laws often carry a stiffer penalty than state laws for the same offense(s). Take, for example, a situation that one city was facing where there was a combination of firearms-related violence, combined with gang activities. In many situations, gang members were found to be in possession of a firearm. Under this particular county's policy, carrying a concealed weapon was often plea-bargained down to a misdemeanor charge where the accused served a short jail sentence. In other situations, defendants were charged with a felony but did very little prison time. Upon release, these short sentences were actually a badge of honor, where the convicted gang members received greater respect from their peers and followers. In essence, the state laws were basically ineffective in controlling violent gang activities. To combat this problem, this particular police agency contacted the ATF, and with their assistance, defendants in firearms-related crimes were now charged and prosecuted under federal law where they received prison terms of up to ten years in the federal prison system. No longer did gang members serve a short term. Prison or jail time was no longer a "badge of honor" or respect among other members in the gang. These harsh sentences served to dramatically reduce and deter gang and firearms-related violence in this particular community.

A second issue deals with those available resources that agencies have to combat firearms-related crimes. Investigations are often a costly venture for many police agencies. Including the federal government in these investigations can serve to reduce the costs associated with investigations, since the federal government will "foot the bill" instead of the financially burdened local government. As this section will also show, the federal government also has expertise and a wide variety of information that is readily available to state and local agencies to assist them in firearms-related investigations.

The Relationship Between State and Federal Firearms Laws

In some instances, state laws are more strict than federal firearm laws. For example, federal firearms laws permit individuals to own and possess fully automatic weapons while some state laws prohibit their ownership (unless they have a federal Curio & Relics license which still limits what automatic weapons they can legally own). Some states also have additional laws related to the purchase and registration of certain firearms. Some states, for example, may require individuals to obtain a permit to purchase and a subsequent safety inspection or registration for their handguns from their local police agency. Since these laws do not conflict or violate existing federal firearms-related legislation (and relevant state laws) they are completely legal.

There can be no state laws and local ordinances that conflict with federal law. There is however, overlap where both federal and state laws prohibit the same activities. In situations where this exists, either the state or the federal government has jurisdiction over the case and can bring charges against the accused. This is known as concurrent jurisdiction. In these cases, factors that may determine who will charge includes politics, available resources (financial, expertise and manpower) and the penalties for the violation(s). For example, in some instances, the state will prosecute the accused. In other situations, police agencies may contact the federal government for their assistance (in some level or capacity) and have the appropriate federal government agency "adopt" the case and have the case heard in the federal court system.

The Interstate Nexus

For the federal government to become involved in a firearms-related case, an interstate commerce nexus must be established. This means that the crime in question must somehow be involved in interstate travel, use the facilities of interstate commerce, or the use the mail as a conveyance device to commit the crime in question. The criteria for the interstate commerce nexus in firearms-related cases was established in *Scarborough v. United States* (1977). In this case, the Supreme Court clarified the requirements of the interstate commerce nexus. In *Scarborough*, the Court held that the proof that possessed firearms had previously traveled in interstate commerce was sufficient to satisfy the statute's "in commerce or affecting commerce" nexus requirement. For example, federal law prohibits the illegal purchase and transport of firearms across state lines. This can include transporting a weapon across state lines by a possessor. It can also include the travel of the firearm, frame or receiver during, or subsequent to its manufacture. For example, if a firearm is manufactured in state A and then it is legally shipped to a distributor in state B, interstate nexus has occurred. At the same time, if person A unlawfully transports a weapon to another state, interstate nexus has also occurred and the federal government has jurisdiction and can intervene in the investigation and subsequent prosecution of the offender(s). Interstate nexus is not limited solely to firearms. It deals with all federal cases. For the federal government to usually become involved in a criminal investigation, an interstate nexus must be established.

Firearms Trafficking

One particular federal and local issue is firearms trafficking. According to Greco (1998), firearms trafficking is "the movement of firearms from the legal to illegal marketplace through an illicit method for an unlawful purpose, usually to obtain profit, power, or prestige or to supply firearms to criminals or juveniles" (p. 9). It is basically the unlawful transportation and trade of firearms. Traffickers, meanwhile, are individuals or groups of individuals who illegally transport firearms and supply these firearms to individuals who cannot, for some reason, get the firearms themselves. These traffickers sell, barter or trade these firearms to criminals, juveniles, and gang members (National guns first, 1999).

Traffickers pose a danger to the police and public as they provide firearms to the criminal element and juvenile gangs. The trafficking of firearms also increases the risk of firearms-related crimes and the level of danger to the citizenry. The diversion of firearms is not the same as trafficking. Firearm's diversion involves any movement of a firearm from a legal to illegal market. A felon who steals a firearm for their own use has diverted a legal firearm (Following the gun, 2000)

A two-year study conducted by the ATF on trafficking has identified five different types of traffickers and trafficking channels. These sources and the frequency of criminal activities associated with each source are shown in Box 2-2.

Trafficked firearms originate from multiple sources. They can come from individuals who purchase weapons with an altered or a fake form of identification (such as a fake driver's license), flea markets and from purchasing firearms from newspapers and other advertising mediums such as the internet (National guns first, 1999). Trafficked firearms also originate from the theft of firearms from residential burglaries and related crimes involving the theft of legitimately owned firearms.

BOX 2-2
TYPES OF FIREARMS TRAFFICKERS

Source of Trafficked Firearms	Description, Nature & Extent of the Problem
Corrupt FFLs (gun dealers)	Corrupt and unlawful gun dealers (who, for example, sell firearms off paper to avoid the proper paperwork [such as the 4473 federal form that is required to be filled out for all firearms purchases]) accounted for only 10 percent of all trafficking investigations. However, they accounted for the largest number of diverted firearms (approximately 40,000 firearms; average of 350 guns per case)
Gun Shows	Both licensed and unlicensed sellers at gun shows account for the second highest percentage of trafficked firearms (Approximately 26,000 firearms; more than 130 guns per case)
Straw Purchasers	Are the most common form of traffickers (26,000 guns; 37 guns per investigation)
Unlicensed Sellers	Range from persons who sell firearms to criminals out of their personal collections to interstate gun runners

BOX 2-2
TYPES OF FIREARMS TRAFFICKERS

Source of Trafficked Firearms	Description, Nature & Extent of the Problem
	who sell firearms to criminals (approximately 26,000; 75 guns per case)
Theft of Firearms	Firearms stolen from common carriers (e.g. UPS), Stores/FFLs and Residences (9,000 cases)

(From: Following the gun, 2000)

Source v. Market Areas

Where the gun originates is a source area. The source area is simply that area where a firearm trafficker has easier access to firearms, where they can transport these guns to other locations. Source areas are characterized by some or all of the following characteristics:

- A high number of Federal Firearm Licensees (FFLs) or legitimate gun dealers
- Lenient state and local gun laws
- Close proximity to urban centers and other places where there is a demand for guns
- Lax law enforcement scrutiny to trafficking

Market areas are those areas where there is a demand for guns. These are often large urban areas with restrictive gun laws and/or areas with a high crime rate, perhaps because of a large narcotics trade. Market areas are defined as geographical areas and are not limited to states. Moreover, a market area's source could be in the same state, or a different city or county within that state. Once the weapon reaches these market areas, they are illegally sold or traded to gang members and other individuals who cannot obtain a firearm legally, or have the criminal intent to avoid obtaining a firearm in a legal manner.

Corridors & Gateways

Different types of transportation methods are used in the trafficking of firearms. They include vehicles, trains, busses, watercraft, the U.S. mail and other package shippers or carriers. A trafficking corridor is that route of transportation that is frequently used by firearm traffickers to transport firearms from source to market areas. It is simply that path or route that connects the source area to the market area. An example of a well-known trafficking corridor is Interstate 95 that parallels the East Coast of the United States. Traffickers transport firearms from the southern states to the more restrictive New York City and New Jersey market area via the I-95 corridor. By being aware of these corridors, police officers can be more alert to trafficking and better prepared to protect themselves and others. This will also lead to better enforcement, apprehension, and suppression efforts related to firearms trafficking. A trafficking gateway, meanwhile, is a border crossing, point of entry, airport, train or bus station that is frequently passed through by firearms traffickers when transporting firearms from a source to market area (Guide to illegal firearms trafficking, 1999).

The "Barbecue Theory" & Trafficking

One way to explain firearms trafficking is through the barbecue theory. This theory uses the analogy of building a barbecue in one's backyard. It takes the position that if the bricks are close by (i.e. the market) to the source (the barbecue under construction), the builder will only carry a few bricks at a time due to their proximity to the barbecue under construction and ease of access to other bricks. If, however, the bricks are quite a distance away (i.e. at the brick store), the builder will make one single trip, hauling a lot of bricks. The same concept can be applied to traffickers. If the source and market areas are in close proximity to one another, the trafficker will carry only a few firearms at a time (i.e. one to three) because they can easily get to the source area to obtain more guns. If there is a greater distance, however, it may be more difficult to get to the source area readily, which will lead to traffickers obtaining and transporting more weapons on every trip (National guns first, 1999).

Straw Purchasers

Straw purchasers are individuals who purchase a firearm for another person with the intent on concealing the second person's identity (Guide to..., 1999). The straw purchaser is that individual who completes the paperwork requirements. The straw purchaser uses their name and identity. However, they have no intent on keeping the firearm for themselves. The key to a straw purchaser is that their intent is to obtain a firearm for someone else – not themselves. Some of the potential indicators of a straw purchaser include: 1) a person who has purchased several firearms in a short amount of time; 2) a person who cannot account for the firearms they obtained; or, 3) a person who has reported the theft of firearms shortly after they purchased them (National guns first, 1999).

49

Tracking Firearms Ownership History

In the course of a career in law enforcement, undoubtedly, the police officer will encounter and seize firearms. It is the responsibility of the police officer and their agency to trace the ownership of these weapons in order to determine if they are crime guns. Title 18, United States Code, Section 922(a)(6) defines a crime gun as a firearm that is illegally possessed, used in a crime, or suspected of being used in a crime. Crime guns may also include abandoned firearms if they are suspected of being used in a crime. Box 2-3 lists the four primary steps that should be followed to identify the legal owner of the firearm.

Tracing a Firearm through the National Tracing Center

Tracing can be defined as "the process of tracking firearms recovered in crimes from the manufacturer to the final purchaser who is either an individual or firearms dealer" (National guns first, 1999). Tracing is not new. It originated in 1934 with the National Firearms Registration and Transfer Act, where the federal government passed legislation against gangster-style firearms (such as the Thompson machine gun) and explosive devices, requiring individuals to register all gangster weapons and pay a transfer tax on these weapons to the Department of Treasury (this legislation is still in effect today) (Greco, 1998). With additional legislation and new technologies, tracing has changed and proves to be a valuable resource for police agencies in investigating, solving, and fighting firearms-related crimes.

BOX 2-3
STEPS IN FIREARMS TRACING

1. Conduct an NCIC Check to determine if the firearm was stolen
2. Check the State Database (if applicable) to determine the lawful owner
3. If steps 1 and/or 2 reveal that the person in possession of the firearm is not the registered or licensed owner, initiate and conduct an investigation
4. Initiate an NTC (National Tracing Center) trace through the ATF. This may provide additional information for the investigation

(National guns first, 1999)

When thinking about tracing, police officers should remember one important point: The vast majority of all trafficked firearms originated at one time from a federal firearm licensee. The only exception would be very old and other firearms that were never registered (pre federal legislation); spoils of war (i.e. "bring backs" from WWI and WWII, Korea and Vietnam). However, even if the firearm was legally registered, officers must also remember that the firearm may have changed hands from the original purchaser. For example, an original purchaser could have sold a rifle or shotgun in the local newspaper, etc. (which is legal in some states), where there is no record of the transaction at times. Nevertheless, the trace will show who the original purchaser was, which will provide the investigator with a lead to further pursue the case.

With the assistance of the Bureau of Alcohol Tobacco & Firearms National Tracing Center (NTC) police agencies in the United States and abroad have access to a comprehensive database where they can trace the origin and movement of the firearm from the manufacturer, to the dealer, and purchaser. The NTC also serves as a reference library to identify firearms, importers, and firearms manufacturers. By tracing firearms, police agencies and the federal government can determine patterns in firearms trafficking and related crimes, establish investigative leads, and solve crimes. In short, the firearm can serve as an "informant" in many cases – some of which may not even appear to be criminal at first glance. In addition to thinking of the firearm as an informant, the serial number should be considered as a fingerprint that can be analyzed and traced (Greco, 1998). With a little investigative work, important information from the NTC will provide investigative leads for police.

The NTC provides a variety of services to police agencies. Of these services, the Firearms Tracing Services (FTS) may be the most useful. The FTS contains multiple databases that includes a stolen firearms database that provides information on firearms stolen from FFL's (Federal Firearms Licensees) and interstate carriers or shippers. The FTS also has a multiple sales database that provides information on individuals who have purchased multiple firearms (3 or more per purchase) from the same dealer(s) within a period of five business days. The FTS also contains a suspect gun database that provides information on stolen firearms related to where the firearm was recovered, and what crimes were committed with it. The FTS also has databases on suspect names and stores information on individuals who are under investigation. The FTS can also conduct queries on individuals and FFL's to determine how many firearms have been traced back to them, and crimes committed with those firearms (National guns first, 1999).

In order to understand the trace process, one must first understand the firearm registration process. Under federal law, each firearm purchaser must complete an ATF Firearms Transaction Record. This form is known as the 4473 and it consists of three sections: 1) a full description of the firearm purchased; 2) a description of the purchaser (i.e. name, social security number, date of birth and address); and, 3) a series of questions to determine if the buyer can legally purchase the firearm(s). Some questions include: if the person is a convicted felon, if they have been adjudicated mentally ill, if they are a citizen of the United States and if they have a court-issued restraining order. If a person falsifies information on this 4473 form in order to obtain the firearm, they are "lying and buying, which is a federal offense (Greco, 1998).

In order to complete a trace, police agencies must submit a trace request form to the NTC. These trace forms can then be faxed to the NTC. Depending upon the type of crime the weapon was used in, trace priorities can be urgent or routine. An example of a priority-based trace would be a homicide. Routine traces would include found property and other non-violent crimes. Trace requests can also be electronically submitted through the National Law Enforcement Telecommunications System (NLETS). Information contained in the trace report includes relevant dealer and purchaser information. For example, the weapon can be traced from the factory to distributor and then to the dealer who sold the firearm. The dealer can provide specific information on the buyer of that firearm from the 4473 form (required by the buyer to complete when purchasing a firearm from FFL dealers) that is required by law for dealers to keep on file (National guns first, 1999).

Information from the NTC will also provide police agencies with additional information including where crime guns are coming from and "time to crime" statistics on how long it took for the firearm to be purchased and used in a crime. Trace information can also provide information on whether particular types of firearms are being traced back to specific dealers or individuals, which could be an indicator of criminal activity by that dealer or individual. Submitted trace information can also assist other police agencies and the federal government in monitoring firearms used in crimes. In some cases, however, trace information may not be completely successful, due to the fact that a dealer may be out of business or the firearm was too old to be traced. Nevertheless, it is important that all firearms that come into the possession of police agencies be submitted to the NTC (National guns first, 1999). At a minimum, it will assist the federal government in monitoring firearms that are seized by the police.

The Use of Force by Citizens

A civilian's authority in the context of the use of force may be different from those powers granted to the police, depending upon the state they live in. Primarily, these differences can be seen in the context of the Duty to Retreat and the defense of one's home, known as the Castle Doctrine. Another difference deals with civil litigation issues, primarily a civilian's exposure to civil lawsuits for their actions.

Like a police officer, a citizen can use force up to and including deadly force to protect themselves and others from great bodily harm or death. Deadly force can be used in the defense of others, based on the totality of the circumstances and on what the defender perceived was objectively reasonable in light of the situation at hand. In order to use deadly force legally, the defender must also be an innocent victim. For example, a defender cannot provoke a person by engaging in a fight with them or any other action that puts himself in danger, and then use deadly force to stop the threat from further attacks against them.

Legislation regulating a citizen's use of deadly force varies from state to state. Some states, such as Wisconsin, do not issue concealed carry permits for civilians. The majority of states have "shall issue" legislation. These are also referred to as "right to carry" states where if a citizen meets the criteria set forth under that state's legislation, a concealed carry permit or license must be issued. Other states such as California have discretionary CCW laws, while Alaska and Vermont have no licensing requirements. Depending upon state legislation, there may be reciprocity between states for CCW holders.

The powers granted to CCW holders also vary from state to state. For example, Michigan's Self Defense Act provides citizens broad powers in the use of force, up to and including deadly force to protect themselves and others from attacks and forcible felonies (i.e. home invasion). This legislation uses the Presumption of Reasonable Fear. This presumption takes the position that a person who has reasonable fear of imminent peril of great bodily harm or death can use defensive force against an attacker/

perpetrator who is in the process of forcibly entering or who had already entered a dwelling, residence or occupied vehicle. It also allows force (up to and including deadly force) to be used anywhere else that person has a legal right to be when they have reasonable fear of great bodily harm or death. A person can also use deadly force when the perpetrator was trying or attempting to remove another person against their will from a dwelling, residence or occupied vehicle. This Self Defense Act does not have a Duty to Retreat requirement. A person can hold their ground and meet force with force, and use deadly force, if necessary. This force would be justified as long as the person reasonably believed that their conduct was necessary to protect themselves or others against another's imminent use of unlawful force. As pointed out earlier, this level of force would also be justified as long as the defender was not engaged in an unlawful activity. Individuals that are justified in using force to protect themselves or others, meanwhile, are immune from criminal prosecution. They are also immune from civil liability. The only way a person can be successfully sued in the civil courts is when it is found that their actions were illegal. For those individuals whose actions are challenged, the courts are required to compensate the defendant (i.e. reasonable attorney fees, curt costs, loss of income) in any civil action, if the court finds that the defendant was immune from prosecution under the legislation.

"Duty to Retreat" Requirements

Other states have "Duty to Retreat" restrictions in their civilian self-defense statutes. Unlike police officers who do not have a legal duty to retreat, if the situation allows, citizens in these states must attempt to retreat before using deadly force. This is based on the argument that the sanctity of life demands that those who are unlawfully attacked attempt to retreat before using deadly force if they can safely do so. Under these types of statutes, the defender must attempt to physically retreat or evade the attack by the suspect if it can be done safely. If, however, the defender perceives or reasonably believes (based on the totality of circumstances) that they are facing great bodily harm, forcible sexual penetration, or death, and they cannot escape or evade the suspect, then they can use force up to and including deadly force to stop the threat.

The only exception to the duty to retreat is when a citizen is in their home and an uninvited person tries to break in or somehow gain entry (i.e. forcibly entering the home) into the person's dwelling. Under this circumstance, a civilian can use deadly force regardless of the fact if they or another is facing great bodily harm or death to protect themselves or others (however, it would be advantageous for the homeowner to do everything possible to avoid the use of a firearm and deadly force in these situations). The underlying principle related to this action is called the Castle Doctrine. The Castle Doctrine is an exception to the duty to retreat rule. It is based on English Common Law belief that "every man's home is his castle." It takes the position that those who are unlawfully attacked in their home do not have a duty to retreat because their home or "castle" provides them more protection than that which they would have if they have outside of their home (Carpenter, 2003). This Castle Doctrine often extends to the curtilage of one's home. Curtilage is defined as that area of ground and dwellings surrounding a dwellinghouse, or that piece of land that is used with the dwellinghouse (Blacks Law Dictionary, 1979).

The Civilian & Civil Liability

Like police officers, civilians can be sued for using deadly force against suspects regardless of if they were justified in the use of deadly force or not. Unlike police officers, however, civilians cannot be sued under USC 42 § 1983. Instead, they will be sued under state tort law. Furthermore, police officers that have used deadly force will be represented by their municipality for their actions. Civilians, meanwhile, will be left on their own, and are personally responsible for their own criminal and civil defense.

There is often the mistaken belief that civilians will be covered under their homeowner's insurance policy if they should, for example, shoot a suspect that has broken into their home. As a general rule of thumb, a homeowner's insurance policy will not cover intentional based torts. This is based on the policy's exclusionary clause, which releases the insurance company from indemnification and the legal costs of representation if the person is sued. In fact, even if the firearm is used in self-defense, it is unlikely that the insurance company will cover any expenses related to the incident.[1] Intentional based torts are those activities where the defendant intentionally engaged in the activity that led to the damage, injury or harm. It does not mean that the person intended to inflict the damage, injury or harm per se. All a plaintiff needs to prove is that the defendant engaged in an activity that a reasonable person would know leads to damage, injury or harm. The plaintiff does not have to prove that they intended to injure or

---

[1]   See for example the Michigan Supreme Court cases Auto Owners v. Churchman, 440 Mich 560; NW2d 431 and Auto-Owners v. Harrington, 455 Mich 377 (1997). In both these cases the Court determined that the insurance company did not have to defend or indemnify the insured.

kill the suspect. In the case of a homeowner shooting an intruder, for example, the homeowner knowingly pointed a loaded firearm at the suspect, subsequently shooting him or her. Pointing the firearm at the suspect was an intentional activity and the person's homeowner's insurance will not cover any expenses related to such incidents. At a minimum the homeowner/civilian will be required to hire an attorney to defend them in this issue. Regardless of if they should win or lose the claim, this could cost the civilian thousands of dollars in legal expenses.

Conclusion

The decision to use deadly force rests on three pillars – the tactical, moral and legal aspects of force. This chapter has shown that even if the level of force used does not rise to the level of deadly force, all force decisions up to and including deadly force must meet the standards set forth under Graham's 4th Amendment "Objective Reasonableness" standard. To assist police officers in making appropriate use of force decisions, use of force or subject control continuums have been developed. These continuums serve as a guideline to assist officers in making objectively reasonable force decisions in light of the totality of the circumstances that they encountered in the particular situation at hand. Nevertheless, when the elements of ability, opportunity, and jeopardy are present, deadly force can be used to stop the threat from causing great bodily harm or death to the officer, their partner or the citizenry. Police officers may have an aversion to inflicting deadly force on a subject, which is often based on cultural and religious factors. To be an effective police officer, these issues need to be addressed prior to a deadly force encounter.

Deadly force policies set forth those conditions in which deadly force can be used. Deadly force can be used in defense of another when the officer has reason to believe that there is imminent danger of death or great bodily harm, and in other occasions covered by departmental policy including shooting injured animals. Other issues related to force also need to be considered. The use of warning shots and shooting at vehicles in order to disable them are also prohibited. The drawing of a firearm, meanwhile, should be limited to those occasions where an officer has reason to believe that their safety or another's is in danger of great bodily harm or death, based on the totality of circumstances. As this chapter has also pointed out, in any force situation a police officer will expose himself and his agency to a civil action. Civil lawsuits can be filed in the state and federal courts. At the state level, claims are filed based on the negligent or intentional actions of the officer(s). For a suit to have standing in the federal courts, meanwhile, the injured party or plaintiff must demonstrate that the police officer's actions violated a constitutionally protected right.

Local and federal agencies must work together to combat firearms-related crimes. For the federal government to become involved in a local firearms-related case, an interstate nexus must exist and be determined. One major issue facing law enforcement agencies is firearms trafficking. Firearms trafficking is the movement of illegal firearms from source to market areas. This trafficking occurs in a variety of ways, and it may involve straw purchasers (individuals who purchase a firearm for another with the intent on concealing this person's identity). In order to combat trafficking, police agencies should work with the federal government and conduct traces on all crime guns.

Last, this chapter has provided a review of federal and state laws related to firearms regulations and violations. In order to be effective, police officers need to have a comprehensive understanding of these laws and regulations. In some cases, state laws are more restrictive than federal laws regarding the purchase and possession of certain firearms. In other situations, federal laws provide harsher penalties for certain firearms-related offenses.

REFERENCES

Atkins v. New York , 143 F.3d 100 (1998).

Blacks law dictionary, (5th edition). St Paul, MN: West publishing.

Carpenter, C.L. (Spring, 2003). Of the enemy within, the Castle Doctrine, and self-defense. Marquette law review, 654-700.

City of Canton, Ohio v. Harris et. al 489 U.S. 378 (1989).

Department of Treasury, Uniform Policy on the use of force, Treasury Order No. 105-12, section (4)(a) (1995).

Following the gun: Enforcing federal laws against firearms traffickers (June, 2000). Washington, D.C.: Department of the Treasury Bureau of Alcohol, Tobacco & Firearms.

Graham v. Connor, 490 U.S. 386 (1989).

Greco, J.P. (September, 1998). Pattern crimes: Firearms Trafficking Enforcement Techniques. FBI Law enforcement bulletin, 67(9), 6-13.

Grossman, D. (1996). On killing. The psychological cost of learning to kill in war and society. New York: Little Brown, and Company.

Grossman, D. (January 4, 2001). The Bulletproof Mind: Mental Preparation for Combat. Firearms/Use of Force Annual Review: Washtenaw Community College, Ann Arbor, Michigan January 4, 2001.

Guide to Illegal FirearmsTrafficking (1999). Washington, D.C.: United States Department of Justice.

Key v. State, App. 2 Dist., 837 So.2d 535 (2003).

Kappeler, V.E. (2001). Critical Issues in Police Civil Liability (3rd edition). Prospect Heights, IL: Waveland.

Mattis v. Schnarr, 547 f.2d, 1007 (1976).

Michigan Criminal Law § 750.204

FIREARMS-RELATED LAWS

Model Penal Code 3.11(2) 1962.

Monell vs. New York Department of Social Services, (436 U.S. 658).

National Guns First: Training for Law Enforcement Officers to Help Reduce Illegal Trafficking of Firearms. (February, 1999). Washington D.C.: U.S. Department of Justice, Office of Justice Programs.

Olson, D.T. (February, 1998). Improving Deadly Force Decision Making. FBI law enforcement bulletin, 67(9), 1-9.

Scarborough v. United States, 431 U.S. 563 (1977)

Tennessee v. Garner, 471 U.S.1, 18 (1985)

The Civil Rights Act of 1871. 42 U.S.C. ß 1983

Wisconsin Statute §939.22 (14).

Chapter 3
FIREARMS NOMENCLATURE

Introduction

F irearms is a field of study where individuals must have an in-depth understanding of the nature, operation, and various types of firearms that exist. There are several reasons why a police officer and student should fully understand firearms definitions and nomenclature.

First, law enforcement is a profession. As a profession, there are expectations that those working in that particular field will have in-depth knowledge and expertise in their subject matter. In many situations, however, students and police officers often confuse common facts related to firearms. Thus, it is important for students and police officers alike to gain a working understanding of the common terms related to firearms.

Second, the failure to properly identify and classify a weapon could result in losing a case, or at a minimum being embarrassed and discredited on the witness stand. One key element of the law enforcement profession is writing detailed and accurate reports that describe the incident at hand. Imagine, for example, that you seize a weapon at a call. This weapon is a revolver. In your report you state that you seized a pistol. As this chapter will reveal, there is a significant difference between a revolver and a pistol. Now, five months later you are testifying in court regarding the incident. Using the facts from your report, you testify that you seized a pistol at the crime scene. The defense attorney, meanwhile, asks you if you are sure that you seized a pistol. You respond "yes." Next, the revolver is presented to the jury. Has this individual presented sufficient doubt to the jury that the weapon perhaps is not the one that you seized? At a minimum, with sufficient probing the officer will be discredited to the point where the rest of his report and testimony may be subject to skepticism by the jury. While a "trivial" point, combined with other issues, the case could be lost as a result of using the wrong descriptive terminology in the initial report.

Third, police officers need to know the basic operations of a firearm for their own safety. Often tragic accidents happen simply because the officer did not understand how the weapon functioned.

Fourth, the proper maintenance and care of a firearm requires that individuals have a working understanding of the various parts or components, as well as the function of both hand and long-guns.

Last, police officers will come into contact with firearms in the course of their duties. Officers will be required to safely secure these firearms as evidence in several instances. If not for evidentiary purposes, they may be turned over to officers as lost property and for disposal and/or destruction. In other instances, officers will come into contact with weapons on routine calls where they will be required to make them safe and secure. All of these activities require that officers have a fundamental understanding of the functions of various types of firearms. Unfortunately, in some situations, officers lack a practical, working understanding of firearms which could lead to tragic consequences for themselves, other officers, and citizens.

Firearm Definitions

Firearm

Per 18 U.S.C. Chapter 44 § 921(a) (3) the legal definition of a firearm is "any weapon (including a starter gun) which will, or is designed to, or may readily be converted to expel a projectile by the action of an explosive." A firearm is also considered to be "the frame or receiver of any such weapon," "any firearm muffler or firearm silencer; of any destructive device."

Consider the following examples. As a police officer, a concerned citizen stops by the police department to turn in a slide assembly and barrel that they found. Is this a firearm? The answer is no. There is no receiver or frame. In another situation, an officer comes across the opposite: A suspect has a frame or receiver of a weapon *without* the barrel and slide assembly. This part of the weapon constitutes a firearm where the suspect could be charged with violating applicable state and/or federal firearm laws.

Semiautomatic Firearm

The semiautomatic firearm has an autoloading action that fires only a single shot for each single function of the trigger. An autoloading action will fire a succession of cartridges, so long as the shooter keeps pulling or depressing the trigger, or until the ammunition supply is exhausted. The semiautomatic designation applies to pistols, rifles and shotguns. It does not apply to revolvers. As the name suggests, an autoloader automatically loads the firearm. By its design and function, the firearm acquires ammunition from an internal or external magazine, inserts the ammunition in the chamber, extracts and ejects the spent cartridge, and then retrieves another cartridge from the magazine. Below are the definitions of each type of semiautomatic firearm as defined in the Federal Firearms Regulations Reference Guide (2000).

- *Semiautomatic Pistol:* Any repeating pistol which utilizes a portion of the energy of a firing cartridge to extract the fired cartridge case and chamber the next round, and which requires a separate pull of the trigger to fire each cartridge.
- *Semiautomatic Rifle:* Any repeating rifle which utilizes a portion of the energy of a firing cartridge to extract the fired cartridge case and chamber the next round, and which requires a separate pull of the trigger to fire each cartridge.
- *Semiautomatic Shotgun:* Any repeating shotgun which utilizes a portion of the energy of a firing shell to extract the fired shell case and chamber the next round, and which requires a separate pull of the trigger to fire each shell.

As each of these definitions reveal, the key to a semiautomatic weapon, regardless of if it is a pistol, rifle, or shotgun, is the fact that a portion of the energy from the fired cartridge works the action of the weapon to extract, eject, and feed a new or live cartridge into the chamber of the firearm. Another key component of the semiautomatic weapon is the separate pull of the trigger: for each pull of the trigger only one round is fired.

Manual Loading Firearms

Opposite of autoloaders are manual loading weapons. Manual loading weapons require that the cartridge or shell be inserted into the chamber of the firearm "with the hands or by means of a mechanical device controlled and energized by the hands" (Federal Firearms Regulations Reference Guide, 2000, p. 79). An example of a manual loading firearm would be a bolt or lever action rifle where the shooter must mechanically manipulate the weapon in order for a cartridge to be inserted into the chamber of the firearm.

Hand-Held Firearms

As the name implies, hand-held firearms can be classified as originally being designed to be fired from the hand — not the shoulder, a bipod, tripod or similar apparatus.

Pistols

Pistols are firearms originally designed, made, and intended to fire a projectile (bullet) from one or more barrels when held in one hand. A pistol also has a chamber as an integral part of the firearm, or the chamber is permanently aligned with the bore(s) of the firearm. In short, a pistol has a grip underneath the bore (or barrel) of the weapon. It was designed and intended to be fired with one hand, and the chamber is fixed. The ammunition for pistols is contained in a magazine that is inserted into the magazine well of the weapon. Pistols can be classified as full-sized, medium and compact.

Revolvers

A revolver, like the pistol, is designed to be fired with one hand. Unlike the pistol, a revolver has a revolving cylinder that holds the ammunition in cylinder chambers. A revolver **does not** have a fixed integral chamber. Instead, ammunition is breech-loaded into the cartridge chambers of the cylinder. When the hammer of the weapon is cocked (or the trigger is pulled or moved to the rear) the cylinder rotates, which aligns the ammunition with the barrel of the weapon for firing. It is easiest to remember that a revolver is a handgun that contains its ammunition in a revolving cylinder. Revolvers can be small, medium or large framed.

Shoulder-Mounted Firearms (i.e. Long Arms)

These are often referred to as long arms. By their very nature and design, these weapons are much longer in length and larger than hand-held weapons. These types of weapons are used in sporting applications including large and small game, bird, and waterfowl hunting. They are also used in military and law enforcement applications. Like handguns, there are several manufacturers of long arms in the United States and abroad.

The simplest way to designate long arms is to divide them into the categories of rifles and shotguns.

Rifles

The term rifle means a "weapon that is designed or redesigned, made or remade, and intended to be fired from the shoulder and designed or redesigned and made or remade to use the energy of the explosive in a fixed metallic cartridge to fire only a single projectile through a rifled bore for each single pull of the trigger" (18 U.S.C. 44 § 921(a) (7)). The key components to consider with the rifle is that they are designed to be fired from the shoulder and they fire a single projectile from a fixed metallic cartridge.

Shotguns

The term shotgun means a "weapon designed or redesigned, made or remade, and intended to be fired from the shoulder and designed or redesigned and made or remade to use the energy of the explosive in a fixed shotgun shell to fire through a smooth bore either a number of ball shot or a single projectile for each single pull of the trigger" (18 U.S.C. 44 § 921(a) (5)). The key definitional components of the shotgun include that it is a weapon designed to be fired from the shoulder. The ammunition used consists of a shell (that are often constructed of brass and plastic) that fires a single (i.e., a slug) or multiple projectiles (i.e., birdshot). While the legal definition states that shotguns have a smooth bore, shotguns can also have rifled bores.

Short Barreled Rifles and Shotguns

In some instances, police officers will encounter long arms that have been modified for some particular purpose. For example, the barrel(s) or stocks on the firearm have been shortened or modified, or a combination of the two has occurred. Often these firearms are modified for easier concealment, for cosmetic purposes (i.e. "they look neat"), or for greater mobility or maneuverability. Regardless of their purpose, those persons in possession of these firearms may be in violation of federal and/or state laws.

Federal law defines a short-barreled rifle as "a rifle having a barrel or barrels less than 16 inches in length" (26 U.S.C. 53 § 5845(a)(3). A short-barreled shotgun, meanwhile is a shotgun that has one or more barrels that are less than 18 inches in length (26 U.S.C. 53 § 5845(a)(3)). Often these shotguns are simply called a "sawed-off" shotgun. While a common term that is readily understood by the criminal justice system and public, the legal term is short-barreled shotgun.

Cutting the overall length of the firearm's stock can shorten the length of a rifle or shotgun. These are referred to as weapons made from a rifle or shotgun. A weapon made from a rifle is defined as "a weapon made from a rifle if such weapon as modified has an overall length of less than 26 inches or a barrel or barrels of less than 16 inches in length" (26 USC 53 § 5845(a)(4). A weapon made from a shotgun is defined as "a weapon made from a shotgun if such weapon as modified has an overall length of less than 26 inches or a barrel or barrels of less than 18 inches in length" (26 USC 53 § 5845(a)(2). If any of these elements are met, the individual in possession of the firearm is in violation of the law, **unless** the holder has a federal license to own and possess these types of weapons.

There are specific procedures to be followed when measuring barrel length and the overall length of a firearm:

Steps in Measuring Barrel Length

1. SAFETY FIRST – Follow all procedures related to the safe handling of firearms. Check, recheck, and have someone else check the firearm to make sure that it is not loaded and it is safe to handle. If in doubt, do not attempt to measure.
2. Close the breech, breechlock, bolt, or cylinder.
3. "Cock" the firearm (if possible) to make sure that the firing pin is withdrawn from face of the bolt.
4. Using a straight rod (such as a wooden dowel to prevent damage to the firearm), insert the rod down the muzzle end of the barrel until it comes into contact with the face of the bolt, breech or breechlock.
5. Mark the wooden rod at the muzzle end. Take the rod out of barrel and measure the rod to see if the barrel is legal length.

Steps in Measuring Overall Length

1. SAFETY FIRST – Follow all procedures related to the safe handling of firearms. Check, recheck, and have someone else check the firearm to make sure that it is not loaded and it is safe to handle. If in doubt, do not attempt to measure.
2. Lay the firearm on a flat surfaced square or rectangular table (or similar setup).
3. Line up the butt of the firearm with the edge of the table and the barrel(s) of the firearm with the adjacent edge.

4. Measure the corner from where the butt is lined up with the edge of the table down to the furthest point of the muzzle. This procedure will provide a true and accurate measure of the overall length of the firearm.

These weapons may be used in the commission of a crime (i.e. a crime gun) or an officer may respond to a call where the weapon is not used in a crime, but the owner has it in his or her possession, for the purpose of home defense. Often the officer may overlook this type of firearm if it is not used in a crime. Nevertheless, the owner is in violation of the law, and the weapon can be confiscated and the person can be charged with a firearms-related crime.

Assault Rifles

When a person thinks of an "assault rifle," they often develop a mental picture of what an assault rifle looks like. Usually this image is that of a military-style weapon that is chambered for what is considered to be an intermediate-sized rifle cartridge (i.e. .223 or 7.62 x 39). The federal government, however, had a specific definition of what a semiautomatic assault rifle was. For a weapon to be considered (and defined as) a semiautomatic assault rifle under the now-expired Assault Weapon Ban of 1994, the firearm had to have a detachable box-style magazine and at least two of the following components:

- A folding or telescoping-styled stock
- A pistol grip that protrudes conspicuously beneath the action of the weapon
- A bayonet mount
- A flash suppressor or threaded barrel that is designed to accommodate a flash suppressor
- A grenade launcher

What often makes this confusing is that many firearms manufacturers in the United States and abroad modified their weapons in order to meet the Assault Weapon Ban of 1994 (that has now expired) that prohibited the importation and manufacture of these firearms in the United States. In order to meet the requirements set under the ban, manufacturers modified the design of their firearms. For example, these firearms may not have a pistol grip. Instead, they may have a match or target style stock that eliminates the pistol grip portion of the weapon. In other cases, flash suppressors and bayonet lugs are eliminated from the design of the weapon. Weapons that look very similar to these assault rifles, but do not meet the true definition of such rifles under the GCA are still manufactured, imported, and legally sold. However, they do not meet the federal government's formal definition of an assault rifle under the Violent Crime Control Act of 1994. This law expired on September 13, 2004. Now, these types of firearms can be imported into and manufactured in the United States again. While the legal definition no longer exists at the federal level, some officers may still refer to these types of weapons as assault rifles.

Machine Guns

A machine gun is considered to be any weapon that "shoots, is designed to shoot, or can be readily restored to shoot, automatically more than one shot without manually reloading, by a single function of the trigger, this includes: (a) the frame or receiver of any such weapon, (b) any part designed and intended solely and exclusively or combination of parts designed and intended for use in converting a weapon into a machine gun; or (c) any combination of parts from which a machine gun can be assembled if such parts are in possession or under the control of a person" (26 USC 53 § 5845(b)). According to the Bureau of Alcohol, Tobacco and Firearms (ATF), "readily restorable" means that it is a firearm that could previously shoot automatically, but it will not in its present condition. The "designed" definition, meanwhile, includes those firearms that did not previously function as machine guns. However, by their design, they could be modified for automatic fire (Federal Firearms Regulations Reference Guide, 2000).

Figure 1a Heckler & Koch G3

Figure 1b Heckler & Koch 416

The key point to the definition of a machine gun deals with the function of the trigger. With machine guns, when the trigger is pulled to the rear, the firearm has the ability to fire multiple rounds until the ammunition supply is used up or the shooter takes their finger off the trigger. As the above definition further explains, a person does not have to possess a fully functional firearm for it to be considered a machine gun. Rather, a person simply has to possess those parts needed to make a machine gun (or convert a firearm to a full-automatic status). In other situations, individuals may have converted their legal firearm to function in a fully automatic capacity. This is also illegal and in violation of applicable state and federal laws.

Figure 2a Colt M4 Carbine

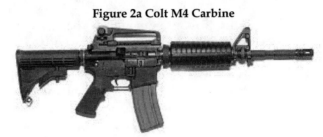

Copyright © Colt Defense LLC. Used with permission

Figure 2b SIG 556

Copyright © SIGARMS. Used with permission

Another term that is often used to describe the machine gun is "full-auto" or "select fire." Full-auto simply means that the weapon will continually fire rounds until the ammunition source runs out or the shooter takes their finger off the trigger. Select fire, also known as "burst fire" is when a firearm is designed to fire a series of rounds with each pull of the trigger. A common select fire configuration includes the three-round burst. Many machine guns offer both options. By simply moving a lever or selector switch that is located on the receiver of the firearm, the operator can change from semi-auto, burst or full-auto. Machine guns are not illegal to own, possess, or sell in some states. Depending upon what state a person resides in, citizens can legally possess machine guns if they have the firearm registered with the federal government and follow state laws and regulations. Shown in Figures 1a and 1b are the German Heckler & Koch G3 and 416 machine guns. Figure 2a shows the Colt M4 Carbine, a variant of the M-16 machine gun, while Figure 2b shows the SIG 556 patrol rifle. Both are chambered for 5.56 caliber ammunition.

Machine Pistols (MPs)

Machine pistols (MPs) are fully automatic weapons that fire a pistol cartridge. Machine pistols are also called submachine guns. Perhaps one of the most well known and most frequently encountered MP in the field of law enforcement is the Heckler & Koch MP5, shown in Figures 4a and 4b. Over 100 different variants of the MP exist. For example, they can be chambered for the 9mm or .40 S&W ammunition. Their trigger assemblies, meanwhile, can be semi-auto, 2 or 3 round burst, or fully automatic, depending upon the variant. Another MP model that is used in law enforcement applications is the UMP45 that is shown in Figure 4c. Like the MP5 the UMP45 can be fully automatic burst (2 or 3 rounds at a time) or semi-automatic only, depending upon the variant. Like machine guns, fully automatic (and/or 2 or 3 round burst variants) can be legally owned in certain states as long as the owner follows all applicable state and federal laws. MPs are not new. Shown in Figure 3 is the German MP40 (this machine pistol was invented in 1940 [hence the designation 40]) by the Germans that was chambered for 9mm(Ingram, 2001). While old, this is the forerunner of the modern-day MPs shown below.

| Figure 3 | Figure 4a |
| MP 40 | Heckler & Koch MP5N |

| Figure 4b | Figure 4c |
| Heckler & Koch MP5K | Heckler & Koch UMP 45 |

Common Firearm Components

Regardless of the type of weapon, these are some of the common components of any firearm. They include the receiver or frame, safeties, trigger pull and travel, and barrels.

The Receiver or Frame

All firearms have a receiver or frame. The ATF defines the firearm frame or receiver as "that part of a firearm that provides the housing for the hammer, bolt breechblock, and firing mechanism, and which is usually threaded at its forward portion to receive the barrel (Federal Firearms Regulations Reference Guide, 2000, p. 79).

The receiver or frame of the firearm is what constitutes a firearm, per federal law. Federal regulations (27CFRSS178.92) require that the serial number of a firearm be conspicuously located on the receiver or frame. Common serial number locations include the side of the frame, on the butt, under the crane (yoke), or on the front strap. This is where the make, model, serial number, proof marks, etc. can be found. It is critical that a police officer uses that serial number that is located on the frame for documentation purposes. In some cases, the weapon could be built from multiple firearms (i.e. a "parts" gun which is legal) where the recovered or seized weapons may have different serial numbers on various parts of the firearm (which is legal). Because of this fact, that unique serial number that is found on the frame is the only serial number that should be used to identify the firearm. This serial number should also be used for tracing the weapon through various state and local databases. However, officers should also consider conducting traces on other serial numbers found on firearms. Using the other serial numbers could reveal that a part of the firearm was perhaps stolen at one time.

Federal law also requires that each firearm manufacturer use a unique serial number for the firearms they manufacture. The exception to this is firearms made prior to the Gun Control Act of 1968. In cases of these earlier manufactured firearms, there may not be a unique serial number. For example, some early firearms manufacturers in the United States did not stamp serial numbers on their firearms. In other instances, foreign manufacturers produced firearms with the same serial number but had a unique date code instead. These weapons may pose a problem to conduct a trace. Under these situations, the police agency should contact the Bureau of Alcohol, Tobacco and Firearms for further assistance.

An altered or obliterated serial number is the result of an individual purposely attempting to remove or alter the serial number of a firearm. There are several ways a serial number can be altered or obliterated through chemical and mechanical means (i.e. acids, drilling and grinding the numbers away). Regardless of the techniques used, if a serial number is in any way altered or obliterated, federal law considers possession of a firearm with an obliterated serial number as an absolute intent to traffic a firearm. Federal law prohibits the possession of firearms with altered or obliterated serial numbers. The possession of such a firearm, regardless of whether the person in possession did not alter or obliterate the serial number, is a crime (18 U.S.C. 44, Sect 44, 922(k)).

Safeties

There are two types of safeties on firearms. Active safeties require manipulation by the shooter. They include grip safeties, tang safeties, slide locks, trigger safeties, cross-bolt and de-cock levers. Passive safeties are internal safeties. These *are not* manipulated by the shooter. The firearm, by its function or operation automatically activates these safeties. Examples of passive safeties include trigger safeties, magazine disconnects, drop safeties and inertia firing pin safeties.

Trigger Pull and Trigger Travel

Trigger pull is the minimum force required to pull the trigger to the rear to fire the weapon. Trigger travel is the horizontal distance a trigger must travel to fire the weapon (Tully, 1996). Trigger pull is measured in pounds. As a general rule of thumb, in single action stage, the trigger has a shorter distance of travel and a lighter trigger pull. In double action mode, meanwhile, there is a longer trigger travel and a "harder" trigger pull, as measured in pounds.

Barrels

Every firearm has some type of barrel. The barrel is what the projectile passes through. Barrels can be smooth bore or rifled. Smooth bore firearms have no rifling. They are associated with antique weapons and modern-day shotguns. To make a firearm more accurate, manufacturers impress the inner surface of the bore of the barrel with spiral grooves. These spiral grooves or twists serve to

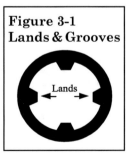

Figure 3-1
Lands & Grooves

Lands

create a "spin" on the bullet/projectile while it is still in the barrel. Once the bullet/projectile exits the barrel, this "spin" continues on, serving to stabilize the bullet/projectile, to make it more accurate and aerodynamic in flight. This process of inscribing grooves or twists in a barrel of a weapon is known as rifling.

A rifled barrel consists of three primary components. These include the lands, grooves and the twist. Lands are the raised portion of the rifle bore. The tops of the lands represent the barrel's internal diameter as measured in caliber. For example, a barrel of a .40 caliber weapon is based on the land diameter. The groove diameter is actually a few one-thousandths of an inch larger (or its metric equivalent) than the land diameter. The groove is the part of the barrel that has been removed through the rifling process. The number of grooves cut in the barrel varies among manufacturer and design. The twist, meanwhile, is the degree of spiral of the lands, per foot of barrel length. For example, one firearm may have a 1 in 8 twist (8 "twists" or spirals per foot) while another may have a 1 in 12 twist. Depending upon the manufacturer, twists can also be left or right-handed (Saferstein, 1990).

Handgun Nomenclature

As was discussed earlier in this chapter, there are two primary groups of handguns: revolvers and pistols. Within these two groups of handguns, there are many different types of firearms, based on design and manufacturer. Pistols and revolvers, by their design operate differently. One of the first issues the reader needs to understand is the difference between single and double action firearms.

Single vs. Double Action Handguns

Handguns can be single action (SA) or double-action (DA). Single action has been traditionally associated with revolvers, where the hammer must be manually cocked for each shot. The manual cocking rotates the cylinder, bringing another cartridge chamber in line with the barrel for firing. The term is also used to describe certain semiautomatic pistols that must be manually cocked prior to firing the first shot. An example of a single action pistol would be the Colt Model 1911 Government .45 ACP (Automatic Colt Pistol). In order to fire this weapon, the shooter must "cock" the hammer or lock the hammer to the rear on the first round. If the hammer is in the forward position, meanwhile, the trigger cannot "pull" the hammer to the rear. The hammer must be physically cocked by the shooter.

Following the first round being fired, the firearm (by its design) automatically cocks the firearm into the single action stage for the next round that is fired.

The definition of a double-action firearm refers to when the hammer on the firearm is "un-cocked" or in the forward position, where it is then mechanically cocked by the function of the trigger. The pulling of the trigger to the rear brings the (internal or external) hammer rearward, eventually dropping the hammer via the function of the internal mechanics of the weapon, and firing the handgun. The shooter does not manually cock the weapon for it to function correctly.

Modern pistols can be double action (DA), single action (SA) or a combination of the two. For example, the first round can be in double-action stage, whereas all subsequent rounds are fired in the single action mode by the design of the firearm. Modern firearms, that often feature the DA/SA stages, often have a de-cock lever to safely bring the hammer to the forward position after using the weapon, in order to prevent an accidental discharge. Depending upon the manufacturer, in some cases, this de-cock lever also serves or doubles as an external safety. Double action and single action firearms have the same consistent trigger pull. In weapons that have a DA/SA option, however, the trigger pull varies. For example, the first round requires a greater distance for the trigger to travel before the hammer releases. The trigger pull (as measured in pounds) is also heavier in the DA stage, in comparison to the next round that is fired in the SA stage. The SA stage usually requires fewer pounds of trigger pull and shorter distance of travel for the trigger to move to discharge the firearm.

There is also what is referred to as the" safe action." Safe action pistols are associated with the Glock® Firearms Company. The safe action trigger pull provides a consistent and even trigger pull (as measured in pounds) for every shot that is fired. It is very similar (if not the same) to the trigger pull in a double action only firearm. This action is also referred to as a striker fire mechanism (Sundstrum, 2000).

Revolvers

Revolvers are older in design than pistols. Revolvers were invented prior to the Civil War, and since that time have had many refinements and modifications to their function and overall design. In comparison to semi-automatics, their design is simple. The key to a revolver is that the ammunition for the firearm is contained or stored in cartridge chambers in the cylinder. The cylinder is mechanically manipulated by the shooter. By pulling the trigger in a rearward direction, the cylinder and the hammer simultaneously engage, causing the weapon to fire.

How a Revolver Functions

- Pulling the trigger to the rear pushes the hammer backwards to a rearward position. In single action revolvers, the shooter must physically pull the hammer to the rear until it locks in the rearward position. When manually cocking the weapon, the shooter will also see the trigger move with the hammer. The trigger and hammer move in unison with one another.

- As the trigger moves to the rear, the hammer compresses a spring that is located in the grip portion of the frame.

- At the same time, a pawl that is attached to the trigger pushes on a ratchet on the rear of the cylinder. This rotates the cylinder, indexing or aligning the cylinder chamber with the barrel of the firearm. At the rear of the barrel, where the cylinder lines up with the barrel's bore, is the forcing cone. This very slight funnel shape "forces" the bullet into the barrel when the weapon is fired.

- When the trigger reaches a certain distance of travel, the trigger lever disengages from the hammer.

- The compressed spring in the frame of weapon forces the hammer forward. The hammer, which usually has a firing pin as part of the hammer assembly, strikes the cartridge's primer. In cases where the revolver has a transfer bar, the hammer strikes the transfer bar, which now "transfers" the energy to the firing pin.

- The primer ignites the powder, driving the bullet down the barrel of the firearm.

- The shooter then lets the trigger travel forward, which begins a new cycle of operation.

When reloading the revolver, the shooter must first activate the cylinder release (in some cases, the shooter must also open the loading gate). The cylinder release unlocks the cylinder. Depending upon the design and manufacturer, the cylinder release is pushed forward or backward toward the shooter. The cylinder, which is attached to the crane part of the revolver, can then swing out. Next, to remove the spent cartridge cases, the shooter needs to push on the ejector rod. The ejector rod activates the extractor that is located in the middle (or center) of the cylinder. When pushing on the ejector rod, the extractor (by its design) pulls the spent cases from the cylinder chamber(s).

Some of the common components of a revolver are shown in Figure 3-2:

- Barrel
- Sights
- Cylinder
- Extractor
- Thumb Piece
- Forcing Cone
- Hammer
- Trigger
- Trigger Guard
- Cylinder Yoke
- Top Strap
- Frame

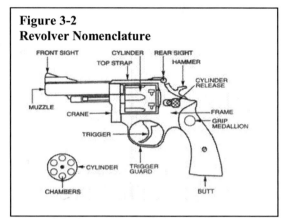

Figure 3-2
Revolver Nomenclature

ATF Guidebook (ATF 5300.17 (08/98)

As a general rule of thumb, large frame revolvers have six cartridge chambers in the cylinder. Small frame revolvers can have 5 or 6 cartridge chambers, depending upon the manufacturer. Revolvers have what is known as a fixed barrel. Unlike pistols that will be discussed later in this chapter, the barrel is permanently affixed to the frame of the firearm. The barrel does not "float" as is the case with pistols. This makes the revolver a more accurate weapon by the nature of its design (not operation). Depending upon the manufacturer, the cylinder in a revolver can rotate clockwise or counter-clockwise. The cylinder on a Smith and Wesson® revolver rotates counterclockwise. The cylinder on a Colt® revolver, meanwhile, rotates clockwise.

Shown in Figure 5 is the Ruger Vaquero® .357 revolver, which is a single-action only revolver. Figure 6, meanwhile, shows the .357 Ruger GP141® medium-framed, double-action revolver.

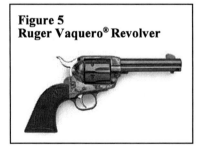

Figure 5
Ruger Vaquero® Revolver

Figure 6
Ruger GP141® Revolver

Pistols

Pistols are often referred to as semi-automatics or autoloaders. This autoloader action is the result of when the propellant gasses or recoiling forces created by the firing cartridge are used to open and close the mechanism of the firearm. The autoloading mechanism extracts each fired case from the chamber, ejects the spent case from the firearm, and then chambers a new, loaded cartridge in preparation for the next shot (Guide to Investigating Illegal Firearms Trafficking, 1997).

How a Pistol Functions

There are eight distinct steps to the cycle or operation of a pistol. They include:

1. Feeding
2. Chambering
3. Locking
4. Firing
5. Unlocking
6. Extraction
7. Ejection
8. Cocking

Figure 7
Beretta Model 92F

Copyright ©2006 Beretta U.S.A. Corp.
Used with Permission

The cycle of operation of a semiautomatic handgun begins with **feeding**. The feeding of the cartridge into the chamber of the pistol takes place when the cartridge is stripped or removed from the magazine. **Chambering** occurs when the slide moves forward, subsequently pushing the cartridge up the barrel feed ramp into the barrel chamber. As this occurs, the base or rear of the cartridge slides up onto the breech face. At the same time, the extractor tooth that is located near the ejection port on the slide engages or locks into the extractor groove on the cartridge. **Locking** occurs when the slide continues to move forward a short distance as it pushes the barrel with it. Depending upon the model and type of weapon, the locking lugs of the barrel assembly index or lock with the corresponding locking recesses in the slide. The firearm is now in battery and is ready to be fired. The **firing** stage occurs when the trigger is pulled in a rearward direction. The trigger assembly presses against a disconnector that pushes a sear, which subsequently disengages the hammer. A mainspring puts pressure on the hammer, forcing it forward, where it

77

engages the firing pin. This, in turn, strikes the primer, causing the primer to explode, which subsequently ignites the powder, pushing the bullet down and out of the barrel.

Unlocking occurs after the weapon is fired. The pressure developed by the expanding gases of the fired round recoils the slide and barrel assembly to the rearward direction. After a short distance, the locking block is disengaged from the slide, the barrel stops against the frame, and the slide continues its rearward movement. **Extraction** occurs as a result of the slide moving to the rear. While moving to the rear, the base of the spent cartridge is still held securely in place on the breech face by the extractor tooth. This extractor tooth pulls or extracts the spent round from the chamber of the pistol. Following immediately after extraction, the cartridge is ejected from the pistol. **Ejection** occurs when the slide moves further back because of the weapon's recoil. As the slide moves further back (the extractor tooth is still locked into the spent cartridge, still holding it against the breech face), the cartridge comes into contact with the front of the ejector rod which is located somewhere on the frame of the weapon. Contact with the ejector causes the cartridge to pivot out of the slide's ejection port, freeing it from the extractor in the process. Last is the **cocking** stage. Depending upon the design and manufacturer, the slide rotates or pushes the hammer in the rearward position as it travels back from the recoil of the weapon being fired. The hammer spring is compressed, and the sear locks the hammer in the rearward position for the next firing cycle. The slide then moves forward under spring pressure from the compressed recoil spring of the pistol, beginning the cycle of operation again.

In some firearms, depending upon their design, when the magazine is empty, the magazine follower forces the slide stop lever upward, that subsequently engages the slide stop notch on the slide. This locks the slide of the weapon to the rear in a "locked back" position. To disengage the slide stop lever (after a loaded magazine is inserted), the operator must then pull the slide to the rear. The slide stop lever can also be physically manipulated by the shooter (to bring the slide forward) by simply pressing the lever in a downward direction.

Figure 3-3 shows a diagram of a semi-automatic pistol. The four main components of a semi-automatic handgun include the slide, barrel, frame, and magazine.

Some of the more common components of pistols include the following:

- Sights
- Barrel
- Slide
- Frame
- Recoil Spring
- Recoil Spring Guide
- Slide Stop
- Bore
- Trigger
- Trigger Guard
- Firing Pin
- Extractor
- Ejector
- Muzzle
- Chamber
- Hammer (internal or external)
- Decock Lever/Safety
- Ejection Port

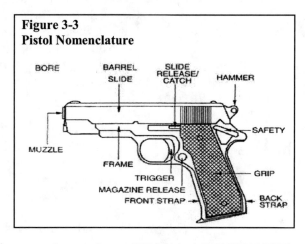

Figure 3-3
Pistol Nomenclature

Source: ATF Guidebook (ATF 5300.17 (08/98)

Another component of any pistol is the barrel assembly. They include the feed ramp, chamber, barrel and bore. This is shown in Figure 3-4. Pistols also have different types of actions. These include the slide and toggle action. The vast majority of pistols that are manufactured are the slide action design. With a slide action weapon, the slide that contains the

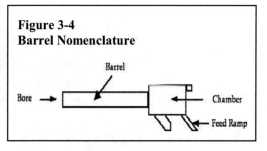

Figure 3-4
Barrel Nomenclature

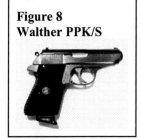

Figure 8
Walther PPK/S

barrel assembly, rides or slides on a track that is located on the frame of the weapon. When the weapon is fired, the complete slide assembly moves in a rearward direction on the frame, actually going over the top of the shooter's strong hand during its cycle of operation.

The toggle action, another variant of a semi-automatic pistol, is more complicated than the slide action. The toggle action does not have a slide assembly. A toggle action, like the slide action, relies upon the recoil of the weapon to operate. Instead of a slide, there is a toggle joint. When this type of weapon fires, the toggle lock "unlocks" and pivots above the bore of the weapon. This allows the breech block, which is part of the toggle assembly to also move rearward and extract and eject the fired cartridge. A return spring then forces the toggle forward where it strips a new cartridge from the magazine, feeds it into the chamber and then locks back into the firing position (Ingram, 2001).

**Figure 9
Luger P-08**

An example of a toggle action would be the Luger P-08 pistol that is shown in Figure 9. This firearm was designed by George Luger. It was sold commercially in the early 1900's and used in the World Wars by Germany. After World War II, this weapon was manufactured in limited quantities as collector's pieces. While considered to be somewhat rare, it can be expected that police officers will encounter these weapons as many of them became souvenirs for WWII veterans and returned with them to the United States.

There are several types of pistols. They include small frame pistols such as the Walther PPK/S as shown in Figure 8 and larger framed pistols such as single action Colt Government Model 1911 .45 ACP (Automatic Colt Pistol) as shown in Figure 10a and the SigSauer GSR in Figure 10b. Other common police duty weapons include the H & K USP 40 and the SigSauer P229 that are shown in Figures 11a and 11b.

**Figure 10a
SIG GSR**

**Figure 10b
Colt Model 1911**

Copyright © SIGARMS. Used with Permission

Copyright © Colt's Manufacturing Company LLC

Figure 11a
HK USP 40

Copyright © HK Inc. & HKJS
GmbH. Used with permission

Figure 11b
Sig P229

Copyright © SIGARMS. Used
with permission

Long Guns

As discussed earlier in this chapter, a long gun is a firearm that is designed to be fired from the shoulder. There are some general classifications of long-guns. These can be broadly categorized into the two main classifications of rifles and shotguns. Within these two families of guns, however, there are a variety of different designs and subsequent actions that need to be understood by police officers.

Rifles

Rifles can be broadly categorized as manually operated (requiring a person to manipulate or work the action of the firearm) and autoloaders (which function the same as a semi-automatic pistol). Some of the more common manually operated weapons include the lever action, bolt action, pump or slide action, and the semi-automatic. These will be discussed in detail in this section.

Lever Action

A lever action is a firearms action in which the user of the firearm must manually operate the lever mechanism, which extracts each fired shell case from the chamber, ejects the spent shell case from the firearm, and chambers a loaded cartridge in preparation for the next shot. The action must be repeated prior to each firing...(Guide to Investigating Illegal Firearms Trafficking, 1997, p. 101). While it requires the physical manipulation of the action, the lever action has several of the same components of the semi-automatic. For example, they have a magazine, feed ramp, chamber, extractor, and ejector.

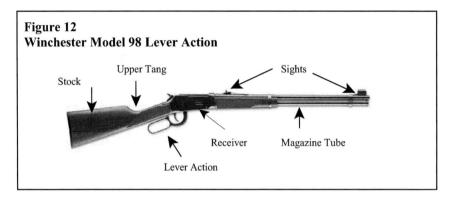

Figure 12
Winchester Model 98 Lever Action

Image: Copyright© Winchester Arms. Used with permission

Bolt Action

A bolt action is a firearms action in which the user of the firearm must manually operate the lever mechanism that extracts each fired shell case from the chamber, ejects the spent shell case from the firearm, and chambers a loaded cartridge in preparation for the next shot. The action must be repeated prior to each firing or function of the weapon (Guide to Investigating Illegal Firearms Trafficking, 1997, p. 100). The bolt action also has the same components of a semi-automatic, including the feed ramp, chamber, extractor and ejector.

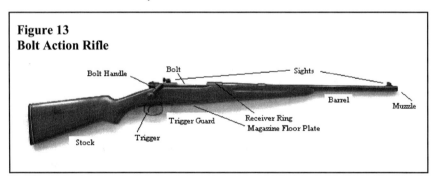

Figure 13
Bolt Action Rifle

Pump Action

A pump action is also referred to as a slide action firearm. It is described as "a firearms action in which the user of the firearm must manually operate the lever mechanism which extracts each fired shell case from the chamber, ejects the spent shell case from the firearm, and chambers a loaded cartridge in preparation for the next shot. The action must be repeated prior to each firing or function of the weapon" (Guide to Investigating Illegal Firearms Trafficking, 1997, p. 101). These types of firearms also have a magazine, feed ramp, chamber, extractor and ejector.

Semi-Automatic

There are also a variety of semi-automatic or autoloader types of rifles. Shown in Figure 14 is the Remington Model 750 that can be chambered for a variety of centerfire cartridges. Figure 15, meanwhile, shows the Ruger 10-22 which uses a .22 caliber rimfire cartridge. These types of firearms essentially have the same cycle or function of the semiautomatic handgun (i.e. feeding, chambering, locking) as previously discussed in this chapter.

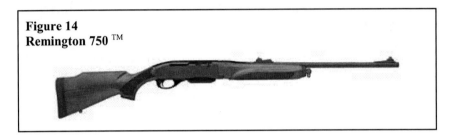

Figure 14
Remington 750 ™

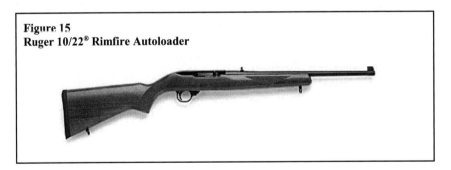

Figure 15
Ruger 10/22® Rimfire Autoloader

Shotguns

Like rifles, shotguns can be a manually operated pump or gas-operated semi-automatic. There are also lever-operated breechloader shotguns and fully automatic shotguns. Two of the more common types of police shotguns include the Remington 870 pump and 11-87 semi-automatic shotgun that are shown in Figures 16 and 17.

Figure 16
Remington Model 11-87™
Semi-Auto Shotgun

Figure 17
Remington Model 870™
Pump Action Shotgun

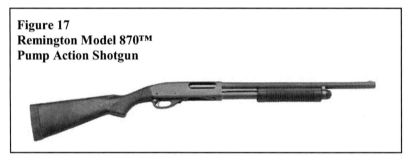

Copyright © Remington Arms Company. Used with Permission

Ammunition Nomenclature

The term ammunition may not appear to be a complex definition. It is. Usually when a person thinks of ammunition, they think of a complete cartridge (i.e. the case, powder, primer and bullet which will be discussed in detail later in this chapter). In other instances, individuals refer to a complete cartridge (i.e. the case, primer, bullet and projectile) as the "bullet." Bullets are a component of ammunition. The complete cartridge should be referred to as ammunition.

Under federal law, ammunition is defined as those components that make up a complete cartridge. Ammunition consists of the following components:

- The cartridge (i.e. the brass or case)
- The Primer
- The Bullet or Projectile
- The Propellant or Powder

Any one of these components alone, or together, constitutes ammunition. While the reader may question the relevance of knowing this definition, take for example one federal law that prohibits the possession of ammunition by convicted felons. If you conduct a vehicle search and find bullets/projectiles or empty cartridges (i.e. "spent brass"), you have a crime.

In some instances a person may come across armor piercing ammunition. The term armor piercing ammunition means "a projectile or projectile core which may be used in a handgun and which is constructed entirely (excluding the presence or traces of other substances) from one or a combination of tungsten alloys, steel, iron brass, bronze, beryllium copper, or depleted uranium." It also means a full jacketed projectile larger than .22 caliber designed and intended for use in a handgun whose jacket has a weight of more than 25 percent of the total weight of the projectile (18USC 44, § 921(a)(17)(B)).

Armor piercing ammunition has military applications. Unfortunately, there are some armor piercing projectiles on the market today that can readily pierce an officer's body armor. What is excluded from the term armor piercing ammunition includes: shotgun shot required by state and federal game regulations for hunting purposes, frangible projectiles used for target shooting, and projectiles that are used in industrial applications.

Caliber

Caliber is a term that is used to describe ammunition. The caliber of a firearm is the approximate diameter of the projectile. In the United States, caliber is usually written in inches (i.e. .30 caliber which is three-tenths of one inch in diameter). In most other countries of the world, caliber is usually written in millimeters (i.e. 7.62 mm which is equivalent to .30 caliber).

Ammunition may be described by its caliber, plus its year of introduction. One commonly encountered size of rifle ammunition is the .30/06 or the "thirty aught six." This is a .30 caliber cartridge that was designed in

85

1906 to be used in the U.S. Army's Springfield rifle. In other cases, it may be the caliber plus the name of the firearm for which it was designed such as the .30 Carbine, a World War II rifle. It can also be based on the designer of that particular sized cartridge. One example would be the .30 Newton. Basically, there is no standardized system for describing ammunition that was designed in the United States. However, most other countries, especially the Europeans, identify specific ammunition by its diameter plus the overall length of the cartridge (7.62 x 63 mm). Ammunition often has a U.S. and metric equivalent. Box 3-1 provides an overview of the some of the more common ammunition calibers and their metric equivalents.

BOX 3-1
CONVERSION OF CALIBER TO MILLIMETERS

- .22, .222, or .223 caliber can be called 5.56 mm
- .25 caliber = 6.35mm
- .264 caliber = 6.5mm
- .284 caliber = 7mm
- .30 and .308 caliber = 7.62mm
- .32 caliber = 7.65mm
- .380 caliber = 9mm short (sometimes called "Corto" or "Kurz")
- .45 caliber = 11mm or 11.4mm

Note: .38 and .357 do not have metric equivalents. 9mm Parabellum does not have a decimal equivalent.

To complicate this discussion of caliber even more, antique or 19th century ammunition is usually classified differently than modern ammunition.

Nineteenth century ammunition was often classified according to the diameter of the projectile and the number of grains of black powder. For example, one 19th century cartridge heavily used by the U.S. military with their Springfield Trapdoor Rifle was the .45-70. The .45-70 denotes a .45 caliber bullet where the cartridge or case is loaded with 70 grains of black powder. Another 19th century designation was the .30-40 Krag (30 caliber bullet with 40 grains of black powder designed by the Norwegian Ole Krag) and the .30-30, which denotes a .30 caliber bullet with 30 grains of black powder loaded into the cartridge. While these are 19th century designations used for 19th century firearms, modern firearms are also chambered with this sized ammunition. While they no longer are loaded with black powder, they still carry the same cartridge designation or name.

Cartridge Components

The primary components of a cartridge include the case, primer, powder and the projectile(s). When all of these components are self-contained, this is referred to as fixed ammunition (Federal Firearms Regulations Reference Guide, 2000). Figure 3-5 shows a cutaway diagram of a typical center-fire rifle cartridge.

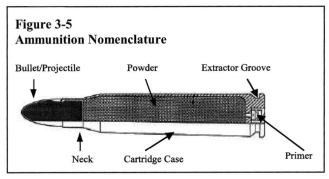

Figure 3-5
Ammunition Nomenclature

Bullet/Projectile   Powder   Extractor Groove

Neck   Cartridge Case   Primer

Adapted From: ATF Guidebook (ATF 5300.17 (08/98)

In other situations, ammunition is not in a fixed cartridge. For example, black powder revolvers require that the shooter load and pack each cylinder chamber with black powder, a cloth patch, and a round lead projectile known as the ball. The percussion cap or primer is then placed over the nipple that is semi-permanently attached to the end of the cylinder or breech that ignites the powder in the chamber. Black powder rifles also follow the same ammunition configuration. This is not a fixed type of ammunition.

Ammunition can be center or rimfire. The majority of cartridges are center fire where the primer is located or centered in the base of the cartridge case in the primer pocket. Rimfire cartridges have the primer materials located within the rim of the cartridge case. A diagram of this type of cartridge is shown in Figure 3-6.

Figure 3-6
Rimfire Cartridge

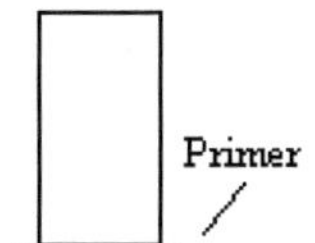

Primer

Ammunition is marked with its caliber on the headstamp, located at the base of the cartridge. The outer margins of the base of the cartridge are stamped with various markings. These markings may indicate manufacturer, batch, caliber, year of manufacture, and type of ammunition. These markings are collectively known as the headstamp. The headstamp may disclose the caliber of the cartridge case and the manufacturer. For example, the headstamp on the center-fire cartridge in Figure 3-7 tells the reader that it is a 30.06 Springfield cartridge case made by Federal Cartridge Company (FC).

**Figure 3-7
Cartridge
Headstamp**

Shotgun Ammunition

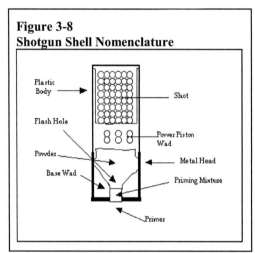

**Figure 3-8
Shotgun Shell Nomenclature**

Plastic Body — Shot

Flash Hole

Power Piston Wad

Powder

Metal Head

Base Wad

Priming Mixture

Primer

The primary components of a shotgun shell include the case, primer, powder and the projectile(s). These, however, are not called cartridges. They are referred to as shells. When all of these components are self-contained, this is referred to as fixed ammunition (Federal Firearms Regulations Reference Guide, 2000).

Figure 3-8 shows a cutaway diagram of a typical shotgun shell.

Some of the major components include the:

- Body
- Shot
- Wad
- Flash Hole
- Primer
- Headstamp
- Metal Head

Gauge is the term that is used to describe the bore diameter of shotguns. Originally shotgun gauges were determined by the number of lead balls that made up one pound of shot. For example, 10 gauge required a total of 10 lead balls per pound, while 12 gauge required a total of 12 balls and so forth. While shot or ball sizes now vary, the term gauge is now used to describe the bore diameter of the shotgun. Unlike rifle ammunition where there are hundreds of different types (based on the diameter of the cartridge and length), the shotgun shell is much more limited in the context of length and gauge. Box 3-2 shows some of the more common gauges and shell lengths (Hawks, 2003).

	BOX 3-2	
	SHOTGUN BORE DIAMETERS & CHAMBER LENGTHS	
Gauge	**Bore Diameters:**	**Chamber Length**
10	.775 inches	2.875 inches - 3.500 inches (if magnum)
12	.729 inches	2.750 inches - 3.500 inches (if magnum)
16	.662 inches	2.750 inches
20	.615 inches	2.750 inches - 3.000 inches (if magnum)
28	.550 inches	2.875 inches
*	.410 inches	3.000 inches

* The .410 is already named for the bore diameter. It is not a gauge.

The Magazine

The magazine is a storage device for ammunition. In the majority of cases, magazines are not permanently affixed to the weapon. They are removable and, most of the time, they are considered disposable. Magazines and the components that make up a complete magazine can

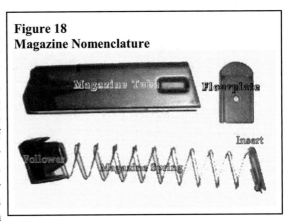

Figure 18
Magazine Nomenclature

be constructed of metal of plastic, or in some cases, a combination of the two. The main components of the magazine as shown in Figure 18 include the magazine tube, floorplate, follower, spring, and insert. Figures 19 and 20 show some different types of magazines.

**Figure 19
Pistol Magazines**

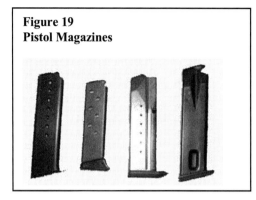

Figure 19 shows some various types of pistol magazines. The number of rounds a magazine can hold varies on the size and the caliber of the firearm they are designed for. Magazines can be single stack designs meaning that the ammunition is stacked directly on top of one another in the magazine tube. Single stacked magazines (such as the two on the left in Figure 19) hold fewer rounds than the staggered-style magazines.

Staggered types of magazines hold more ammunition because the ammunition is staggered or stacked in the magazine in a "zig zag" style. These are also referred to as high capacity magazines because they hold more than 10 rounds of ammunition.

Shown in Figure 20 are some examples of rifle magazines. They include (from lower left to right): 5-round Mini 14 .223 Magazine; 20-round .223 M-16 Magazine; 30-round .223 M-16 magazine; and a 20- round .308 Heckler & Koch G3 Magazine. Regardless of if the magazine is designed for a pistol or a long arm, they have similar components.

**Figure 20
Rifle Magazines**

Magazines are not clips. The clip is a metal device whose purpose is to hold a number of rounds, making it easier and faster to load the firearm. Clips are simple metal devices that do not fully encase the ammunition. Some older-style handguns such as the Colt and Smith and Wesson revolver use clips to hold ammunition together to make loading easier. These were often referred to as half-moon clips because each small metal clip held 3 rounds around the extractor groove of the cartridge case forming a half circle, making loading easier.

**Figure 21
M-1 Rifle Clip**

The clip is best associated with some bolt action and semi-automatic rifles where the extractor groove of the cartridge case slides onto a disposable metal strip, often called a stripper clip. When this strip of cartridges is inserted into the internal magazine of the weapon, the metal strip is removed, while the cartridges remain in the magazine of the firearm. In other cases, the clip may be more than a simple strip of metal. For example, the M-1 Garand Clip in Figure 21 encases the rear of the cartridges. When the last round is fired from this clip, it is then automatically ejected from the rifle's internal magazine.

REFERENCES

18 U.S.C. 44 Sect 921 (a)(5)

18 U.S.C. 44 Sect 921 (a)(7)

26 U.S.C. 53 Sect 5845(a)(2)

26 U.S.C. 53 Sect 5845(a)(3)

26 U.S.C. 53 Sect 5845(a)(4)

18 U.S.C. 44 Sect 921 (a)(17)(B)

Federal Firearms Regulations Reference Guide (2000). Washington, D.C.: U.S. Department of Justice

Guidebook: Importation and verification of firearms, ammunition and implements of war. Washington, D.C. U.S. Government Printing Office.

Guide to Investigating illegal firearms trafficking (1997). Washington, D.C.: U.S. Department of Justice

Hawks, C. (2003). Introduction to shotgun shells. www.chuckhawks.com/intro_gauges.htm. Last visited: October 28, 2003.

Ingram, M. (2001). The MP 40 submachinegun. Osceola, WI: MBI Publishing.

Sundstrum, A. (May, 2000). Equipment performance report: 1999 Autoloading Pistols. Washington D.C.: National Institute of Justice.

Tully, E.J. (July, 1996). Unintentional discharge of police weapons: Part one. Beretta USA leadership bulletin, 2(4), 1-8.

Introduction

T here are countless factual stories involving police officers who handled firearms in an unsafe manner. One off-duty police officer shot a hole in his wife's vehicle's gas tank while unloading his weapon. Another shot himself in the calf while re-holstering. Another example of careless handling comes from an old Associated Press wire story about a police officer that shot himself in his right foot not once, but twice in a period of two weeks.

A quick review of incidents from Officer Down Memorial WebPage also shows the unfortunate consequences of the poor handling and the dangers associated with firearms. Stories on this web page abound reflecting the careless handling of firearms by police officers that resulted in their or another's death. Consider for example, the following incidents:

- A deputy sheriff was accidentally shot and killed by another deputy when responding to a shots fired/home invasion call.

- An officer was accidentally shot in the head during a training exercise by another officer. All of the officers at this training exercise were supposedly using non-lethal training rounds.

- A California officer who was shot in the head and killed by his own weapon when he accidentally dropped his holstered weapon on the ground, causing it to discharge.

This chapter will provide the reader with a review of the fundamentals of firearm's safety. Firearms-related accidents can happen to anyone at any time. The only common denominator associated with an accident, whether it is a one-year probationary employee, or a firearms instructor with several years of experience is *complacency*. *Never* take firearms safety for advantage. If this occurs, you can be guaranteed that there will eventually be a firearm's safety mishap ranging from a careless oversight to the serious wounding or death of yourself, a citizen or fellow officer. **Firearm safety begins and ends with you**. It is also the responsibility of **all individuals** who are involved in training or have some degree of contact with firearms.

Firearms safety is everyone's business and responsibility. It is imperative that an officer does not trust anyone regarding the condition of the firearm. It is their sole responsibly to ensure that the firearm is safe.

The Four Fundamentals of Firearms Safety

All civilians and police officers that have an interest in firearms MUST abide by the four simple rules of firearms handling. These cardinal rules are listed below in Box 4-1.

BOX 4-1
THE CARDINAL RULES OF FIREARMS HANDLING

- Treat all firearms as if they are loaded at all times
- Point the muzzle in a safe direction
- Keep your finger off the trigger and outside the trigger guard until you are on target and ready to shoot
- Be sure of your target, backstop and beyond

CARDINAL RULE #1   TREAT ALL FIREARMS AS IF THEY ARE LOADED AT ALL TIMES

Firearms are ALWAYS Loaded. Keep this permanently ingrained in your mind and live by this statement. Check and double-check the condition of a weapon when:

- It is handed to you
- You hand a firearm to someone else
- You are you putting a firearm away or in storage
- You are getting ready for duty/training

Accidents can happen anywhere and at any time. They can happen on and off-duty, while cleaning a firearm, or confiscating a firearm that was used in a crime. Because firearms are part of an officer's job, police officers become quite relaxed, and perhaps complacent, around firearms, taking some things for granted, such as the safe handling of firearms. Regardless of the situation, the expertise level of the officer in the context of firearms, and the situation at hand, all officers must follow and enforce this rule.

This rule may be difficult to enforce at times. Take for example the seizure of firearms. While officers may have an interest in examining these weapons, police officers should not allow fellow officers to examine confiscated weapons. The sharing or examining of seized or confiscated weapons is a fundamental violation of this Cardinal rule. There are several reasons why. First, one should never examine, play with, or experiment with weapons. This is what leads to accidents and death. Second, this weapon could be a crime gun. By showing other officers this firearm, the chain of custody could be corrupted and the evidentiary value of the firearm could be jeopardized in later court proceedings. Third, a person does not know the condition or integrity of the firearm. The mechanics of the weapon could be faulty. For example, the owner(s) of the weapon could have modified it, rendering any safety features defective, and a second or third party does not know the condition of that firearm.

CARDINAL RULE #2   POINT THE MUZZLE IN A SAFE DIRECTION

What constitutes a safe direction? A safe direction is determined by the officer who is handling the firearm. It can be best described as that direction where if a discharge should occur, there would be no personal injury and little, if any, property damage.

In some situations, it is not easy to determine what constitutes a safe direction. For example, a hard concrete or linoleum floor is not a good surface to point the firearm at because of the potential for ricochet. You as an officer is in control of this situation. Take for example, where a police officer needs to load his/her firearm for duty. Would he/she do it in a crowded locker room? Unfortunately some do, and the outcome can be clearly seen by bullet holes in lockers, nicks on the floors, and holes in ceilings. A simple solution would be to holster the weapon in the locked back position (which will be discussed later in this chapter) and move to a more appropriate and safer location where there is a designated weapons loading station.

Take, for example, an encounter the author had at the Federal Law Enforcement Training Center. While standing in line in at the reception building to check into the facility, an agent ahead in line was told to clear his weapon prior to entering the training facility. In a lobby filled with many individuals, this agent stepped out of line, and cleared his weapon in the crowded lobby by pointing it toward the linoleum floor. People scattered while many expressed their concerns to this agent regarding his reckless conduct. There was a dedicated weapon clearing station located behind this building to ensure everyone's safety.

In other cases, pointing the muzzle down and toward a wall may not be appropriate. In many residential and office settings, walls are simply constructed of thin drywall (composed of gypsum) that a bullet can easily penetrate. By pointing the weapon in this direction, a person violates the 4th cardinal rule: Know your backstop and beyond. The backstop in this case is a thin piece of drywall. Ask yourself: what is behind that wall - an occupied bedroom or office?

Pointing the firearm in a safe direction also applies to when an officer is on duty. For example, officers may have their handgun drawn during building searches. They may also use shotguns and rifles in situations that also require that the muzzles be pointed in a safe direction. It also applies to off-duty use where officers will need to point their weapon in a safe direction when unloading, storing, and securing their firearms.

The Laser Rule

One way to remember to point the firearm in a safe direction is to consider that there is a laser that is located inside the barrel of the firearm. This laser emits a deadly beam of light that is projected out of the muzzle. This laser beam is always on, and it will destroy anything that it passes by or touches. Wherever this weapon is pointed and whatever it is pointed at, this laser will destroy that object in its path.

A common "laser rule" violation during both low and high-risk police operations is "sweeping" individuals with the muzzle of the firearm allowing the laser to touch or cross another person. This may be a special concern with long arms that may be more difficult to control because of their length or size. Remember: Whatever that laser beam comes into contact with will be destroyed.

The laser rule does not apply just to "lasering" other people. Students and officers also need to be aware that they will often "laser" themselves when they are using their firearm. This often occurs during an improper draw, reload, and re-holster of the firearm. The laser rule also applies to objects. Accidental or unintentional discharges may also cause property damage. Through proper training, attention, and due diligence by handlers, these issues can be easily overcome and avoided.

CARDINAL RULE #3   *KEEP YOUR FINGER OFF THE TRIGGER AND OUTSIDE THE TRIGGER GUARD UNTIL YOU ARE ON TARGET AND READY TO SHOOT*

The shooter has more than enough time to index their trigger finger on the trigger as they are aligning the firearm's sights on the threat and establishing a sight picture. With proper training, this should become a reflexive action, where the shooter does not necessarily have to think through the process—it simply becomes a spontaneous response that is learned by establishing muscle memory—just like catching a ball—you do not have to think through the process every time you do this.

In other cases, where the firearm's sights are already aligned with the threat, as is the case in a felony stop, the trigger finger is not on the trigger. Instead, the trigger finger is resting outside the trigger guard and is aligned with the frame of the firearm, and pointing at the threat. If a decision is made to fire the weapon, all the shooter has to do is move their trigger finger to the inside of the trigger guard and index it on the face of the trigger. This does not take long period of time. In fact, a study conducted by Tobin and Fackler (2001) found that the average time for an officer (who already has their weapon drawn and pointed at a target) to fire their weapon with their finger outside the trigger guard was 0.677 seconds. Of course, this reaction time can be even faster through attentiveness, proper training, and practice.

CARDINAL RULE #4   *BE SURE OF YOUR TARGET, BACKSTOP AND BEYOND*

You, and only you, are responsible for the shots fired from your weapon. This requires some points to consider: First, you must identify the target as a threat. Do not rely upon others to determine if it is a threat. In some cases, for example, it will be. In other cases it may not. Since you are responsible for the shots you fired, you need to personally assess the threat potential of your target. Second, the shooter must make sure that the area around and behind the threat is clear of people and objects that could be injured or damaged by gunfire.

The backstop must effectively stop a projectile. At a minimum, the backstop must prevent the projectile from traveling great distances, and prevent damage, injury, or harm to people and property. Police handgun rounds as well as shotgun and rifle ammunition have the ability to travel great distances. As a result, in some cases, the projectile(s) may penetrate or miss the backstop, so an officer needs to consider what is beyond the backstop that could cause personal and property damage and expose the officer and agency to civil liability and perhaps, criminal charges.

The following are some common examples of a backstop:

- Distance – bullets/projectiles will drop (i.e. gravity) as distance and time increase. Because of this fact, distance from objects and people can be considered a backstop
- Solid, non-penetrable walls
- Wooded Areas – trees and brush may slow and stop a bullet from traveling long distances
- The sky – the safest direction (believe it or not) in some cases would be to angle a shot upward to avoid damage, injury and/or harm

Making Firearms Safe

In many of these situations, officers will be required to check and clear weapons that have been seized or used in the commission of a crime. While these firearms will vary in type and function, one critical issue that needs to be understood is that the officer cannot rely upon the integrity of found and unfamiliar weapons. Many firearms may be quite old, and they may have not been properly maintained. In other cases, they have been modified, which could affect the safety mechanism(s) of the firearm. If there is any doubt regarding the function or integrity of the weapon, the officer should not attempt to make the firearm safe.

Making Pistols Safe

The steps associated with making pistols safe are:

- Adhere to the 4 Cardinal Rules of Firearms Handling
- Visually inspect and study the firearm prior to picking it up (if applicable) to gain an understanding of what type of weapon it is and how it functions. If in doubt, ask for assistance from someone else
- Pick up the weapon, using the master grip & point it in a safe direction. Keep your finger off the trigger and outside the trigger guard
- If the firearm has an external safety, engage the safety

Making A Pistol Safe Checklist:

At a minimum the operator must:

- ✓ Activate Safety (if present)
- ✓ Remove the Magazine
- ✓ Work the Slide
- ✓ Lock Slide to the Rear
- ✓ Visually & Manually Inspect
- ✓ Reholster/Secure

- Remove the magazine from the weapon & secure it
- Check the condition of the hammer (if present). If the hammer is in the rearward position or in single-action stage, it must be returned to the forward position. If the firearm is cocked, the following guidelines should be followed

  - Do not trust the de-cock lever on unknown firearms! The weapon may be defective or modified, causing an accidental discharge when the de-cock lever is activated. Instead, while maintaining a grip on the weapon:

    - Place a pencil or other small diameter object between the hammer and the frame or slide of the weapon
    - Place the strong hand thumb on the hammer spur to control the fall of the hammer. Keep the thumb on the hammer to control the movement of the hammer as it travels forward
    - Pull the trigger to the rear to allow the hammer to move slightly forward until it can no longer move forward
    - Keeping rearward tension on the hammer, slowly remove the small diameter object and ease the hammer down the rest of the way
    - This firearm is now out of single action stage

- With the support hand, pull the slide to the rear using the "hand over" technique
- Work the slide/action. Using the "hand over" technique, work the slide back and forth a couple times
- Lock the slide to the rear by engaging the slide stop lever (if there is one) on the frame or receiver of the firearm
- Visually and physically check the chamber and magazine well of the firearm to make sure there is no ammunition in the firearm

If the firearm is seized or being used for evidentiary reasons, it must be made so it cannot readily function. There are several ways to make sure a firearm cannot be readily restored, and to indicate to others that it is safe. Some of the more common methods to secure a pistol include:

- Trigger Locks
- A cable lock or flex cuff through the magazine well and ejection port to make sure a magazine cannot be inserted into the firearm

- A cable lock or flex cuff through the barrel and chamber to make sure the action will not close and a round cannot be fed into the chamber
- Disassembling the weapon/removing the slide and barrel from the frame

Making Revolvers Safe

The steps associated with making revolvers safe are:

- Adhere to the 4 Cardinal Rules of Firearms Handling
- Visually inspect and study the firearm prior to picking it up (if applicable) to gain an understanding of what type of firearm it is and how it functions. If in doubt, ask for assistance from someone else
- Pick up the firearm, using the master grip & point it in a safe direction. Keep your finger off the trigger and outside the trigger guard
- If the firearm has an external safety, engage the safety
- Check the condition of the hammer (if present). If the hammer is in the rearward position or in single-action stage, it must be brought back to the forward position. If the firearm is cocked:

  - Place a pencil or other small diameter object between the hammer and the frame of the firearm
  - Place the strong hand thumb on the hammer spur to control the fall of the hammer. Keep the thumb on the hammer to control its movement
  - Press/pull the trigger to allow the hammer to move slightly forward until it can no longer move forward
  - Keeping rearward tension on the hammer, slowly remove the small diameter object and ease it down until it is in its most forward position
  - The firearm is now out of single action stage

- With the strong hand thumb, push or pull (depending upon the manufacturer) the cylinder release and swing the cylinder out
- Use the ejector rod to remove the ammunition out of the cylinder chambers
- Secure the ammunition
- Visually and physically check the cylinder chambers to make sure there is no ammunition left in any of the cylinder chambers

If the revolver is seized or being used for evidentiary reasons, it must be made safe so it cannot readily function. There are several ways to make sure this revolver cannot be readily restored, and to indicate to others that it is safe. Some of the more common methods are shown here:

**Figure 22
Trigger Locks**

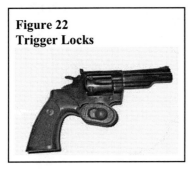

**Figure 23
Cable Lock through cylinder**

**Figure 24
Cable lock through barrel**

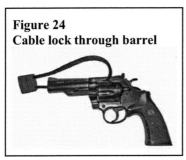

**Figure 25
Handcuff through top strap**

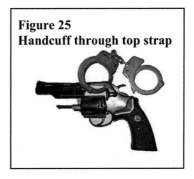

Making Semi-Automatic & Manual Long Arms Safe

The principles related to making a semiautomatic and manual long arm safe, whether it is a rifle or shotgun, are similar to making pistols and revolvers safe. HOWEVER, there are some differences that need to be considered. For example, in some cases (because their size) some of the steps in making the long arm safe can be conducted without physically picking up the firearm. This may be a safer alternative for officers to consider.

The procedures to be followed for making a semi-automatic long arm safe are:

- Adhere to the 4 Cardinal Rules of Firearms Handling
- Visually inspect and study the firearm *prior* to picking it up (if applicable) to gain an understanding of what type of weapon it is and how it functions. If in doubt ask for assistance from someone else
- Find the external safety. Engage the safety to the "on" position

101

- Remove the magazine (if applicable)
- Secure the magazine and ammunition
- Activate the action to remove the ammunition from the chamber
- Lock the slide action open
- Visually and physically check the weapon's chamber and magazine to make sure it is clear of any ammunition
- Secure the firearm and ammunition

With semiautomatic shotguns the procedure for making them safe is different from that of a rifle. Usually semiautomatic shotguns do not have an external box-style magazine. Usually the shells are stored in a tubular magazine that is located under the barrel of the firearm. To safely clear these types of weapons, the officer must physically activate the shell stops that are located in the receiver of the shotgun. While these may be difficult to locate and manipulate, an officer should NEVER cycle the live ammunition through the firearm to empty the magazine. Cycling the weapon to extract and eject live rounds could easily result in an accidental discharge.

Making a Manual Long Arm Safe

The steps in making a manual long arm safe are very similar to making a semiautomatic safe. One of the primary differences between the two is that usually the manual long arm does not have a detachable box magazine. Instead, there may be an internal magazine that is located in the receiver of the weapon, or there may be a tubular magazine that needs to be safely unloaded. As is the case with making the semiautomatics safe, a person should NEVER, cycle or feed live rounds through the action of the firearm to empty the magazine. If the firearm has some type of non-detachable internal magazine, the following procedures should be followed:

- Adhere to the 4 Cardinal Rules of Firearms Handling
- Visually inspect and study the firearm prior to picking it up (if applicable) to gain an understanding of what type of firearm it is and how it functions. If in doubt ask for assistance from someone else
- Locate the external safety. Engage the safety to the "on" position
- Activate the action to remove the ammunition from the chamber of the weapon
- Lock the action in the "open" position, so the chamber is open
- Manually remove the ammunition that is contained in the magazine (if applicable). DO NOT cycle the weapon.
- Visually and physically check the weapon's chamber and magazine to make sure it is clear and empty of ammunition
- Properly secure the weapon and ammunition

Traditional lever action firearms also require a different series of procedures. Common lever actions have a tubular magazine that is located under the barrel of the firearm. To make this type of firearm safe, the officer has to cycle the weapon to extract and eject the ammunition contained in the magazine. Besides cycling the firearm, another way to remove cartridges in the magazine tube is to dismantle the magazine tube, which requires some advanced knowledge and skill.

Range Safety

Everyone on the range is responsible for safety. Many individuals make the faulty assumption that range instructors are completely responsible for safety on the range. While this is one of their primary duties, **everyone** on the range is responsible for one another's safety. Unfortunately what often occurs in range training is the building of poor safety habits. These poor habits are then practiced on the street and off-duty. The building of the safe handling of firearms begins with range training.

One of the key safety concerns involves the conduct of officers on the range. The great majority of accidents occur on the range because of inattentive behaviors and horseplay. Another primary cause of accidents is the failure of individuals to realize that they are responsible for safety on the range. Safety cannot be delegated away.

Following is a list of some of the other common range rules a shooter will encounter:

- If you observe an unsafe condition, you must immediately take appropriate action to stop the training activity. *Anytime you observe an unsafe act that could endanger someone, you have the responsibility and authority to shout "CEASE FIRE"*
- Firearms will only be handled during a course of fire or under the direction of the range master
- Every time a firearm is picked up for any purpose, open the action (if not open already) and make a manual and visual inspection to make sure that it is not loaded. Never trust your memory and consider every firearm as loaded until you have proved otherwise
- Do not leave a loaded firearm unattended. Un-holstered firearms will have actions open at all times when not being used, with the magazine removed

- Dry firing (firing a weapon with no ammunition in it) is allowed only at the firing line and under the supervision of an instructor
- The muzzle of all firearms will be pointed downrange at all times when not holstered
- Do not handle a firearm on the firing line when there is someone downrange
- No conversations are allowed between shooters while on the firing line. This causes distractions for other shooters that could lead to a safety issue
- The use of alcoholic beverages and/or narcotics is prohibited. Alcohol and other controlled substances do not mix with firearms
- If a firearm is accidentally dropped, report this immediately to an instructor who will inspect the firearm to ensure that it is safe to use. Let it lie and notify an instructor
- Holstered firearms will have the keeper snapped or shroud locked down at all times. The safest place for a firearm is in a secured holster
- Do not bend over to retrieve dropped items. A shooter will be permitted to do so after the line has been declared safe
- Do not fire at a target that has been turned to the edged position, and only fire at the proper target
- All shooters must wear ear protection while engaging in live firing on the range
- All shooters must wear shatter resistant eye protection at all times on the range, even when they are not shooting
- All shooters must wear eye protection when cleaning weapons
- Any injury sustained during firearms training, regardless of how minor it may seem, will be reported to an instructor immediately
- If the weapon fails to fire, it will be the shooter's responsibility to clear the stoppage and continue the stage of fire
- Participants are not allowed to take an equipment tray or box to the firing line. All equipment and ammunition will be carried on the shooter in an approved manner
- Never leave or turn around at your assigned firing position or move forward of the firing line unless directed to do so
- Be sure your firearm and ammunition are compatible
- No one may leave the firing line unless approved by the instructor
- On a "COLD RANGE" (all weapons are unloaded) do not load until the command is given
- On a "HOT RANGE" (weapons are loaded) once the initial command to load is given, the shooter will maintain their guns in a loaded condition

- Shooters must follow all other range rules established by that particular range
- Never anticipate a command

Training Tip: Many range-related accidents are the result of the range itself. Make sure the range is cleared of all obstructions to ensure a safe range environment. Be especially careful of spent cartridges and shells on the ground that could cause a slip-and-fall-related injury.

Firearms Safety & Lead Exposure

Shooters need to be aware that they will be exposed to lead. A primary component of a bullet is lead. While used heavily in the manufacture of bullets, lead is **highly** toxic to the human body. To one extent or another a person's entire body, especially the face, arms and hands will be covered with lead when engaged in firearms training.

Lead, a natural element (Pb on the periodic table of elements) is a systemic poison that serves no known useful function once absorbed by the body. Taken in large enough doses, it can kill a person in a matter of days. According to OSHA, most exposures occur with inorganic lead. Inorganic lead is not metabolized by the body. It is directly ingested, distributed and excreted. The rate of ingestion depends on its chemical and physical form and on the physiological characteristics of the exposed person (e.g. nutritional status and age). Lead adversely affects numerous body systems, and causes health problems and diseases which arise after periods of exposure as short as days or as long as several years. Lead is distributed primarily in the blood, soft tissues (kidneys, bone marrow, liver, and brain) and mineralizing tissues (bones and teeth) (Substance Data Sheet for Occupational Exposure to Lead, 2003 (1926.62 App A)).

Short & Long-Term Effects of Lead Poisoning

Lead poisoning has both long and short-term effects. However, there is no sharp dividing line between rapidly developing acute effects of lead, and chronic effects which take longer to acquire. A short-term exposure to large quantities of lead can lead to acute encephalopathy (en-ceph-a-lop-athy) which is a disease of the brain. Short-term occupational exposures of this magnitude are highly unusual, but not impossible.

Long-term or chronic overexposure to lead may result in severe damage to the blood-forming cells, nervous system, urinary, and reproductive systems. Below is an excerpt from OSHA's Substance Data Sheet for Occupational Exposure to Lead (1926.62 App A)):

Some common symptoms of chronic overexposure include loss of appetite, metallic taste in the mouth, anxiety, constipation, nausea, pallor, excessive tiredness, weakness, insomnia, headache, nervous irritability, muscle and joint pain or soreness, fine tremors, numbness, dizziness, hyperactivity and colic. Damage to the central nervous system in general and the brain (encephalopathy) in particular is one of the most severe forms of lead poisoning. Chronic overexposure to lead also results in kidney disease with few, if any, symptoms appearing until extensive and most likely permanent kidney damage has occurred. Chronic overexposure to lead also impairs the reproductive systems of both men and women. Overexposure to lead may result in decreased sex drive, impotence and sterility in men. Lead can alter the structure of sperm cells raising the risk of birth defects. There is evidence of miscarriage and stillbirth in women whose husbands were exposed to lead or who were exposed to lead themselves. Lead exposure also may result in decreased fertility, and abnormal menstrual cycles in women. The course of pregnancy may be adversely affected by exposure to lead since lead crosses the placental barrier and poses risks to developing fetuses. Children born of parents either one of whom were exposed to excess lead levels are more likely to have birth defects, mental retardation, behavioral disorders or die during the first year of childhood. Overexposure to lead also disrupts the blood - forming system resulting in decreased hemoglobin (the substance in the blood that carries oxygen to the cells) and ultimately anemia. Anemia is character- ized by weakness, pallor and fatigability as a result of decreased oxygen carrying capacity in the blood.

Lead poisoning occurs in two ways: inhalation and ingestion. Both these methods of delivery will occur to some extent during firearms training. According to OSHA, lead (except for certain organic lead compounds such as tetraethyl lead) **is not absorbed through the skin**. Organic (tetraethyl and tetramethyl) lead, which was added to gasoline up until the late 1970s, is not commonly encountered.

Lead inhalation is one issue to consider. According to OSHA, "when lead is scattered in the air as a dust, fume, or mist it can be inhaled and absorbed through the lungs and upper respiratory tract. Inhalation of airborne lead is generally the primary source of occupational lead absorption." Modern forms of gunpowder or accelerants are considered to be smokeless. However, on the range a shooter can readily see smoke or gasses exiting the muzzle of the firearm after it is fired. A great deal of this gas is composed of lead-based fumes. These lead gasses are created as a result of the bullet design. In the context of jacketed bullets, for example, the jacket does not entirely encase the bullet. In many cases, the base of the bullet does not have a jacket. The lead base is directly in contact with the powder. When the powder rapidly burns, this lead actually converts into a molten state on the surface, which in turn creates a lead gas that later exits the muzzle of the firearm. Hence, shooters are inhaling a great deal of lead in the form of gas.

A person can also ingest lead. After shooting in an open or confined area, lead dust will have settled or deposited on a person's skin and clothing. This can easily be transferred to the mouth, swallowed and be absorbed through the digestive system. If a person handles food, cigarettes, chewing tobacco, and other foodstuffs, lead residue could be transferred to the mouth through these products. If the shooter uses make-up and lotions such as sunscreen, lead can also cling to these oily surfaces, eventually ending up on the hands, and enter the mouth and digestive tract.

A significant portion of the lead that is inhaled or ingested gets into the blood stream. Once in the blood stream, lead is circulated throughout the body and stored in various organs and tissues. Some of this lead is quickly filtered out of the body and excreted. However, some remains in the blood and other tissues. As exposure to lead continues, the amount stored in the body will increase if the person is absorbing more lead than what the body is excreting. Even though a person may not be aware of the immediate symptoms of lead poisoning, this lead that is stored in the tissues can slowly cause irreversible damage. Damage begins first to individual cells, then to the organs, and eventually entire body systems (Substance Data Sheet, 2003).

In some cases, a shooter may become quite complacent regarding lead exposure on the range. They may reason that they are only on the range for a short period of time, which is probably true. However, when one considers the fact that they are on the range on a bi-monthly or quarterly basis, the exposure time to lead dramatically increases. A shooter also needs to consider the fact that like in many poison situations, it is the repeated, prolonged exposure to a toxin that leads to serious health problems. Hence, when lead exposure is compounded over a police career, these relatively "small" exposures constitute a great amount of exposure to lead. Consider the following example of a police officer that spends a minimum of 10 hours on the range per year, not including their initial academy or firearms training.

Over a 25-year period, this would add up to 250 hours of exposure. This does not include secondary exposure to the toxin in the context of having lead residue on the uniform that is transferred from their clothing and shoes, and to their vehicles, homes, and furniture. Consider this point: If someone told the reader that they would be exposed to 250 hours of lead exposure, would they be concerned? The answer would be an unequivocal **yes**.

Many police agencies and ranges have recognized the hazards of lead and the costs associated with OSHA requirements for lead clean up. Some agencies have prohibited the use of lead-based ammunition and have gone to environmentally friendly or "green" ammunition. In other cases, however, police officers will still be exposed to lead on the range. For those individuals and agencies that use lead-based ammunition, there are some ways to limit lead exposure. These methods are listed below:

- Do not smoke on the range. Smoking causes the bronchial tubes to dilate or expand. This will result in lead being deposited "deeper" into the lungs, making it more difficult to later expel through the normal respiration process
- Do not eat on the range. Food will become contaminated with lead dust. A person's hands will also be contaminated with lead dust and other toxins that will easily rub off and transfer to foods
- Do not place your fingers in your mouth or rub your eyes until you have washed your hands. This will reduce the risk of ingesting lead and other range toxins
- Do not collect fired brass in baseball hats. Used brass will contaminate the cap with lead dust. This lead dust will then be deposited in and on one's hair, hands, food, etc.
- Do not collect used brass in pockets. In some situations, after the training is over, shooters will police the range and collect used brass in their pockets. This will result in lead dust being deposited into the pockets and later being transferred to their hands and mouth
- In some "primitive" ranges, water and other means to clean oneself is not available. If water is not available, shooters should consider carrying a box of diaper or handiwipes, and/or a bottle of water and towels for the purpose of removing lead residue from their exposed skin and hands
- Consider applying all lotions and sunscreen prior to arrival at the range to minimize lead exposure. If a person applies lotions or sunscreen after being exposed to lead, they will essentially "sandwich" the toxins between their skin and the lotion(s). The

lotions will prevent the toxins from naturally falling off the body and essentially trap them, where later they may be transferred to the mouth, clothing, upholstery and other individuals, to name just a few sites where the toxins will end up

Shooters also need to consider the fact that they may be contaminated with lead after their training. According to OSHA, at the greatest risk are children under the age of six because they are undergoing rapid neurological and physical development. In order to avoid any issue regarding lead poisoning at home, consider the following points:

- Be aware that the hair and clothes are contaminated with lead and other toxins
- Change your shoes/take your shoes off before entering your home in order to avoid tracking in toxins
- After training, shooters should wash all exposed skin thoroughly with cold water and plenty of soap. Cold water is preferred to warm or hot, because warmer water temperatures expand the skin pores, depositing the lead deeper into the skin's pores, making it a little more difficult to remove all traces of lead
- Avoid physical contact with family members until after a shower, shampoo, and change of clothes

Other Range Toxins

There are other toxins in a range environment besides lead that shooters will be exposed to. For example, primers often contain highly sensitive base metals including mercury fulminate, which is toxic to the human body. When firearms are discharged, minute traces of this and other elements are present. A variety of solvents used to clean firearms are also toxic. These toxins can also be inhaled, ingested and absorbed through the skin, causing short and long-term health risks. To limit exposure to these toxins, shooters should wear rubber gloves when cleaning firearms and follow other rules associated with lead contamination.

Hearing & Eye Protection on the Range

It is always easy to identify the retired police officers. They are the one's who suffer from a hearing loss from the prolonged exposure to gunfire. The stories regarding "early" forms of hearing protection are sometimes humorous in nature, but tragic. In one police department, for example, officers would take their spent .38 cartridges and use them as earplugs. Not only did these not serve well to prevent hearing loss, but it also resulted in these officers probably ingesting more lead into their system.

One of the most common ways hearing protection is measured is by the Noise Reduction Rating (NRR). Hearing protection must have an acceptable NRR level, and it must be capable of keeping noise exposure below 85 decibels. The higher the NRR number, the better the level of hearing protection. For example, a NRR of 29 is better than a NRR of 20. However, the NRR is calculated under controlled laboratory conditions, and they may overestimate "real world" NRR's by 140 to 2000 percent (Berger, 1996). Other studies have found that ear plugs yield only 25% of the labeled NRR, while foam plugs and earmuffs may yield only 40% of the labeled NRR values (Berger, 1998). Several factors could affect the overall performance of the hearing protection. They include overall fit and comfort, compatibility with the activities being performed, and the belief that the device(s) will prevent hearing loss (Criteria for…, 1998). In other situations, the shooter may not want to wear the hearing protection because they are not "in fashion."

In order to prevent hearing damage from the prolonged exposure to gunfire, shooters should wear both muff-style cups that encase or completely cover the ear and plugs that are inserted into the ear canal. By "double-plugging", shooters will be better ensured that their hearing will be protected, as the two sources of protection will compliment one another. When shooting rifles or shotguns for example, the stock of the weapon may cause the muff-style protection to move or create a gap, which could lead to hearing damage. By wearing both, if this would occur, the shooter will still be protected by the ear canal plug. While a concern may arise that "double-plugging" could lead to a safety concern because officers to some degree will not be able to hear range commands, this concern can be readily addressed by using a PA system on the range.

Eye protection is also another mandatory safety item. Eye protection should met all NIOSH Standards. The glasses should meet American National Standards Institute (ANSI) Z87.1 certified industrial eye protection that is marked "Z87" (or "Z87.1") on the frame or lens. They should also have some form of side protection, such as side shields or a wrap-around styled lens. It is also recommended that safety glasses be treated for anti-fog (Eye safety, 2003).

Regardless of if the shooter is on the line shooting or "off-line" loading magazines or waiting to shoot, there is the potential that they can be struck

110

in the eye by debris. In many situations bullets will fragment, causing small pieces called "spall" to propel back at the shooters (remember—for every action there is an equal and opposite reaction). Additionally, this spall may also fly over the shooters and strike non-shooters on the range. This may be particularly dangerous when shooting at shorter distances and on steel targets. For example, in one incident, a range instructor, who was standing approximately 10 yards off the firing line was struck by the jacket of a bullet that penetrated his pants and lodged in his skin. This required medical attention.

Eye protection is also required when cleaning weapons or being around weapons that are being cleaned. As pointed out earlier in this chapter, many cleaning solvents are toxic. Eye protection will assist in preventing aerosol mists from getting in the eyes. Eye protection will also ensure that a person does not get struck from flying parts and other debris such as powder residue and gun parts. For example, some pistols do not have captured recoil springs. Instead, the recoil springs extend their full length. When disassembling these weapons, there is the risk that these springs will launch themselves (and the recoil guide rod), which could lead to an eye injury. A good rule of thumb is to have a mandatory policy of requiring eye protection at all times while on the range.

Other Safety Equipment

All safety equipment (including body armor) should also be worn when cleaning firearms. Unfortunately, there have been documented cases of accidental discharges in cleaning rooms. When cleaning weapons, shooters should also make sure that this is done in a well-ventilated area in order to avoid breathing in large quantities of solvents and other toxins. Unlike lead, many of these solvents can be absorbed through the skin. As previously discussed, shooters should also wear rubber gloves when using these chemicals to prevent poisoning.

Accidental/Unintentional Discharges

An accidental discharge (AD) occurs when the user of the weapon does not intend to discharge the firearm. Nevertheless, the firearm does discharge. Accidental discharges are the result of the careless handling of firearms. Very rarely can one "blame" the design or integrity of a firearm for an accidental discharge. An accidental discharge is the result of the user. They failed to follow the second fundamental rule of the safe handling of

111

firearms: They did not keep their finger off the trigger and outside the trigger guard.

According to Edward Tully (1996), there are four primary causes of unintentional or accidental discharges of semiautomatic firearms. These include: carelessness; poor weapon design; involuntary muscle movements; and, the lack of familiarity of the firearm. These are discussed in detail below.

Carelessness

Tully (1996) writes that carelessness just doesn't happen. Instead, it is a common human trait. "It is the result of a lackadaisical attitude that has developed over the years in many things they do" (p. 2). Handling a firearm requires great care and training in being particularly cautious in order that a person can react in a safe manner under crisis situations or conditions. Unfortunately, there are numerous examples of the careless handling of firearms.

Weapon Design

Tully (1996) proposes that some weapons by their design have too light a trigger pull for law enforcement applications and are unforgiving "of human error and rough handling"(p. 4). Meanwhile, others have a very short trigger pull that could also lead to an AD. Combined with the fact that in his opinion the majority of police officers do not receive enough firearms training (which this author also supports) these issues could lead to an AD.

Consider the following example: At a law enforcement meeting, a Chief of Police was attributing a recent accidental discharge of a firearm at his range because the weapon by its design was "inherently dangerous." The chief explained to his audience that the officer, while disassembling his off-duty firearm, pulled the trigger, subsequently discharging a round from the firearm. Was the weapon inherently dangerous by its design? NO. The weapon design was perhaps a contributing factor. Carelessness and poor training by the operator was the primary cause of the accidental discharge.

Involuntary Muscle Movements

Involuntary muscle contractions (contractions not controlled by the brain) may also account for accidental discharges. Involuntary muscle movements or contractions are caused by signal receptors that are found throughout the human body. These sensory cells under certain conditions can stimulate the nervous system and activate nerve cells that control muscle movements, eliciting the involuntary muscle contraction(s). In essence the brain is bypassed. A person does not think about these movements. They just happen, such as blinking one's eyes.

According to Tully (1996) there are three conditions that can cause these involuntary muscle contractions. They include sympathetic contraction, loss of balance, and startle reaction. These are explained in detail below:

Sympathetic Contraction

Sympathetic contraction is a condition that occurs when an individual who is exerting near or maximum force with one hand, has the same muscles in the opposite limb involuntarily react to that force by as much as 20% of the maximum force being used in the other hand. This is due to neural overflow, which is a term that is used to describe how a person's neural drive provided by the brain spreads to other muscles. What basically occurs is that there is "sensory overflow" to associated muscles when an involuntary contraction occurs.

Take for example this real-life example of sympathetic contraction. A local police officer while enacting an arrest had his weapon in his right hand and his finger on the trigger – a cardinal rule violation. When he forcefully grabbed the suspect with his left hand, the neural overflow "spread" to his adjoining or opposite muscles in his right hand. This caused him to pull the trigger to the rear and subsequently shoot out a store front window. Fortunately, nobody was physically injured in this mishap.

Loss of Balance

Loss of balance occurs when an individual loses their balance and the body automatically attempts to adjust itself. This does not require involvement of the brain since it is so rapid in nature. This loss of balance may also cause compensatory responses, where for example, forcefully grabbing something with a right hand may cause an involuntary muscle contraction in the opposite hand with enough pounds of pressure to pull a trigger or discharge a weapon. Tully (1996) proposes that these compensatory responses are enhanced under conditions of heightened excitability including foot chases and arrests—relatively common activities by police officers.

Startle Reaction

A startle reaction is a rapid response to a stimulus that is not commanded by the brain. For example, if there is a loud explosion, one may "jump" or be startled. These types of reactions are considered to be global in nature. They affect the entire body to some degree and are not limited to one limb or muscle group. In short, the entire body reacts to some type of stimulus.

Lack of Familiarity

As discussed in the Nomenclature chapter, there are a variety of firearms that police officers will encounter over the course of their career. Depending upon the type of firearm, its manufacturer, as well as any modifications to the firearm, a police officer may lack familiarity with its function and any safeties it may have. In order to avoid any safety issues or accidents, officers should adhere to and follow one simple rule. If an officer is not completely familiar with the firearm, do not handle it. Let other individuals who have more-depth knowledge of the firearm deal with it to prevent any accidents.

Ammunition Safety Issues

Besides safety issues related to the handling of firearms, ammunition may also be a safety issue or concern. Some of the common safety concerns related to ammunition are highlighted here:

- Individuals must inspect their ammunition for defects and the presence of lubricants. Defects, such as a damaged or cracked cartridge case could cause the firearm to malfunction. Excessive lubricants on cartridges could also cause ammunition to fail as these chemicals could foul or contaminate the propellant or powder.
- Make sure the ammunition is clean and will function in the weapon. Duty ammunition is exposed to a variety of environmental contaminants on a daily basis including rain, heat, cold, dirt, etc. This will affect the performance of the ammunition over time. Dirty ammunition could also feed and introduce dirt and other contaminants into the firearm, causing a malfunction and/or safety issue.
- Make sure the ammunition is the same caliber as the firearm. Figure 26 shows an example of a expanded cartridge case. This

9mm case was accidentally loaded into a .40 caliber magazine. This ammunition fit into the magazine, fed into the weapon, and fired. However, the pistol did not properly eject the spent cartridge, causing a malfunction. As can be seen by the photo, the cartridge brass expanded to the diameter of the chamber.

Figure 26 Expanded Brass

- If there is any doubt regarding matching the correct caliber ammunition to the weapon, do not attempt to use it.

Reloaded Ammunition

In some situations shooters may use reloaded ammunition. Reloaded ammunition is also called re-manufactured ammunition. Several issues need to be considered when using re-manufactured ammunition. These are listed below:

- Many manufacturers will void the warranty on the firearm if reloaded ammunition has been used.
- Improperly reloaded ammunition could lead to excessive pressures exerted on the weapon's action, frame and other components, causing premature wear and damage to the firearm.
- Under no circumstances should a police officer use reloaded ammunition as a duty round. Reloaded ammunition simply does not have the same quality as new, factory-loaded ammunition from a reputable company.
- There are also some issues regarding using reloaded ammunition for a training round (remember: we fight the way that we train). As a rule, police officers should train with that ammunition they will use on duty. The same type of ammunition should be used as one may experience a different feel or recoil among various types of ammunition. Take for instance a training round that has a lighter bullet weight and slower muzzle velocity. This ammunition will have a different feel in the context of recoil than the duty round (which could have a heavier feeling recoil to it). Now, under stressful conditions, accuracy and handling of the weapon (such as getting the sights aligned and back on target because of increased recoil) could be affected because the shooter did not train with their duty ammunition. Because they did not train with duty ammunition, they were unaccustomed to the heavier recoil or "kick" the weapon had with their particular duty ammunition.

115

Modern loading machinery and quality controls by ammunition manufacturers produce top quality ammunition. Nevertheless, shooters still need to inspect their ammunition for defects. In some rare cases, for example, the author has found cracked cartridge cases and primers that have been loaded backwards into the primer pocket of the cartridge case.

Common Ammunition Failures

Some of the more common issues related to ammunition failures include barrel obstructions, squib rounds, hang fires, and faulty primers.

Barrel Obstructions

A fully obstructed barrel, also known as a lodged or stuck round, is considered a catastrophic weapon failure. This weapon will simply not function with the obstruction in it. Under this type of situation the shooter needs to contact a certified armorer who will remove the obstruction and check the integrity of the firearm. In an actual gunfight, the shooter has one other option—shoot the obstruction out of the barrel. Depending upon the recommendations of the manufacturer, this may be a viable option.

There are two primary reasons for an obstructed barrel. First, there can be cases where there is not enough energy or gas to force the projectile out of the barrel. This could be on account of the fact that there may not have been enough (or no) powder in the cartridge case, or the powder may be somehow contaminated. In the case of a cartridge with no powder, for example, the energy from the primer can force the bullet into the barrel, while the casing can still be extracted and ejected from the firearm. Second, an obstructed barrel could be the result of foreign objects somehow disrupting the exit of the bullet from the barrel of the firearm.

Squib Round

The difference between a squib and an obstruction is that the squib round has exited the barrel of the firearm. A "squib" occurs when there is a defect with the powder in the cartridge. This defect could be attributed to no powder, not enough powder (under-loaded) or contaminated powder. Regardless, the primer is ignited and there is enough energy based on the powder that is available to push the bullet out of the barrel. In a squib round situation, the shooter will hear a loud "pop." This sound will be distinctly different from the loud "bang" traditionally associated with the weapon firing.

116

Consider the following example. In one instance, during a training session where the training staff was using reloaded ammunition (because the administration was cheap and went low bid against the training staff's recommendations), there were several squib rounds. Upon inspection of the ammunition, it was discovered that the manufacturer had used an excessive amount of case lubricant in their reloading process. This excess amount of oil contaminated the powder to the point where in some cases, there was not enough uncontaminated powder or propellant left to ignite and to push the bullet out of the barrel, causing a barrel obstruction. In other cases, the bullet did have enough energy to leave the barrel of the firearm. However, inspection of the bullet's impact on the paper target showed that in many cases there was not enough energy to force the bullet through the ¼ - inch plywood backer. The bullets stuck into the backer, failing to penetrate it.

Hang Fire

What happens in a hang fire situation is that the primer does not successfully ignite all of the powder in the cartridge simultaneously. Instead, the powder may burn slow, where eventually the remainder of the powder in the cartridge ignites and the firearm successfully discharges. What basically occurs is that the shooter will feel and hear a "pop" of the primer igniting and a simultaneous bang a fraction of a second later. The hang fire can be compared to shooting a black powder rifle. There is the ignition of the primer, followed by a "hang" or delay until the primer is successful in igniting the powder. A hangfire can be caused by a faulty primer, an obstruction in the cartridge's flash hole, and defective powder.

There are two remedies to deal with a hangfire. The first method is to keep the weapon pointed downrange in a safe manner. Remember, the powder may ignite causing the weapon to discharge. If the weapon discharges, there is no problem or issue. The second technique is used if the powder fails to ignite. With this second technique, the shooter should clear the weapon, using the tap-rack method and reengage the target if appropriate (this will be discussed in detail in the Malfunctions chapter). Remember: you are responsible for the condition of your own weapon ("we fight the way that we train"). Any other remedy such as stopping and raising your hand for assistance from the range master or instructor(s) is contra-training. In a real gunfight, you are solely responsible for maintaining the condition of your weapon. You must learn to do this on the range yourself.

Faulty Primers

In some situations, the cartridge's primer may be defective. The primer may not function, where even though the striker or firing pin did impact the primer, it did not detonate, resulting in the powder not igniting and the weapon not firing. This could be attributed to a defect in manufacturing or the primer becoming contaminated with moisture or solvents. In rare instances, primers can also be accidentally installed backwards into the cartridge case during the production process.

Other Conditions

Ammunition can pose other safety problems. While rare, the following issues could occur:

- Ammunition could be improperly sized. Improperly sized ammunition means that the ammunition is too large in diameter for the cartridge to correctly chamber. In cases where it is too small, this ammunition may chamber and fire. However, the weapon may fail to properly extract the case from the chamber.
- In other cases, the overall length of the case may be too short or too long. Both of these issues, of course, will cause problems for the shooter.

Conclusion

What makes safety particularly challenging for police officers is that they are in a double bind. The officer MUST ALWAYS safely handle firearms. At the same time, the officer needs to respond to a threat that suddenly appears. This requires that officers, often under high stress situations, safely use their firearms. Both of these objectives can easily be met by following the fundamental rules of firearms safety that were reviewed in this chapter. Officers must always follow the four cardinal rules of firearms safety.

They include:

- **TREAT ALL FIREARMS AS IF THEY ARE LOADED AT ALL TIMES**
- **POINT THE MUZZLE IN A SAFE DIRECTION**
- **KEEP YOUR FINGER OFF THE TRIGGER AND OUTSIDE THE TRIGGER GUARD UNTIL YOU ARE ON TARGET AND READY TO SHOOT**
- **BE SURE OF YOUR TARGET, BACKSTOP AND BEYOND**

This chapter has reviewed firearms safety primarily in the context of range safety. The principles of range safety also carry over into the safe handling of firearms on duty. The safe handling of firearms also applies to off-duty and civilian applications. In addition to range safety, this chapter also reviewed the major points in making pistols, revolvers, and a variety of long-arms safe. Regardless of the type of weapon that is being made safe, all of the fundamentals of the safe handling of firearms must be followed.

Concerns over lead exposure were also reviewed in this chapter. As pointed out, one of the primary concerns with lead poisoning is how it is inhaled and ingested into the body. In order to minimize the risk of lead poisoning, shooters should be aware that their body, and clothing worn while training, is contaminated with residual lead deposits. However, some common sense practices (i.e. changing one's clothes, not putting the fingers in one's mouth) can limit the amount of lead that is ingested. In addition to lead, meanwhile, shooters should always wear eye protection on the range. Shooters should also wear appropriate hearing protection and consider "double-plugging" to further protect their hearing.

This chapter also concluded with a review of the causes of accidental discharges and safety issues related to ammunition. Accidental discharges can be the result of carelessness, weapon design, and involuntary muscle movements. These involuntary muscle movements include sympathetic contractions, loss of balance and startle reactions. In the context of safety issues with ammunition, shooters should avoid using reloaded or re-manu-factured ammunition, while being aware that some of the common ammunition failures include barrel obstructions, squib rounds, and hang fires.

REFERENCES

Berger, E.H. (1998). A new standard for measuring hearing protection. Retrieved from www.cahoc.org/updateearticles/winter98/ansi.html. Last visited November 5, 2003.

Berger E.H., Franks JR, Lindgren F [1996]. International review of field studies of hearing protector attenuation. In: Axelsson A, Borchgrevink H, Hamernik RP, Hellstrom P, Henderson D, Salvi RJ, eds. <u>Scientific basis of noise-induced hearing loss</u>. New York: Thieme Medical Publishers, Inc., pp. 361-377.

Criteria for a recommended standard. Occupational noise exposure (June 1998). Washington D.C.: Cincinnati, OH: U.S. Department of Health and Human Services.

Eye safety: Emergency response & disaster recovery (2003). (www.cdc.gov/niosh/eyesafe.hmtl#1).

Substance Data Sheet for Occupational Exposure to Lead - 1926.62 App A. Regulations (Standards - 29 CFR)

Safety and Health Topics: Construction: Lead U.S. Department of Labor Occupational Safety & Health Administration <u>www.osha.gov</u>

Tobin, E.J. & Fackler, M.L (Fall, 2001). Officer reaction – response times in firing a handgun. <u>Journal of the international wound ballistics association,</u> 3(1), 6-9.

Tulley, E.J. (July, 1996). Unintentional discharge of police weapons: Part one. Beretta USA leadership bulletin, 2(4), 1-8.

Chapter 5
BREATHING

Introduction

B reathing is a physiological necessity. It is a life process that is often taken for granted, even though a person breathes quite a few times a minute. Perhaps the only time that a person realizes that they are breathing is when they have physically exerted themselves and they are out of breath. It is a simple fact that the muscles and organs require oxygen to properly function and survive. The heart and brain, which play an important role in the control of blood flow and respiration, rely solely upon aerobic metabolism to properly function (Rowell, 1993). Organs including the eyes are also sensitive to the loss of oxygen, while muscle groups, such as the fingers, require a constant and regulated flow of oxygen in order to properly function.

All body functions are respiratory-related (that is why this is the first chapter of the firearms fundamentals). As a consequence, controlling the breathing is a necessary component for marksmanship and combat-related shooting. There are two primary issues that will affect breathing. First, under normal, low stress training situations, a person needs to be concerned about breathing properly to control oxygen and carbon dioxide levels in their blood. Under high stress situations, meanwhile, a shooter needs to be concerned about how sympathetic nervous system activation (the body's fight or flight response) affects their breathing and their oxygen and carbon dioxide levels in the blood.

This chapter will provide the reader with an understanding of the importance of breathing when shooting. It will review the respiratory process, including issues related to improper breathing that could cause Alkalosis and Acidosis. This chapter will also review the effects of stress on the respiration process and discuss ways a person can better control their breathing. It will also provide ways to control the body's stress response through the use of abdominal breathing techniques.

Respiratory Physiology

Respiration is an exchange system where oxygen (O_2) and carbon dioxide (CO_2) molecules are transported within and expelled from the human body (Hlastala & Berger, 2001). Breathing is part of the autonomic system—it is mostly spontaneous or automatic in nature. Breathing is controlled and initiated by the central nervous system, particularly the medulla, which is part of the brainstem (McKinley & O'Loughlin, 2006).

The volume of air inhaled and exhaled in a natural breath is called the tidal volume. Each inhalation (known as an inspiration) and exhalation (or expiration) is measured in units per minute, which are referred to as tidal values. Generally, high tidal values per minute (or volume) occur during periods of exercise and stressful situations. Low tidal values per minute, meanwhile, are associated with activities including resting and sleeping. The average human breathes about 12 times a minute, producing a tidal minute volume of about 500 milliliters per unit (i.e. per breath depending upon body size and metabolic needs). As this chapter will point out, the tidal volume is an important component of the respiratory process. When there is a rapid or slow tidal volume, there is a loss of heart-breath rhythm, which can have serious effects on the performance of the human body (Fried, 1999).

The primary goal of respiration is to transport oxygen to the tissues in the human body. Oxygen is transported to the tissues two ways. The majority of oxygen (approximately 80-90%) is transported in the bloodstream and rapidly combines with the hemoglobin molecule in the blood. These molecules transport the oxygen to metabolically active tissues in the body. Second, oxygen is dissolved in the blood where it basically floats in the bloodstream and does not bond to any blood cells (Hlastala & Berger, 2001).

There are other gasses besides O_2 that are important in ensuring that the human body operates effectively. One of these gasses is carbon dioxide (CO_2) which is basically the main regulator of the respiratory process, which controls the respiration rate (McKinley & O'Loughlin, 2006). CO_2 is a gas waste product of cellular metabolism. On average, air is composed of approximately 21 % oxygen, .03 % carbon dioxide, 78 % nitrogen, and other trace gasses (Fried, 1999). When oxygen molecules are inhaled, they combine or bind with the hemoglobin in the bloodstream (capillary beds) and are delivered throughout the body. Metabolizing cells in the body exchange oxygen for their CO_2 waste, diffusing CO_2 into capillary blood.

This waste CO_2 is then carried through the circulatory system and exhaled by the lungs (Slomin & Chapin, 1967).

Oxygen and carbon dioxide levels must be properly maintained by the respiratory system. When a person exhales, their breath contains about 5 % carbon dioxide (Fried, 1999). The respiratory system must also maintain a proper acid-base balance or pH level. As pointed out, one of the primary waste gasses is CO_2, which is an acid. However, human blood needs to be slightly more of a base than an acid. To achieve this balance, the body contains and secretes a variety of substances including bicarbonate (a base) to buffer the acids it produces (Levitzky, 1999). Levels of CO_2 are automatically regulated by chemoreceptors that protect the body against hypoxia or too much CO_2 in the blood system (Hlastala & Berger, 2001). At the same time, if CO_2 levels drop, chemoreceptors supply the central nervous system with information that adjusts the respiration rate to restore the proper acid-base pH balance (Levitzky, 1999).

If this acid-base balance is thrown off for some reason, the human body develops an acid-base disorder that will impact the respiration process to some degree. To regulate the pH levels, the respiratory system and kidneys play an important role. However, the respiratory system is primarily responsible for pH regulation (Fried, 1999). It is responsible for the fast adjustments or compensation of pH levels during sudden shifts (Respiratory alkalosis, 2005). The kidneys only account for approximately 15% of the pH regulation (Fried, 1999) and take 1-2 days to become maximally effective in regulating the body's acid-base. They are effective for long-term disorders, including emphysema and other respiratory disorders and diseases (Respiratory alkalosis, 2005).

While the autonomic system regulates respiration, it can be altered unconsciously to a great degree by the actions of a shooter. Two conditions that are greatly affected by the respiratory system include alkalosis and acidosis. The symptoms of these two breathing disorders are shown in Box 5-1.

Alkalosis (Hyperventilation)

When alkaline (basic) levels get too high in the bloodstream, it is called alkalosis. A more common name for respiratory alkalosis is hyperventilation. Alkalosis is caused by the loss of carbon dioxide in the bloodstream (less than 4 % of CO_2 concentration in the bloodstream causes alkalosis). Breathing too much or too fast makes the body lose excessive amounts of CO_2, causing the body to shift its acid-base balance where the blood becomes too alkaline. When the blood becomes more alkaline-based, the hemoglobin molecules (that part of the blood that carries oxygen) retain oxygen instead of releasing it to tissues that need oxygen to perform and survive. Basically, the hemoglobin holds or attracts oxygen instead of delivering oxygen to the tissues that need it to function properly. This is known as hypoxia, which is the reduced oxygenation of body tissues (Fried, 1999). When this occurs, there is an increase in the body's sympathetic activity, including the secretion of stress-related hormones that increase the heart rate and cardiac output (Mohan, Golding & Patterson, 2001).

Hyperventilation causes a series of cascading and interrelated events in the human body. First, fast shallow breaths result in lower tidal volumes. When a person takes shallow or small breaths, this means that they will have to breathe more to secure the correct amounts of oxygen in the bloodstream. Breathing faster to get more oxygen increases the respiration rate per minute, which in turn further reduces the level of carbon dioxide in the body. The result of the loss of proper levels of CO_2 in the blood causes the autonomic nervous system to adjust respiration, heart rate, and blood flow where blood flow to the large skeletal muscles increases (i.e. the proximal muscles), while blood flow to external (i.e. distal) extremities, such as the hands and feet decrease (for example, cold hands can be the result of constricted blood vessels due to low blood carbon dioxide levels). The vascular beds in the brain are also affected. Arteries in the brain constrict, reducing the flow of blood (and oxygen), which in turn could make a person feel faint or dizzy (Fried, 1999). Other symptoms are shown in Box 5-1.

Acidosis (Hypoventilation)

Another acid-base disorder is acidosis. Respiratory acidosis, also referred to as hypoventilation, is caused by too much carbon dioxide in the blood, due to decreased breathing (Respiratory alkalosis, 2005). The blood, in effect becomes too acidic. Respiratory acidosis occurs because the body is not excreting enough CO_2 out of the bloodstream in comparison to the level of CO_2 produced by the body (Priestley, Levine & Litman, 2003). In this condition, CO_2 in the body bonds with water and forms carbonic acid, increasing the acidity level of the blood (Respiratory alkalosis, 2005).

The effects of acidosis vary. High concentrations of CO_2 in the blood as the result of hypoventilation cause an increased respiration rate because the reduced pH level in the bloodstream stimulates the respiratory system. Higher concentrations of CO_2 cause vasodilation (the blood vessels expanding) resulting in severe headaches, because of increased cranial pressure. Some other symptoms include restlessness, faintness, and dulling of consciousness. If CO_2 levels get above 15% in the blood, a person can experience tremors, muscular rigidity, and even the loss of consciousness (Levitzky, 1999).

The effect of acidosis is primarily neurological. Acidosis depresses the central nervous system. At first, the peripheral nerves are affected where muscles and nerves begin to be stimulated spontaneously. As a result of this stimulation, a person may experience muscular (or tetanic) contractions as well as extreme nervousness, or even convulsions if severe enough (Respiratory alkalosis, 2005). Respiratory acidosis is also a systemic vasodilator, and it causes the body to release epinephrine and norepinephrine, causing the heart to beat faster, creating a higher cardiac output. Because blood is now flowing faster, tissues do not have time to capture the oxygen, and in the process, they become oxygen deprived, further affecting their performance. CO_2 has also been found to diffuse rapidly across the blood-brain barrier, leading to an accumulation of CO_2 in cerebrospinal fluid. Increased elevations in CO_2 in the cerebrospinal fluid can cause confusion and headaches, while higher levels can cause drowsiness, depressed consciousness or even a coma and death (Priestley, Levine & Litman, 2003).

"Accidental" acidosis can be readily seen in persons who hold their breath while shooting. When they finish their string of shots, for example, they can be physically seen gasping for air. When engaged in this type of behavior, the shooter is causing self-induced hypoxia. In other situations, meanwhile, a person may have a case of the "shakes." If it is not due to muscle fatigue, a person is experiencing hand tremors because they are not breathing enough, subsequently increasing their CO_2 levels in the bloodstream, which in turn, causes certain parts of the body to shake, including the hands.

	BOX 5-1 ACIDOSIS & ALKALOSIS PATHOPHYSIOLOGY AND SYMPTOMS	
Condition	**Pathophysiology (Causes)**	**Symptoms**
Acidosis (Hypo- ventilation)	• Too Little Breathing • Increase of CO_2 in the bloodstream and tissues • Vasodilation/Increased blood flow to certain regions	• Increased Heart Rate/Pulse • Increased Respiration Rate • Decrease in Blood Pressure • Mental Cloudiness • Shortness of Breath, Easy Fatigue, Chronic Cough or Wheezing • Anxiety, confusion or memory loss, headaches • Sighing
Alkalosis (Hyper- ventilation)	• Too Much Breathing • Loss of CO_2 in the bloodstream • Hyperventilation (decreased levels of CO_2) • Vasoconstriction/decreased cerebral blood flow	• Lightheadedness • Inability to Concentrate; Confusion • Numbness & Tingling • Nervous Stimulation & Hyperexcitability of nervous system leading to spasms, muscular contractions, extreme nervousness and convulsions

Adapted from discoveryhealth.com; Medline.com; Fried, 1999; Hlastala & Berger, 2001; Rowell, 1993; and, Levitzky, 1999

In both these situations, the heart rate can easily rise to over 100 beats per minute. When this occurs, the sympathetic nervous system auto-matically engages, further compounding issues related to respiration, including hyperventilation, to restore proper respiration rates (Rowell, 1993).

The Stress Response & Its Effect on Breathing

As pointed out earlier in this chapter, breathing is controlled by the autonomic nervous system. This system regulates the body and keeps it in balance (or homeostasis) by releasing a wide variety of chemicals. The autonomic nervous system of the human body can be divided into the sympathetic (i.e. the "emergency" fight or flight system) and parasympathetic (the "stabilizer," "rest and digest" system) divisions. These two divisions are always working to some degree to regulate body functions; they are antagonistic to one another. That is, they work in opposition to one another to keep the human body constantly balanced or in homeostasis (Cacioppo & Tassinary, 1990).

The part of the brain that regulates autonomic activities such as breathing, heart rate, and body temperature is the hypothalamus (Adams, et al, 1997). The hypothalamus basically serves as a link between the nervous system and the endocrine system (a series of ductless glands) that adjust the body's functions. It can be considered as the "central command" of the body. The hypothalamus regulates and controls bodily functions by sending messages to the pituitary gland. The pituitary gland (which is actually connected to and is part of the hypothalamus) secretes chemicals called hormones into the bloodstream. These chemicals stimulate various organs and other endocrine glands, including the adrenal gland, that release additional chemicals, including epinephrine and small amounts of norepinephrine, into the bloodstream when the body's stress response is activated (Carrasco & VandeKar; 2003; Rowell, 1993).

The body has a variety of sensors that react to stress. Some of these include the visual, olfactory, gustatory (taste), enteroceptive (intestinal), and auditory sensors (or receptors) (Cacioppo & Tassinary, 1990). Stress can also be psychologically constructed. A person can psychologically react to something (i.e. fear of dogs or heights) or have anxiety disorders or panic attacks based on psychological factors. Regardless of whatever stresses a person, there are a series of neural and endocrine adaptations known as stress responses that the body activates.

Under "fight or flight" or stress situations, the hypothalamus (i.e. central command) activates two systems - the Hypothalamic-Pituitary-Adrenal (HPA) axis and the sympathetic nervous system (SNS) (Miller & O'Callaghan, 2002). Through the HPA axis, the adrenal gland secretes epinephrine (also known as adrenaline) which serves as a vasodilator (expanding the size of blood vessels) in certain parts of the body. For example, bronchial tubes in the lungs will expand to take in more air (Hlastala & Berger, 2001), while blood flow increases to certain parts of the body. The HPA also activates the release of small amounts of norepinephrine (a vasoconstrictor) into the bloodstream, that also affect various organs and regions in the body (Levitzky, 1999).

In addition to the HPA axis, the SNS also secretes norepinephrine (a vasoconstrictor) directly to specific regions or components of the human body through nerve endings via the nervous system — not the blood stream. Often SNS activation is considered to be an "all or none" approach, where under some type of stressor, the full extent of SNS activation occurs. This statement is not accurate. SNS activation is occurring all the time in the human body (through exercise and regulation of bodily processes, for example). SNS activation is not like throwing the "master switch," where the entire body is equally affected. Instead, SNS activation can be specific and target different regions or parts of the body (Hohen-Saric & McLoed, 1988). For this reason, the SNS response is not massive. Rather, it is refined, specific, and graded to the intensity of the stressor (Cacioppo & Tassinary, 1990).

At the same time, emotional arousal (i.e. psychological factors independent or combined with physiological factors) will also increase SNS activity. That is, if a person feels the effects of SNS activation, their degree or level of emotional arousal could actually serve to intensify the SNS arousal (Hugdahl, 1995). When considering the fact that many stressors are psychologically constructed and vary in intensity among people, it is the officer's psychological perception of the response that will affect their breathing. For example, a new recruit could be quite anxious on a traffic stop, simply because it is something new and unknown to them. This psychological anxiety could affect their breathing and activate the stress response. A veteran officer, meanwhile, may be less psychologically anxious. Since they are not as anxious, their body will not initiate the stress response.

SNS activity also depends upon constitutional (physical and psychological) and hereditary factors. In other cases, the degree of change is often subjective in nature where a person recognizes the changes "but not the degree of change." For example, a less anxious person may have a more flexible autonomic response, where they can respond better to stressful situations, and then recover faster than those individuals who have a more anxious personality (Hohen-Saric & McLoed, 1988).

As pointed out earlier in this chapter, when the heart reaches 100 beats per minute, the stress response is automatically initiated. When this occurs, about 70% of all vascular blood flow is directed to skeletal muscles which make up 40% of the total body mass. Because of this change, blood flow to the skeletal muscles can increase from 1,000 to 22,000 ml per minute, causing dramatic changes in the body. However, the stress response is equipped to deal with these changes. Sensors including chemoreceptors and baroreflexors located in those specific parts of the body's circulatory system respond to the epinephrine and norepinephrine and increase or decrease blood flow to certain regions (i.e. vascular beds) by constricting or expanding to keep up with the increased demand for oxygen-rich blood. Basically, it "shifts" blood flow to critical areas including the large muscle groups, heart and lungs, and blood vessels in these areas vasodilate to allow the flow of more blood into these regions. In other regions, including the mesenteric (the digestive system) and cutaneous (the skin), meanwhile, vascular beds constrict and reduce blood flow because these parts of the body in a time of "emergency" are not needed for survival (Hugdahl, 1995). Blood flow is also reduced by about 25% in the splanchnic region (liver, gastrointestinal tract, spleen and pancreas) and in the renal/kidney (20% reduction) and skeletal (20% reduction) systems. Vasoconstriction in these areas also serves to increase the body's arterial blood pressure and flow due to the decrease in diameter and increased resistance in the bloodstream (Hugdahl, 1995; Rowell, 1993).

Several physiological changes also occur. As already pointed out, the heart and respiration rates increase. Some of the other changes the body experiences include dilation of the bronchioles in the lungs and the pupils in the eyes, constriction of the blood vessels, inhibition or suppression of the gastrointestinal system, and increases in blood pressure, stroke volume, cardiac output, and perspiration. In total, there may be over 1,400 physio-chemical changes associated with the body responding to a stressor (Cacioppo & Tassinary, 1990). All of these changes may also draw out psychological responses to some degree, increasing the intensity and duration of the stress response.

When the stressor goes away, the parasympathetic system shuts off production of HPA and SNS-related chemical hormones. The heart and respiration rates, meanwhile, return to a normal state (Conlan, 1999). Research has shown that the heart rate and blood pressure returns to normal levels soon after the stressor goes away (Hugdahl, 1995). For example, research on vagal rebound and recovery (the recovery of heart rate) found that the parasympathetic nervous system decelerates the heart rate rapidly within the first minute after the stressor is removed or eliminated (Mezzacappa, et. al, 2001).

There are two explanations for this rapid shutdown. As pointed out earlier, SNS activation does not secrete norepinephrine directly into the bloodstream. Rather, presynaptic vessels store this chemical until they are stimulated by nerve impulses, which then release the chemicals to reactor sites that stimulate specific organs and parts of the body (Adams, Victor & Ropper, 1997). The majority of this chemical is then immediately reabsorbed back into the nerve endings. Second, chemicals secreted from the HPA axis induce receptors in the body to produce steroids, including cortisol, to readily stabilize and restore homeostasis to the body (Slominski, 2000). At the same time, norepinephrine and epinephrine in the bloodstream are metabolized in a variety of pathways and among various organs and tissues, including the liver (Eisenhofer & Pacak, 1999).

Controlling the Breathing

When the SNS response is activated, it is often beyond the direct control of the person, due to the infusion of various chemicals into the bloodstream. Even though this is a physiological response, it should also be remembered that breathing is also a psychological process. Because the shooter reacts psychologically to the stress response, it can be controlled to a certain extent. Swartz (2003) points out that somatic (physiological) and psychological stress are autonomous and interrelated. For example, activities including jumpiness, being startled, agitated, restlessness, pain in the muscles, and other uncomfortable physical sensations are somatic in nature because the body is eliciting a physiological response regarding the change or disorder. However (and at the same time), anticipating and dealing with these physiological changes are psychological in nature. Unlike the somatic symptoms that are objective, psychological symptoms are primarily subjective. That is, individuals react differently to the uncomfortable physical sensations they are experiencing, which in turn could affect the degree and extent of the body's response to the perceived stressor.

These points suggest that a person has a great deal of control over their breathing and the body's stress response even though they may think that they do not. Therefore, a person can have a direct impact on their breathing in how they react to the physiological processes that occur under the stress situation. For example, under a high stress situation, the stress response increases the heart and respiration rate. This could cause hyperventilation. The lack of oxygen being delivered to the brain and other body tissues could also cause graded hypoxia, which is a less severe form of hypoxia that will cause neural and physiological changes in the body (Fried, 1999). Some of the other changes in respiration because of stress are shown in box 5-2. According to Hugdahl (1995), this cycle of events will continue, and hyperventilation will increase in intensity and effect until the person passes out from hyperventilation or they take control of their breathing.

BOX 5-2
NEGATIVE CHANGES IN BREATHING
BECAUSE OF STRESS

- Irregular breathing (both inhaling and exhaling)
- Increase in respiration rate/Hyperventilation
- Increase in air flowing in and out of the lungs
- Decrease in release of CO_2 being exhaled

Adapted from Fried (1999)

Even after the stressor is eliminated, and regardless of the fact that the parasympathetic nervous system has rapidly restored the body back to a homeostatic state, a person can disrupt their breathing through hyper-ventilation. This is due to their psychological response to the stressor, independent of the physiological changes that they may experience. This point suggests that a person must regain their psychological composure immediately after a stressful event. They must purposefully focus and con-centrate on controlling their breathing (which is now a psychological process) in order to get their O_2 and CO_2 levels back to normal levels to prevent the stress response from re-engaging. In fact, physiologically there are no barriers because the body's stress response is deactivated. Now, it is psychological in nature.

Since a stressor can also be "created" because of a psychological mani-festation or construct, a person must also concentrate on their breathing prior to a stressful event. For example, a police officer may become anxious prior to responding to the actual call. This anxiety may create changes in their breathing, and if severe enough (when the heart exceeds 100 beats per minute), they could actually cause the body to initiate the stress response (HPA & SNS activation) prior to the call. This could affect their performance on the call to some degree, further spiraling the body's response to the stressor in a negative direction, enhancing the severity and length of the stress response. Thus, by controlling breathing prior to the stress response, the officer can actually prevent the stress response from engaging.

Signs of Bad Breathing

There are many signs of "bad" breathing, which are shown in Box 5-3. For example, rapid breathing speeds up the heart rate. If a person can prevent hyperventilation, they can prevent their heart rate from reaching 100 beats per minute. Keeping the heart rate below 100 beats per minute can prevent the stress response, preventing sympathetic responses beyond the control of the officer.

BOX 5-3
SIGNS OF BAD BREATHING

- Sighs — Right after a stressful event a person may hear or see a person take a deep breath. Sighing is a sign of hyperventilation as the person is taking a deep breath and letting it out too fast
- Short Breaths/Shallow Breathing — causes hyperventilation and a loss of CO_2
- Irregular Breathing
- Chest Heaving — is a sign of chest breathing and not belly breathing
- Unable to Catch One's Breath
- Dizziness

Adapted from Fried (1999)

A shooter could also disrupt their breathing simply because they are not concentrating on their breathing. This can be readily seen in mild cases of alkalosis and acidosis, which may be occurring throughout a person's day irregardless of if there is stressor in the environment (Fried, 1999). Effective breathing can be achieved and mastered just like any of the other fundamentals of shooting.

Breathing requires practice and concentration. By controlling the breathing, a person can avoid the stress response. Through effective breathing, a person can actually become healthier by maintaining correct levels of O_2 and CO_2 while reducing their body's response to stress which releases a variety of potentially destructive chemicals into the bloodstream.

Developing Proper Breathing

There are two types of breathing. They include chest (or thoracic) and abdominal (diaphragmatic) breathing. In chest breathing, the chest simply rises up and down. Chest breathing is the result of the rib cage raising and lowering, allowing gasses to enter and leave the lungs. Chest breathing does not cause a lot of air to enter the lungs. Because there is less air volume in the lungs under this form of breathing, a person may hyperventilate. This is because they are trying to maintain the correct tidal volume. In the process, however, they are expelling too much carbon dioxide from their body (Fried, 1999).

> **Training Tip:** In order to see the positive effects of controlled abdominal breathing, purposefully engage in strenuous dynamic activities while training with firearms. Be sure to concentrate on effective breathing in combination with shooting.

There is also abdominal or "belly breathing." Abdominal breathing results in a greater tidal volume of air because the contraction of the diaphragm and abdominal muscles increases the space in the chest and lungs. By creating more space in the chest cavity, the lungs can expand more, and take in more gas in the process. Since the lungs can take more air, the respiration rate will be much slower, averaging between 3 and 5 breaths per minute. This, in turn, will also reduce the heart rate and blood pressure (Fried, 1999).

This controlled breathing is known by a variety of names. Siddle (1996) refers to controlled abdominal breathing as "combat breathing." This procedure is also called autogenic breathing. Under the concept of autogenic training, for example, the individual is in an almost meditative relaxed state where they are in cue with their body, especially their breathing. By controlling their breathing, they will be able to then control their pulse rate and other bodily functions, including blood pressure. Autogenic training as a means to control breathing is not new. It has been used in sporting activities and the martial arts for years to increase performance and to reduce stress (Respiratory alkalosis, 2005).

Robert Fried, in his book *Breathe Well, Be Well*, provides some key points on autogenic breathing. The keys to effective breathing, according to Fried, is to always breathe from the diaphragm, regardless of it is a stressful or non-stressful event. By training oneself to always breathe from the abdomen, a person can increase their oxygen intake (or tidal volume) and reduce their tidal values per minute. Proper breathing will also reduce the pulse rate and issues related to alkalosis and acidosis which could lead to an increase in the pulse and respiration rate, and lead to the body initiating the stress response.

Abdominal Breathing Techniques

Fried (1999) points out that there are some specific procedures that a person must follow when engaging in correct abdominal breathing. Some of the "musts" or fundamentals include the following:

- Breathe through the Nose

A person should always breath through their nose. Breathing through the nose prepares the air for the lungs. Mucous membranes and hairs in the nose filter and collect dirt, dust and germs. Air entering the nasal cavity is also warmed and moisturized in the nose and nasal cavity.

> **Proper Breathing Checklist**
>
> ✓ Always Breathe Through the Nose
> ✓ Always Breathe from the Abdomen - Not the Chest
> ✓ Inhaling & Exhaling Should be the Same Volume & Tempo
>   Breathe in on a four count, exhale on a four count…

Breathing through the nose also regulates the amount of air entering the lung and prevents hyperventilation.

- Always breathe from the abdomen—not from the chest

Breathing from the chest results in short breaths that have a low tidal volume. Short speedy breaths could lead to hyperventilation, and they will not provide the proper amount of oxygen that is needed to slow the heart rate down. One quick way to check to see if a person is breathing correctly is to place one hand on the chest and the other on the abdomen. If the abdominal area is not expanding and contracting while the chest wall is rising and falling, this is a sign that the person is chest breathing only, which is the incorrect way to breathe.

- Inhalation & Exhalation should be the same volume and tempo

The inhalation and exhalation rate (I/E) should be the same rate and volume. For example, if it takes four seconds to breathe in, it should take four seconds to fully breathe out. Concentrating on the I/E rate will make sure that a person is not taking "short" breaths and hyperventilating. The breathing should also be smooth where there is no pause between the inhalation and exhalation stages.

- Breathe in for a four count; exhale on a four count (one, two, three, and four).

Abdominal breathing is not "fast breathing." The person should inhale on a four count and exhale on a four count. The person should be focused on letting the abdomen extend out as far as possible when inhaling and pulling back on the abdomen as far back as it will go when exhaling. While doing this, the person should also make sure that their chest is not rising. While the respiration rate may appear to be slower under four-count abdominal breathing, the lungs are actually receiving more oxygen, since they are expanding a lot more in comparison to chest breathing.

- Autogenic Breathing Requires Training and Concentration

A person must concentrate and "teach" the body to respond to their explicit commands. Until it is fully mastered, a person must concentrate and tell him or herself to breathe correctly. Over time, this practice of telling oneself to breathe will become automatic and reflexive in nature. When a person has reached this stage, they have mastered autogenic breathing.

A shooter should also keep in mind that there are other factors that could impede their breathing:

- Wear Appropriate Clothing

Fried (1999) also states that tight clothes can affect breathing. Tight clothes may cause a person to take short or shallow breaths, which could lead to hyperventilation. This point requires that police officers and shooters should wear clothing that is comfortable for them. Officers should not wear a clothing size that they "wish" they would fit in. Rather, they should select that size of clothing that allows for mobility of movement, is comfortable for extended wear, and allows them to breathe correctly. For example, tight pants can restrict breathing to some degree, especially when sitting. The same applies to body armor. If the body armor is too tight, it will restrict breathing under both normal and high stress situations.

- Make sure autogenic breathing is not impeded in any way.

Some positions, such as sitting or shooting prone for example, could impede autogenic breathing to some degree. A person must practice their autogenic breathing while in these positions to determine what, if any, constraints on their breathing exist. If any problems are discovered, they can then experiment and modify their shooting positions to make sure that they can properly breathe.

- Physical Fitness & Smoking

Of course, a person's physical fitness levels also affects their breathing. Obese people, for example, may have greater respiratory problems in the context of acidosis. Related to fitness, of course, is smoking. Smoking forces more CO_2 into the respiratory system, causing respiratory acidosis. Individuals suffering from emphysema also experience problems associated with respiratory acidosis (Respiratory alkalosis, 2005).

Autogenic Breathing and Firearms Training

As pointed out earlier in this chapter, autogenic breathing should become part of an officer's daily life. This also means that autogenic breathing must be a major component of firearms training.

Consider, for example, using autogenic training when shooting. While shooting a weapon, a person may hold their breath for a variety of reasons (i.e., poor training, poor attention to detail, anxiety). Often this is seen on the range where a shooter holds their breath to maintain a perfect sight picture to get the "perfect shot." Teaching a person (or even allowing them) to hold their breath is contra-training. A shooter must never alter their breathing to get the perfect shot. In a gunfight, the perfect shot is the one that hits center of mass and stops a threat. A person can easily do this while breathing. Thus, the proper technique is that the shooter should breathe and shoot at the same time. Under proper "belly breathing" techniques, the chest should not rise and fall to a great degree. Since it is not moving too much (instead, the lower abdominal area is), sight alignment and the sight picture should not be disrupted.

In order to avoid these and other respiratory-related problems, a shooter should use autogenic training strategies to control their breathing. While off the firing line and in the course of other range activities, shooter's must practice autogenic training to control their breathing which, in turn, will control their pulse rate. However, in many situations a person may practice or concentrate on their autogenic breathing just prior to shooting. While it may be somewhat helpful, the person that just does autogenic training prior to shooting misses out on the long-term benefits of this type of breathing. They are also training themselves wrong. This type of breathing is not sporadic. It should be a habitual, where the person abdominally breathes at all times

Autogenic Breathing & Police Work

The research suggests that autogenic training will work to reduce stress levels before and after a stressful event. Anecdotal information from police trainers has revealed that concentrating on breathing prior to a stressful event (qualifying on the range, a dynamic entry, etc.) serves to calm officers down. Additional information from the police literature also shows the benefits of autogenic breathing. Grossman (2001) writes about using autogenic breathing to calm individuals when recalling a stressful event in their lives, while Street Survival seminars also recommend autogenic breathing for high stress situations. Research involving military pilots has also found that autogenic feedback training exercises improves a pilot's performance (Cowings, Kellar, Folen, Toscano & Burge, 2001).

Like all of the techniques reviewed in this book, autogenic breathing is something that must be practiced and incorporated into training and in the daily lives of officers. Without practicing and incorporating it into training, it will not become habit or ingrained as muscle memory. If it is not practiced and eventually incorporated into the daily lives of individuals, under a high stress situation, it will be very difficult, if not impossible, to use autogenic breathing techniques to calm and control the respiratory process. In fact, concentrating on autogenic breathing will most likely be the least of the officer's concerns in these settings.

As pointed out earlier, autogenic training is not something that is used only under high stress situations and for a short period of time. Autogenic breathing must be used prior to and throughout an encounter to be effective. A person cannot just use this technique for a few minutes after an encounter and then return back to their normal, and perhaps irregular breathing cycle. To achieve mastery, autogenic breathing must be practiced and used in all daily activities. With practice, then under a high stress situation, a person will be able to better "tell" him or herself to control their breathing. In a best-case scenario (which the readers of this book should strive for) it should become a new way of breathing where the person is always using autogenic breathing techniques on and off-duty. The benefits of this type of breathing extends far beyond stressful occasions. Mastering autogenic breathing also reduces blood pressure and prevents irregular breathing patterns, and it will lead to a better homeostatic state (Fried, 1999).

Conclusion

The need to control the breathing is based on the body's need to maintain the proper levels of oxygen and carbon dioxide in the bloodstream. As pointed out in this chapter, under high stress situations, the body experiences a variety of physiological changes because of the body's stress response which includes the activation of the HPA and sympathetic nervous system. Two specific respiratory disorders include alkalosis and acidosis, which could lead to hyper or hypoventilation. If serious enough, these self-induced respiratory disorders could trigger the body's stress response. It should also be remembered that the shooter may also experience respiratory-related problems simply because they do not breathe correctly, unrelated to the stress of the situation.

To avoid these problems, a shooter must properly breathe. However, both physiological and psychological factors, acting independently, and in conjunction with one another at times affects the breathing process. Under the stress response, the body will activate the HPA and SNS responses, which will release a series of chemicals into the bloodstream. The shooter will feel the effects of these chemicals, eliciting a psychological response, independent of the true affects of the physiological impact the chemicals have on the body. When the stressor is eliminated, the stress response shuts down rapidly. Now that the parasympathetic system has taken over, the officer can devote more attention to their breathing, where they must address the psychological factors, and engage in proper breathing to make sure the body has the proper balance of oxygen and carbon dioxide in order to rapidly recover. This requires that the officer must follow through on their breathing, mentally concentrating and telling him or herself that they need to breathe correctly.

This chapter has also pointed out that regardless of if a person is engaged in non-stressful or high stress situations, the shooter should learn how to breathe from their abdomen, not their chest. Chest breathing is a very common practice that results in low tidal volumes and a lower intake of oxygen into the lungs. This causes a series of respiratory problems including hyperventilation and other side effects that can impair a person's neural and physical performance. Effective breathing requires abdominal or belly breathing, that when done correctly, lowers the respiratory rate per minute, blood pressure and heart rate, while ensuring the correct balance of oxygen and carbon dioxide in the bloodstream. Abdominal or autogenic breathing must be mastered just like any other basic in firearms. Through the mastery of this type of breathing, a person can control their breathing prior to, during, and immediately after a stressful event, allowing the control of, and the fast recovery of physiological and psychological responses that may occur.

REFERENCES

Adams, R.D.; Victor, M. & Ropper, A.H. (1997). Principles of neurology (6th ed.) New York: McGraw-Hill.

Cacioppo, J.T. & Tassinary, L.G. (1990). Principles of psychophysiology. New York: Cambridge University Press.

Carrasco, G.A. & VandeKar, L.D. (February, 2003). Neuroendocrine pharmacology of stress. European journal of pharmacology, 463(1-3), 235-272.

Conlan, R. (1999). States of mind. New York: John Wiley & Sons, Inc.

Cowings, P.S.; Kellar, M.A.; Folen, R.A.; Toscano, W.B. & J.D. Burge, (2001). Autogenic feedback training exercise and pilot performance: Enhanced functioning under search-and-rescue flying conditions. International journal of aviation psychology, 11(3), 303-1315.

Eisenhofer, G. & Pacak, K. (April, 1999). Biochemical diagnosis of Pheochromocytoma. Bethesda, MD: National Institute of Health.

Fried, R. (1999). Breathe well, be well. New York: John Wiley & Sons.

Grossman, D. (2001). The bulletproof mind. Jinesboro, AK:

Hlastala M.P. & Berger, A.J. (2001). Physiology of respiration (2nd ed.). New York: Oxford University Press.

Hoehn-Saric, R. & McLoed, D.R. (June, 1988). The peripheral sympathetic nervous system. Its role in normal pathological anxiety. Psychiatr Clin North Am. 11(2), 375-386.

Hugdahl, K. (1995). Psychophysiology: Cambridge, MA: Harvard University Press.

Levitzky, M.G. (1999). Pulmonary physiology. New York: McGraw-Hill.

Lewis, S.M.; Collier, I.C. & M.M. McLean (1996). Medical-surgical nursing (4th ed.). St. Louis, MO: Mosby-year book, Inc.

McKinley, M. & O'Loughlin, V.D. (2006). Human Anatomy. New York: McGraw-Hill.

Mezzacappa, E.S.; Kelsey, R.M.; Katkin, E.S. & R.P. Sloan (2001). Vagal rebound and recovery from psychological stress. Psychosomatic medicine, 63, 650-657.

Miller, D.B. & O'Callaghan, J.P. (June, 2002). Neuroendocrine aspects of the response to stress. Metabolism, 51(6 suppl 1), 5-10.

Mohan, R.M.; Golding, S. & D.J. Patterson. (2001). Intermittent hypoxia modulates nNOS expression and heart rate response to sympathetic nerve stimulation. American journal of heart and circulatory physiology, 281, 132-138.

Priebe, H.J. & Skarvan, K. (2000). Cardiovascular Physiology (2nd ed.). London: BMJ Books.

Priestley, M.A.; Levine, G. & Litman, R. (January 21, 2003). Respiratory Acidosis. Emedicine (electronic journal).

Respiratory alkalosis. Retrived from emedicine.com. Last visited: January 10, 2005.

Rowell, L.B. (1993). Human cardiovascular control. New York: Oxford University Press.

Siddle, B. (1996). Sharpening the warrior's edge. Milstadt, IL: PPCT Management Systems, Inc.

Slominski, A.; Wortsman, J.; Luger, T.; Paus, R. & S. Solomon. (July, 2000). Corticotropin releasing hormone and proopiomelanocortin involvement in the cutaneous response to stress. Psychological reviews, 80(3), 979-1020.

Swartz, C.M. (March, 2003). Sympathy for the sympathetic (nervous system). Psychiatric times, 20(3), 48-51.

What is autogenic training? Retrieved from emedicine.com. Last visited January 10, 2005.

Chapter 6
STANCE

Introduction

The stance is an important fundamental that a shooter must master to become proficient in the use of their firearm. The stance (also known as the base or shooting platform) deals with how a shooter positions their body to shoot and effectively control their weapon. It is simply not positioning the feet. The stance is the relative positioning of the entire body when shooting to ensure that it is completely balanced throughout the course of fire. The stance or base can be thought of as the vice to which the firearm is mounted. Inasmuch, this stance should be as solid as possible in order to ensure the delivery of accurate and controlled fire at the threat. This chapter will introduce the reader to the basic stances used in police firearms training. These include the weaver, isosceles, and modified isosceles.

Principles of an Effective Stance

An effective stance is basically that stance chosen by the shooter, which provides the most stable shooting platform as possible. An effective stance is also one that is tactically sound. That is, it allows the shooter to deliver controlled and accurate fire at the threat in static or dynamic setting. This stance must also properly control the firearm's recoil. It should also be able to be used with different types of weapons, including longarms.

All firearms have some degree of recoil (i.e. "kickback") against the shooter when the gun discharges. In some cases, individuals may think that there is a great degree of recoil. Usually, however, this is not the case. Recoil depends upon a variety of factors including the weight of the gun, the mass of the bullet and the bullet's velocity. It is also dependent upon the design of the firearm and the physical size of the shooter. For example, the recoil system on a pistol is designed to absorb momentum through the action of the slide moving to the rear and the barrel slightly moving rearward. Considering this point that the semiautomatic firearm will absorb a great degree of this momentum through its design (i.e. the slide moving), the degree of momentum (energy) exerted against the shooter is not extreme. In fact, recoil can be easily controlled, regardless of one's size, *IF* they have a stance that will work in controlling that momentum.

The following are some points to consider in controlling the recoil of a firearm through a proper stance. They include:

- It must provide as much balance as possible.
- The chest, shoulders and head must be properly centered and balanced above or on the hips and feet.
- The head should always remain upright and as level as possible.
- It should be simple. The stance should be similar to the way a person walks and stands.
- It should provide both lateral (side to side) and forward/backward support.
- The stance should be designed to absorb as much recoil as possible. This recoil should be absorbed through the bones; the majority of the recoil should not be absorbed through the soft tissues. This concept is called the "bone bridge" — letting one's skeletal structure support the firearm and absorb the recoil from the firearm. By forming a "bone bridge" a stronger, more stable shooting platform will be established. Using the skeletal system will reduce muscle fatigue while transferring and absorbing the recoil from the firearm to the bones.
- It should create an isometric-shooting platform. Isometrics basically means resistance, where the muscles of the body operate in opposition to one another. This opposition or force against one another creates a solid base from which the firearm may be held, allowing for the smallest amount of movement. This creates a strong and stable shooting platform.
- It should be comfortable. The shooter needs to find that body position which places their weight evenly on their feet in such a manner that it allows them to stand for long periods of time without the body swaying. In many force situations, officers may have to hold cover or "cover down" on a suspect for a long period of time until backup arrives. The stance should use gross (or large) rather than fine or complex muscle movements that can become more easily fatigued.
- Shooters should choose their own stance, after experimenting with all of them. If a shooter feels uncomfortable with the stance, there is probably something wrong with it. If it is not comfortable, meanwhile, it will not be used and it will be avoided.
- The stance should be consistent with good defensive tactics techniques.
- It must be designed so the shooter grips the weapon with *both* hands.

- The stance should be able to be used with various types of firearms, with little or no modifications.
- The stance should be rigid but relaxed. It should not be tense (for example, the shooter should be able to wiggle their toes), yet, it must be a firm, solid stance.

Shooting Stances

The Weaver Stance

The weaver stance is a traditional law enforcement stance. Photographs of this stance are shown in Figures 27 through 29. It is often described as the field interview stance. The key to this stance is that the body is angled toward the suspect/threat, offering less body profile to the threat. Because of the position of the body in this type of stance, relative to the threat, it also provides protection of the shooter's gun side against assailants. Since the firearm is angled away from the suspect when holstered, this stance could protect the gun (to some degree) from being stripped away from an officer.

Figure 27

These are the principles of the weaver stance:

- Feet, hips & shoulders quarter the target at a 45 degree angle – the strong foot is back.
- Feet are flat on the ground.

- Feet are approximately shoulder width apart.
- The majority of the shooter's weight should rest on the balls of the feet. This will assist in the body absorbing and working with the recoil of the firearm.
- Knees are slightly bent, creating a little spring in one's step. The knees should not be locked.
- Shoulders are slightly forward of the hips.
- Back is straight.
- Hips are slightly back, relative to the shoulders and knees.

Figure 28

- Head is level, not cocked or angled, and fully upright.
- Strong arm is locked out. The wrist, elbow, and shoulder joints are "locked" forming a straight line, allowing the recoil of the weapon to operate against this solid "bone bridge." The strong arm, to some degree, also angles across the shooter's body.
- The weak/support arm elbow is bent down and toward the ground, pulling back on the gun. The elbow of the support arm does not point outward. Pointing the elbow outward provides little support. When doing this, the shooter relies upon muscles (soft tissues) instead of the bones for support. This could lead to increased fatigue when supporting the firearm.
- The strong hand/arm is pushing the weapon outward while the weak/support arm & hand is pulling backwards. This creates the isometric-shooting platform.

Figure 29

Commonly Encountered Problems

Some of the common problems with the weaver stance deal with balance. They include:

- Shooters "crouching" and/or leaning forward too much.
- The hips and buttocks are thrust out too far in a rearward direction, while the shoulders are too far forward.
- Bending or squatting at the knees too much.
- Having the hips forward and the shoulders pulled back, causing a bow in the lower back.
- Positioning the hips and feet at a 45 degree angle to the threat while the upper torso and shoulders are squared (or perpendicular) to the threat.
- Too wide or too narrow of a stance (feet spread too far apart or too close together).
- The head and eyes going to the firearm instead of the firearm coming to the eyes. This will lead to a shooter "turtling" or tucking their head between their shoulders. This could lead to an unbalanced stance while limiting the shooter's field of view.

All of these issues will lead to an unbalanced shooting platform. They will also result in the shooter becoming more fatigued while shooting, based on the simple fact that they are using too many muscles to perform relatively simple tasks and movements.

In other situations, there are issues related to the shooter's arms when using the weaver stance. Shooters may forget to lock their strong arm out or they may become fatigued from holding the gun too long and pull their elbow into their body to provide additional support for the gun. Additionally, failing to lock out the strong arm will result in the shooter not being able to effectively control the firearm's recoil. It will also lead to accuracy issues. In the context of the weak arm, meanwhile, in many cases it is not pulling straight back, subsequently providing little or no support for strong hand and arm. Shooters should also make sure that the elbow of the support arm is pointing down. Locking the elbow down (as mentioned earlier) forms a "bone bridge" where the bones, not just the muscles, are providing the necessary strength and support to the strong arm, hand, and firearm.

Benefits & Drawbacks of the Weaver Stance

One of the benefits of the weaver stance is that it is consistent with the field interview stance that is often taught to recruits and heavily used by police officers. If this is the case, then the weaver stance provides simplicity for the officer, since they only have to learn and remember one basic stance for the majority of their activities (with some modifications for shooting). They have the same stance for both the field interview and deadly force situations. If properly applied, the weaver stance is also a comfortable stance for shooters and it provides a stable base for skill building in firearms. In comparison to one-handed methods (that this chapter does not address because they lack the control related to the two-handed stances), the weaver also provides a strong shooting stance and effectively controls the recoil of the firearm. In fact, many individuals feel that the best component of the weaver stance is using the support arm elbow as a power control device. By pulling the elbow down, it creates positive counter-pressure, serving to considerably dampen the recoil of the weapon.

There are some disadvantages to the weaver stance. One disadvantage is related to officer safety. With the body angled toward a threat, the officer's body armor may not offer the same degree of protection from projectiles. There may be a gap between the front and rear panels, and no coverage at all in the armpit region of the body. If the body is angled, the shooter essentially exposes this gap between their body armor panels to the threat. Furthermore, the weaver stance is considered to be a target stance only. It is not a combat stance. Because it is a stationary stance, a shooter cannot maintain the weaver stance when moving, due to the fact that the feet are at approximately a 45 degree angle to the threat.

Another disadvantage is related to vision. Because the body and head are angled toward the threat, the head and eyes may not be looking directly at the threat. Due to this fact, there could cause some loss of the peripheral field of vision, slowing down the officer's visual acuity to identity and engage the threat.

Another issue is related to balance. The weaver is not a natural stance. It is not consistent in how a human being naturally walks and moves. A person cannot maintain a correct weaver stance and move in a forward or rearward motion because the hips are at a 45-degree angle to the threat. The weaver stance is also difficult to maintain with lateral (side to side) movements. The weaver stance also requires the use of more fine and complex muscle movements in comparison to other stances. With the strong arm locked out and supported by the weak hand (with the hips, shoulder and feet positioned at a 45 degree angle to the threat) it also places more motion on the firearm (it tends to bounce up and down) in comparison to other stances that provide a better isometric shooting platform. The weaver is also not as instinctual as other forms of stances. Because of this, it will require more training to become proficient when using this stance.

When using long arms with the weaver stance, there may also be issues with accuracy and control. Because the body is angled toward the threat, the recoil of the weapon is not operating against a completely solid surface per se. When using a long arm, such as a shotgun for example, in many cases the shooter places the butt of the weapon directly on the shoulder joint (which is wrong). Now, the recoil is working against a flexible joint, while the body itself is angled toward the threat. When firing multiple rounds, for example, the firearm's recoil will have the natural tendency to climb at an upward (and outward) angle away from the body with this stance. For example, a right handed shooter that positions a shotgun on their right shoulder will most likely experience the shotgun climbing high and right as they fire multiple shots. This is because the recoil of the firearm does not have a solid, but angled, surface to work against.

The Isosceles Stance

The isosceles stance can be best described as forming a triangle with the strong and weak arms in relation to the body. Examples of the Isosceles

Stance are shown in Figures 30 through 32. Some of the primary differences between the weaver and isosceles stance deal with the arm, hip and foot placement. Below are the principles of the isosceles stance:

- Feet, hips & shoulders are perpendicular or "squared" to the target.
- Feet are flat on the ground.
- Toes are aligned with one another.
- Feet are approximately shoulder width apart or wider.
- Knees are slightly bent, creating a little spring in the step. The knees should not be locked out. This will cause unnecessary fatigue.
- Shoulders are slightly forward of the hips.
- Back is straight.
- The shooter's weight is slightly forward, resting on the balls of the feet.

Figure 30

- Hips are slightly back; buttocks are pushed slightly to the rear.
- Head is level, not cocked or angled, and fully upright (chin is up and not tucked toward the neck).
- Both the strong and support arms are locked out. A triangle is formed with the arms and the line of the shoulders.
- The wrist, elbow and shoulder joints are "locked" forward. Locking the joints allows the recoil of the weapon to operate against a solid "bone bridge," instead of the soft tissues that can become fatigued. The strong hand "pushes" the handgun forward, while the support hand "pulls" the gun to the rear, forming an isometric platform.

Figure 31

- The outstretched arms and hands (gripping the weapon) are then centered in front of the chest and are brought up to eye level.

Figure 32

Commonly Encountered Problems

Some of the common problems associated with the isosceles stance, like the weaver stance, deal with balance issues. They include:

- The upper body leaning too far forward or backward.
- Squatting or bending the knees to much while thrusting the buttocks too far to the rear.
- Having feet positioned too far apart or too close together.
- Using the isosceles stance from the waist up, and positioning the hips and feet in the weaver stance.
- The head and eyes going down to the firearm instead of the firearm coming up to the eyes. Having the head and eyes directed downward causes the shooter to roll their shoulders forward where the head "turtles" or in between the shoulder blades. "Turtling" will limit the shooter's field of view and it could also lead to an unbalanced stance.
- The strong and support arm elbows and wrists are not locked out.
- Not maintaining the same consistent stance throughout the course of fire (i.e. standing upward/erect, bending the knees just before or after the gun fires).

Benefits and Drawbacks of the Isosceles Stance

One of the primary benefits of the isosceles stance is that the shooter is able to use both eyes to enhance their binocular vision. As mentioned in the sight alignment chapter, humans are designed to see three-dimensionally using binocular vision. Under high stress situations, the sympathetic nervous system will automatically adjust the body to receive as much information as possible. This means that the body will automatically shift to a stance that allows for a greater amount of visual information — the isosceles — where binocular vision will be optimized (Siddle & Breedlove, 1995).

This means that visual processing time will be faster with the isosceles stance. This is because the entire body, including the head and eyes, are aimed or pointed directly at the threat. This is in contrast to the weaver stance where the head is slightly angled in line with the angle of the shoulders, where the shooter's visual processing time may be slowed because they are not using both eyes to their maximum potential. This slowed visual processing could then mean a slower response time.

There are other benefits. Another benefit is the fact that with the isosceles stance, the shooter's body armor will offer full protection against the threat. In comparison to the weaver stance where shooter's side may be exposed because of a gap between the front and rear panels, directly facing the threat offers maximum protection for the shooter because their body armor (and the trauma plate which exists in many models of body armor) will provide maximum protection from projectiles. A person may be able to move more effectively using this stance. Lateral or side to side movements are easier to perform. All a shooter has to do is side shuffle their feet to the side, which will not disturb their balance, sight alignment, and sight picture to a great degree. Walking in a forward or rearward motion is also easier with the isosceles stance. This is because the feet are pointed forward — not sideways toward the threat.

There are some disadvantages with the isosceles. One issue that is often raised is that the shooter exposes their entire profile to the threat, in comparison to the weaver that provides a smaller threat profile. Another possible issue (that can be readily overcome) is that some shooters may perceive that there is greater recoil control problems with the isosceles, in comparison to the weaver stance, since their support arm is extended outward, instead of bent and pointed downward.

The Modified Isosceles

The Modified Isosceles is also referred to as the Index Shooting Platform or the Universal Shooting Platform. Photographs of the Modified Isosceles are shown in Figures 33-35. This type of stance is a combat stance where one's body assists in aiming the firearm. One simple way to describe this stance is to place it in the context of an everyday activity — walking. Walking is natural, simple and comfortable and it does not require a person to think about the movements associated with this motor activity. These movements are also instinctual in nature. The shooter does not have to think about the activity. It simply happens.

Figure 33

The key to the modified isosceles is to make the stance as simple as possible to reduce the time it takes to react and respond to the threat. Some of the key points of the modified isosceles are listed below:

- Feet, hips and shoulders are perpendicular or "squared" to the threat.
- Knees are slightly bent (not locked out) with a little spring in them.
- The buttocks are pushed slightly backwards, relative to the shoulders and feet.
- The feet should be positioned in the normal walking stance (shoulder width apart), with the toes pointed toward the target. Feet should be positioned "heel to toe" in a natural stride position. This stance is narrower than the traditional isosceles stance.
- The tops of the shoulders are positioned just forward of the hips and over the balls of the feet.
- Shoulders are slightly hunched to tighten up the arms.
- The back and spine are straight and not bent forward at the shoulders.
- Strong side foot is back (behind the support foot), positioned "toe to heel" with the strong foot. The shooter should make sure that the placement of the strong foot to the rear does not rotate their hips from the forward position.

Figure 34

- Head is level (not cocked) with the body, looking straight ahead (head and eyes are on the sights).
- Hands and arms are brought into the line of vision. The head does not go down to the gun. The gun comes to the eyes and the field of view. The head is as high as possible (but still in a natural pose).
- The firearm is as close to the center of the body as possible.
- The strong arm is locked out, "pushing" the firearm outward, while the weak arm is "pulling" the firearm back and is bent at the elbow, pointing down toward the ground. The weak arm elbow should not be pointing outward from the body (no "chicken-winging").

Figure 35

- The shooter's body weight should be leaning slightly forward. Leaning slightly forward and into the firearm will help control the weapon's recoil.

One way to visualize the modified isosceles is to think of a boxer's stance. The fighter is looking at the threat straight on and their weight is forward with the majority of it resting on the balls of their feet. The person's weight is transferred forward. This does not mean that the shooter is on their toes. This simply means that the majority of the shooter's weight (not all of it is resting on the balls of the feet) is transferred forward (i.e., weight forward transfer).

This stance combines the best elements of the isosceles and weaver positions. Like the isosceles, the feet, hips, and shoulders are perpendicular or "squared" to the threat. The arms are also centered to the body. However, the feet are not even or squared to the threat. Instead, the strong foot is directly behind the support side foot, in a shortened heel-to-toe stride. Like the weaver, the strong arm is pushing outward, while the support/weak arm is pulling back with the elbow pointing down. By keeping both the elbows "down and in", this motion creates a bone bridge to support the firearm and absorb the weapon's recoil. Like the other stances, the energy from the recoil of the weapon firing is transferred down and through the bones, instead of through the soft tissues that are not as resistant to recoil and fatigue. This stance may also create a smaller profile to the threat, in comparison to the isosceles and weaver stances, since the shooter's body is a little more "tucked" with this stance.

Commonly Encountered Problems

Some of the common problems associated with the modified isosceles are similar to the isosceles and weaver. They include:

- Issues with posture (ex: leaning too far forward).
- Squatting too much because the knees are bent too much, while the buttocks may be pushed rearward too far.
- Feet are too far apart or too close together.
- Using the isosceles stance from the waist up, and positioning the hips and feet in the weaver stance.
- The head and eyes going to the firearm instead of the firearm going to the eyes. This could cause a shooter to "turtle" or tuck their head between their shoulder blades. It could also lead to an unbalanced

stance and limit the shooter's field of view of the threat environment.

- Not positioning the feet "heel to toe."

Advantages & Disadvantages of the Modified Isosceles

This stance is better suited for dynamic situations that are often encountered in a gunfight. It allows for increased support of the firearm and a more stable shooting platform, in comparison to other stances. For example, by keeping the elbows down and tucked closer to the body, the shooter can support the firearm for longer periods of time, in comparison to other types of stances, such as the isosceles. Besides the smaller profile to the threat, the practice of keeping the elbows tucked down and closer to the body makes it easier to maneuver without the fear or concern of disrupting the sights. This technique allows a shooter to move through doors and other narrow openings, lowering the possibility that the arms and elbows will strike against doorsills or other objects that could throw off the stance. Walking in a natural stride (because of the heel-toe placement) also ensures that the sight picture and sight alignment may be less disturbed because the gun may be "bouncing" less in the shooter's hands.

Other advantages to the modified isosceles include:

- It concentrates on the use of gross muscles, instead of fine and/or complex muscle movements
- It is consistent with the field interview stance. It does not require the shooter to readjust their stance when drawing their firearm under a deadly force situation.
- By its design, shotguns, rifles and MP's can be used from this same stance. It does not require the shooter to adjust to or use a new stance when using long arms.

Perhaps one of the primary drawbacks of this stance is that it is more advanced in nature than the weaver and isosceles stances. As a consequence, it may be more difficult for some inexperienced or novice shooters to immediately master. This stance is also not readily accepted and used in police firearms training. It is often seen in advanced and specialized training that is dynamic, rather than static-based.

Conclusion

This chapter has provided the reader with a review of the basic stances that are used in the field of law enforcement. Regardless of the specific stance, an effective human shooting platform must provide a strong, stable base from which the shooter can deliver controlled and accurate fire to stop a threat. The stance should be instinctual, comfortable and simple. Shooters should also consider selecting and using one stance for all weapons (regardless of if the officer is using their defensive sidearm or an offensive-based shotgun or rifle) that they use. In a gunfight an officer does not have time to readjust their stance according to the type of weapon they are using. By using (and training with) one universal stance, a very complex and dynamic situation can be simplified, giving the officer the tactical advantage to win the deadly force encounter.

While this chapter has provided the reader with the basics of the "perfect stance," a shooter may also modify their stance to fit their individual needs. Every stance will vary to some degree, based on body type and shooter preference. The key is that whatever stance is used, it should provide as stable a base as possible from which a shooter can effectively use and control various type of hand and/or long guns.

REFERENCES

Siddle, B.K. & Breedlove, H. (May/June, 1995). How stress affects shooting stance. <u>Police marksman</u>, 16-20.

Chapter 7
THE GRIP

Introduction

T he grip controls and stabilizes the firearm. It provides a means to hold the firearm in such a way that it will not slip or move in the shooter's hand. An effective combat grip also requires the use of two hands, used in conjunction or in harmony with one another to stabilize the firearm as much as possible.

This chapter will address how to properly grip the semiautomatic handgun using the two-handed combat grip. As this chapter will point out, an effective combat grip requires the shooter to use both the strong and weak support hand in conjunction with one another to create a stable shooting platform. This chapter will also provide an overview of the basics of the strong and support hand grip technique, including a review of the issues and concerns related to the combat grip.

Principles of a Good Grip

In law enforcement, the grip is made up of two hands — the strong and the support hands that work in unison with one another. Through the combination of these two hands, a combat grip is established that provides a means to hold the firearm in such a way that it will not slip or move in the hands when the firearm is held and fired. Creating and maintaining equal pressure from four different directions at the same time accomplishes this. For example, the strong hand should push forward, creating forward pressure. The support hand, meanwhile, must wrap around the front of the strong hand and exert rearward pressure towards the operator. At the same time the hands are exerting the "push-pull" principle, they are also exerting side-to-side lateral pressure, to further stabilize the firearm. This conscious process of applying equal pressure in four different directions at the same time around the firearm's grip needs to remain consistent throughout the course of fire.

157

Some points to consider when developing and properly using the combat grip include the following:

- Grip Uniformity. The grip must be the same each time the firearm is drawn, fired, and returned to the holster.
- It must be firm. The weapon cannot slip or move around in the hand. The master grip should be about handshake strength.
- It must be comfortable. If the grip is uncomfortable, a shooter will not use it. Through practice, comfort can be established.
- It must be instinctual. Shooters must practice using a correct grip. Through practice and repetition, muscle memory will be developed.
- The grip should ensure that the firearm comes back on target after each round is fired.
- Thumbs are not involved in the grip of the weapon. The thumbs should point forward and be relaxed.

The Master Grip

The master grip is that grip that is applied using the strong or primary hand. For example, if a shooter is right-handed, the strong hand is the right hand. At the same time, if the right-handed shooter needs to fire the weapon using the left hand for some reason, the strong hand has now become the left hand. The primary role of the master grip is to control the function of the firearm, beginning with the draw, fire, and eventual return of the weapon to the holster. The master grip is also responsible for stabilizing the firearm in conjunction with the support hand. In other cases, however, where speed is essential, the strong hand may be the only hand that is gripping and stabilizing the firearm. This one-handed grip only occurs in a point-shoot or in a contact-shot situation where the shooter engages the target immediately from the holster, having no time to use the support hand to further stabilize the gun. This last point makes learning and mastering the fundamentals of the master grip even more important.

Establishing the Master Grip

One key consideration is that the master grip is established *in the holster*, prior to the drawing of the weapon (as shown is Figure 36). This same master grip is maintained through the draw and the firing of the firearm and upon reholstering. The master grip is never given up or adjusted until the firearm is returned and secured in the holster. Unfortunately, this rule is often violated, which will be discussed later in this section.

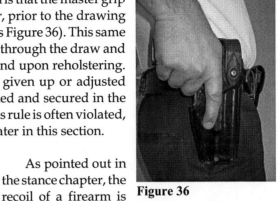

**Figure 36
The Master Grip**

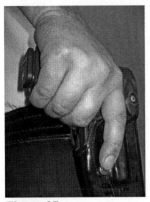

Figure 37

As pointed out in the stance chapter, the recoil of a firearm is easy to control. In the context of the grip and recoil, this means that properly gripping the firearm does not require a great deal of strength or force to control the recoil of the weapon. However, in many instances, shooters have the misconception that a person needs to exert a great deal of force or strength against the gun's grip when shooting. This is not correct. In fact, the amount of force or grip strength that should be exerted on the grip of the firearm should be equivalent to a comfortable handshake that has a nice, even firm pressure. Regardless of the level of strength exerted on the grip, a firearm will always have some degree of recoil of "jump" to it. However, the shooter will become accustomed to the recoil over time, and they will soon learn how to work with (and not against) the recoil to get the sights back on target rapidly, if necessary.

Establishing the master grip is easy. From the holster, the middle and ring finger (and if the handgrip is large enough, the "pinky" finger) should wrap around the grip of the handgun while it is still in the holster (see Figure 37). These fingers should be kept together. They should not "web" out. The shooter should imagine that the fingers are all glued or sewn together, forming a mitt. The index finger should be indexed on the outside of the holster where it is positioned parallel with the holster, pointing down toward the muzzle. When the firearm is then pulled out of the holster, the index finger should come to a natural position, resting on the side of the

159

frame of the weapon, outside the trigger guard, pointing straight ahead. From this position, the index finger can readily move inside the trigger guard and onto the trigger if conditions warrant the use of deadly force.

As shown in Figure 38, a major portion of the palm of the strong hand should cover and overlap the rear of the handgun's grip, which is known as the backstrap. The master grip should also be as high up on the backstrap as possible, without interfering with the slide action of the firearm. The strong hand, meanwhile, will not entirely come into contact with the grip. When the back of the hand is properly wrapped around the grip, there should be a small air gap between the center of the palm of the hand and the grip. This gap is usually large enough where a shooter could actually insert a pencil between the handgun grip and the palm of the hand.

Figure 38

The "V" notch of the hand (between the index finger and the first joint of the thumb), meanwhile, is positioned directly in line with the frame and slide of the firearm (see Figure 38). The placement of the palm of the hand on the backstrap should ensure that the front sight, rear sight and wrist (which is locked out) are all in a straight line with the arm bones. Ensuring that

Figure 39 – Finger Placement

the placement of the gun in the hand is lined up straight with the long bones of the arm will result in the arm and gun having a "natural point." To better understand this point, extend the strong arm straight out while making a fist with the fingers, pointing the index finger at a threat. The firearm should fit solidly in the "V" notch in the web of the hand, resulting in the gun having and have a "natural point."

The fingers serve multiple roles in the context of the master grip. The index finger of the strong hand is respon-

Figure 40 – Finger Placement

sible for the firing of the weapon. The thumb on the strong hand, meanwhile, is responsible for manipulating the slide stop lever, magazine release, de-cock, and safety levers, if applicable. The ring and middle fingers, in the meantime, are responsible for gripping the firearm (see Figures 39 and 40). The "pinky" finger exerts little pressure around the grip. It simply wraps around the grip of the weapon. The thumb of the strong hand also has a limited role in the support of the weapon. The thumb is wrapped around the backstrap of the firearm and points straight-forward. It should be parallel to the index finger (which is on the other side of the gun) where it is relaxed, and pointing at the threat. The thumb should not exert any pressure against frame of the firearm. Likewise, it cannot interfere with the function of the slide. If the thumb, for example, is pressed against the slide (or somehow impedes the action of the slide), it could cause a shooter-induced malfunction that could lead to a failure to feed and/or fire.

The Role of the Support Hand in Gripping the Firearm

The support hand has a fundamental role in the combat grip. Its primary responsibility is to support the firearm and the strong hand. Without the use of the support hand to assist in gripping the weapon, the shooter will have an unstable shooting platform. Like the strong hand, the support hand is critical for the control of the weapon's recoil. While the strong arm controls the rearward direction of the recoil, the support hand must control the unstable upward recoil. To achieve this, the support hand should exert about 60% of the control on the gun, while the remaining 40% comes from the strong hand. Through this "push-pull" process, the upward movement of the firearm will be reduced.

Figure 41
Support Hand
Placement

Besides recoil control, the support hand is also responsible for charging the firearm, stoppage clearing, and magazine changes.

The placement of the support hand is also important. The palm of the support hand should come into contact with the grip of the firearm and provide side-to-side

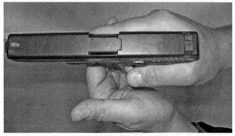

Figure 42
The Support Hand Mitt

161

or lateral pressure against the grip. Since the strong hand is providing lateral side pressure in the opposite direction, the end result is that both the palms provide side-to-side or lateral pressure that stabilizes the firearm. The four fingers of the support hand, meanwhile, should wrap firmly around and over the strong hand fingers. Like the strong hand, the shooter should imagine that the hand is a mitt where all four fingers are connected or sewn together that wrap around the front of the strong hand. The hand and fingers then form a solid pocket in which the strong hand slides into, to form a solid two-handed grip as shown in Figure 41.

The support hand's index finger should be placed directly underneath and touch the outside bottom of the trigger guard. In some cases, the front of the trigger guard has a knurled indent where the shooter can place their index finger. For beginners, the index finger should not be placed in this location because the shooter may inadvertently place too much pressure on the front of the trigger guard. This action could unintentionally pull the frame of the weapon and the muzzle downward, causing accuracy problems.

As pointed out in Figure 42, another way to imagine the correct placement of the support hand is to think of it as a pocket that the strong hand slides into during the draw. To create an effective pocket, the knuckles of the four fingers should be lined up underneath the trigger guard and point toward the threat. Using the push-pull principle, the support hand

Master Grip Checklist
✓ High on Backstrap
✓ Aligned with Long Bones of the Arm
✓ Handshake Strength Only
✓ Fingers Should Form a Mitt
✓ Thumb is Relaxed
✓ Finger Off Trigger & Outside of

should be pulling back toward the shooter, while the strong hand is pushing forward. Depending upon the size of the firearm, the shooter should be pulling back with the index, middle and ring fingers. The "pinky" finger should not be exerting a lot of rearward pressure. This push-pull forward and rearward pressure, combined with the lateral or side-to-side pressure, will create a strong and stable isometric shooting platform. Using this "pocket" concept, the support hand should firmly hold the strong hand and not increase its degree of force against the strong hand during the course of fire. Cinching down or increasing one's grip strength with either hand just before, during, or after the shot is fired will lead to shot placement and/or accuracy problems.

The thumb of the support hand, like the strong hand, should be relaxed as possible and point toward the threat. The support hand thumb should be directly underneath and touching the strong thumb, which drapes or rests over or on top of the support thumb. The support hand thumb should not exert any pressure against the frame or slide, as this could cause a malfunction. Additionally, if too much pressure is exerted against the frame, the muzzle of the weapon could also unintentionally cant at an unintended angle just before the shot breaks, causing problems in accuracy.

Issues & Concerns Related to the Combat Grip

As this chapter has shown, combat shooting requires the use of both hands to create a stable shooting platform. Shooters must remember to use that grip that provides forward, rearward and lateral resistance to stabilize the weapon. There are several issues that a shooter must be aware of with the use of the combat grip. These problems can be associated with the strong hand only, the weak hand only, or a combination of the two. By reviewing some of the common concerns, these issues and problems can be easily overcome and avoided.

Improper Thumb Use & Placement

The thumbs of both hands, in the context of the combat grip, do very little in stabilizing and holding the firearm. As discussed earlier, the thumbs should remain relaxed and point toward the threat, while the strong thumb "drapes" over the support thumb.

There are two primary issues regarding the thumbs. First, the thumbs cannot interfere with the function of the weapon. One of the most commonly seen errors is when the support and/or strong side thumb presses against the frame or slide of the firearm. Pressure from the thumbs resting forcibly against the frame of the weapon could force it to go in the direction of the force exerted against the frame. This could lead to problems with accuracy. If the shooter's thumbs come in contact with the slide, it could also impede the action of the slide to the point where an officer could have a shooter-induced malfunction. These malfunctions could include the failure to extract and eject and/or a failure to feed.

Another common mistake is crossing the thumbs. Wrapping or crossing the support hand thumb over the top of the strong arm thumb may cause some downward pressure against the strong arm thumb. This downward

163

pressure could cause the firearm to cant or move in a sideways/downward angle toward the support side hand, causing problems with accuracy. Crossing the thumbs may also pull the support hand palm away from the grip, causing a "power leakage" or gap between the support hand and the grip of the weapon. This could subsequently lead to problems in controlling the recoil of the weapon.

In other cases, a shooter may wrap their support hand thumb around the top of the support hand, behind the slide of the firearm. This will result in the thumb getting struck to some degree by the slide action of the weapon when the pistol fires. A common injury, for example, is two parallel cuts from the slide mechanism (specifically, the rails) across the top of the support hand thumb. These are often referred to as "railroad tracks." They are painful and embarrassing. If severe enough, there could also be some tissue and/or bone damage to the support thumb.

Improper Hand Placement - Strong Hand

Besides improper thumb placement, the shooter's hand may also be improperly positioned on the grip of the firearm. In some cases, the palm of the strong hand may not properly rest on the backstrap or spine of the firearm's grip. This could be attributed to the fact that the weapon is too large for the shooter's hand, or the shooter has strength and/or fatigue issues, where they readjust the weapon to compensate for their lack of strength by moving the index finger deeper into the trigger. Now, instead of using the pad on the first joint, they rest the second joint of their index finger on the face of the trigger. Improper hand placement can also be attributed to sheer carelessness. In other cases, meanwhile, the shooter has positioned their strong hand too low on the gun's grip where there is a gap between the hand and the tang. To properly control the weapon, however, the hand must be positioned as high up on the grip as possible.

What usually happens in cases of improper hand placement is that the weapon is repositioned in the hand so the first knuckle of the strong hand thumb is lined up with the frame and slide of the firearm. Instead of the palm of the hand firmly holding the firearm, now, the only portion of the strong hand that grips the firearm is essentially the thumb portion of the hand. Besides not having enough "hand on the gun," this type of grip also disrupts the natural point or aim of the gun. For example, if a right-handed shooter holds the weapon in this manner, and then "naturally points," they would see that the muzzle of the weapon is dramatically shifted to the right. And, depending upon distance, the sights may no longer be lined up on the threat. In a high stress situation, where speed and accuracy is critical, a shooter using this type of grip would be at a disadvantage to the point where they could actually miss hitting the threat because of their poor grip.

Improper Hand Placement - Support Hand

In other cases, the shooter may have some issues with the correct placement of their support hand. In some instances, for example, instead of pulling straight back with the support hand, a shooter may only use the fingertips of the support hand to pull back. Using the support hand fingertips only could result in the shooter not properly stabilizing the firearm, where the firearm could inadvertently be pulled at an angle instead of straight to the rear. Or, it may not have enough support to control the weapon's recoil.

Figure 43
"Cupping"

Another common mistake with the support hand is known as "cupping" the firearm, as shown in Figure 43. Cupping occurs when the shooter places or cups their support hand palm underneath the grip, covering the magazine well. This provides limited lateral, forward, and rearward support of the weapon. This technique also blocks the magazine from being removed from the firearm. Another non-combat related handgrip is the wrist support method (see Figure 44). Wrist supporting occurs when the shooter wraps their support hand around the strong arm's wrist to supposedly provide more support to the strong hand and firearm. In effect, what the shooter is doing when using this technique is that they are trying to control upward motion associated with the recoil of the gun. While it may serve to hold the arm in place, this type of grip does nothing to provide counter-pressure to actually control the firearm's recoil.

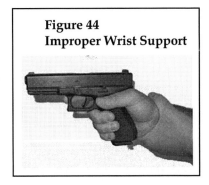

Figure 44
Improper Wrist Support

Readjusting & Changing the Grip

As pointed out earlier, the shooter must maintain the same combat grip throughout the course of fire. However, in some cases, shooters adjust their grip on the firearm immediately after it is drawn. In other cases, the grip is also adjusted between shots or when time permits. This can occur with both the strong and support hands combined, or with the strong and support hand separate of one another. Readjusting the combat grip should not occur, regardless of which hand is involved. There must be economy of motion, where the same grip is maintained throughout the draw, fire, and re-holstering of the gun.

There are several reasons why the master grip should not be adjusted. First, it takes time to adjust the grip. A police officer does not have time in a gunfight to adjust their grip. Readjusting the grip after the gun is fired slows down the ability to get back on target. It also leads to an inconsistent grip between shots, which could lead to problems with accuracy. In other cases a shooter may change their grip strength just before or during the course of fire. This problem is known as "milking" the weapon. It is usually associated with the shooter anticipating the recoil, and it will lead to problems with accuracy. Milking may occur with either the strong and weak hand or in combination of the two. While usually associated with the strong hand, milking can also occur with the support hand where the shooter inadvertently increases their grip strength just prior to or during the course of fire which will cause the sights to be disrupted to some degree.

Gripping the Firearm Too Tightly

In some cases, a shooter may not realize that they are gripping the weapon too tight. Holding onto a firearm and controlling the recoil does not require a "death grip." Gripping a weapon too tightly will constrict the flow of blood (particularly oxygenated blood) to various parts of the hand. It will also decrease the time in which the muscles in the hands become fatigued. This is primarily a problem associated with the strong hand. However, it can also occur with the support hand.

Too strong a grip leads to hand tremors, which is the involuntary trembling or shaking of the hands. To illustrate this point, consider the following example: In a combat stance, with the strong arm outstretched, make a fist and close the hand as tight as possible, using the index finger as the sight, pointing it at the target. It will only take a few seconds for the shooter to see that their hand is beginning to tremble a certain degree. Now, in the same position, relax the grip. The shooter will soon see that the hand tremor decreases because the degree of muscle exertion is reduced and oxygenated blood can now travel easier to the fine muscles.

One way to check to see if a person is gripping a weapon too tightly is to look at the hand immediately after the firearm is re-holstered. If the shooter can see an indentation of the grip (and grip medallion) in their hand as a result of the capillaries in the blood stream not being able to be refill (because of the pressure against the skin), the weapon is being held too tight. Watching the blood flow back into those constricted areas (capillary refill) is an indicator that the firearm is being held onto too tight. In order to prevent this problem (and fatigue associated with it), the shooter should only grip the weapon with enough force or strength to control the recoil of the weapon.

Fatigue & Strength Issues

In other instances, a person may be simply too weak to grip and operate the firearm in an effective manner. In some cases a person cannot effectively pull the trigger to the rear because they are too weak to do so. In other situations, the lack of strength in the strong hand will cause hand tremors, and a shooter will not be able to pull the trigger to the rear in a consistent and smooth manner shot after shot. Tremors may also occur because the muscles in the hand and arm are fatigued from overuse.

A person may also become fatigued because they are not using their support arm and hand in an appropriate manner. As pointed out in this chapter, the combat grip requires two-hands to properly control the weapon. Using the support hand (in a push-pull principle) serves to reduce fatigue associated with the strong hand grip. The weak arm/hand may compensate (to a certain degree) for any weakness with the strong hand, arm and shoulder on account of the isometric resistance (push-pull) it creates. If not the isometric resistance, using the support arm in an appropriate manner will simply provide additional strength to support the weapon for prolonged periods of time.

Besides fatigue, in other cases the shooter simply lacks that level of physical fitness or stamina to safely and effectively use a firearm. Firing a handgun or any other type of firearm requires physical exertion. It requires the use of the shoulder, arm, and hand muscles that may not be used and/or exercised on a daily basis. Because it requires some level of physical exertion, the shooter must also have a degree of cardiovascular fitness. Regardless of the causes of the lack of strength, one thing is certain: the consequences of the lack of strength and fitness will be reflected in accuracy and safety issues on the range.

Improper Tactics

Improper tactics are another issue. One of the most common problems in the context of improper grip tactics is not using the support hand properly. The shooter, for example, may actually fire the weapon from a Camp Perry or one-handed grip (and a different stance in addition to other unusual or unsound tactics). While it may work for target-related and point-shoot tactics, it is not a tactically sound grip for a dynamic gunfight. This type of grip offers little stability for the gun, making it more difficult to fire successive rounds accurately in a timely manner. This is because the recoil of the gun cannot be controlled as well in comparison to the two-handed grip. If not shooting one-handed per se, another common tactical error is not exerting enough rearward pressure with the support hand. Not exerting enough rearward pressure with the support hand will cause the gun to "jump" more in the shooter's hands, increasing the amount of time it takes to re-establish sight alignment and the sight picture.

Weapon Size

In other cases, a shooter may experience problems related to the grip because of the weapon's size, relative to the size of their hand. The firearm should fit naturally into the shooter's hand. This applies to both the strong and support hands (as a shooter may have to use their support hand under emergency conditions if the strong is injured, etc.) where the shooter should be able to naturally hold the gun. If the gun does not "fit" a shooter, he or she will not be able to handle, manipulate, and shoot it. Having too large a gun is like trying to run a mile in size 14 shoes when the runner has size 11 feet. It may work, but it will be a clumsy and slow process.

Checking the fit of the gun to one's hand is easy. All a person has to do to check fit is to properly grip the gun, making sure that the firearm's grip is positioned in the "V" of the hand while ensuring that it has a natural point. In this position, if the index finger cannot come into positive contact with the trigger, this is an indicator that the weapon is too large for the user. While a shooter could still use this weapon, what often occurs is that the shooter will compensate for the size of the weapon by improperly positioning their strong hand around the grip. This often leads to the trigger finger and entire hand becoming fatigued. Too large a grip could also psychologically defeat the shooter. Because the gun cannot be properly gripped, a person could become overly anxious and frustrated, and give up on concentrating on the basics of shooting, which could result in a mediocre performance.

Conclusion

This chapter has provided a review of the basics of the combat grip. The complete combat grip uses both hands that work in unison with one another to create a solid and stable shooting platform. One of the keys to an effective grip is to maintain the master grip that is applied using the strong hand. The master grip is responsible for controlling and stabilizing the handgun. A shooter never gives up the master grip until the firearm is re-holstered. The same grip is maintained through the entire sequence of the draw, firing, and the return of the gun to the holster. The support hand also has an important role. In fact, it is primarily responsible for stabilizing and controlling the recoil of the gun. Under the push-pull principle, the strong hand is pushing away from the shooter's body, while the support hand pulls rearward, or toward the shooter. At the same time, there is side-to-side or lateral pressure against the firearm by both the strong and support palm regions of the hands.

There are some issues to consider when establishing and maintaining the master grip. First, there must be grip uniformity. The way a handgun is held makes the difference between hits and misses. The master grip must be the same each time the firearm is drawn from the holster. In many instances, however, there are some problems associated with the grip. Problems can originate from both the strong and support hands. Some key considerations deal with finger and palm placement, and the role of the thumbs when shooting. Shooters should also consider issues related to strength, and make sure that they are using a tactically sound and effective combat grip to ensure speed and accuracy in a gunfight. Any problems with the grip of the weapon will lead to accuracy issues, increased frustration, and perhaps psychological defeat when shooting.

Chapter 8
SIGHT ALIGNMENT

S ight alignment is one of the most important shooting fundamentals. When thinking of sight alignment, consider it in the perspective that if the sights are not lined up, the shooter will not be able to accurately place their shots on the intended threat or target. In this context, sight alignment is one of the keys to becoming an excellent shooter. Combined with the fact that a gunfight is often a sudden and dynamic event, a shooter also needs speed and accuracy which often begins by "getting on the sights."

In order to gain a better understanding of the concept of sight alignment, this chapter will review some of the basic physiological properties associated with vision. This chapter will also provide the reader with an understanding of the importance of sight alignment and the sight picture in becoming a proficient shooter.

The Physiology of the Human Eye

The eyes are the computer programmer for the brain. They transmit information to the brain from the outside world. The brain meanwhile, determines where the eyes will look. It also makes decisions based on visual stimuli from the eyes. Vision can be divided into static and dynamic visual acuity. Static visual acuity is the ability to see a non-moving fixed target. Take for example the reading of an eye chart. This is static visual acuity, and it is measured in the context of what a person can see at 20 feet. If a person has 20/20 vision, this means that they can see at 20 feet what most other people see at that same distance. If a person has 20/40 vision, meanwhile, this means that they can see at 20 feet what most people can see at 40 (Palay & Krachmer, 1997). Unlike static visual acuity, dynamic visual acuity is learned. It deals with how people respond to various stimuli they encounter. It could range from a professional hockey player striking a hockey puck that is traveling at 100 miles per hour to a police officer identifying, tracking, and responding to a threat with a preprogrammed response. Dynamic acuity requires visual concentration, identifying threat cues, and reacting to those threats — often in a split-second.

Basic Components of the Human Eye

Some of the basic components of the human eye include the cornea, iris, pupil, retina, photoreceptor cells (composed of rods and cones), and the optic nerve. The cornea is the protective cover of the eye. The iris, which is visible through the cornea, is that part of the eye that gives it its color. In the center of the iris is the pupil. The pupil regulates and allows light to reach the retina, which is located in the back of the eye. Behind the iris is the lens. The lens focuses light on the retina (Cassel, Billig & Randall, 1998). The retina consists of layers of complex sensory tissue that are located adjacent to the inside rear of the eye. Within the retina are rods and cones, which are photoreceptor cells. They gather light and transform this light into a nerve impulse that is sent through the optic nerve to the brain. The macula of the eye (which is located directly behind the lens) has the greatest concentration of cones that provides the most acute or accurate vision in humans. This portion of the eye is used for central and color vision because cone photoreceptors have the ability to distinguish color. The sides of the inner eye (or the peripheral retina) have large concentrations of rod photoreceptors. Rod photoreceptors do not distinguish colors. They can only distinguish varying shades of gray. This region of the eye is used primarily for night and peripheral vision. Both cones and rods are important. Daylight vision is mediated primarily by cones. Night vision is mediated by rod photoreceptors, while twilight vision is mediated by a combination of rods and cones (Vaughan, Ashbury & Riordan-Eva, 1999).

Binocular Rivalry

One of the first issues that needs to be addressed, in gaining an understanding of vision, is the concept of binocular rivalry, where the eyes "compete" for focus on a specific target. In essence, both eyes attempt to focus on the same object at the same time. An example of binocular rivalry can be seen below:

> *These right and left circles can be superimposed by looking toward or between the two circles. When fixated between the two circles, a slightly blurred circle will appear between the left and right circles. When viewed for a few seconds, binocular rivalry occurs:*

Now, imagine that you have both eyes open and you are trying to focus on the front sight by looking through the rear sight. The shooter will inadvertently experience binocular rivalry (you may comment that you see two front sights, for example). To overcome binocular rivalry, the shooter must **use their dominant eye** to properly sight the weapon.

The Dominant Eye

All individuals possess a dominant eye. The dominant eye is basically that eye that takes priority over the other eye when focusing on an object. The dominant eye can be considered to be the lead eye. This lead eye is the first to focus on a specific point or object. The non-dominant eye then "follows" the dominant eye.

In the context of shooting, a person must know which one of their eyes is the dominant eye. To test for eye dominance, pick a small object several feet away. With both eyes open, form a circle with your fingers creating an"O.K." symbol with the right hand and fingers. Center the object in the circle, keeping both eyes open. Then extend your arm outward. Close the right eye. If the image is no longer in the ring created by your finger, you are right eye dominant. Then, open your right eye and close your left eye. If the object remains in position, you have confirmed that you are right eye dominant. Alternatively, if the image appears to "jump" to the right where you can no longer see it, you have confirmed left eye dominance.

Crossed Dominance

It is a fortunate condition when a shooter's dominant eye corresponds to their strong hand. In some cases, however, the strong hand and the dominant eye do not correspond. For example, a person may be left-eye dominant and a right-handed shooter or vice-versa. This is known as crossed dominance. This can be a common issue. Some research has found that approximately 20% of the general population is crossed dominant (Dargent-Pare, DeAgostini, Mesbaj, & Dellatolas, 1992).

Many individuals may not realize that they have crossed dominance because they have continually trained by closing one eye when shooting. While this technique may work under low-stress target shooting scenarios, under a high stress situation, the human body will not allow the shooter to close an eye because of the stress response. In this situation, the shooter may encounter problems associated with binocular rivalry. They will not be able to rapidly focus on their front sight, especially if they always used their non-dominant eye when shooting. To avoid this problem, police officers need to keep both their eyes open at all times so they can properly aim and shoot.

Crossed dominance can create problems for a shooter in some situations. One study that researched crossed dominance found that individuals do not learn marksmanship skills as fast as those who had matched hand and eye dominance (Jones, Classe, Hester and Harris, 1996). Through proper training and practice, however, crossed dominance can be easily overcome and corrected. In fact, one of the simplest ways to correct this condition is to make sure that the sights of the weapon are always aligned with the dominant eye. In the case of the right-handed shooter/left eye dominance, for example, all the shooter has to do is train themselves to bring the weapon over to their dominant left eye when sighting the weapon.

One- or Two-eyed Shooting?

Often the question arises from police officers and recruits if they should close one eye when shooting at close ranges of less than 10 yards. Traditionally, recruits, police officers, and civilians have been taught to shoot with one eye closed. This can be referred to as monocular-based shooting (monocularity is a term that means having vision with only one eye). Monocular-based shooting can be attributed to the fact that it may be easier to gain sight alignment and a sight picture with one eye closed. In other situations, monocularity is the result of ocular occlusion—being taught to, and deliberately closing one eye when shooting. While this method is appropriate for lower-stress and marksmanship-building skills at distances greater than 10 yards, one-eyed shooting is an inappropriate and unacceptable training method in law enforcement for high stress, close-range, combat-related shooting. In fact, it is contra-training.

To judge the above point, consider any dynamic fast-paced sporting activity that the reader has ever engaged in. Did you close an eye during this event to make yourself better? No. Like these sporting events, a gunfight is a visually guided dynamic event. It requires both static and dynamic visual acuity. The outcome of this event depends upon the relationship between visual and motor events. Thus, monocular-based shooting at close distances (less than 10 yards) is unacceptable for the following reasons:

- The Physiological Impact of Stress on the Human Body

In the context of vision, when a shooter encounters a high stress situation, they experience what is known as perceptual narrowing. Due to changes in the human body associated with the stress response, the human eye actually changes shape and bulges outward from the eye socket because of increased blood pressure and other physiological changes. Because of these physiological changes, the shooter loses a great deal of their peripheral (side) vision (Reeves & Bergum, 1972). This change in the shape of one's eye can be so extreme that a shooter wearing hard contact lenses may actually have their contacts pop out of their eyes under high stress situations.

Combined with the change in the shape of one's eyes, Siddle and Breedlove (1995) point out that an individual exposed to a high stress situation will not be able to keep and/or force an eye shut. This is the result of physiological changes in the body during high stress situations and the activation of the body's stress response (that cannot be easily controlled). These are due to the sympathetic response from the body. As pointed out earlier in this book, the sympathetic nervous system is part of the autonomic system that influences the heart, smooth muscles, and glands. Individuals have very little control over the stress response. It is activated during high stress flight or fight situations. In essence, the body is now in survival mode and is on autopilot. Meanwhile, the brain is demanding as much information as possible, and it will simply not perform the physiological function of limiting visual information that it depends upon for survival.

Figure 8-1
The Peripheral Field

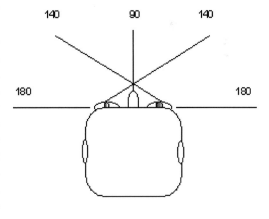

What is even more interesting is that the human eye cannot focus under high stress situations. Siddle and Breedlove (1995) point out that during high stress situations where the sympathetic response occurs, the eye cannot focus at short distances and a shooter will not be able to clearly see the front sight. While the shooter may be able to see the front sight, for example, it will be out of focus.

- The Peripheral Visual Field

The extent of a human's visual field using binocular (both eyes) vision is approximately 180 degrees. When controlling for the size of a person's nose, an individual could lose up to 20 to 40 degrees (because of nasal defect or blockage of vision) of their peripheral field in comparison to their temporal or strong side. With regard to this visual field and a person's "nasal defect," it can be assumed that the monocular human has a total of 140 degrees of peripheral vision. The equivalent monocular field would be 50 degrees on the nasal side and 90 degrees on the temporal side (Westlake, 2001). This loss of peripheral vision could be corrected with head movements to compensate for the difference. In force situations, however, this cannot be done for two reasons that include: 1) the officer is focused on a specific threat, and, 2) the shooter has already lost some of their peripheral vision due to the body's stress response and the resulting perceptual narrowing of their visual field.

Figure 8-1 provides an example of the benefits of peripheral vision, based on the angles that were discussed earlier. By examining this figure, a shooter may lose at least 40 degrees of vision (i.e. 180-140 = 40) through ocular occlusion (in combination with other sensory information that will be discussed below).

- Binocular Summation

Vision is better under binocular viewing conditions than viewing with either eye monocularly. This can be explained in terms of probability and neural summation. According to Westlake (2001), "….Probability summation occurs because when using two eyes, twice the number of photoreceptors are stimulated at corresponding retinal points within the visual field, compared to monocular viewing…Neural summations occur higher up the visual pathway as a result of additive neural input into binocularly-driven cells" (p. 620). A shooter must remember this simple point: There is no binocular summation in an occluded (one-eyed) individual.

- The Physiological Blind Spot

As discussed earlier in this chapter, the retina of the eye is made up of photoreceptors known as rods and cones. The retina is found on the inner surface of the back of the eye. One area of the retina where the optic nerve and blood vessels are found lack these photoreceptors. This area is known as the blind spot. Research by Westlake (2001) has found that a blind spot of 6 degrees results in a scotoma of over 2 meters at 20 meters (imagine looking approximately 60 feet away and you have a black hole in your visual field about 6 feet in diameter). With monocularity, however, there is the potential that this blind spot could interfere with the shooter's vision. While head and eye movements may serve to alleviate or correct the problems associated with the blind spot, combined with the fact that humans experience ocular refixations that occur between three and five times a second, the blind spot may still be an issue if someone were to shoot with one eye closed (Mourant & Rockwell, 1970; Crundall, Underwood & Chapman, 1999).

- Depth Perception

Depth perception is the visual ability to see the world in three dimensions, allowing the individual to see and accurately determine the distance to an object. Depth perception takes place in several different ways in human beings. One way is by using monocular depth cues that involve the use of one eye. When using monocular cues to judge depth or distance, some of the cues an individual uses include the relative height of objects and familiar size. For example, a person can generalize how far an individual is standing away from them, based on their relative height. At the same time, a shooter can estimate the distance of a paper target based on the size difference of the target when it is 3 yards away from them relative to when it is 15 yards away (Lincoln & Lincoln, 1988).

Humans also use binocular depth cues. In fact, humans are "built" to use binocular vision. A person's eyes, unlike grazing animals, for example, are positioned on the front of the skull. This eye placement allows humans to use binocular cues more effectively than those animals whose visual fields do not overlap very much (we are built to be hunters and predators). This is a much more powerful cue to depth than monocular vision. By using both eyes, an individual sees two similar but different images on account of the fact that the distance between the pupils causes two different images of the world (Campbell, Reece & Simon, 2004). This difference depends upon the relative distance of the object from the eyes. For example, an

177

image closer to the shooter's face shifts more if they look at it with alternating eyes than images that are far away from the individual. This is known as binocular disparity. On account of this binocular disparity, each eye basically captures its own view of two separate images. These images are then sent to the brain where they "melt" together and create a three-dimensional stereo image. The results of binocularity (i.e. stereovision), allows an individual to better see where objects are in relation to him or herself. It also allows the shooter to judge depth more accurately. That ability to judge depth is known as stereopsis (Sekuler & Blake, 1994).

- Temporary Visual Loss

The possibility of temporary visual loss further requires one to learn how to be a proficient shooter with *both* eyes open. Consider, for example, a situation where a shooter has experienced some type of temporary visual loss, ranging from a chemical restraint (OC Spray) or a foreign object in the eye. In the same manner, consider the situation where a shooter has always trained by keeping their right eye shut. In a gunfight, however, the left eye is somehow injured, where the shooter now has to use the other eye. In both of these examples, changing eyes to shoot under a high stress situation would be very difficult to accomplish. Therefore, learning to shoot with both eyes open would be a better training alternative.

Principles of Sight Alignment

As shown in Figure 8-2, A shooter should consider sighting a firearm in the context of a four-point line. There is the eye, the rear sight, the front sight and the threat (target). Shooters should maintain this four-point line when shooting. However, the key to sight alignment is the front sight. The front sight is critical in determining where the projectile will hit the target. In fact, the front sight must remain in clear, sharp focus throughout the course of fire.

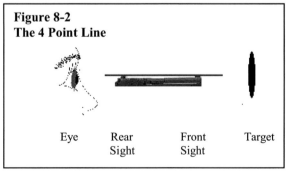

Figure 8-2
The 4 Point Line

| Eye | Rear Sight | Front Sight | Target |

There are some simple steps that should be followed when lining up the sights First, the shooter must "pick up" or focus on the front sight. Once the front sight is in focus, the shooter should then align the rear sight with the front sight. Once the sights are then aligned, then the shooter can position these sights on the threat (see Figure 8-5). Another key consideration with sight alignment is that the gun goes to the eyes; the eyes do not go to the gun. That is, the shooter must maintain an effective stance, keeping the head level. In order to keep the head level and not "shrug" and position the head between the shoulder blades, the shooter should make sure that head remains level and the gun is raised to their normal visual field. Another way to remember to keep the head level is to make sure the chin is not tucked to the neck. Instead, the chin should be raised or pushed forward and toward the threat.

**Figure 45
Proper Sight
Alignment**

Types of Sights

There are a variety of different sights that can be used on firearms. Two of the more common sights are the peep and the aperture or partridge-style sights, which are shown in Figure 8-3. The peep sight is often referred to as a "ghost ring" sight. Basically, the rear sight is simply a ring or loop that the shooter looks through when focusing on the front sight, which is centered in the ring. The partridge-style sight, meanwhile, is simply a square notch rear sight with a square front blade. Depending upon the manufacturer, these types of sights may also have dots or squares on them to assist the shooter in acquiring proper sight alignment. Despite the types of sights that are used on a weapon, the fundamentals of sight alignment remain the same—"front sight focus."

What Is Sight Alignment?

The term "sight alignment" refers to the alignment of the front and rear sight. It *does not* apply to the sights' relationship to the target or threat. Sight alignment exists when the front sight is centered in the rear sight notch, with the top of the front sight level with the top of the rear sight.

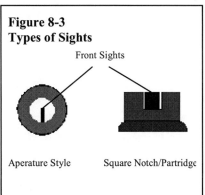

**Figure 8-3
Types of Sights**

Front Sights

Aperature Style   Square Notch/Partridge

179

The rear sight always serves as a "window" for the front sight. It serves as a frame. The shooter must look through this window and focus on the front sight. Regardless of the type of sights, the front sight must be evenly framed in the rear sight. Any movement of the front sight during the sequence of the firing will be reflected by accuracy issues on the target.

Figure 8-4 provides an example of correct sight alignment. Correct sight alignment (A) is when there is equal distance or light on each side of the sight in relation to the rear post and when the top of the front sight is level with the rear sight. The projectile will strike high under condition B, because the front sight post, while having equal distance or light on each side, is higher than the rear sight. A projectile will impact to the right under condition C, while the projectile will impact low/left under condition D.

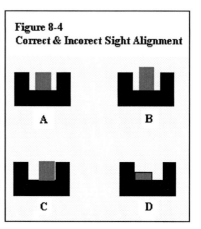

Figure 8-4
Correct & Incorect Sight Alignment

A   B

C   D

Training Tip: To visualize proper sight alignment with the standard partridge-styled sights, imagine an "E" lying on its back.

When looking at the front sight through the rear sight, (and the front sight is centered in the rear sight notch, with the top of the front sight level with the top of the rear sight), the shooter has proper sight alignment (Position A). The shooter must continue to look directly at the front sight and maintain sight alignment until the trigger releases and the shot is fired.

The large majority of the shooter's attention must be focused on "front sight focus." The sights must stay aligned all the way through the pull of the trigger and after the round has been fired. The four point line must be maintained until the shooter has asked themselves the following two questions: 1) Did it hit the threat? and, 2) Did it work? If either or both of these two questions are answered in the negative or "no," then the shooter will need to fire more rounds to stop the threat, requiring immediate sight alignment to achieve this goal.

Some key points to consider with sight alignment:

- Sights must be perfectly aligned. If there is a slight variation where the front sight is not even with the rear sight (i.e., too high or uneven side to side) the bullet will not impact the intended point of aim. This is true even if there is a minute difference. At close ranges, a minute difference will be forgiving. When this slight difference is calculated over several feet or yards, the bullet will be off several inches from the intended point of aim. For example, if a shooter would disrupt their sight alignment only 1/32 of an inch, at 30 feet, this would mean that the bullet would strike approximately 1 inch from of the intended point of aim.

Sight Alignment Checklist
✓ Head Level
✓ Pick up Front Sight
✓ Align w/Rear Sight
✓ Establish Sight Picture

- Sight alignment must be maintained throughout the entire function of the weapon.
- The shooter must continue to look directly at the front sight and maintain sight alignment until the shot is fired. It applies throughout the continual pull of the trigger to the rearward position, until the trigger releases and the round leaves the barrel.
- Sight alignment also applies to getting back on the sights immediately (i.e. follow through) after a round is fired. The shooter must follow through and re-establish the sight picture immediately.
- The head must remain level and upright when sighting the weapon. In many situations, the shooter may "cock" or angle their head or bring the head down to the sights to establish sight alignment. The shooter must also bring the sights up to their field of view, not the other way around. In situations where the shooter brings their head down to their sights, the head is bent forward, reducing the shooter's peripheral vision, balance, and stance.

"Eye Sprint" & Sight Alignment

One of the common problems in sight alignment is called eye sprint. As pointed out earlier, the shooter must maintain "front sight focus." However, what often occurs is that the shooter focuses on the threat, the front sight, and then back to the threat. Because the human eye can only focus on one thing at a time, it must change its focus from the target to the sights and back. This is known as eye sprinting, which is when the focus is changed and moves between the threat and front sight. Because of the change in focus from the target to the front sight, sight alignment becomes disrupted and the bullet does not hit the intended point of aim.

Eye sprinting is a common problem in shooting. It can be attributed to the simple fact that shooters are anxious to see their point of impact on the target. Because they are anxious, they lose their concentration on the front sight. If this activity should become repetitive, it will then become habitual, where the shooter will not even realize that they are eye sprinting. This type of contra-training is, of course, wrong. In a real gunfight this will consume a lot of time that a shooter does not have. Shooters must maintain front sight focus until they have stopped the threat. It is not necessary to see if the intended target was hit. A shooter needs to be confident and "trust their sights" that the bullet or projectile hit where they intended it to strike the threat. The only way to overcome eye sprinting is to realize it occurs and to overcome this practice. Again, the last thing a shooter should remember after the round has been fired is "front sight focus."

Arch of Movement & Sight Alignment

Every shooter has some movement in their body when shooting. It may be based on not properly applying the basic fundamentals of shooting (i.e. stance and grip) or because they may not have enough strength to maintain a perfect and balanced stance. This unintended motion of one's body is referred to as the arch of movement. Because of this arch of movement, the firearm's sights are going to "float," "wobble," and move to a certain degree on the target. It is the shooter's responsibility to "settle into" their arch of movement, minimizing it as much as possible by concentrating on the basics to shoot nice, tight groups.

Arch of movement can be controlled to some degree. As the shooter becomes balanced and locked out, their arch of movement will be minimized in comparison to when they first established sight alignment and the sight picture, because the shooter "settled into" their shooting platform. Nevertheless, as the shooter begins to build up pressure on the face of the trigger, the sights may still slightly "float" or move around the intended point of aim. Often what happens in these cases is that the shooter tries to anticipate their arc of movement, when they simply snap a round off when they think the sights are lined up on the target. In other cases, the shooter can become fatigued from holding the gun up too long for the "perfect shot." Waiting too long could actually increase the arch of movement due to fatigue, where the shooter could subsequently jerk the trigger or "let the round off" with an unstable trigger pull when they think that the sights are perfectly aligned as they float around. Of course, both of these actions (as well as others) will result in inconsistent shot patterns on the target, due to the misalignment of the sights. What the shooter needs to do instead, is to concentrate on the basics of marksmanship to minimize their arch of movement to the least amount possible. The shooter also needs to accept the fact that there may always be some movement or "floating" of the sights, and learn to work with their arch of movement to get the best, controlled shot possible. In fact, the sequence of events that should occur when shooting, in the context of sight alignment and wobble is: first concentrate on trigger control, establish a sight picture, let the sights (and gun) wobble, and then pull the trigger to the rear. The shooter needs to remember that they are combat shooting. As long as the arch of movement or "wobble" is center mass, their shots will be deadly.

Sight Picture

The sight picture is the relationship between the aligned sights and the threat or target. A shooter has a sight picture when the sights are lined up on the threat. Take for example, Figure 8-5 which shows a sight picture using the "six o'clock" hold. The six o'clock hold position is the placement

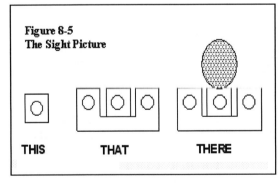

Figure 8-5
The Sight Picture

THIS   THAT   THERE

of the front sight just below the intended point of impact. To establish a sight picture, the shooter must first "get on the front sight." Second, the shooter should line up the rear sight with the front sight. Last, the front sight should be aligned at the "six o'clock" hold position relative to the threat. The rear sight, meanwhile, must have equal light on each side and be level with the front sight.

Another option related to the sight picture is the center hold. As the name implies, center hold alignment is when the sights are aligned directly with the intended point of impact. For example, a center hold on Figure 8-5 requires that the shooter place the front sight in the direct center of the shaded region.

Often the question arises: How can the shooter hit the threat if it is not in focus? The response to this question is that while the threat or target may be out of focus and blurry, the shooter will still be able to accurately place their shots center of mass on the threat. The threat will be large enough in the sight picture to ensure that the rounds will hit the intended point of aim, if proper sight alignment is maintained throughout the course of fire. A deadly force situation does not necessarily require precise shooting. It requires survival shooting, or placing the shots center of mass on the threat to ensure rapid incapacitation.

Conclusion

Sight alignment refers to the alignment of the front and rear sight. It is one of the most important fundamentals of shooting. Without correct sight alignment, the shooter will not be able to accurately place rounds on the intended target or threat. Sight picture, meanwhile, is the relationship between the aligned sights and the target.

Several issues need to be considered with sight alignment. First, the sights need to be aligned with the dominant eye. The dominant eye is that eye that takes priority over the other eye when focusing on an object. Second, individuals should learn to shoot with both eyes open at close distances. As this chapter has pointed out, under high stress situations the human body will not allow one eye to be closed. Monocular or one-eyed shooting also limits peripheral vision, prevents binocular summation, and limits depth perception, to name just a few issues related to monocular or one-eyed shooting.

Proper sight alignment requires the shooter to look through the rear sight and focus on the front sight throughout the entire cycle of the weapon, even after the weapon has been fired. The shooter's focus must remain on the front sight. One of the common problems with sight alignment is known as eye sprinting where the shooter shifts their focus from the front sight to the threat. This will result in the sights no longer being aligned with the threat, causing the projectile to miss the intended point of aim. Through proper training and concentration, however, this can be readily overcome. Regardless of the type of weapon and sights used, shooters must concentrate on the basic principle of "front sight focus."

REFERENCES

Campbell, N.A., Reece, J.B. & E.J. Simon (2004). Essential biology with physiology. Upper Saddle River, NJ: Pearson.

Cassel, G.H., Billig, M.D. & H.G. Randall. (1998). The eye book: A complete guide to eye disorders and health. Baltimore: Johns Hopkins University Press.

Coren, S. & Ward, L. M. (1989). Sensation and Perception. San Diego, CA: HBJ.

Crundall, D., Underwood, G., Chapman, P. (1999). Driving experience and the functional field of view. Perception, 28, 1075-1087.

Dargent-Pare, C., DeAgostine, M., Mesbah, M, & G. Dellatolas (September, 1992). Foot and eye preferences in adults: Relationship with handedness, sex and age. Cortex, 28(3), 343-351.

Jones, L.F., Classe, J.G., Hester, M., & K. Harris (May, 1996). Association between eye dominance and training for rifle marksmanship: A pilot study. Journal of the American Optometric Association, 67(2), 73-76.

Lincoln, K.R. Lincoln, J. E. (Eds.) (1988). Engineering data compendium: Human perception and performance. (Vols. 1-4). Wright-Patterson AFB, OH: Armstrong Aerospace Medical Research Laboratory.

Mourant, R., Rockwell, T (1970). Mapping eye movement patterns to the visual scene in driving: An exploratory study. Human factors, 12, 81-87.

Palay. D.A. & Krachmer, J.H. (1997). Ophthalmology for the primary care physician. St Louis: Mosby.

Reeves, F.B. & Bergum, B.O. (December, 1972). Perceptual narrowing as a function of peripheral cue relevance. Perceptual and motor skills, 35(3), 719-724.

Sekuler, A.B. & Blake, R. (1994). Perception. New York: McGraw-Hill.

Siddle, B.K & Breedlove, H. (1995). How stress affects vision and shooting stance. Police marksman, 16-20.

Vaughan, D.; Asbury, T., & P. Riordan-Eva (1999). <u>General ophthalmology</u> (15th ed). Stamford, CT: Appleton & Lange.

Westlake, W. (May, 2001). Is a one eyed racing driver safe to compete? Formula one (eye) or two? <u>British journal of ophthalmology, 85,</u> 619-624.

Introduction

A ccuracy involves trigger control and sight alignment in that order. Trigger control is the key to effective shot placement. It is also the hardest skill to master. Because of this fact, it is the most important skill that a shooter needs to perfect.

To effectively place rounds on the target, the weapon must be fired without disturbing the sights so the projectile will hit the intended target or threat. To accomplish this task, there must be effective trigger control. To illustrate this point, consider that in many situations the sight picture can be disrupted to the point where the bullet may not hit the intended point of aim, but be slightly off because of some wobble in the sight picture. In the context of poor trigger control, meanwhile, snapping or jerking the trigger, depending upon the distance to the target, can result in the bullet completely missing the target. Thus, trigger control should be the main focus of effective shot placement.

Trigger control is a conscious, physical process that requires mental concentration in order to create a smooth and consistent trigger pull. At the same time, pulling the trigger is also a physical process. Unlike some of the other basics that you need to be proficient in, mastering the trigger requires getting "the feel" of a moving mechanical device that requires physical manipulation by the strong hand's index finger. Because there is physical manipulation of the trigger mechanism, greater attention must be given to making trigger control an automatic and smooth action, based on muscle memory. Because of these two issues, trigger control is perhaps one of the more difficult firearms fundamentals to master.

In its most basic sense, trigger control is quite easy. The shooter should imagine "pulling" the front sight through the rear sight. The front sight must stay in perfect alignment until the trigger releases or "breaks," surprising the shooter when the gun discharges. Additionally, the shooter should concentrate on the fact that when pulling the trigger to the rear, the front sight cannot "touch" the sides of the rear sight. At the same time, the top of the front sight must stay perfectly level with the top of the rear sight (as shown in Figure 8-5).

Several issues related to trigger control will be explored in this chapter. This chapter will begin with a review of the principles of trigger pull and travel. Next, the importance of finger placement to ensure effective trigger control will be reviewed, followed by the importance of maintaining positive trigger pressure and using the trigger reset when shooting. Some of the specific problems related to trigger control, especially jerking, flinching, snapping, and having too much or too little finger on the trigger will also be reviewed

Principles of Effective Trigger Control

Regardless of the type of semi-automatic handgun, there are some fundamentals related to trigger control that a shooter must master. These include getting the "feel" of the firearm's trigger pull and travel, establishing proper finger placement, maintaining positive pressure with the trigger finger and using the trigger reset.

Trigger Pull & Trigger Travel

Trigger pull is the weight or pressure required for the mechanics of the weapon to fire. It is "the force that must be applied to the trigger to fire the pistol" (Sunstrom, 2000, p. 16). This force is usually measured in pounds. The weight of the trigger varies according to manufacturer, modification, how well the firearm has been maintained, and the trigger action of the weapon. For example, a double action pistol will generally have a heavier trigger pull (up to or more than 12 pounds) than single action pistols (which may be 4 to 5 pounds). Trigger travel, meanwhile, is the length a trigger must move (as measured in distance) before the weapon fires. The amount the trigger travels also depends upon design and manufacturer. As a general rule of thumb, single action pistols will have a shorter trigger travel than double action pistols. This shorter trigger travel generally reduces the amount of time it takes to fire the weapon.

Shooters must consider issues related to trigger pull and travel. Too heavy a pull could move the sights out of alignment (i.e. what happens to a handgun that weighs approximately 1 pound when the shooter has to apply over 5 pounds of pressure to move the trigger?). Too heavy a pull could also lead to strength issues, as a shooter's trigger finger may fatigue faster because of the physical exertion needed to pull the trigger to the rear.

This could also lead to safety concerns. At the same time, too light a pull could also lead to issues, including accidental discharges. As a guideline, the National Law Enforcement and Corrections Technology Center recommends that duty weapons should have no less than 3lbs or more than 8lbs in single action mode; 18lbs in double action mode; and, no less than 5lbs and no more than 15 lbs in striker-fired firearms (Sundstrom, 2000).

The same issues apply to trigger travel. Too long a travel could pull the sights out of alignment. This is based simply on the fact the trigger has to travel further, increasing the risk of the sights getting out of alignment. Too short a travel, meanwhile, could also lead to safety problems, especially accidental discharges.

Finger Placement

The strong hand index finger is responsible for trigger control and firing the weapon. Accordingly, the proper placement of the index finger on the face of the trigger is critical for accuracy and shot placement. This also means that the shooter must maintain a positive grip on the weapon. They must make the action of pulling the trigger a conscious and deliberate activity, concentrating on the pull, while "telling" their trigger finger to pull the trigger to the rear.

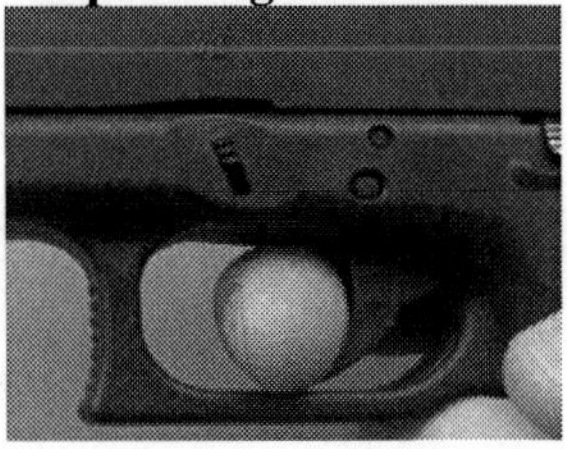

As discussed in the chapter on the grip, a shooter must maintain a proper grip on the firearm. At the same time, the shooter must have proper finger placement on the trigger of the weapon without changing the grip. There are two recommendations for finger placement. One recommendation is that the first joint (the distal joint) of the trigger finger should rest on the face or front of the trigger. Another recommendation is to place the first

Figure 46
Proper Finger Placement

pad of the index finger on the trigger. Either one is correct depending upon shooter preference. Basically, the only requirement is that the finger must be comfortable and consistently placed on the face of the trigger. Comfort is based on the size of the weapon, relative to the shooter's hand and trigger finger. For example, the gun must naturally fit the hand (including the support hand), and the index finger must naturally rest on the face of the trigger. In the context of consistency, meanwhile, each and every time the shooter places their finger on the face of the trigger, it should be in the same exact location.

Regardless of if the shooter uses the first knuckle or pad of the index finger, the key is that the placement of the finger should ensure that the trigger is being pulled straight back to the rear each and every time in an even and consistent manner. There must be a smooth and consistent trigger pull throughout the entire trigger pull, where the shooter is somewhat surprised when the trigger releases and the weapon fires. In order to achieve this, the shooter must be relaxed and imagine that they are pulling the front sight of the weapon through the rear sight, where the sights must stay perfectly aligned throughout the pull of the trigger.

The shooter must also have the strength to pull the trigger and have the ability to control the movement of the trigger under spring pressure. This requires that the finger be properly placed on the face of the trigger. In some cases, for example, the shooter may position the finger too far down on the trigger where part of the finger is on the trigger and the remainder is resting on the inside of the trigger guard. Since only a small portion of the pad or joint is resting on the trigger, it could be more difficult to maintain a smooth, consistent pull. When coupled with the fact that the principle of leverage requires more strength to pull the trigger from this location, problems with accuracy will occur. At the same time, the lateral or side-to-side pressure exerted on the trigger face must be equal. Unequal pressure (i.e. too much or too little finger on the trigger face) and/or strength issues will cause the front sight of the weapon to move either to the left or to the right a minute distance. As pointed out in the sight alignment chapter, this slight movement (calculated over several feet or yards) will result in the projectile being off several inches (or feet in some cases) from the intended point of impact.

Positive Trigger Pressure

A shooter must also always maintain positive trigger pressure. They must keep their finger on the face of the trigger in a gunfight. Trigger pressure (or the finger's contact on the trigger) must be constant, even, quick and smooth. It can be compared to taking a photograph where the operator slowly and evenly presses down on the shutter button to make sure that the photo is not blurred by their actions. It is a pull, straight backward and then forward (imagine squeezing a lemon with the index finger with enough force and/or consistency to only get one drop of lemon juice). It should be thought of as a rolling motion that is continual, nonstop, and uninterrupted until the shooter has determined that the threat has been stopped, where he or she can then consciously take their finger off the trigger and move it outside the trigger guard. This nonstop motion is backward and forward. When pulling the trigger to the rear and then releasing it forward under spring pressure, the same speed and motion must be maintained.

In some situations maintaining the same even trigger pull may be difficult. In many situations this can be attributed to the design of the trigger mechanism itself. For example, many pistol triggers are two stage triggers. With a two-stage trigger system, the first stage (often referred to the "take up") occurs when the shooter takes up the slack of the trigger, where there is little or no resistance from the trigger bar and sear. At stage two of the trigger travel, meanwhile, the shooter encounters a degree of resistance because the trigger is actually moving the trigger bar or sear. Depending upon the weapon, stage two can be a long or short pull. Often, what will occur with this type of trigger system is that the shooter incorrectly increases the speed of their trigger pull because of the increased resistance on the trigger at the second stage. What a shooter should do, instead, is that they should pull through the first stage of the trigger, and when the "stop" or resistance is reached, the trigger pull should be the same speed and consistency until the trigger "breaks" and the weapon fires.

> **Training Tip:** To improve trigger control, take up the "slack" in the trigger, until resistance is encountered. Then, begin a smooth and consistent trigger pull

Trigger pressure must also be maintained after the weapon fires. However, a common mistake made by shooters is to immediately take their finger off the trigger after the weapon fires. This may be the result of the recoil forcing the finger off ("bouncing") the trigger, or the shooter inadvertently taking the finger off the trigger and perhaps outside the trigger guard. Repositioning the trigger finger back on the trigger to fire successive rounds takes time. However, the shooter does not have time to do this in a gunfight. Furthermore, under high stress situations, if a shooter keeps readjusting their finger, this may lead to the rounds not accurately hitting the intended target because of inconsistent placement of the trigger finger on the face of the trigger.

The Trigger Reset

Another reason why positive trigger pressure should be constantly maintained is on account of the design of the firearm. In all firearms, to one degree or another, there is trigger slack. Trigger slack can be best described as movement in the trigger before any mechanical pressure is placed on the trigger mechanism. For example, in some handguns, a shooter can pull the trigger in a rearward direction a certain distance where they may feel very little or no resistance at all from the trigger mechanism. In fact, the shooter may also see and feel the trigger "wiggle" backward and forward. Consider, for example, a double/single action firearm. Double action requires a longer distance of trigger travel (the distance the trigger must move before the weapon fires). When the weapon goes into single action mode, the trigger (if positive pressure is not maintained) will travel to its most forward position (i.e. back to double action stage). However, there is a great deal of slack (up to or more than 1/4" in some models) before the trigger mechanically engages, where the shooter can start to feel pressure or resistance. This play or slack in the trigger is useless and unnecessary. At times it can also interfere with accuracy. If, for example, a shooter would let the trigger travel to its furthest forward point, it could cause the shooter to "slap" the trigger, which will lead to errors in accuracy.

In all firearms there is also a trigger reset. The trigger reset is basically the mechanism in the handgun that resets the trigger so the weapon can be fired again. If a shooter maintains positive pressure on the trigger between shots (i.e. does not take their finger off the trigger or let it "bounce") and lets the trigger move forward under spring pressure, they will feel and perhaps hear a "click." This is the trigger reset, and the "click" feel or sound indicates that the trigger assembly has been re-engaged, and the weapon is ready to be fired again (the practice of stopping the forward movement of the finger when feeling the trigger re-engage is referred to as "catching the link"). Even though the trigger will travel further, there is no need for it to do so. Any more forward movement of the trigger is unnecessary and is simply "slack."

In short, the shooter should not allow the trigger to move any further forward than the reset. Mastering the trigger reset will allow a shooter to become faster and more accurate in firing the weapon. It can be easily achieved by concentrating on the function of the weapon, developing muscle memory, and practice. Getting a feel for the reset can be accomplished on the range under live fire and in dry fire exercises. All the shooter has to do is hold back the trigger, release the trigger to the reset point, and then take the next shot. Through practice, muscle memory will be established and the shooter will see the effects of using the trigger reset, as evidenced by tighter groups and a faster rate of accurate and controlled fire at the target.

Practice, Practice, Practice

Repetition and practice are the keys to developing trigger control. Based on this concept, firearms training should be considered a sport. Like all sport-related activities, the participant needs to be physically and mentally prepared for the game. To be a top performer, a person must also practice. Through practice and repetition, the participant develops muscle memory and mastery of that particular activity.

One of the best methods for diagnosing problems and developing proper trigger control is through dry firing the firearm. Dry firing, as the name implies, is when a shooter manipulates the trigger and "fires" an unloaded and safe weapon. Through dry firing, the shooter will not have to worry about the weapon firing and the subsequent recoil. It also allows the shooter to see any mistakes with trigger control that they may not readily see under live fire situations, due to the recoil of the weapon hiding undesirable movements. Even through the firearm is not loaded with live ammunition, all of the rules regarding firearms safety must be followed to avoid and prevent any accidents.

Problems with Trigger Control

Like the other firearms basics, a shooter can encounter several problems associated with trigger control. Some of the more common problems associated with trigger control is "jerking" or 'flinching" and having too little or too much finger on the trigger. Another problem is using the entire hand to pull the trigger.

Jerking

Jerking and flinching are unintentional muscle movements. Causes of jerking include fatigue, strength issues, and the failure to concentrate. Regardless of the cause, it is a total loss of trigger control, and it must be overcome. Jerking is defined by Webster's Dictionary as "a quick single motion of short duration or an involuntary twitching." In the context of trigger control, this means that while the shooter may think that they are pulling the trigger in an even and consistent manner to the rear, they actually are not. Instead, the shooter unconsciously increases the speed of the trigger pull just before the weapon fires because they are anticipating the weapon's recoil. In other cases, jerking may occur as the result of the shooter meeting some mechanical resistance on the trigger (i.e., when the trigger engages the trigger bar mechanism). As a result of this resistance, the shooter then increases the speed and intensity of the pull. In both of these situations, the shooter "jerks" the trigger, the muzzle dips downward (or sideways), and the projectile subsequently misses the intended point of impact on the threat or target. Often jerking the trigger is thought to occur only under conditions where the shooter pulls the trigger too fast to the rear. However, jerking the trigger also occurs during slow movements of the trigger to the rear. To avoid jerking, a shooter must not anticipate the weapon firing and its subsequent recoil.

Flinching

A flinch, meanwhile, can be understood as the muscles in the body tensing up. This may be the trigger finger itself, or in some cases the entire hand or body may "tense" in anticipation of the weapon firing. For example, one common cause of flinching is that the shooter's muscles in their hand and arm tense up just before the weapon fires, leading to a flinch. Like jerking the trigger, flinching is caused by changes in the trigger speed at the last moment before the weapon fires. This is because the shooter is most likely anticipating the recoil of the weapon. Regardless of if a shooter jerks or flinches, the end result will be that the projectile did not hit the intended point of aim on the threat.

Snapping

Like jerking the trigger, snapping the trigger is also an unintended action by the shooter. Unlike jerking, which is the result of uneven side-to-side and rearward pressure on the trigger, snapping the trigger occurs when the shooter allows their finger to come off the face of the trigger between shots. Because the shooter's finger comes off the face of the trigger, when placing their finger back on the trigger, they inadvertently "snap" the trigger rearward, often with a fast and inconsistent trigger pull. This trigger control problem will also result in the bullet/projectile not hitting the intended point of aim on the target or threat.

Too Much or Too Little Finger on the Trigger

Often there are problems associated with too much or too little finger on the trigger. As pointed out earlier in this chapter, strength and control are two key ingredients to effective trigger control. The trigger finger must be positioned squarely on the face of the trigger. If not, the trigger may be difficult to pull straight to the rear. At the same time, if a shooter has too much or too little finger wrapped around the trigger, this could cause the muzzle of the weapon to move laterally to the left or right. The consequences of this will be readily seen when a person examines their target. The impacts will be left or right of the intended point of aim. This issue will be discussed in greater detail in the Target Analysis chapter.

Using the Entire Hand

Another commonly encountered problem with trigger control is when the shooter uses their entire hand to pull the trigger to the rear. Effective trigger control requires that the shooter should only use their index finger to pull the trigger. The shooter should not "squeeze" the trigger by using the hand or arm muscles. Using additional hand and arm muscles will result in the front sight of the firearm becoming disrupted just before the trigger releases, leading to problems with shot placement. The only thing that moves during the pull of the trigger is the index finger!

Conclusion

Only through patience, hard work, concentration and self-discipline will mastery of the trigger be achieved. Effective trigger control requires the development of muscle memory through perfect practice. With diligence and practice, mastering trigger control can be easily and readily accomplished. And, it will become an unconscious reflex when firing the weapon. Shooters must "teach" the finger how to properly pull the trigger to the rear. It must be pulled to the rear in a smooth, consistent, and even manner. Pulling the trigger can be compared to the accelerator on a vehicle. A driver simply does not "slam" their foot on the accelerator. Instead, they make contact with the accelerator and then slowly build up pressure on the face of the pedal. The same concept applies to the trigger, where the operator must slowly build up pressure on the face of the trigger until it releases.

There are some other essential elements related to trigger control. One of the first issues a shooter needs to consider is how the trigger pull, or the weight of pull required to fire the weapon, will affect trigger control. The shooter will also need to consider that the distance the trigger travels will also have an effect on trigger control. Trigger control also requires proper finger placement. In addition, a shooter must also maintain positive trigger contact and pressure until they have determined that they have stopped the threat. Then, they can take their finger off the trigger (if the threat is stopped or no longer poses a danger). Positive trigger pressure is also needed to master the trigger reset, since all weapons, by their design, have trigger slack that must be controlled by the trigger finger.

Some of common problems with trigger control include jerking and flinching which will disturb sight alignment. In most cases, jerking and flinching is attributed to anticipating the recoil. This problem can be overcome through both live and dry fire training, and through practice. Another common problem is using the entire hand (and perhaps the arm muscles) to pull to trigger to rear. To avoid this problem, the shooter should concentrate on pulling the trigger to the rear with the use of their index finger muscles only.

REFERENCES

Sundstrom, A. (May, 2000). Equipment performance report: 1999 auto loading pistols. Washington, D.C. National Institute of Justice.

Webster's new collegiate dictionary (1974). Springfield, MA: G & C. Merriam company.

Introduction

The principle of follow through is what the person does after an event, in the context of the actions he or she performs. Consider for example a golfer who "follows through" on their swing. Once the clubface comes into contact with the ball, the golfer does not abruptly stop. Instead, the golfer's body and club continue to move together in a controlled and relaxed motion. The same can be said in the sport of basketball. When shooting a free throw, the player lets their arms, hands, and wrists continue to move after the ball is released. Just flipping the ball up and lowering their arms and hands down rapidly would affect the shot. The same can be said for baseball: after the player hits the ball, their body and bat continue to rotate, with their back eventually facing home plate. While the sports differ in technique, the common element of each of them is that their actions do not come to an abrupt stop. Rather, the participant deliberately allows their body to follow through after the actual event, creating a natural flow and feel in the sequence of events.

Like the above examples, when an individual fires a weapon, the action of shooting (and/or the gunfight) is not over. In fact, one could argue that it has just begun. As pointed out in Chapter 1, a gunfight is a dynamic event. Because a gunfight is dynamic and fluid in nature, the shooter needs to be tactically prepared for anything that could happen next. In the context of a gunfight, this means that the police officer must be tactically prepared to deliver additional controlled shots at the threat. This means that they must continue to apply all of the fundamentals of shooting after firing the shot, following through on the shot, making sure that their movements are smooth and controlled.

Principles of Follow Through

Follow through, in the context of firearms, means doing the same thing after each shot is fired, thereby ensuring that there is limited movement or no change regarding the fundamentals of shooting. The fundamentals of firearms never change—they are basic and constant. That's why they are called "basics."

Unlike these athletic examples where there is continued motion as the result of prior body movements, the follow-through is a matter of maintaining the basics, limiting movement, maintaining control, and letting the force of the weapon's recoil work with the body – not against it.

Follow Through Checklist

✓ Move in Natural Rhythm w/Gun
✓ Focus on Fundamentals
✓ Stay on the Threat
✓ Scan & Cover

Some of the key points of the follow through include:

- It is a Natural Process
- The Recoil from the Weapon Must Be Controlled
- Sight Alignment and Sight Picture Must Be Maintained

The Follow Through is Natural

One of the keys to an effective follow through is that movements must be natural. When watching a proficient shooter one will immediately see that they appear to be relaxed and comfortable when shooting. This is because they are. This does not mean that the shooter is inattentive and not following the basics of marksmanship. Rather, they are comfortable with the firearm (ex: "you and the gun are one") and they are in a natural rhythm with the gun's recoil.

Achieving a "natural" feel for the firearm requires concentration on the basics. By concentrating on what happens after the shot (i.e. the follow through), the shooter can detect any errors in their basics, such as sight alignment and sight picture, and they can correct them after the follow through has been completed. These correct movements also build positive muscle memory.

In some cases, a person may observe and actually sense some unnatural movements in the follow through stage. For example, the shooter may see and feel a great deal of "climb" where the handgun moves to the left, right, or in an upward direction. At first glance, an individual may assume that the recoil is forcing it in that particular direction. However, what is actually occurring is that the shooter is unconsciously over-compensating the recoil. This may be also referred to as "riding the recoil." Subconsciously, the shooter is physically moving their arms far above and beyond the force that the recoil of the weapon is actually exerting against their body. At a minimum, these actions will lead to the building of incorrect muscle memory and accuracy problems.

198

Work With the Recoil—Not Against It (Recoil Control)

Another key to the follow through is controlling the recoil. It is a fact that the recoil from the firearm will affect sight alignment. The sights of the firearm will no longer be perfectly lined up after the firearm discharges. This also means that the recoil from the firearm will also disrupt the sight picture. The shooter, however, has a great deal of control over recoil, and the actions of the follow through will determine just how much the sights will be disrupted. The key behind working with the recoil is that a shooter has to learn how to subconsciously return the sights to the same spot each and every time after the weapon fires.

Learning to follow through on the recoil is easy. Through mental concentration and practice, a shooter can train him or herself to immediately recover from the recoil of the weapon and re-establish the sight picture as fast as possible. This is because the recoil of the weapon is very consistent. The gun will move or "jump" in the same direction basically every time. At the same time, the body should also work with the recoil in a consistent manner. While the hands will also move a little (the grip will remain solid though) and the body may rock to a certain degree with the firing of the weapon, the body will return to a natural shooting position. All a shooter needs to do is to maintain an effective grip on the weapon, while letting their entire body absorb and work with the recoil. At the same time, the shooter must use their muscles to resist the recoil to a certain degree. That is, the shooter must use enough muscle resistance to ensure that the weapon returns back to its original position as soon as possible. By concentrating on the basics and the follow through, the shooter will see that the weapon will naturally "fall" back into sight alignment. The front sight, for example, will rise a small degree and "plop" right back into a perfect sight picture.

As an example of using the muscles to ensure that the weapon returns to its normal position, establish a normal shooting stance. With the arms extended outward in a normal shooting stance (without the weapon in the shooter's hand), establish a point of aim and then have somebody purposely slap or push the arms away from that point of aim. With a correct amount of muscle resistance, the arms should naturally return to the same position every time, regardless of if the person pushes the arms laterally or horizontal.

Mental Focus

Working with the firearm requires that the shooter focuses on his or her actions. Shooters must concentrate on the basics, making sure that they are not disturbed or changed to some degree when operating the firearm. This mental focus must be on technique. It does not concentrate on the outcome or the "score." By mentally focusing on the technique over outcome, over time a shooter will see a dramatic improvement in their outcome. Technique improves outcome. Outcome does not improve technique, per se.

To ensure mental focus, the shooter must create a "mental checklist" to make sure that all of the basics are being followed **prior** to firing the weapon. Using this checklist, the shooter can then assess their fundamentals after the weapon fires, to make sure that nothing has changed. If something has changed (such as shifting one's feet, leaning too far forward or changing the grip), the shooter should make a mental note and correct those issues. If not corrected, the consequences of these unintended changes will be seen in the shooter's ability to accurately hit and stop the intended threat.

Mental focus also means staying on the threat. In traditional target practice, this is quite easy because the threat is stationary and easy to locate. In a gunfight, however, the threat and the officer are both moving. To address this issue, shooter's must mentally train themselves to "stay on the threat," by mentally telling themselves to reestablish the sight picture as fast as possible. While maintaining the basics and following the threat, the principle of follow through also requires that the shooter mentally asks himself two questions. They are:

- Did It Hit?
- Did It Work?

If the shooter can answer these questions in the affirmative (yes) then s/he now follows through on the total threat environment through the "scan and cover" stage of the follow through.

The Scan & Cover Stage

The "scan and cover" is another essential component of the follow through. It involves a slow and deliberate examination of the threat environment to ensure the threat(s) have been stopped, and to provide cover fire, if necessary. The purpose of the scan and cover is to make sure that the threat has been stopped and there are no additional threats, and that the threat environment is now secured and made safe by the actions of the officer(s). There are several different methods of the scan and cover technique. That method that will be used will depend upon safety issues and department policy.

**Figure 47
Scan & Cover**

One of the first issues with the scan and cover is whether the shooter should maintain sight alignment. Depending upon tactical preference, one technique is to fully maintain sight alignment during the scan and cover stage, where the head, eyes, and weapon move together, scanning the environment for additional threats. This technique would allow for the shooter to establish the sight picture on the threat quite fast. This technique is shown in Figure 47.

In another scan and cover technique, the shooter gets off the sights and lowers the firearm slightly below the field of view, no more than 12 inches below the line of sight. As pointed out in the chapter on Sight Alignment, under high stress situations, a person experiences perceptual narrowing or a loss in their peripheral field of view. Since the arms and the handgun will block the field of view to some degree, purposely lowering the weapon just below the field view (while maintaining the other basics) can serve to improve or open up the shooter's field of view.

**Figure 48
Tactical Ready**

**Figure 49
Low Ready Position**

Lowering the firearm just below the field of view is called the tactical-ready or threat-ready position. From this position, the officer can still readily reengage that threat. Depending upon departmental preference, one technique calls for the eyes and firearm to follow one another. This could lead to a faster acquisition of the sight picture, if necessary. Instead of the combined technique, where the head, eyes, and firearm work together, a shooter could also keep their weapon directly in front of them, while the head and eyes move.

201

This may allow the shooter to respond to threats to the left or right of center faster since the weapon is centrally located.

Once the threat environment has been determined to be safe, the shooter can then lower their weapon to the low-ready position as shown in Figure 49. The low ready position can be best described as pointing the weapon down toward the ground at approximately a 45-degree angle. Depending upon the tactical situation, the shooter can then reholster the weapon from this position.

Finger Placement and The Scan & Cover

During the scan and cover stage of the follow through, another issue is finger placement. There are two schools of thought regarding finger placement in the scan and cover stage. One perspective proposes that the shooter take their finger off the trigger and outside the trigger guard. This is based on the premise that the only time the finger enters the trigger guard and comes into contact with the trigger is when the shooter has determined that there is a threat and the threat must be stopped. In the scan and cover stage, however, there may not be a threat, or the threat may be already stopped. The argument for keeping the finger off the trigger is based on the fact that the officer could still rapidly respond to a threat since they are practicing sound tactics and they are mentally and physically prepared to reengage the threat(s) if necessary. It is also based on safety-related issues. Since it is probably a high stress situation, moving the finger off the trigger and outside the trigger guard could prevent an accidental discharge.

Other techniques call for the shooter to keep their finger on the trigger. This is based on the assumption that the threat may not be completely stopped, and he or she could still pose a danger to the officer or others. It is also based on the premise that there may be multiple threats that the officer has not yet identified and perhaps engaged. Because of these points, the finger must be kept on the trigger in order to rapidly respond to the threat. The danger of this technique is that (as it is a high stress situation) it could lead to an accidental discharge.

Problems with Follow Through

In many cases, the principles of follow through are not adhered to. If not followed, the shooter will not be tactically prepared to reengage the threat in a gunfight. Some of the more common problems associated with the principles of follow through include the failure to: 1) concentrate; 2) stay on the sights; and, 3) scan and cover.

Failure to Concentrate

One of the most common errors of new shooters (as well as some experienced ones) is the failure to concentrate on the basics during the follow through. An effective shooter must keep their mind switched on. Most people feel that follow-through is simply maintaining the basics until the projectile has cleared the muzzle of the firearm. This is wrong. An effective shooter will analyze and sense everything that they did prior to and after the weapon fired, to make sure that the projectile hit the intended target. This, of course, requires concentration on the basics of marksmanship.

Failure to Stay on the Sights

What often occurs with shooters is that, immediately after firing their weapon, they lower the muzzle and look downrange to see how well they did, failing to stay on the threat. The shooter is more concerned with the outcome rather than their technique. This is dangerous and it equates to contra-training. While shooters may be anxious regarding their outcome, they must remember to hold the front sight on the threat. The shooter must "stay on the sights" and ask two questions: Did It Hit/Did It Work? After answering in the affirmative, then they (depending on choice of tactics) can lower the weapon to the threat-ready and/or low-ready position and scan for additional threats.

Another issue related to not staying on the sights occurs when shooters finish their particular course of fire, and they immediately bring the weapon down to the low-ready position (muzzle at a 45 degree angle to the ground), failing to stay on their sights and control the threat environment. When doing so, the shooter often changes their field of view toward the ground and away from the threat environment. During this process, they may also change their grip and stance too (as well as other basics).

These actions, as well as others the shooter may engage in after rounds are fired, are wrong, dangerous, and again are an indicator of contra-training. Perhaps the best way to look at this issue is to consider it in the context of a gunfight: Would a police officer ever move to the threat and/or low ready and change any of their fundamentals, especially sight alignment, before they determined that they stopped the threat and there were no other threats in the area? No! Only after determining that the threat environment is completely under their control can a police officer lower their firearm and get off the target.

Failure to Scan and Cover

Combined with not staying on the sights and immediately looking down range, in other situations, a shooter may not perform an effective scan and cover. Instead, they may simply "wag" the gun back and forth, neglecting the basics of combat shooting in the process. In several cases, for example, a shooter will relax their stance to the point where their arm is no longer locked out. They may also break their wrist to the left or right when conducting the scan and cover. This again is a form of contra-training. Considering the fact that a person fights the way they train, this activity in a real-life deadly force encounter is tactically unsound and unacceptable. In a real life situation it will put the officer, their partners, and other innocents in danger.

Conclusion

Follow through deals with what the shooter does after the weapon is fired. Follow through is making sure that the person does the same correct thing every time a shot is fired, to ensure accuracy and consistency of their shot placement. The key to an effective follow through is that all of the fundamentals of firearms are correct in style and function, and they work in unison to create a natural flow in the process of firing the weapon. An effective follow through is the result of all the firearms basics put together in a good, effective rhythm. The follow through is natural. It must be comfortable and smooth flowing.

To master the follow through, the shooter must work with the recoil and mentally focus on the actions that they are performing. The follow through also requires that the shooter stay on the threat and maintain the sight picture until they have determined that the threat has been stopped. Once the threat is stopped, the next stage of the follow through is to scan and cover for additional threats. Some of the more common errors in the follow through include the failure to: concentrate on the basics; stay on the sights (i.e. front sight focus); and, conduct an effective scan and cover.

Chapter 11
The Draw

Introduction

Winning a gunfight is not entirely dependent on delivering rounds accurately at a threat downrange. Winning the gunfight first means that a shooter must get their firearm out of the holster and on target as soon as possible (following all of the basics), to deliver accurate and controlled fire at the threat. This fact requires that the shooter has an effective draw. One of the best ways to describe an effective draw is that it should be a holster-to-stance reflex (Felter, 1988). Another way to look at the draw is to consider it a continuous unbroken cycle of events.

The Holster & the Draw

An effective draw begins with the holster. The type or design of the holster that the officer is wearing will affect their draw performance to some degree. In order to ensure an effective draw, the following points should be considered when selecting a holster.

- It must secure the firearm. As pointed out in Chapter 1, officers are often assaulted and killed by their own weapon. The firearm needs to be secure from the criminal element. To properly secure the weapon it must be holstered. In fact, the safest place for a firearm is in a secured holster.
- There are some different types of security or retention levels for police holsters. The general rule of thumb is the higher the retention value, the better the weapon is protected. These levels include:

  - Level I: Thumb Break Device
  - Level II: Ring Finger Break or Shroud Style Device
  - Level III: Internal Indent/Rear Tilt Style Retention Device

In some situations, police officers may complain that the higher the retention level, the more difficult the weapon is to draw. While the retention level does make it a little more difficult to draw the firearm out of the holster, this issue can be readily overcome through proper training.

- It must fit the firearm. The holster should be designed for that specific model and make of firearm. There are many generic holsters on the market. These generic holsters will not ensure that the holster is properly fitted to the firearm. An improperly fitted holster could also lead to issues related to if the weapon is properly secured in the holster. It may also affect the speed of the draw.
- Regardless of the retention device on the holster, its design should allow the shooter to release the retention device simultaneously, while obtaining the grip with one hand.
- It should allow the shooter to obtain a master grip while the firearm is still in the holster. Some police agencies still carry the flap-style holster, where the flap completely covers the grip of the firearm when it is in the holster. While it may secure the firearm (and prevent it from being exposed to the elements), this type of holster is not tactically sound. Instead, it is simply a decorative storage device for the gun.
- It should ride high enough on the hip so the officer can readily grasp and protect the weapon. As a general rule of thumb, the holster should ride high enough so that the officer can index the grip of the weapon with their strong arm elbow. Indexing basically means that while the officer is in the field interview stance with their hands out in front of them, they can use their strong arm elbow to "index" or touch reference the firearm. Additionally, when the holster is positioned in this nature, the elbow (combined with other moves) can trap or retain the gun if a suspect were to try to take it away from the officer.
- The holster should be designed so the shooter can pull the weapon straight up and out of the holster. The holster should not be angled forward or backward, as this leads to a tactically poor draw. A forward or backward angled holster could also lead to safety issues as a suspect could "strip" the firearm from the holster. It may also impede weapon retention tactics.
- The holster should not move. A shooter has to know where the firearm is at all times. Any movement in the holster could disturb any muscle memory that the shooter has developed in the context of drawing their weapon under high-stress combat conditions. At a minimum, the holster should always be kept in place with belt keepers on each side of it, regardless of the belt design and if the holster is secured to the belt with set screws. Using keepers not

only serves to prevent the holster from moving, but it also prevents an officer from having their duty belt torn off their body.

- The holster needs to be properly positioned on the shooter's strong side. To ensure proper alignment, while standing with the strong arm draped down the side of the leg, the holster should be positioned between the hip and underside the arm. Another way of checking to make sure that the holster is properly aligned on the body is that it should be lined up with the seam of the pant leg, or in some cases, it should be lined up with the striping on the uniform pant leg.
- A cross-draw style holster should not be used. Because the shooter is reaching and drawing the firearm across their body, the speed of the draw may be slower in comparison to holsters mounted on the strong side. These types of holsters are also tactically unsound.
- The shooter should be able to operate the holster with one hand. This applies to both drawing the firearm and reholstering.

The Four Principles of the Draw

There are four distinct, but interrelated components of an effective draw that forms a cycle of events. This cycle of events is shown in Figure 11-1. The four stages or elements of the draw:

1. Push;
2. Pull;
3. Point; and,
4. Punch

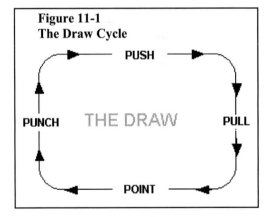

Figure 11-1
The Draw Cycle

PUSH

PUNCH   THE DRAW   PULL

POINT

The four-point draw, however, should not be looked upon as four separate stages. Instead, they are four inter-related events that, if done correctly, will lead to a smooth cycle, beginning with the draw and ending with the weapon returning to the holster. This four-point draw can also be performed from a sitting and kneeling position, if necessary.

There are some assumptions with the four-point draw. First, it requires that the shooter be in the field interview stance with their hands out in front of them. It also requires that the shooter be balanced, tactically alert to their surroundings, and prepared to engage an adversary in a potential deadly force encounter, if necessary. Some of the essentials of the four-point draw include the following:

- *Economy of Motion.* The key behind wining a gunfight is economy of motion. All unnecessary movements related to the draw should be eliminated. The shooter must concentrate on developing a smooth, fast, and consistent draw stroke.
- *Focus on the Threat Environment.* The shooter must maintain their focus on the threat environment - not on the draw of the weapon. A shooter should never look at their holster when drawing and reholstering.
- *Muscle Memory.* The draw must also become a reflex, where it is performed without thinking every time it is drawn.
- The draw must be smooth, fast and controlled.

Push

Regardless of manufacturer and the retention level of the holster, the first stage in the draw is the "push." In the push stage, the shooter establishes the master grip on the firearm while it is still in the holster (see Figure 50). To maintain the smallest profile to the threat, the inside bicep and tricep of the strong arm should touch the rib cage. Meanwhile, the strong arm elbow is hinged, pointing straight behind the shooter—not outward. The support hand and arm is also in a good field interview position, where the hand and forearm are elevated at hip level (or higher) and in front of the shooter's body. This arm/hand placement allows for a faster response to the threat. It will also serve to increase the speed in the later stages of the draw.

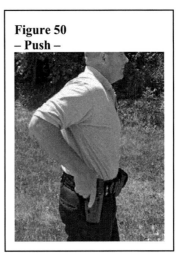

Figure 50 – Push –

While in this aggressive combat stance, the shooter (while looking toward the threat and not at the firearm) pushes down with their strong hand on the grip of the firearm to establish the master grip. The index finger and the thumb are both pointing down while the "V" of the hand is open, so the shooter can position the "V" of the hand correctly on the grip's backstrap. While pushing down to establish the grip, the shooter is simultaneously "breaking" or releasing the holster's retention device with the thumb. With a traditional thumb break holster, for example, the strong hand thumb is pushing down on the thumb break snap. With a rocker-style shroud retention device, meanwhile, the strong thumb is pushing down on the thumb lever while rocking the shroud forward. Regardless of whether the retention device is a thumb break or shroud-style, the strong hand thumb is solely responsible for manipulating the retention device. With those holsters that do not have a top shroud or thumb break, the thumb has a limited role in the draw. Its role is similar to that of the index finger where it rests on the outside of the holster. The rest of the fingers (with the exception of the index or trigger finger that is resting on the outside of the holster and pointing down) are wrapped around the grip, to establish the master grip on the firearm, while it is still in the holster.

Pull

The next stage of the draw is the pull. While still maintaining the master grip on the weapon, the shooter pulls the firearm straight up and out of the holster, until the muzzle clears the top of the holster. The firearm should not be pulled up any higher. This is referred to as the "belt level" position (Felter, 1988). While pulling the firearm out of the holster, the wrist is locked. The strong arm, meanwhile, hinges at the elbow joint, bending upward, while still pointing directly behind the shooter. The forearm, meanwhile, is almost perpendicular to the ground. If the firearm is pulled from the holster correctly,

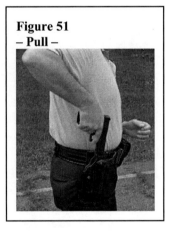

Figure 51
– Pull –

the muzzle will be canted forward of the shooter, pointing at a slight angle toward the ground. The shooter should not raise the muzzle of the weapon any higher. Any additional movement is simply a waste of time and a tactical error. Remember: This is the pull stage only.

Point

Next in the draw cycle is the "point," as shown in Figure 52. As the name implies, the key to this movement is that the firearm must point at the threat. Immediately after the muzzle clears the holster, the shooter must cant or rotate the muzzle forward and upward until the muzzle is horizontal. The firearm is still positioned next to the strong side of the shooter, just above the holster at the belt level position. It is not yet extended outward. From this position, the shooter's body is protecting the firearm. It is important to keep the gun in this location since it is not yet fully stable or secure because the support hand has not made any contact with the gun.

Figure 52
– Point –

The point stage does not deal with fully extending the arm outward and establishing a completed shooting platform. Additionally, at this stage the firearm is not raised to establish sight alignment and a sight picture. It stays level just above the hip where the muzzle is horizontal to the ground, pointing forward. In this stage the shooter should imagine that they are rotating the elbow of the strong arm straight down from a rearward position, down to the top of the holster. By rotating the elbow down, the muzzle of the firearm naturally moves from the low-ready position to the waist level position. From this position, a shooter can then readily and easily deliver controlled shots at a threat, if necessary.

This stage is critical. The reason why the muzzle should be level or pointed toward the threat is based on the fact that many deadly force encounters are sudden and unexpected. As pointed out in Chapter 1, many deadly force encounters occur at a very short range where the police officer simply does not have the time to get into their final combat stance with their hands and arms positioned outward to deliver effective and controlled fire to stop the threat (keep in mind that the shooter may already be at a disadvantage in the context of reaction time, proximity to the threat, and availability of tactics, including cover and concealment). For example, an officer who is dealing with a charging suspect or wrestling with a suspect, where deadly force is warranted, will have to literally "shoot from the hip" or point-shoot. In other instances, the officer may have to deliver what is known as a contact shot. A contact shot is when the officer physically places the muzzle of the weapon against the suspect, and from this position, shoots the suspect at point blank range.

Punch

The last stage of the draw cycle is the punch (Figure 53). As the name implies this is where the shooter "punches" the weapon straight out and completes the combat stance. The firearm should not be swung sideways or at an angle. Recall that in the point stage, the shooter rotates their elbow downward that causes the muzzle of the firearm to rotate upward and point forward or horizontally toward the threat. In the "punch" stage, the shooter brings the firearm to eye level, establishing sight alignment and a sight picture, locking out the strong-arm shoulder, elbow, and wrist, while using the support hand to further secure and stabilize the firearm. One of the keys to the punch stage is to keep the head level where the weapon "goes to the eyes" – not the "eyes to gun" (which would disrupt the shooter's stance).

The punch stage requires synchronizing the support hand with the movement of the strong hand and firearm. Just as the shooter begins to punch out the firearm, or when the firearm starts to clear the body, the support hand must cross the body, and establish the support grip. It is crucial that the support hand establishes a grip on the firearm before it is fully extended and punched out. The firearm must be secured as soon as possible with both hands. Getting both hands on the gun as soon as possible will also stabilize the firearm (through the push-pull principle) as it is being punched out. This is important since a shooter may have to fire the weapon from this position, if necessary, to stop a threat.

**Figure 53
– Punch –**

This procedure is actually quite easy to do. Already, the shooter's support hand should be out in front of their body in the field interview stance (not at their side). All the shooter needs to do is to slightly move the support hand palm over to the strong side of the body while the firearm is moving forward). While doing so, the shooter then wraps the support hand around the front of the strong hand that is gripping the handgun. Once secured around the strong hand, then the weapon can be fully extended and punched out. Like the strong hand, the grip established by the support hand during the punch stage must not change as the arms lock out and the shooter prepares to engage the threat.

The Principles of Reholstering

The reholstering stage is slow and deliberate, where the shooter should be concentrating on the threat environment and not on the holster. One fundamental reason why the reholstering stage is slow and deliberate is based on safety. After a high-stress situation that required the drawing of the firearm, an officer may inadvertently have their finger on the trigger. Additionally, clothing or even part of the holster may snag on the trigger, causing an accidental discharge. Being slow and deliberate can prevent accidents of this nature from happening simply because the officer will be better aware of, and able to detect any obstructions.

Reholstering is simply the reverse of the draw cycle, without the pull stage. The specific procedures that must be followed to ensure a smooth, safe and consistent reholster are discussed below.

"Unpunch"

After the shooter has determined that the threat environment is safe and secure, they can end their sight alignment and picture and bring the firearm back into the point stage of the draw. All a shooter has to do in this stage is to pull the firearm straight back while maintaining the grip with both hands. What basically occurs is that the shooter breaks the elbows of both arms and pulls them straight to the rear, until both forearms come in contact with the shooter's chest/abdominal region of the body. At this stage, the firearm's muzzle is pointing straight forward while the firearm is at the belt/abdominal level height. It is important to keep the muzzle pointed forward (and not

Figure 54 – Unpunch –

down); the shooter can readily re-punch the weapon out from this position to reengage the threat, if necessary.

212

"Unpoint"

**Figure 55
– Unpoint –**

At this stage, the shooter releases their support hand from the firearm, and rotates the strong arm elbow in an upward direction. The support hand should remain in the field interview stance out in front of the shooter. It should not be positioned down at the side of the body. With the strong-arm wrist still locked, the shooter should pull their elbow backwards and in an upward direction. This movement will naturally pull the firearm to the rear, while pointing the muzzle in a downward direction toward the ground and at the top of the holster. When the muzzle of the weapon reaches belt level, and is clear of the top or mouth of the holster, it is then ready to be reholstered and secured.

Push

At the push stage of reholstering, the shooter pushes the firearm back into the holster. While still maintaining the master grip, and keeping their vision on the threat environment (while not looking at the holster), the shooter should push the firearm back into the holster until it physically stops. This may require some force to get beyond the thumb break (that usually moves back to its "secure" position). During this stage, the index finger and thumb will naturally follow and rest on outside of the holster. Particular emphasis should be placed on making sure that the finger is not on the trigger or inside the trigger guard. If the pistol does not have an external hammer, the shooter

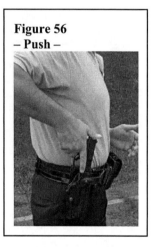

**Figure 56
– Push –**

should also place their strong hand thumb on the back of the slide to make sure that it stays in battery when it is reholstered (see Figure 56).

Now, the shooter can give up the master grip and secure the firearm in the holster. With the strong hand only, and while watching the threat environment, the shooter should use their strong hand to secure the holster's retention device. Depending upon design, the shooter may have to use his thumb and index finger to secure the snap on the thumb break, or they may simply have to pull the shroud to the rear with their thumb or index finger. Without looking, the shooter should then "feel" that the retention device is activated by pushing on the shroud or feeling to see if the snap is secure. The weapon can be further checked to make sure it is properly secured by using the elbow of the strong hand through touch reference.

Problems with the Draw

As with the fundamentals of marksmanship, there are issues that need be addressed with the draw. All of the issues that are listed below will somehow impede the draw and/or reholster of the firearm, making the shooter tactically unsound, unsafe, and slow in responding to a threat. In order to prevent the building of bad habits on the range (that will later be used on the street), these issues must be identified, addressed, and avoided.

- Not maintaining a master grip through the draw cycle

  While already addressed in the chapter in the Grip, a shooter must maintain the same grip throughout the draw, fire, and reholstering of the weapon. In some situations, however, during the draw cycle, the shooter is adjusting the strong, and/or support hand grip. This is not acceptable and it is a poor technique that will lead to poor tactics on the street. Shooters must concentrate on and develop the master grip at the draw stage. This will save time and increase the shooter's draw speed and accuracy.

- "Windmilling"

  "Windmilling" for lack of a better term, is associated with not punching the weapon straight out during the draw. Often, when the weapon is pulled out of the holster, the shooter pushes the gun straight down beyond the bottom of the holster, and subsequently locks their elbow out. With their elbow locked out, the shooter then lifts or "windmills" the firearm in an upward direction, extending it straight out in front of their body, rotating the arm from the shoulder joint, instead of from the elbow joint. This is tactically wrong. It adds unnecessary movement in the draw cycle. It is also dangerous because the shooter is now extending (or virtually handing) a weapon that is not fully secured toward the threat. The threat, if close enough, could easily strip it from the shooter. Compounded with the fact that if the threat and officer are very close, the officer may not have room to level the weapon at the threat. Instead, the firearm may be pinned in a downward direction between the officer and the threat.

- Using Two Hands to Draw and Reholster

    In some situations, a shooter will use their support hand to assist the strong hand in releasing the retention device on the holster. As pointed out earlier, retention devices are designed for one-handed use. With practice, the shooter will learn how to become proficient in manipulating the retention device one-handed.

    Another common mistake is involved with reholstering the firearm, where the shooter uses both hands. The shooter, for example, may use their support hand to try to spread apart the thumb break retention device or push down on the shroud, out of concern that the weapon will get hung up on the device at the push stage. What often happens when using both hands is that is that the shooter often ends up "lasering" himself because the muzzle will naturally cross the support hand's wrist area. Using both hands also means that the support hand is not readily available to defend oneself, because it is no longer out in front of the body.

- Looking at the Holster

    In other instances a shooter may inadvertently look at the holster when drawing and holstering. There is no need to look at the holster when drawing and reholstering. The shooter's attention must be directed toward the threat zone at all times.

Training Tip:

To make sure that the fundamentals of the draw are achieved without any problems, follow the STOP method:

- ▸ Start Slow – be slow and deliberate to master each stage of the draw.
- ▸ Train – It may takes 100's of perfect draws to master the draw.
- ▸ Observe – Have another individual critique your draw stroke to help you catch any issues. Otherwise, consider videotaping your draw so you can review your own movements.
- ▸ Be Patient. It takes time to master the draw. The draw speed will come in due time.

- Not Clearing the Holster Correctly

  Another common problem is that the shooter does not fully clear the holster in the pull stage. If the firearm is not pulled to the belt level and the muzzle is not properly "cleared," it will catch or hang up on the top of the holster. When "snagging" on the holster, the shooter also inadvertently breaks their wrist to compensate for this problem. This often causes the muzzle to subsequently point backwards, further disrupting the draw cycle.

- Not Using the Support Hand Correctly

  The establishment of the support hand grip happens immediately after the point stage, when the firearm begins to be punched out. A common error that is often encountered is that the strong arm is fully extended outward and then the shooter then brings their support hand up to establish the complete grip (imagine extending both hands out and bringing them together). If this occurs, the weapon is not immediately stabilized and secured, leading to both accuracy and safety issues. When reholstering, meanwhile, the support hand must also stay with the weapon back to the point stage. By keeping the support hand with the strong hand, the weapon is better secured and stabilized.

- Keeping the Finger on the Trigger when Reholstering

  In some instances, a shooter will keep their finger on the trigger and not outside the trigger guard when reholstering. This is a VERY DANGEROUS activity, as the finger will catch the top of the holster and push the trigger to the rear, causing an accidental discharge. Keeping the finger on the trigger and not outside the trigger guard is a violation of the fundamentals of firearms safety!

216

Conclusion

This chapter looked at combining the fundamentals of shooting with an effective draw cycle. An often-overlooked component of firearms training is the draw. It is often not practiced, not taken seriously, and, in many cases, the end result is that shooters are quite clumsy and slow when drawing the firearm from the holster. A shooter must be able get the weapon out of the holster as fast as possible, while concentrating on the basics. Like the fundamentals of shooting, the draw requires consistency, economy of motion, and the development of muscle memory. The draw must be smooth, consistent and fast. To gain speed in the draw, one must first work on technique. Once the technique is mastered the shooter will see a significant increase in their draw speed.

As pointed out in this chapter, the draw is an unbroken sequence of events. It consists of the: 1) Push; 2) Pull; 3) Point; and, 4) Punch. In addition, the draw is not over once the firearm is used. The draw stage also deals with effectively returning the firearm back into the holster and securing it, where the draw cycle is simply reversed and the shooter's actions are slow and deliberate. It is a complete cycle of events from start to finish.

This chapter has also revealed some issues related to the draw cycle that the shooter needs to avoid. These include using two hands to draw or reholster the pistol, and looking at the holster when reholstering. An effective draw also requires the shooter to clear the top of the holster, using the support hand correctly during the draw, and keeping the finger off the trigger when reholstering.

REFERENCES

Felter, B.A. (1988). <u>Police defensive handgun use and encounter tactics</u>. NJ: Englewood Cliffs. Prentice Hall.

Introduction

A n essential tactical requirement in law enforcement is to have the ability to reload a pistol in an effective and fast manner, while controlling the threat environment. This chapter will first begin with a review of the basic principles of conducting reloads, discussing the importance of the position of the magazine pouch, the placement of the magazine in the pouch, and the proper magazine grip. It will also emphasize the importance of using the hand-over technique when reloading the pistol. Next, it will review the three types or reloads a shooter can use, depending upon the tactical setting. After reviewing the administrative, tactical and combat loads, this chapter will also review some of the common problems related to reloads.

Principles of Reloads

There are some general principles that must be followed, regardless of the type of reload that is conducted. They include:

- The reload must be done in an efficient and smooth manner.
- The reload must be done without looking at the pistol.
- Reloading, like other firearm's skills, requires practice and the development of muscle memory.
- All reloads must be conducted from the magazine pouch. Always reloading from the magazine pouch builds muscle memory and speed, which is, of course, useful in any type of reload.
- The support hand is primarily responsible for manipulating and reloading the firearm.

In addition to these general principles, the position of the magazine pouch on the duty belt, and how the magazine is placed in the pouch is important.

Positioning of the Magazine Pouch

The magazine pouch must be accessible from the standing, kneeling and prone positions. It must also be positioned to allow for economy of motion when extracting the magazine from the pouch. The best position where an officer can get at their magazine(s) is when the magazine pouch is mounted on the operator's support side. Based on economy of motion and tactics, the pouch should be mounted vertically with the magazines perpendicular to the ground, facing down, and positioned over the front pocket area of the pant.

There are, however, other ways to position the magazine pouch on the duty belt. Some trainers propose that mounting the magazine pouch horizontally on the support side with the pouch flaps pointing forward or backward will provide more comfort for the officer. Some officers, for example, may complain that the magazine pouch may cut into the groin area, or it may be uncomfortable to wear vertically in some shooting positions. However, if the duty the belt is riding high enough on the officer (it should be just below the belly button), the officer will be able to sit, kneel and/or squat without the pouch cutting into the groin area when mounted vertically.

Another method among some agencies and officers is to horizontally mount the pouch on the gun side, in front of the holster, with the pouch flaps facing forward. Another way is to mount it vertically on the strong side, in front of the holster. Often, this method is used for veteran officers who were originally trained with revolvers and then transitioned to semi-automatics. Since these officers were accustomed to reloading their revolvers from speed loader pouches located in front of the holster, they have subsequently mounted their magazine pouches flap forward on their gun side. When considering the fact that magazines must be drawn rapidly with the smallest amount of movement possible, placing the magazine pouch vertically on the support side is the best option.

Magazine Placement

The principle of economy of motion requires that the pistol magazine be properly inserted into the magazine pouch. The best way to reduce movement in reloads is to make sure that the toe of the magazine is facing forward when it is in the magazine pouch. Another way to remember if the magazine is properly placed in the pouch is to make sure that the bullets are pointing forward, toward the threat.

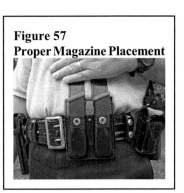

Figure 57
Proper Magazine Placement

Fully Topped Off Magazines Only

Only fully topped off magazines should be placed in the magazine pouch. By following this rule, officers will always be guaranteed that they do not have partially loaded or empty magazines in their magazine pouch. In some cases, officers could develop bad habits with their magazines and magazine pouch. During range qualifications, for example, officers may pick up and place empty or partially loaded magazines back into their pouch. In cases where they are on-duty during training or qualification sessions, they may inadvertently go back on the street with empty or partially loaded magazines in the magazine pouch.

The simplest way to avoid this contra-training issue is to follow the simple rule that at all times, only fully topped off magazines will be placed in the magazine pouch. At the same time, the magazine pouch should always hold the maximum number of magazines it was designed to hold. An officer should never begin a shift with a partially filled magazine pouch. If the pouch is designed to hold two magazines, then it must hold two magazines.

Proper Magazine Grip

Like the master grip on the firearm, a shooter must also establish a master grip on the magazine with their support hand. Considering the fact that magazine changes are conducted under high-stress situations where lighting may be limited and there is movement involved, establishing a master grip on the magazine is very important to ensure that the magazine can be held, stabilized, and inserted into the magazine well of the firearm.

Some of the steps in properly drawing and gripping a magazine are shown in Figures 58 - 61:

**Figure 58
Magazine Grip**

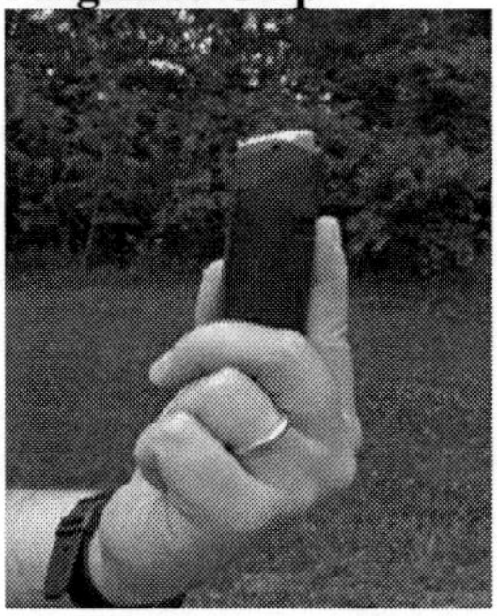

**Figure 59
Support Hand Finger Placement**

- The support hand is responsible for magazine changes (as well as other functions).
- The support hand index finger should be indexed alongside and on the outside of the magazine pouch.
- The middle and ring fingers are responsible for unsnapping the flaps on the pouch (if present).
- Pull the magazine straight up and out of the pouch. The index finger should rest on the front the magazine tube with the index finger positioned just below the nose of the bullet. Having the index finger near the top of the magazine will assist the officer in finding the magazine well through touch reference if it is a low-light situation. Having the index finger on the front of the magazine also serves to further stabilize the magazine to make sure that it is properly fed into the magazine well of the firearm. The thumb, meanwhile, should be behind the pouch or flap and grasp the side of the magazine when it is extracted from the pouch.

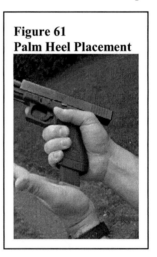

Figure 60
Finger Support

Figure 61
Palm Heel Placement

- Once the magazine is extracted from the pouch, the support hand wrist should rotate upward and toward the center of the chest, so the ammunition in the magazine is pointing forward, and the spine of the magazine is facing the officer's chest.
- The remainder of the fingers should support the magazine and slightly wrap around the spine of the magazine, with the first pads of the middle, ring and pinky fingers gripping the spine of the magazine.
- The toe or floorplate of the magazine should be centered in the palm of the hand to further stabilize the magazine.

- After aligning the magazine with the magazine well of the firearm visually (and perhaps through touch reference), the fingers of the support hand should peel away from the magazine, allowing it to be inserted and firmly seated in the magazine well by the palm of the support hand.
- The palm of the support hand and fingers should then rotate upward, wrapping around and re-establishing the support hand grip on the firearm. This should be a fluid motion.

Reloading Using the Hand-Over Technique

The hand-over technique, as shown in Figure 62, requires that the operator use their support hand to properly load and clear the firearm. The hand-over technique uses the larger hand muscles to manipulate the slide. A proper hand-over technique requires that the operator of the pistol place the palm of their hand on one side of the slide, while the fingers wrap around the top and grasp the other side of the slide. This ensures that the palm area of the hand and fingers are fully gripping the slide, guaranteeing that there is enough strength and muscle mass to pull the slide to the rear under all conditions. This technique also decreases the chance that the support hand will accidentally slip off the slide when reloading. One way to make sure that the hand-over technique is being properly used is to check the thumb placement of the support hand. The support hand thumb should be on the back or rear of the slide: the operator should be able to see their support side thumb and thumb nail that is positioned on the back of the slide when reloading.

There are some key points to consider when conducting the hand-over technique. First, the support hand cannot cover the ejection port. If the hand (or part of the hand) is covering the ejection port, part of the operator's hand could get pinched between the ejection port and barrel assembly as the slide moves forward. It could also cause a malfunction/ stoppage.

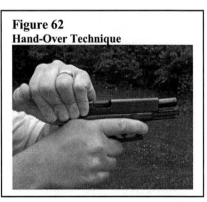

Figure 62
Hand-Over Technique

Second, when using the hand over technique, the operator must maintain their field of view on the threat environment. In many cases, the

223

operator may lower the muzzle of the firearm to the "low ready" position. Pointing the muzzle down, instead of at the threat or threat environment will also force the operator's field of view toward the ground and away from the threat. If this happens, the operator has lost a degree of control on the threat environment, and they are now at a tactical disadvantage in the gunfight. In order to prevent this issue from occurring, the operator must remember this simple point: The user should work around the gun and not move the gun to operate around them. This means that the operator keeps the muzzle pointed down range and as horizontal as possible, toward the threat environment.

Administrative Reloads

An administrative load can be considered as that loading procedure that prepares the firearm for duty. This type of load is conducted at the beginning of the shift or when the officer is reloading the firearm. It is conducted in a static or controlled setting, such as on the range when training or when the officer is loading their firearm at the beginning of their shift. The basic steps in conducting the administrative load are listed below:

- The pistol should be in the holster with the slide locked to the rear.
- Using the support hand, properly grip and extract the fully topped off magazine from the magazine pouch, as shown in Figures 58 and 59 (this will serve as additional practice in properly gripping and extracting the magazine from the pouch as this is often neglected in firearm's training).
- Transfer the magazine from the support to the strong hand.
- With the strong hand, insert the magazine into the magazine well of the pistol while it is still holstered, as shown in Figure 63.

Figure 63
Magazine Insertion

- Make sure the magazine is properly seated or secured in the firearm. This can be achieved by simply tugging on the floorplate of the magazine with the strong hand to make sure the magazine is locked (or seated) in the firearm.
- Establish the master grip on the pistol with the strong hand. Draw the firearm and point it in a safe direction.

- Using the hand-over technique, release the slide forward, allowing it to go into battery under its own spring pressure. Do not allow the hand to "ride the slide." Keeping the hand (and some degree of resistance, thereof) on the slide could interfere with the slide action of the firearm, causing a shooter-induced malfunction. Do not use the slide stop lever. Using the slide stop lever, instead of the hand-over method requires the use of fine motor skills. This technique should be avoided.
- Properly secure the pistol in the holster.
- While the pistol is secure in the holster, activate the magazine release and extract the magazine from the firearm with the strong hand.
- Top off the magazine with an extra round of ammunition (i.e. the "Barney Bullet"), and reinsert the magazine into the firearm.
  - Now, the pistol is fully topped off. It has a round in the chamber and the magazine is also fully loaded, since the operator has replaced that round that was stripped from the magazine that was fed into the chamber of the pistol.

Training Tip: Develop a routine when drawing new magazines from the mag pouch. On the first mag change, for example, always take the magazine that is in the front divider pocket of the pouch. On the second change, take the mag from the next divider. Getting into a routine of drawing from the same divider every time will develop muscle memory and increased speed in mag changes

---

- Check to make sure the magazine is properly seated in the firearm by tugging on the floorplate.

In other cases where the firearm is already in battery and there is a round it the chamber, the steps in the administrative load will be slightly different. Below are the steps in administratively reloading the firearm when it is in battery and there is a round in the chamber.

- With the pistol properly secured in the holster, activate the magazine release and extract the magazine from the firearm with the strong hand.
- Secure this magazine somewhere on the body. Do not place the partially loaded magazine in the magazine pouch. Always place the magazine in the same place on the body (ex: cargo side pant

pocket) to establish muscle memory, so a shooter does not have to "search" for the magazine.

- Using the support hand, properly grip and extract a fully topped-off magazine from the magazine pouch. This will serve as additional practice in properly gripping and extracting the magazine from the pouch, as this is often neglected in firearm's training.
- Transfer the magazine from the support to strong hand.
- With the strong hand, insert the magazine into the magazine well of the holstered pistol.
- Make sure the magazine is seated into the firearm by tugging on the magazine floorplate.

Regardless of the type of administrative load that is conducted, the last stage in the administrative load is to replenish the magazine pouch. The officer should transfer a fully loaded third magazine from their pocket or another location, where it is kept, to the magazine pouch.

The Press Check

Another component of the administrative load that the operator of the firearm may want to conduct is the press check. The press check is a method to make sure that there is ammunition in the chamber of the pistol. A press check occurs when the operator pulls the slide to the rear just far enough to see that there is ammunition in the chamber. The operator then permits the slide to travel forward under its own spring pressure to lock back into battery.

There are several different ways to conduct the press check. One of the safest ways to conduct the press check is to use the support hand technique that is listed below. Using this technique ensures that there is little risk that the support hand will be in front of, or cross the muzzle.

- While establishing and maintaining the master grip, and following all the rules of the safe handling of firearms, draw the firearm and point it in a safe direction.
- Use the hand-over technique to grasp the slide, making sure that the ejection port is not covered by the support hand.

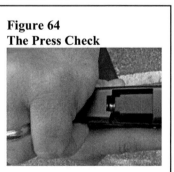

Figure 64
The Press Check

- Slowly pull the slide to the rear, just enough so the operator can see a cartridge in the chamber. If the firearm has a DA/SA configuration, and has an external hammer, do not allow the slide to set or lock the hammer to the rear (if this happens, use the de-cock lever to release the hammer forward to the double action mode).
- Visually check to see if there is ammunition in the chamber.
- Let the slide travel forward under its own spring pressure to lock the firearm back into battery. Do not assist the slide moving forward by keeping the hand on the slide. In fact, immediately take the hand off the gun to prevent a shooter-induced malfunction.
- Reholster the pistol, if appropriate.

Tactical & Combat Reloads

Figure 65
Elbow in to Reload

Tactical and combat reloads are conducted in a dynamic setting. The purpose of the tactical and combat load is to "keep the gun going" in a gunfight by ensuring that the firearm will always have ammunition. Both of these types of reloads require only a slight modification of the shooting stance where the hands and arms only move. Everything else related to the shooting stance basically stays the same, where the officer still keeps their attention on the threat environment. Both combat and tactical loads should be conducted from a position of cover and/or concealment. They should never be conducted out in the open.

The Combat Reload

In a combat load situation, the slide stop lever of the pistol has been activated, locking the slide to the rear. The firearm has run out of ammunition, and it is the responsibility of the officer to reload the firearm in a smooth and fast manner (i.e. magazine in/magazine out) while controlling the threat environment. The stages of the combat load are shown in Figures 65 - 69. The basic steps in conducting the combat load are:

- Lower the firearm slightly off target. Keep the muzzle of the firearm horizontal and pointed toward the threat.

- Bring the strong arm elbow in toward the chest allowing it to rest against the rib cage. As the strong arm elbow is moving back toward the rib cage, activate the magazine release with the strong hand thumb. Slightly cant the weapon so the magazine well is angled toward the operator's support side to facilitate a faster reload. This technique provides additional support for both the firearm and the subsequent magazine change. This movement also makes the magazine change easier to do since the officer does not have to fully extend their support arm out to conduct the magazine change.
- From this position, the operator should find that position where they can see the threat environment, the muzzle and the magazine at basically the same time, while still keeping the head and eyes downrange to control the threat environment (if necessary, the operator can take a quick look at the magazine well, as shown in Figure 67).
- At the same time that the elbow is breaking and moving back toward the ribcage and the magazine release is being activated, the support hand should "strip" or pull the magazine from the magazine well of the firearm.

Figure 66
Extract Magazine

Figure 67
Reload

- Allow the empty magazine to freely fall to the ground. DO NOT attempt to save the magazine. Magazines should be considered disposable (consider this point: is your life worth the value of an empty magazine?).
- As the support hand is stripping the magazine from the firearm, it will naturally move at an angle down and toward the magazine pouch that is located on the support side.

- Obtain a new magazine from the magazine pouch, properly gripping the new magazine in the process.
- With the support hand, insert the magazine into the firearm. Make sure the that magazine is properly secured by firmly seating the magazine into the firearm with the palm of the hand.
- Using the hand-over technique as shown in Figure 68, pull the slide to the rear, deactivating the slide stop lever in the process.

Figure 68
Hand-Over

Figure 69
Back on Target

- Allow the slide to move forward under spring pressure only. Do not allow the hand to "ride the slide." Keeping the hand (and some degree of resistance, thereof) on the slide could interfere with the slide action of the firearm, causing a shooter-induced malfunction.
- Do not use the slide stop lever to release the slide forward. Using the slide stop lever requires the use of fine motor skills. Fine motor skills erode fast under high stress situations, and a person may be unable to activate the slide stop lever under these conditions. Additionally, many slide stop levers are quite small and may be difficult to locate and use under a high-stress situation.
- Rotate the support hand back into the position used for supporting the handgun. This should be smooth and natural.
- Get back on the target/threat by locking the strong arm out, assuming a normal shooting stance.

The Tactical Reload

In a tactical load situation, the firearm has not run out of ammunition. The pistol is still in battery, with a round in the chamber. However, the shooter has decided, based on the tactical environment (and perhaps realizing that s/he is running low on ammunition in the magazine), that they need to reload the firearm with a fully loaded magazine. Consider, for example, an officer who is engaged in a gunfight. This officer has sought cover, and based on his tactical assessment of the situation, he has time to insert a fully loaded magazine from his magazine pouch into the firearm. By engaging in this type of tactical reload, the operator now has a fully "topped off" magazine in their pistol to reengage the threat, if necessary.

The tactical load is very similar to the combat load, with the exception of having the option to save the partially loaded magazine for future use (depending upon how the officer is trained at their agency). Listed below are the steps in conducting a tactical reload:

- Lower the firearm slightly off target. Keep the muzzle of the firearm horizontal, pointed toward the threat.
- Bring the strong arm elbow in toward the chest allowing it to rest against the rib cage. As the strong arm elbow is moving back toward the ribcage, activate the magazine release with the strong hand thumb. Slightly cant the weapon so the magazine well is angled toward the operator's support side to facilitate a faster reload. This technique provides additional support for both the firearm and the subsequent magazine change. This movement also makes the magazine change easier to conduct, since the officer does not their support arm fully extended outward.
- At the same time that the elbow is breaking and moving back toward the ribcage, and the magazine release is being activated, the support hand should "strip" or pull the magazine from the magazine well of the firearm.

Following the above steps, depending upon the tactical situation, the operator has 2 options regarding the partially loaded magazine. These options include a tactical load with a "save," or a tactical load, "no save."

Tactical Load - "Save"

In a tactical load "save," the partially loaded magazine is stored somewhere on the shooter's body. The logic behind a tactical load – save is that the officer may need this partially loaded magazine if the gunfight should continue. The operator may also need to conduct additional magazine changes due to a malfunction/stoppage. The steps behind a tactical load-save are shown in Figures 70 - 73.

**Figure 70
Strip Magazine**

**Figure 71
Save Magazine**

One common location to place the magazine is between the duty and under-belt, near the magazine pouch or in a pants pocket. The key consideration is that the partially loaded magazine should be placed in the same location on the body every time, so muscle memory can be established to retrieve that magazine, if necessary. Because a uniform may change according to season, the officer should find that position on their uniform that remains consistent across seasons. For example, placing the magazine in a jacket pocket would be wrong, based on the fact that a jacket is probably not worn year-round. Instead, storing the magazine between the duty belt and waist, or a cargo pocket on the support side may be a more appropriate tactic.

**Figure 72
Insert New Magazine**

**Figure 73
Back on Target**

Regardless of where the magazine is saved, the following steps should be followed:

- Once the support hand strips the magazine, establish a firm grip on the magazine. Properly store the magazine somewhere on the support side of the body.
- Immediately after the magazine is stored and secured somewhere on the support side, extract a fully loaded magazine from the magazine pouch with the support hand, making sure that the magazine is properly gripped.
- With the support hand, insert the magazine into the firearm. Make sure the magazine is properly secured by firmly seating the magazine into the firearm with the palm portion of the hand.
- Reestablish the proper support hand grip on the firearm.
- Get back on the target/threat.

Tactical Load - "No Save"

A tactical load, "no save," occurs when the operator does not attempt to save the partially loaded magazine for future use. Instead, the operator simply lets the magazine drop to the ground. The steps for the tactical load - "no save" are shown in Figures 74 - 76. The following steps should be followed for a "no-save" tactical load:

- As the support hand is stripping the magazine from the firearm, let the magazine fall, allowing the support hand to move at an angle down and toward the magazine pouch.
- Obtain a new magazine from the magazine pouch, properly gripping the new magazine.
- With the support hand, insert the magazine into the firearm. Make sure the magazine is properly seated in the firearm with the palm of the hand.
- Rotate the support hand back into the position used for supporting the handgun. This should be smooth and natural.
- Get back on the target/threat by locking the strong arm out, assuming a normal shooting stance.

Figure 74
Strip Magazine

Figure 75
New Magazine

Figure 76
Back on Target

Problems with Reloads

Like other firearms tactics, in some situations a person may become lax and inattentive in the quality of their magazine changes. If, however, the basics of a reload are not properly followed, the shooter will be tactically unprepared for a gunfight. Some of the more common problems associated with the principles of reloading include: 1) improper magazine placement; 2) an improper grip on the magazine; 3) placing magazines in the pouch backwards; 4) not concentrating on the threat environment during reloads; and, 5) not using the hand-over technique.

- Improper Magazine Pouch Placement

The magazine pouch cannot move. It must be in the same location on the duty belt at all times so when the magazine change is conducted, the support hand automatically sweeps down, extracts a new magazine from the magazine pouch, and feeds it into the firearm. If the magazine pouch moves, this will disrupt that muscle memory that has been established, changing the shooter's concentration (and perhaps visual field) from the threat environment to the magazine pouch.

Figure 77
Improper Magazine Grip

- Improper Grip on the Magazine

  Magazines are relatively small. They can be oily and, combined with the loss of some motor skills in a stressful situation, they can easily fall out of a person's hand. To avoid this, the magazine must be properly gripped. One of the more common mistakes is that a person will only grip the bottom of the magazine, at times actually curling their fingers around the floorplate (as shown in Figure 67). This will lead to the magazine being unstable in the hand, making it very difficult to insert into the magazine well. To avoid this issue, the support hand fingers should be fully wrapped around the magazine tube with the index finger aligned on the front on the magazine.

- Placing Magazines in the Pouch Backwards

  In some cases a person may place their magazines in the pouch backwards, so the floorplate and/or bullets are pointing to the rear. Placing the magazine in the pouch backwards requires the operator to rotate their support hand wrist on the reload, slowing down the reloading process.

- Not Concentrating on the Threat Environment

  Visual control of the threat environment while conducting the reload is vital. During a reload an officer may inadvertently lower their field of view away from the threat environment, to the area directly down and in front of them. Often this is attributed to the officer pointing the muzzle of the pistol down in front of them, which forces the operator to change their field of view from the threat environment to the ground. The easiest way to avoid this problem is to make sure that the muzzle is as horizontal as possible, while still pointing toward the threat environment. This will ensure that the operator can still keep an eye on the threat environment, while conducting the reload. Depending upon weapon design and the type of reload the operator is conducting, they can readily shoot from this position, if necessary.

- Not Using the Hand-Over Technique

  Rather than using the correct hand-over technique, in some situations a shooter may use what is called the "sling shot" technique of charging the firearm (see Figure 78). The "sling shot" technique, as the name implies, occurs when the operator uses their support hand thumb and index finger to pull the slide to the rear. Basically, the operator pinches the slide with the first pad of the index finger and thumb, only using fine muscles instead of their larger gross muscles in the hand. Under a high-stress dynamic situation, however, a person's fingers could easily slip off the back of the slide, and in the process, not charge the weapon. In other cases, meanwhile, they may actually cause a shooter-induced stoppage, such as a failure to feed.

**Figure 78
"Slingshot"**

- Reloading with Strong Arm Fully Extended Outward

   In some situations, a shooter may fail to bring in their strong arm elbow inward when reloading. Reloading with the strong arm fully extended is difficult. This difficultly can be attributed to the fact that the gun is not supported well, in comparison to having it slightly tucked against the body. Because the arm and gun may be unstable, it will be more difficult to extract and insert a fresh magazine into the pistol in timely manner.

Conclusion

   Without mastering the reload, especially in a threat situation, a police officer can be at a serious disadvantage in a gunfight. This chapter has pointed out that reloading the police firearm can be conducted in both static and dynamic settings. The administrative load is associated with a static training environment, such as, when an officer is preparing for duty. In a dynamic setting, meanwhile, depending upon the condition of the weapon and the factors in the force encounter, the officer may use either the combat or tactical reload. If the firearm is out of ammunition, a combat load is required. If an opportunity in the gunfight to reload exists, then a tactical reload (with or without a save) would be the appropriate tactic to ensure that the officer has a fully loaded firearm to re-engage the threat, if necessary.

This chapter also highlighted some of the common issues associated with reloads. Some common problems associated with reloads include not positioning the magazine pouch correctly on the duty belt, placing magazines backwards in the magazine pouch, and not concentrating on the threat environment. Another common problem is not using the hand-over technique, where instead the operator "sling shots" the slide. Like the other firearms basics and tactics, mastering the reload takes mental focus and practice. Through perfect practice, however, a shooter will master those skills associated with the reload.

Introduction

A malfunction can be defined as a mechanical failure that prevents the pistol from firing. A stoppage, meanwhile, is an unintentional disruption of the cycle of operation of the firearm that can somehow be cleared by the user (HP White Laboratories, 2004). In short, malfunctions and stoppages are unexpected and unwelcome occurrences. Malfunctions/stoppages are a relatively rare event when using a modern high-quality firearm and ammunition. However, they do occur, and it is the responsibility of the operator to clear the malfunction/stoppage in a fast and effective manner, while controlling the suspect and threat environment.

This chapter will provide the reader with an analysis and explanation of what causes malfunctions (the term malfunction will also include stoppages in this chapter) with the police handgun. It will also provide a review of the various types of malfunctions that occur with the semi-automatic firearm. Since it is the sole responsibility of the operator to clear these malfunctions, methods of clearing malfunctions and stoppages will also be reviewed, emphasizing the principle of immediate action to get the firearm back into the gunfight in a timely and efficient manner.

Causes of Malfunctions & Stoppages

Several events can lead up a malfunction or stoppage. These can be broadly categorized into four main areas that include: 1) The Gun Itself; 2) The Magazine; 3) The User; and, 4) Ammunition.

The Gun Itself

In some cases, the gun itself is the cause of the malfunction. This is because the pistol is a mechanical device that is constructed of components that will eventually wear out, fatigue, or break. For example, springs may break or lose some degree of their strength or resistance, affecting the operation of the weapon. In other cases, metal parts will wear out (i.e. trigger bars and strikers) and eventually break because of the lack of proper care and maintenance, or simply because that part of the firearm has met its engineered life. One easy way to avoid malfunctions of this nature is to properly maintain the firearm, have it annually inspected by an armorer to check for any defects, and keep the firearm clean, following the guidelines set forth by the manufacturer.

The Magazine

In several types of malfunctions/stoppages, the magazine is often the cause of the problem. Often the magazine is overlooked as a critical component of a well-operating firearm. The magazine can be in-directly and directly responsible for various malfunctions and stop-pages. Indirectly, for example, a dirty maga-zine will transfer dirt

> **Training Tip:** Magazines take a lot of abuse. To avoid damage to the magazine(s), police officers should have separate training and duty magazines. Training magazines will get beat up and abused, as they are continually dropped when conducting proper magazine changes. The duty magazines, meanwhile, should only be used during the course of the officer's shift to make sure that they are in perfect condition.

and debris into the action of the firearm. As a direct cause, a magazine spring may become weak, causing problems in feeding ammunition into the chamber. Other common problems with the magazine include damaged or bent feed lips that impede the ammunition from being stripped from the magazine and fed into the firearm. The magazine may also have a broken follower (as many of these are constructed of plastic) that may also cause a malfunction/stoppage.

The User

In other cases, the user is to blame for the malfunction/stoppage. When the operator is directly responsible for the malfunction, it is called a shooter-induced malfunction. Some examples of shooter-induced malfunc-tions include a failure to feed, eject, and extract. The causes of these malfunctions vary. However, in many cases they can be attributed to the fact that the operator failed to follow one or more firearm's fundamentals. For example, the operator may not have solidly locked out their strong arm wrist, where the resulting "limp wrist" caused the malfunction, because the recoil from the pistol did not have a solid surface to work against. In other instances, the operator's thumbs may interfere with the movement of the slide, or they may fail to properly seat the magazine when reloading.

Shooter-induced malfunctions are also the consequence of the operator's sheer negligence in the proper care and maintenance of the firearm and magazine. Because the operator has not performed routine cleaning and maintenance on the firearm and magazine, they may be so dirty that the function of the firearm is affected.

Ammunition

Modern factory-loaded ammunition is quite dependable. However, under some circumstances there may be problems with ammunition, ranging from improperly sized cases, fouled or defective powders, and cracked or broken cartridge cases. In instances where the operator is using reloaded or remanufactured ammunition, the risk for these and other problems associated with ammunition failures may increase.

Two of the more common problems (although these are quite rare) associated with ammunition malfunctions include the hangfire and faulty primers. As pointed out in the chapter on safety, a hangfire is the delayed ignition of the powder in the cartridge. As a general rule of thumb, when a hangfire occurs, the operator should wait a minimum of five seconds to make sure the round does not ignite outside of the gun, if it were to be extracted and ejected. However, in a dynamic setting a person does not have five seconds to wait. In these situations, the operator will simply have to take the risk that the round may ignite when extracted and ejected from the pistol.

In a situation involving a faulty primer, for example, the primer may be inserted backward into the cartridge case in the production process. In other situations, the primer may not detonate due to the fact that it is defective. Also, it may not detonate because there is a defect with the firing pin or striker mechanism, where even though the primer was struck, there was not enough force to detonate it. Whatever the case is with the primer, the operator should not attempt to re-fire the cartridge. In no instance should an officer re- insert this ammunition into their magazine. It the primer did not ignite on the first try, most likely it will not fire on the second attempt.

In order to avoid problems with ammunition, the operator should consider the following points:

- Use factory loaded ammunition from a reputable manufacturer.

- Using reloaded and remanufactured ammunition (in both training and duty settings) could increase the risk of an ammunition-induced malfunction and/or damage to the internal components of the firearm. Reloaded or remanufactured ammunition could also void the firearm's warranty.
- Ammunition must be clean and free from dirt and any other type of debris. Any dirt & debris on the shell case and projectile will transfer to the magazine, and then into the action of the firearm.
- Always visually inspect ammunition before loading it into the magazine. If the ammunition looks or feels wrong (i.e. it is dirty, tarnished and/or feels lighter than the others), do not use it.
- Make sure that the ammunition is compatible with the firearm (i.e. the same caliber).
- Properly store the ammunition in a clean and dry environment. High humidity environments could lead to the propellant becoming fouled. This, in turn, could lead to a failure to fire or type of malfunction/stoppage.

Types of Malfunctions & Stoppages

There are several types of malfunctions/stoppages with the semiautomatic pistol. These can be categorized or based on how the malfunction/stoppage interrupts the function of the firearm. The four main categories include

1. Failure to Fire;
2. Failure to Extract;
3. Failure to Eject; and,
4. Failure to Feed.

Other malfunctions/stoppages that will also be reviewed is the failure of the slide to lock to the rear, and the failure to lock/unlock. All of these malfunction/stoppages and their causes and remedies are shown in Table 13-1.

Failure to Fire

A failure to fire occurs when a live round is chambered, but does not fire. With this type of malfunction the shooter may hear the striker mechanism/firing pin strike the primer. Nevertheless, the cartridge does not discharge. Common causes of a failure to fire include: defective ammunition, a broken striker/firing pin and/or spring mechanism, a broken trigger bar (that would result in the trigger assembly not being reset), and no round in the chamber. It could also be attributed to a dirty firearm. If the pistol has an external active safety, another reason why the firearm may fail to fire is because the safety has been activated.

Failure to Extract

A failure to extract occurs when a spent cartridge is not completely extracted from the firearm. Some of the problems associated with a failure to extract include: improperly sized ammunition, a broken or defective extractor tooth, the rim of the case separating from the remainder of the cartridge (i.e. case head separation), a dirty extractor, and a shooter-induced malfunction.

**Figure 79
Failure to Extract**

Failure to Eject

**Figure 80
Failure to Eject**

A failure to eject occurs when the ejector rod is unsuccessful in fully ejecting the spent cartridge from the ejection port of the firearm. Common causes include a broken or bent ejector rod, faulty ammunition (not enough powder to work the recoil of the firearm, for example), a shooter induced error, or simply a dirty firearm.

A common failure to eject is known as the stove pipe (as shown in Figure 80). In this type of malfunction, the spent cartridge is successfully extracted from the chamber. However, it is only partially ejected from the firearm. The slide mechanism has somehow pinched the spent round in the ejection port to the point where the cartridge case looks like a stove pipe protruding from the top or side of the ejection port.

With this type of malfunction the shooter should perform a Stage I Clearance Drill ("Tap-Rack-Assess"). Another common technique other than the Stage I Clearance is to "salute" or "rake" the firearm. Using this technique, after the operator has identified that it is a stovepipe, they partially wrap their support hand around the slide (being careful not to place it in front of the muzzle) pulling their support hand toward

241

themselves. With this process, the shooter's hand serves as the extractor which snags the cartridge and forces it out of the ejection port.

Failure to Feed

A failure to feed occurs when a live round is somehow impeded from being fed into the chamber of the pistol. In some cases, the nose of the bullet will bind up on the feed ramp of the chamber (due to the ammunition itself or the fact that the feed ramp is dirty). In other cases, the ammunition may resemble a stovepipe, where the bullet end of the cartridge protrudes out the

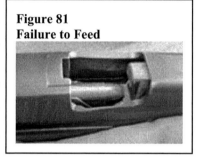

Figure 81
Failure to Feed

top of the ejection port or lodges on the top of the pistol's chamber wall. Usually, this problem is related to a defective magazine.

Another common failure to feed is called the double-feed. A double feed occurs when two rounds of ammunition (instead of one) are fed into the chamber at the same time. The primary cause of this type of failure to feed is that the lips on the magazine are damaged and are spread too far apart to properly hold or secure the ammunition that is contained in the magazine. Because of the increased gap between the magazine lips, two rounds, instead of one, are fed into the pistol at one time.

A failure to feed can also be attributed to a broken magazine follower, which results in the ammunition improperly aligned with the feed ramp of the firearm. An improperly seated magazine, using the wrong ammunition (too small or too large a caliber), and shooter-induced errors, such as blocking the ejection port, are additional reasons for a failure to feed. In rare occasions, meanwhile, a failure to feed can also be attributed to a broken extractor. Because the extractor is broken, it failed to extract the spent round. Because the spent round did not extract, the new live round failed to feed into the chamber of the firearm.

TABLE 13-1
SEMI-AUTOMATIC HANDGUN MALFUNCTIONS

Type of Malfunction	Causes	Symptoms	Remedy
Failure to Fire	• Defective Ammunition • Defective Firing Pin * • Broken Trigger Bar * • Round in Chamber • Dirty Weapon • Active Safety is "on"	• Weapon will not fire • Round lodged in chamber	• Tap-Rack-Assess
Failure to Extract	• Broken Extractor* • Case Head Separation* • Case Expansion* • Slide Impeded by Shooter • Dirty Weapon	• Double-Feed • Slide locked into battery & will not release/function	• Tap-Rack-Assess • Lock Slide to the Rear, Remove Magazine, Insert New Magazine.
Failure to Eject	• Broken Ejector * • Shooter Induced Error (i.e. limp wristing the weapon) • Faulty Ammunition • Slide Impeded by Shooter • Dirty Weapon	• Spent round will not fully eject from the weapon (i.e. "Stove Pipe")	• Tap-Rack-Assess • If Stove Pipe is visible, rake round out of ejection port with support hand ("salute" the weapon)
Failure to Feed	• Broken/Defective Magazine Follower • Magazine not properly seated • Ammunition not compatible with weapon • Chamber Feed Ramp is dirty	• Slide not in battery • No cartridge in chamber • Ammunition does not feed appropriately into chamber	• Tap-Rack-Assess • Insert New Magazine

Type of Malfunction	Causes	Symptoms	Remedy
Slide Will Not Lock to the Rear/Back	• Broken Slide Stop Lever* • Shooter Induced Error • Broken/Defective Magazine Follower • Weak Magazine Spring • Dirty Weapon	• Slide will not lock to the rear	• Replace Magazine
Failure to Lock(into Battery)	• Mechanical Failure(s) (i.e. Recoil Spring)* • Shooter Induced Error • Improperly Sized Ammunition • Dirty Weapon	• Slide will not lock into the forward/battery position	• Tap-Rack-Assess
Failure to Unlock	• Dirty Weapon • Improperly Sized Ammunition • Under or Overpowered Ammunition • Case Head Separation • Mechanical Failure(s)	• Slide will unlock out of the forward/battery position	• Tap-Rack-Assess

* Denotes a catastrophic failure that cannot be resolved by the shooter

Slide Not Locking to the Rear

Another malfunction is the failure of the slide to lock to the rearward position when the magazine is empty. The reasons for a slide not locking to the rear can be based on the shooter and the failure of various mechanical components on the pistol or magazine. An example of a shooter-induced malfunction would be when the operator's thumb(s) interfere with the slide stop lever (because of placement and/or the recoil of the weapon) that, in turn, inadvertently engaged the slide stop lever. A mechanical malfunction, meanwhile, could include a broken slide stop lever. In many cases, however, it can be attributed to the magazine follower. Besides being responsible for correctly feeding ammunition into the chamber, the follower, by its design (in many types of pistols), is also responsible for mechanically activating the slide stop lever after the last round is fed and fired from the pistol. If the follower is cracked or somehow broken, it may fail to activate the slide stop lever, whereas the slide will travel forward and lock into battery without ammunition in the chamber.

Failure to Lock/Unlock

A failure to lock (or go into battery) occurs when the barrel assembly does not lock into battery because the slide has not returned to its most forward position. Since the barrel assembly has not completely locked, the striker/firing pin may or may not be able to release and strike the cartridge primer (depending upon the tolerances of the gun). A failure to lock can be attributed to a dirty firearm and/or ammunition, a weak recoil spring, or because the shooter, through their own actions (i.e. their thumbs prevented the forward motion of the slide) prevented the slide from traveling forward into complete battery. A failure to lock can also occur because of oversized ammunition that only partially fed into the chamber, preventing the slide from locking into battery.

A failure to unlock, meanwhile, occurs when there is a failure to extract the spent cartridge from the chamber. A failure to unlock can occur because of a dirty gun or a broken extractor. It can also occur because of improperly sized ammunition that is too large in diameter, but is nevertheless forced into the chamber, which then cannot be extracted. A failure to unlock can also be caused by overpowered or underpowered ammunition. Overpowered ammunition (i.e. too much powder) could cause a partial case head separation, where the extractor is unable to mechanically remove the case from the chamber because the rim of the cartridge has broken off. In the case of underpowered ammunition, meanwhile, the lack of powder could reduce the recoil of the slide to the point where it could fail to properly unlock and cycle the slide.

Clearing Malfunctions & Stoppages

There are some different types of corrective actions that can be used to address malfunctions and stoppages. This section will address the three levels of corrective action that can be performed. It will also address the responsibilities of the operator in the context of immediately clearing the malfunction/stoppage using the Tap-Rack-Assess technique to clear both stage I and II malfunctions/stoppages.

Levels of Corrective Action

HP White Laboratories (2004) categorizes malfunctions/stoppages according to the type of action that is required to correct the problem. The three levels of corrective action are:

- **Type I:** Is correctable by the operator without tools or implements. A Type I malfunction is correctable within 10 seconds.
- **Type II:** Is correctable by the operator without tools. A Type II malfunction requires more than 10 seconds to complete and it may require the operator to field strip the weapon (i.e. remove the slide assembly).
- **Type III:** This type of malfunction requires the use of tools, parts, or instructions to fix the malfunction/stoppage. It requires the firearm to be disassembled beyond field stripping. A Type III corrective action is also called a catastrophic failure, since the firearm will not function, and the operator cannot readily fix the weapon.

The Principle of Immediate Action

One of the keys to effectively dealing with a stoppage/malfunction is that the operator of the firearm must take immediate action to diagnose and fix the problem. This principle of immediate action also takes the position that the operator is solely responsible to get the firearm back in operation as fast as possible.

A malfunction/stoppage clearing should never be done in the open. Immediate action should always be done from a position of cover and/or concealment to protect the operator from the threat(s). Since "we fight the way we train", the principle of immediate action requires that these clearance techniques are followed and practiced during training. Through practice and repetition, muscle memory will be established and the activity will become reflexive in nature.

Stoppage Clearing Using "Tap-Rack-Assess" Drill

When a malfunction/stoppage occurs, the first thing the operator should do, regardless of the actual problem, it to take immediate action by conducting a Tap-Rack-Assess drill as shown in Figures 82-84. A person does not have time in a gunfight to lower the weapon, examine it, and then deal with the problem. Instead, they should immediately Tap-Rack-Assess. This Tap-Rack-Assess must become instinctual in nature.

Figure 82 "Tap"	**Figure 83** "Rack"	**Figure 84** "Assess"
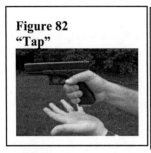		

The Tap-Rack-Assess clearance drill requires the use of the hand-over technique in working the slide with the support side hand. When conducting the hand-over technique, the operator must make sure that their support hand is not blocking the ejection port. If the ejection port is blocked, it will be very difficult, if not impossible, to clear an obstruction from the chamber and/or ejection port. In fact, it may cause an additional malfunction, such as a double feed. The two clearance drills that require the use of the Tap-Rack-Assess clearance technique are listed below.

Stage I Clearance Drills

- **TAP** - With the support hand, while maintaining the master grip and staying on the target and threat environment (do not lower the pistol), use the palm portion of support hand to firmly tap the base of the magazine to make sure that it is properly seated in the firearm. This tap does not have to be exaggerated. For example, the shooter does not have to lower their support hand one or two feet under the magazine and firmly slap the magazine to make sure that it is seated. All the shooter has to do is rotate their support hand under the grip, and apply upward pressure, combined with a sight "slap" against the base of the magazine, to make sure that it is properly seated.

- **RACK** - Using the hand-over technique, pull the slide to the rear, making sure that the hand is not blocking the ejection port. At the same time that the slide is being pulled to the rear, slightly rotate the pistol in the direction of the ejection port (which is usually to the right) to have gravity further assist in removing any obstruction in the ejection port. Allow the slide to move forward under spring pressure only. Do not allow the hand to "ride the slide." Keeping

247

the hand (and some degree of resistance, thereof) on the slide could interfere with the slide action of the firearm, causing a shooter-induced malfunction. Rotate the support hand back into the position used for firing the handgun and re-establish the sight picture. This action should be smooth and natural.

- **ASSESS** - This stage requires that the operator determine if there is still a threat that must be stopped. As a deadly force situation can de-escalate rapidly, the operator must determine if deadly force is still an appropriate tactic to use to stop the threat, based on the threat's actions.

If this clearance technique does not work after the second attempt, do not keep performing this drill. Instead, the operator must perform a Stage II Clearance Drill.

Stage II Clearance Drills

The key behind a Stage II clearance drill is to remove the magazine from the firearm. Below are the steps in a Stage II Clearance:

- **TAP** - With the support hand, while maintaining the master grip and staying on the target and threat environment (do not lower the pistol), firmly tap the base of the magazine with the support hand palm to make sure the magazine is properly seated in the firearm. Another option to this move is it to bring the strong arm elbow toward the chest so the operator has greater support and control of the firearm when conducting the tap stage.

- **RACK** - Using the hand-over technique, pull the slide to the rear. At the same time that the slide is being pulled to the rear, slightly rotate the pistol to the right to have the benefit of the force of gravity assist in removing any obstruction in the ejection port. Most, if not all pistol ejection ports are located on the right side of the slide mechanism. Allow the slide to move forward under spring pressure only. Do not allow the hand to "ride the slide." Keeping the hand (and some degree of resistance, thereof) on the slide could interfere with the slide action of the firearm, causing a shooter-induced malfunction. Move the support hand back into the position used for firing the handgun. This should be smooth and natural.

If there is still an obstruction, repeat the Tap-Rack one more time before moving on to the next steps.

Figure 85
"Tap"

Figure 86
"Rack"

- **LOCK THE SLIDE TO THE REAR** - Locking the slide to the rear will make it easier to extract the magazine from the firearm. In some instances, a cartridge may be partially fed into the chamber of the firearm, while still being held in the magazine by its feed lips. In order to reduce the pressure that the slide is exerting on the cartridge and follower, the slide must be locked open or to the rear. While locking the slide to the rear, rotate the pistol to the right to have the force of gravity further assist in removing any obstruction that may be located in the ejection port.

Figure 87
Lock Slide to Rear

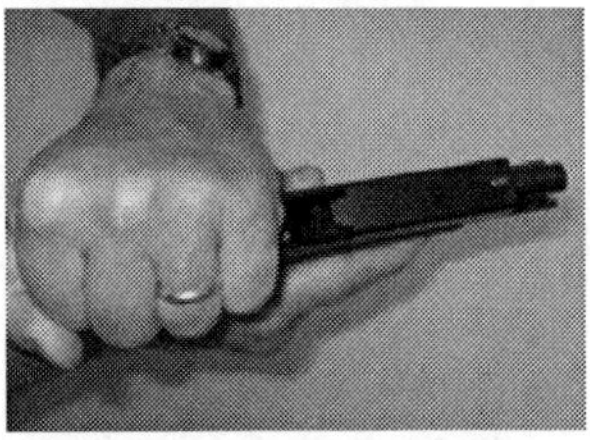

- **REMOVE THE MAGAZINE** - Strip the magazine out of the firearm using the support hand. Let the magazine fall to the ground. In many cases, the magazine is the culprit for the stoppage. Based on this point, it would be ridiculous to insert the same magazine into the firearm that may have been the cause of the initial stoppage/malfunction. The only exception to this rule would be when this is the last magazine the officer has. Then, the operator must trust that the magazine is not defective. Immediately after removing the magazine, the operator must also conduct a quick visual check of the ejection port and the action of the firearm to make sure that is it clear of any obstructions.

249

- **INSERT NEW MAGAZINE** - Insert a new, fully loaded magazine into the magazine well of the firearm, using the hand-over reload. Using the hand-over technique allows the slide to travel forward under its spring pressure to chamber the round.

Figure 88
Insert New Magazine

- **ASSESS** - Determine if there is still a valid threat that requires the use of deadly force.

Common Mistakes in Clearing Malfunctions & Stoppages

Like other fundamentals and tactics, there are some common mistakes made in clearing malfunctions/stoppages. Some of the more common mistakes include: 1) not properly working around the gun; 2) not recognizing a malfunction/stoppage has occurred; 3) relying upon others to fix the problem; 4) not tapping or seating the magazine; and, 5) repeatedly using the Tap-Rack-Assess drill to try to clear the malfunction/stoppage. These common mistakes are discussed in detail below.

Work around the gun - Not the gun around you

The operator of the firearm should always work around the gun. The gun should not work around the operator. In some instances, however, the operator will move the gun off target and away from the threat environment, subsequently moving their field of view from the threat environment to the gun in the process. These types of movements result in the gun moving around the operator, causing them to lose control of the threat environment, as they will often look down toward the ground instead of forward at the threat environment. To prevent this from occurring, the operator must learn how to clear all malfunctions by working their support hand around the gun and not the gun around their support hand and body. The pistol should stay pointed toward the threat environment, which will allow the operator to readily reengage the threat, if necessary.

250

Not recognizing that a malfunction/stoppage has occurred

In other situations an operator may fail to recognize that a malfunction/stoppage has occurred. For example, even though the slide is out of battery, and there is a double-feed or stovepipe, the operator maintains a sight picture and continues to pull the trigger to the rear with no results. Recognizing that there is a malfunction/stoppage is simply based on being attentive to the operation of the firearm and through practice. When the malfunction/stoppage does occur, all the shooter has to do is to recognize and diagnose the problem, take immediate action, and conduct a Stage I clearance drill.

Relying upon others to fix the malfunction/stoppage

As mentioned earlier in this chapter, in some cases the operator will lower their firearm, raise their hand and look to others to assist them in clearing the firearm. This technique is simply wrong. The operator is fully responsible for the condition of their firearm at all times and they are solely responsible for maintaining its operation, including properly clearing a malfunction/stoppage if it should occur. Remember: we fight the way we train. Who is available to fix your gun in a gunfight? Only you.

Not "Tapping" the Magazine

Tapping the base of the magazine is crucial in clearing malfunctions/stoppages. What often occurs with a malfunction/stoppage, however, is that the shooter immediately uses their support hand to rack the slide without first firmly tapping the magazine with their support hand palm to make sure it is properly seated. The Tap-Rack-Assess clearance drill requires that the operator first makes sure that the magazine is properly seated, since the magazine is often the cause of the malfunction/stoppage.

Only Attempt a Stage I Clearance Twice

A common mistake for operators is to become hyper-vigilant when attempting to clear the firearm. In this state or condition, the operator places all of their concentration on the malfunction and repeatedly attempts to clear the firearm multiple times, with no success. If the Stage I clearance technique does not work after the second attempt, do not keep performing the drill. If it did not clear on the second attempt, odds are it will not clear on a third, fourth, or fifth (or even more) attempts. Instead, the operator must transition to a Stage II clearance drill.

Conclusion

A malfunction can be defined as a mechanical failure that prevents the pistol from firing. A stoppage, meanwhile, is an unintentional disruption of the cycle of operation of the firearm that can somehow be cleared by the user (HP White Labs, 2004). There are several causes of stoppages and malfunctions. These can be broadly categorized into four main areas that include the gun itself, the magazine, the user, and ammunition. The magazine is often the culprit of the stoppage, followed by the user who is directly responsible for

> **Training Tip**: One way to train officers to take immediate action is to have them insert "dummy" rounds into their magazines when training. This dummy/training round will create a failure to fire, requiring the officer to Tap-Rack-Assess. Over time, this clearance drill will become a reflexive action, where officers will instinctively "tap-rack-assess" on malfunctions.

shooter-induced malfunctions/stoppages, as well as malfunctions/stoppages associated with the poor care and maintenance of the firearm and magazine(s).

There are several types of malfunctions/stoppages. They include the failure to fire, extract, eject and feed. Another common malfunction/stoppage is that the slide will not lock to the rear after the last round is fed from the magazine into the chamber of the gun and fired. There are also three levels of corrective action to take when dealing with a malfunction/stoppage. Level I is immediately correctable by the operator, taking just a second or more (if that) to complete. Like level I, level 2 is correctable by the operator, but takes more time to clear or correct. A level III malfunction is a catastrophic failure that requires disassembly of the firearm beyond field stripping.

Regardless of the malfunction/stoppage, the operator must take immediate action to correct the problem. One of the best ways to clear the malfunction/stoppage is through a Stage I clearance drill, requiring the operator to "Tap-Rack-Assess." If a Stage I clearance does not work after a second attempt, then the operator must perform a Stage II clearance drill that requires the removal of the magazine from the firearm. Through practice, these clearance drills will become second nature and instinctual if a malfunction/stoppage were to occur.

MALFUNCTIONS

There are also some common errors in malfunction/stoppage clearances. Not working around the gun, not recognizing the problem, and relying upon others to fix the problem are some. Not following the Tap-Rack-Assess drill and repeatedly attempting the Stage I clearance drill, instead of using the procedures in a Stage II clearance drill to correct the problem are additional mistakes made by operators. Like the other fundamentals and tactics discussed in this book, proper training and practice is the key to mastering the clearing of malfunctions and stoppages in the semi-automatic pistol.

REFERENCES

HP White Laboratories (2004). Glossary of Gun Malfunctions, HPW-TP-0103.00. Retrieved January 20, 2004, from www.hpwhite.com.

Introduction

A police officer should always think in a tactical perspective. This tactical perspective occurs prior to and during the one's shift. Thinking in a tactical perspective should occur on the way to the call, during the call or traffic stop, and when an officer is made aware of a situation. Part of this tactical planning involves using cover and concealment in order to prevent oneself from being seen -- "If you can be seen, you can be shot."

This chapter will begin with a review of the principles of using cover, providing the reader with a review of the initial points on using cover. It will also review the principles of concealment and review the cover and concealment hierarchy. This chapter will also review the fundamentals of using the glancing and controlling methods of shooting from cover, from the standing, kneeling and prone positions.

Cover

**Figure 89
Forms of Cover**

Cover can be thought of as anything that will stop a projectile or bullet. It can protect all or part of a person's body. Some examples of cover in an urban environment include large tree trunks, fire hydrants, street curbs, brick walls, cement dividers on highways and construction zones, telephone poles, and steel posts. Other trainers propose that body armor itself is a form of cover as it is designed to stop a projectile. While body armor will usually stop a projectile, a police officer, however, should never rely upon their body armor solely as a form of "moving cover." Body armor as a form of "moving cover" should be considered only as a secondary form of cover.

In some cases, what one person may consider as cover is not actually cover. Take for example, a police vehicle. In many instances, police officers perceive that their vehicle is an armored personnel carrier. It is not. Some parts of the police vehicle may stop a projectile; others will not. Consider, for example, a car door. A typical car door is constructed of lighter gauge sheet metal and plastic. It will not readily stop a projectile. On the other hand, if the officer can place himself between the threat and the engine block of the vehicle (that is built of cast iron and other dense objects), this will usually serve as cover and stop a projectile.

Initial Points on Using Cover

Some points to consider when using cover include:

- If you have a choice always select cover.
- Be behind cover whenever you can.
- Use cover when initiating any action at all.
- If an officer cannot aggressively use cover, make sure there is always a form of cover between the officer and threat that the officer can move to, if necessary.
- Never give up cover unless forced to do so. Even if a suspect is "down" or incapacitated, for example, the officer should not give up cover and approach the threat. The officer using cover should call for backup, if available, and let the backup approach the downed threat while the cover officer "covers down" on the threat to protect the approaching contact officer.

Moving from Cover

While an officer should never give up cover, in some situations, an officer may be forced to move from cover when the existing cover is somehow defeated or when there is a better form of cover that the officer can safely and tactically move to. The officer may also be required to move from a position of cover to protect others from the action(s) of the offender or to get a better angle of attack. For example, if there is an active shooter, the officer may be forced (because of their duty to protect others) to move from their position of cover to aggressively pursue and stop the threat, using that cover and concealment that is available to them.

If an officer has determined that they need to move from cover, some points to consider include the following:

- Only move from cover when forced to do so.
- Decide where to go in advance. An officer must plan their movements prior to moving from the existing position of cover. It does not make sense tactically to move out from cover and then search for cover while in an exposed position.
- Check the amount of remaining ammunition in the firearm before moving, if time and tactics allow. Depending upon the situation, a tactical reload can be conducted before leaving the protection of cover. This will ensure that the officer has a fully loaded firearm if they need to engage the threat while moving to the new position of cover.
- If possible, and when the situation allows it, the officer should inform fellow officers of where they are moving.
- Movement to cover should be erratic and short in duration. An officer does not want to expose himself for long periods of time. They need to stay under the threat's reaction time when moving. The officer should also move fast toward cover.
- The officer must be prepared to deliver controlled and accurate fire at the threat, if necessary, when moving from cover to cover.
- If advantageous and safe to do so, an officer should move to a better form of cover. The new cover, for example, could be larger in size, protecting the officer's entire body. It may also be located in a better tactical position.

Concealment

Concealment is an object or effect that will hide all or part of the body. Concealment does not provide protection from projectiles or bullets. It offers limited, if any, protection from the threat. The purpose of using concealment is to make sure that the human body is more difficult for the aggressor to see. Using concealment also allows an officer to observe suspect movements and locations, and more time to locate and identify a position of cover (and move

Figure 90
Forms of Concealment

to it) in a tactical manner. It also allows an officer to direct the positioning of other officers responding to a call. While concealment may be effective, an officer should always attempt to replace concealment with cover, whenever possible.

Concealment can be a physical object and/or an effect. As an object, concealment is something physical that will "break up" or conceal all or part of the body. Some examples of physical forms of concealment include bushes, the car door on a police cruiser, angles, elevations or depressions (such as ditches on the sides of the road), high grasses, and walls that may not be a form of cover. It may also include furniture in a house and bar stools in restaurants. Various types of fences can also be considered concealment. For example, chain link and picket fences cannot be expected to stop projectiles. These objects, however, will break up the image of an officer who is trying to tactically approach a home or retreat from a potentially dangerous encounter.

Concealment can also be an effect. An effect is a non-physical property that can be thought of as anything that creates an illusion. Types of concealment include fog, darkness, and even distance. Consider for example, the use of depth as a form of concealment. In many situations a police officer may be observing the movements or actions of a potentially dangerous subject from inside a structure, looking out a window. If an officer stands directly in front of the window, they can be easily seen. If, however, the officer stays "deep" in a room and looks out the window, distance as an effect, combined with lighting factors and the glare from the window, could offer a degree of concealment from the threat. In other cases, concealment could simply consist of an officer changing their profile, so they could not be readily seen by the threat. Instead of standing, for example, an officer could simply crouch down, crawl, or position themselves in a prone shooting position.

One common concealment effect that is heavily used in law enforcement is light. On traffic stops, for example, officers use their "take down" lights and/or spotlights to illuminate the interior of the stopped vehicle, so they can easily see into the interior to identify any potential threats that exist in the vehicle's compartment. At the same time, the spotlight's glare prevents the suspect from looking in the direction of the patrol car and advancing officer. In many cases, however, police only use this tactic in low light situations. In the context of using light as a form of concealment, however, lights can be used tactically in daylight situations. In full daylight, for example, if a suspect should exit the vehicle with a firearm and face the police vehicle, they may be temporarily blinded by the lights, simply because the take down lights are brighter than the existing daylight. At a minimum, the bright lights would require the suspect's eyes to adjust, giving the officer the opportunity to react to the threat and move to cover/concealment. In dim light or nighttime situations, meanwhile, the use of "take down" lights would allow the officer to retreat from the brightly lit area to an area of darkness. In this situation, the suspect would be fully illuminated and their eyes would again have to adjust from the bright light to darkness, giving the officer time to react.

Other Concealment Effects

The Police Uniform – Does the uniform & its accessories serve to conceal or reveal the officer? Consider how the color of the uniform and various "shiny" objects on the uniform (hat badge and shield) may serve to reveal an officer's position.

Sound – In many instances police officers have loose change in their pockets and keys that rattle. These and other sounds may reveal an officer's location and/or alert a threat that the officer is approaching them. To avoid this issue, officers should conduct a sound test: jump up and down. If something makes noise, secure it so it doesn't, or get rid of it.

As pointed out in these examples, concealment can be used in a variety of dynamic and/or high-risk settings. Concealment can also be used in static or low-risk settings. An officer can use concealment tactics in their everyday activities. These tactics may be as simple as not walking out in the open when approaching homes. As an alternative the officer could follow tree lines or hedges to partially conceal themselves as they approach the location of the call.

An officer should also recognize the limitations of concealment. Some of the limitations include:

- It provides no protection from lines of fire.
- It provides little or no protection if the threat(s) observed the officer's movement into the position of concealment.
- The officer's profile may still be able to be partially seen by the threat.

The Cover & Concealment Hierarchy

As pointed out in this chapter, cover and concealment is very beneficial. One of the most important benefits is simply the fact that if an officer cannot be readily seen, it will be very difficult for a perpetrator to shoot the officer. Cover/concealment also provides time for target identification, and it provides a greater amount of time for the officer to mentally and physically prepare for an encounter and evaluate a situation. Cover/concealment also

259

provides the best location from where a police officer can issue verbal challenges and commands to threats, conduct reloads, and clear malfunctions. It is simply the best place to be in a gunfight. In the open position, meanwhile, an officer has none of the above advantages.

A police officer should always use cover/concealment whenever it is available (remember: "if you be seen, you can be shot"). To ensure full protection, an officer should follow the cover & concealment hierarchy, which is shown in Figure 14-1.

**Figure 14-1
Cover & Concealment
Hierarchy**

| **COVER** |
| *Use Whenever Available* |
| **CONCEALMENT** |
| *Use When Cover Is Not Available* |
| **OPEN POSITION** |
| *NEVER be out in the Open* |

As pointed out in Figure 14-1, an officer should never be out in the open. An officer must always think tactically and place either a form of cover or concealment between himself and the potential threat. Cover is always the best tactic to use because it will stop a bullet/projectile. Concealment, meanwhile, is the next best alternative. The worst alternative is being out in the open, which an officer should never allow himself to be in.

A key to remember when using and considering this hierarchy is the fact that in the majority of situations, the officer has a great deal of control over the threat environment. For example, an officer can reposition himself to ensure that they have a form of cover/concealment between himself and the potential threat.

The use of cover and concealment must also be considered in a 360-degree perspective. When considering cover and concealment in a 360-degree perspective, an officer may be exposed without knowing it. For example, an officer may believe that they are completely behind cover; nevertheless the top of their head is exposed because the threat has the benefit of elevation, where they can

Training Tip: A good tactical mindset combined with the C& C hierarchy can be practiced off-duty. When off-duty, look for forms of Cover and Concealment and visualize how and when you would use cover or concealment in a force-related situation. These mental exercises could save your life in a real-life situation.

see over the top of the officer's cover. In building searches, meanwhile, officers should also be aware that a threat could be above and/or below their field of view because the building is multistoried. The same issue could exist in responding to residential calls where the threat could be located in a basement or on the second floor, while the officer is on the first floor. At the same time, however, an officer can use this 360-degree perspective as a tactical advantage. An officer, for example, could position himself above a threat, or they could keep cover behind them (as well as in front of them). They could even use forms of concealment above them (i.e. trees and stairways) to further protect or conceal their movements.

Using Cover

In some situations, individuals may perceive that shooting from behind a position of cover is more difficult than shooting from an open position. It is not. Regardless of if the officer is equipped with their pistol, rifle or shotgun, any type of firearm can be effectively used from a position of cover, as long as the officer follows the fundamentals of shooting and the basic points of using cover. While this section reviews the principles of shooting from a position of cover, these same moves apply when shooting from a position of concealment.

One of the keys to moving from a position of cover is that the movements must be fluid, smooth and fast. Shooting, meanwhile, should be accurate and controlled with an emphasis on trigger control and sight alignment. The movements should also be as similar as possible to those movements already used by shooter when not using cover. As this section will point out, the vast majority of the shooting fundamentals do not change. All that does change, however, is that the officer now has some type of barrier between himself and the threat that he must learn how to work around, using sound tactics, combined with the principle of the economy of motion. Listed below are the major points of using cover.

- *Use cover aggressively*

  Cover should be considered in the following context: Cover will protect you - not the threat. Let the threat invade your cover. This means that the shooter must use cover in a tactically aggressive manner. A general principle related to the use of cover is that the officer should never be closer than arm's length to it. By keeping some distance from the edge of cover, the field of view (based on angles) and response time increases, giving an officer the tactical edge. Using cover aggressively also means that the shooter is

261

prepared for the threat to emerge or break into their area of cover. This means that the shooter must maintain sight alignment behind cover in anticipation that the threat may "charge" or break into the officer's area of cover.

A shooter should never use cover passively. Using cover in a passive manner is when the shooter is not using cover to their fullest tactical advantage. The shooter, for example, may be too close to the cover (i.e. their back against the wall or sucking up right next to it) where they are simply hiding behind cover and are not tactically prepared to engage the threat. In other situations, meanwhile, the officer may not even have their gun drawn to engage the threat, or they may not be focused on the edge of cover in anticipation of the threat's aggressive actions.

- *Never give up cover*

  Once cover is achieved, the officer should not give that cover up. The only time cover is given up is when there is better cover available and the officer knows that they can safely move to that form of cover to gain a tactical advantage. Another reason to give up cover is simply because the officer was forced to do so.

- *Never extend the firearm past cover*

  The unknown/danger area is beyond the plane or edge of cover (as shown in Figure 14-2). In some instances, for example, an officer may accidentally extend the firearm in front of the wall or other form of cover. Extending a firearm into unknown territory could result in the weapon being stripped from the officer and possibly used against them.

- *Establish sight alignment prior to breaking the plane or edge of cover*

  With sight alignment already initiated behind cover, all the shooter will have to do is establish a proper sight picture when breaking the plane of cover. If an officer waits to establish sight alignment after they break the edge of cover, their actual exposure time to the threat will increase, due to the time it takes to acquire proper sight alignment and the subsequent sight picture.

- *Make sure you are under the reaction time of the offender*

One of the keys to breaking cover is that the shooter must stay under the threat's reaction time. This can be easily achieved if the officer is prepared for and plans his movements before he breaks the edge of cover and exposes himself to the threat. Without planning in advance, the officer will have to make decisions and take appropriate action beyond the edge of cover. This decision making, of course, will take too much time, allowing the threat to react to the officer's actions.

- *Never come out from cover from the same position or location twice in a row*

An officer must mix up or change his shooting position when exposing himself to the threat environment. Coming out from the same exposure or edge of cover consecutively (regardless of what technique is used), could lead to the threat anticipating and expecting the officer to reappear from the same location. Knowing where the officer will appear from the edge of cover will decrease the threat's response time to the officer's actions, placing the officer in a tactical disadvantage.

- *The officer must stay underneath the threat's reaction time when breaking the edge of cover*

The key to using cover is to adopt the proper stance from behind cover, mentally prepare to engage the threat, break the edge of cover, establish the sight picture, shoot (if deemed necessary) and immediately move back behind cover. However, in many cases an officer will "hang out" from the edge of cover (depending upon their tactics) after delivering controlled and accurate fire to the threat. This is a poor tactic, since it allows the threat the time to react to the officer's actions, subsequently allowing the threat to possibly deliver accurate and controlled fire toward at the officer.

- *Expose as little of the body as possible for the shortest period of time*

An officer should make his profile to the threat as small as possible. A smaller profile means a smaller target for the threat to shoot at, increasing the odds that the officer will not be struck by the bullet or projectile. An officer should strive to make sure that as little of his body is exposed to the threat as possible when breaking the edge of cover.

- *Never use the cover as support for the firearm*

In some situations, an officer may rest the frame of their firearm against the edge of cover. This is a tactically unsound and an outdated technique. Techniques such as this one should **never** be done. Resting a firearm (revolver, pistol or even a long arm) on the side, top or edge of cover will disrupt the normal "feel" of the recoil of the firearm. This will affect the ability of the shooter to effectively follow through with more shots, if necessary. In the case of pistols, resting a firearm against a surface could also impede the function of the slide, causing a shooter-induced stoppage/malfunction.

> **Training Tip:** Always use both the glancing and controlling techniques in the standing, kneeling and prone positions when training. This will ensure that in an actual gunfight, you will be prepared for and be able to use any position possible. Remember – we fight the way we train. If we never practiced the technique, we probably won't use it in a gunfight.

- *Never come out over the top of cover*

An officer should always emerge from the edge of cover from the sides, not the top. Officers should avoid emerging from the top edge of cover on account of the fact that the top of the head will emerge first before the eyes (and gun) can establish sight alignment and the sight picture. Because the top of the head is exposed before the gun, the officer will have a slower reaction time in relation to the threat. The threat, for example, may see the top of the head emerge from cover, react, and shoot at the officer before he, in turn, could shoot back.

The Glancing and Controlling Techniques

There are two primary methods of using cover while shooting. They include the glancing and controlling techniques. What specific technique that will be used depends upon the situation that the officer has encountered and the type of cover and concealment that exists. With either technique, however, the officer must give up a certain degree of cover and consider four essential factors. These include 1) staying under the reaction time of the threat; 2) the relative position of the officer to the threat; 3) maintaining a tactical advantage; and, 4) to always be prepared to shoot, if warranted. The specific techniques for the glancing and controlling techniques are described below.

The Glancing Technique

The glancing technique, as the name implies, is when the police officer glances or "peeks" out from around the edge of cover to check the other (or unknown) side of cover for potential threats. After checking the other side of cover, the officer then quickly moves back to a position of cover. When using the glancing technique, an officer can "break" from cover using several different exposures or positions. These positions can include strong and weak side standing, kneeling, and the prone position. The term "strong side" refers to the shooter coming out from the edge of exposure that is the same as their gun hand. "Weak side" meanwhile, means that the officer comes out from the edge of cover, opposite of their strong hand.

Regardless of what shooting position is used, the principle of economy of motion must be observed. The shooter must also maintain a balanced shooting platform in all of these positions, making sure that the upper body and shoulders are positioned correctly above the hips and feet when standing or kneeling. The specifics of each shooting position are described below.

Strong & Weak Side Standing

When using the strong and weak side standing exposure, the officer is in a standing position where they rock out from the edge of cover to check and react to potential threats that may be present on the other side of cover in the unknown or danger zone. Depending upon the position of the threat in the "danger zone," all a shooter has to do is lean out on their strong side and identify and engage the threat, if necessary, exposing as little of their body as possible in the process. Some of the specific points that an officer needs to consider when standing and using the glancing technique are listed below.

- The stance does not change when shooting from behind cover. All that changes is the simple fact that there is some form of cover between the threat and officer.

- Sight alignment must be established prior to breaking the edge of cover. Establishing sight alignment on the edge of cover provides the shooter the tactical edge to engage any threat that should try to overtake his or her cover. Having the sights lined up on the edge of cover with proper sight alignment also ensures that the officer will be able to rapidly acquire a sight picture when breaking the edge of cover.

- When breaking the edge of cover, the officer should expose as little of his or her body as possible to the threat. The officer should strive to only have part of the firearm and part of the head/eyes exposed to establish a proper sight picture when breaking the edge of cover. The entire body does not have to be exposed to deliver controlled and accurate fire. The only thing that needs to be exposed is one or both eyes, and the pistol.

Figure 91
Breaking the Plane of Cover

- The officer should be positioned as close as possible to the edge of cover, making sure that no part of the body (such as an elbow or knee) is exposed to the threat from the position of cover.

- To break the plane of cover in the standing position, all the shooter needs to do is to bend that knee that is closest to that side of cover that they are engaging the threat from. Depending upon the stance, the officer will need to bend their knee forward or perhaps slightly to the side. By bending the knee, the body will naturally break the plane of cover (as shown in Figure 91) where the officer will be able to see the threat environment and if necessary, deliver accurate and controlled fire at the threat. Nothing else regarding the stance, etc. should change. For example, the feet should not shuffle or move. To move back to the position of cover, meanwhile, the officer can simply straighten their knee, which results in the body effortlessly moving back behind the edge of cover.

Figure 92
Stepping out from Cover

- Eye dominance and the strong hand do not change. The shooter should not switch their eyes, depending upon the edge of cover they are coming out from. They should also not switch hands. Instead, they should adjust their stance to accommodate for the slight differences they may encounter with barricade shooting.

If the threat is beyond the initial break in the plane of cover, the shooter needs to further extend their body out from the edge of cover to locate and perhaps stop the threat. To accomplish this task, all the shooter has to do is to lean and then step out sideways from the edge of cover to check their unknown/danger area as shown in figure 92. To accomplish this task, the shooter must economize their movement, only moving those parts of the body that need to be moved. To step out, the shooter will have to step and move either their right strong foot (if coming out on the right) or their left strong foot (if coming out on the left) sideways. Their other foot, meanwhile, should not move. It should stay firmly planted on the ground. The shoulders, meanwhile, should remain as level as possible and be positioned over the hips to maintain an effective and balanced stance. Immediately after checking the unknown area/danger zone the shooter must return back to a position of cover, reversing their movements in the process.

Strong & Weak Side Kneeling

The kneeling position, when properly conducted, provides a solid shooting platform. Some of the steps that need to be performed to ensure economy of motion and speed with the strong and weak side kneeling position include the following:

- The knee that is closest to the edge of cover is resting on the ground. The long bones of that leg are perpendicularly lined up with the edge of cover. For example (and as shown in Figures 93 and 94), an officer intending to break the right-hand plane of cover will have their right knee on the ground while the femur and tibia bones (the long bones of the leg) are perpendicular with the edge of cover. If an officer is going to expose himself by coming out on the left, the left knee should be on the ground.

Figure 93
Strong Side Kneeling

Figure 94
"Kneel"

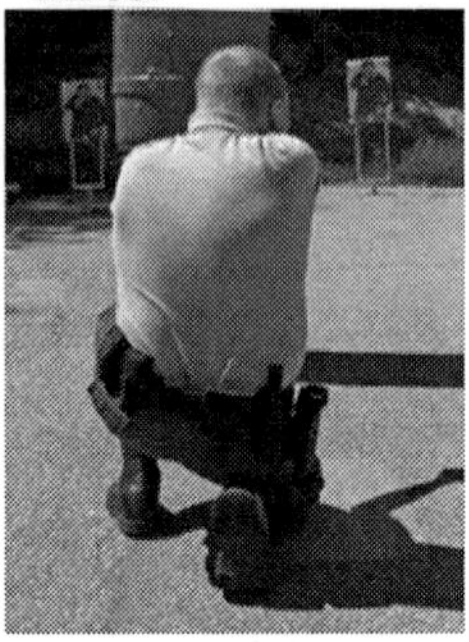

Figure 95
"Rotate Knee Out"

Figure 96
"Knee Out, Butt off
Heel"

- The weight of the body is resting on the heel of the strong foot and on the support side foot that is resting flat on the ground. The entire weight of the body must be directed straight down (not at an angle) to the ground.
- The strong foot toe is rolled under the foot, while the buttocks is resting on the heel of the strong side foot. Resting the buttocks on the heel of the boot ensures that the shooter's weight is transferred straight down through the foot and to the ground. Having the body's weight bearing on the heel of the foot is also important because the strong side foot needs to rotate on its toes and because the strong side knee needs to be able to freely rotate.
- The toe of the strong foot remains rolled under the strong side foot throughout the course of fire.

- The officer's weak side foot is flat while the heel is planted firmly on the ground. This leg is not kneeling. The knee is upright and is pointing toward the threat. To make sure that the heel remains firmly planted on the ground, the support side heel should be lined up and evenly aligned (i.e. heel to knee) with the strong side knee.

- The legs should be about shoulder width apart. The officer's stance should not be open, or forming an open "V" to the threat. If the stance is in an open or "V" shape, it may impair the shooter's movement when breaking the edge of cover.

- The back is straight, as if the officer were sitting in a straight-backed chair. The shoulders should remain level (forming a "T" relative to the hips), to ensure proper balance. Leaning too far forward (which will also displace the officer's weight forward) will result in an improper and unstable shooting base, causing a loss of balance and perhaps poor sight alignment.

- The head should remain level (chin thrust outward and not tucked to the neck) to ensure balance, proper sight alignment, and a proper sight picture.

- Eye dominance and the strong hand do not change. The shooter should not switch from using their dominant eye. Also, they should not switch hands. Instead, they should adjust their stance to accommodate for the slight differences they may encounter with barricade shooting to effectively use their dominant eye and master grip.

Figure 97
"Butt Back on Knee"

Figure 98
"Rotate Knee In"

If the threat is beyond the initial break in the plane of cover, the shooter needs to further extend their body out from the edge of cover to locate and perhaps stop the threat. To accomplish this task, the knee needs to be extended from the edge of cover to a certain degree in order to increase the officer's angle of attack. This will require following all of the basics of shooting from the kneeling position with some minor modifications that are listed here and shown in Figures 94 - 98.

- To make sure that the knee can rotate out from the edge of cover, the weight of the shooter's body should be resting on the strong side heel, not the knee. This will allow the knee to pivot.
- As the knee rotates outward, in order to gain additional distance, the officer's buttocks comes off the heel of the boot. The back remains straight or perpendicular to the ground during this movement. In effect, the shooter picks their body up after the knee rotates outward.
- At the same time that the knee is rotating outward, the shooter should be lifting their body by pushing against the ground with their weak side foot, whose heel is firmly planted on the ground, which is in line with the knee that is resting on the ground (see Figures 95 & 96). Pushing off with the weak side foot, in conjunction with lifting the body straight up, will naturally angle the body outward, increasing the angle of attack.
- The head remains upright (chin out), while the shoulders remain as level or as parallel to the ground as possible, making sure that the shoulders remain positioned above the hips and knees as much as possible.
- To move back to a position of cover, all the officer needs to do is to rotate the knee inward, back behind the edge of cover and return their buttocks back on the heel of the strong foot (see Figures 97 & 98). Because the majority of the body's weight is placed back on the heel, it is quite easy to rotate the knee back behind cover, closing the stance in the process. This should be a quick, fluid movement.
- Throughout this process, the support side foot should remain firmly planted. It should not move. The weight on the support side foot should be on the heel - not the toes. If the majority of the weight is transferred to the toes or balls of this foot, it could cause a balance displacement (and sight alignment) issue since the majority of the body's weight is transferred forward.

Prone Position

Depending upon the use of available cover, an officer may be required to break the edge of cover from a prone (or lying down) position. The prone position may be a little difficult to perform because the officer's mobility is more impaired, relative to other positions, due to the fact that the bulk of their body is on the ground. Nevertheless, the prone position can be effectively used behind cover, if necessary. Like the standing and kneeling positions, shooting prone requires balance, coordination, and practice. Some of the points to consider when using the prone position are listed below.

- The body's profile should be as small as possible.
- Eye dominance and the strong hand do not change. The shooter should not switch from using their dominant eye. They should also not switch hands. Instead, they should adjust their stance to accommodate for the slight differences they may encounter with barricade shooting.
- The head should be upright and level. The chin should not be tucked, but thrust outward to increase the shooter's field of view.
- The shoulders should be aligned with the spine at a right angle. The shooter should imagine that their shoulders form a "T" with the spine. Keeping the shoulder's square with the spine, instead of having an arched or angled position, will increase comfort and reduce muscle fatigue.
- The body should be angled inward approximately 10-20 degrees from the edge of cover. Angling the body inward from the edge of cover will ensure that it is not exposed to the threat environment.
- The legs should be spread about shoulder width apart to provide additional stability for the body.
- The feet should be relaxed and flat. The arches of the feet should rest on the ground, or the heels should face inward. Resting the feet on their sides creates a more stable shooting platform. In some instances, for example, a shooter may attempt to rest their toes on the ground. Attempting to balance the toes on the ground, however, creates muscle tension, and an unstable base.
- Both elbows are bent and resting on the ground. Using the bones, instead of the muscles, to support the body ensures a solid foundation. It also reduces muscle fatigue.
- The support side knee, depending upon comfort, may be bent inward and angled in toward the crotch. Bending the knee may reduce the pressure from the weight of the body on the abdomen and chest, increasing comfort and the ability to breathe correctly. For example, if the shooter is coming out of the right side, they may want to angle their left knee upward, toward the crotch, to improve their level of comfort and breathing.
- With the sights lined up on the edge of cover, the shooter can then slightly roll their body beyond the edge of cover. The elbow that is on the edge of cover should not come off the ground. The opposite

271

elbow, meanwhile, should cant, rotate, and follow the motion of the body, stopping when the edge of cover is broken.

- To return to the position of cover, the officer can then shift their weight in the opposite direction, rolling back behind cover and return to the original prone position.

The Controlling Technique

The goal of the controlling technique is to gain and own property. Unlike the glancing technique where the officer moves back in behind cover, with the controlling technique, the officer does not retreat back behind cover unless they are forced do so. Instead, the officer holds their position. Like the glancing technique, an officer must maintain a balanced stance, regardless of if they are shooting from the standing, kneeling or prone positions.

The objective behind the controlling technique is to gain and keep "property" through the use of angles. More specifically, the goal is to reduce the size of the unknown area or danger zone in a controlled, tactical manner. In order to gain control of this unknown area, the police officer must slowly increase their angle of control (or attack) into the unknown area. While gaining control of this unknown or danger area, meanwhile, the officer should expose as little of their body as possible to the potential threat.

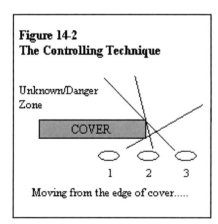

Figure 14-2
The Controlling Technique

Unknown/Danger Zone

COVER

1   2   3

Moving from the edge of cover.....

Perhaps the easiest way to gain an understanding of the controlling technique is to consider this technique as "cutting the pie" or turning cover. Figure 14-2 provides an example of cutting the pie to gain control of the unknown area or "danger zone." As shown in Figure 14-2, as a shooter moves further right from the edge of cover (From position 1 to position 3), their angle of control increases, reducing the size of the unknown area or danger zone where a threat may be located. Achieving this angle of control can be accomplished through a variety of stances or positions reviewed earlier in this chapter. An officer, for example, can readily gain control of the "danger zone" in a normal standing stance, a kneeling position, or even in a prone position.

To "cut the pie" in a tactical manner, the officer should use cover aggressively and not "hug" or be too close to it. Allowing distance between oneself and cover allows more time to react to any threats that may be on the other side of cover. It also decreases the size of the angle, reducing the size of the danger zone, while increasing the zone of control.

Consider, for example, if the reader has ever bumped into somebody when walking around a blind corner. Perhaps it was because the corner was cut too tight, and in the process, they reduced their response time to the person coming from the other direction (who was behind cover). Turning cover wide will also result in getting a better angle of observation and control on the other side of cover.

Conclusion

A police officer should always have a tactical mindset. Part of operating in a tactical perspective is using cover and concealment. Cover is anything that will stop a projectile or bullet. Cover can completely or partially protect a person, depending upon its size. Concealment, meanwhile, is an object or effect that entirely or partially hides a person. However, it provides no protection from projectiles. To be tactically sound, a police officer must know the difference between cover and concealment, and use them at all times, if possible.

The cover and concealment hierarchy calls for the use of cover first. If cover is not available, then the officer should use concealment. A police officer should never be out in the open, fully exposing himself to a threat. When using cover and concealment, depending upon the situation, the glancing or controlling technique can be used to break from the edge of cover. The glancing technique requires the officer to "peek" or glance on the other side of cover for a threat and then move back into a position of cover. The controlling technique also requires an officer to move from a position of cover. Unlike the glancing technique, however, the officer slowly moves out from the edge of cover, decreasing the angle of the threat or danger zone by "cutting the pie." The goal behind this technique is to occupy space (i.e. owning and keeping real estate), decrease the threat zone by increasing the officer's angle of observation, and not give up this newly acquired territory unless forced to do so. If necessary, however, the officer can then tactically retreat back to their position of cover.

Introduction

A police-related shooting is a serious event for everyone involved. On an individual aspect, a shooting will impact those officers who are directly and indirectly involved in a variety of physiological and psychological ways before, during, and after the event. In fact, research has shown that police officers rank shooting and killing someone as the top stressor in their profession (Swanson, Territo & Taylor, 2005). At the same time, a police-related shooting can also be examined from a legal and administrative aspect. Police administrators and the prosecutor's office will need and want to ensure that all applicable policies and procedures were followed and that the shooting conformed to all laws. As a result of these demands, a police shooting is a complicated and stressful event for both officers and administrators.

This chapter will examine some of the common procedures that must be followed after a police shooting. It will begin with a review of some of the major points related to managing the scene in the context of tactical, administrative, and legal concerns. This chapter then provides the reader with an understanding of the physiological and psychological processes that occur with officers who are directly and indirectly involved in a shooting. It also includes various counseling interventions that are provided to officers who are involved in shootings. This chapter also covers post shooting administrative and legal procedures in addition to those specific rights that officers have during a post-shooting investigation.

Managing a Post-Shooting Scene

A shooting is a sudden and dynamic event that is often short in duration. Managing a post-shooting scene, however, is slow and time consuming, requiring a series of slow and deliberate actions for the officer's safety. This process must also be slow and methodical in order to ensure the safety of other officers and civilians in the area, and to guarantee that various administrative and procedural requirements are followed. Some of the key points that a police officer needs to consider include using proper tactics, calling for backup, securing suspects, providing first aid, and preserving the crime scene.

Proper Tactics

Immediately following a shooting, the officer(s) should adhere to all sound police tactics. As pointed out in the Follow Through chapter, an officer should make sure that the threat has been stopped, and scan the threat environment for additional threats or adversaries. Consistent with the issues reviewed in the Cover and Concealment chapter, the officer(s) must also maintain

> **Training Tip:** Incorporate the key points of managing a post-shooting scene into your firearms training. Have officers use training guns (no actual firearms ammunitions, etc. on the range) and have them go through a mock shooting (using all firearms tactics) where they have to request backup, secure the suspect(s), provide first aid, process the scene and write detailed incident reports.

a position of cover and not give up cover unless they are forced to do so. It is very important that the officer holds a position of cover and issues all verbal commands from behind the edge of cover. This is based on the assumption that the suspect may not be completely incapacitated. As a result of this fact, officers must determine if the threat has been neutralized or stopped from a position of cover. A common response toward a suspect that has only been wounded and not completely stopped, however, is to immediately break cover and approach and secure the suspect. This would be a tactically unsound and dangerous action. Officers should also consider the fact that the suspect could be feigning unconsciousness, waiting for the officer to give up cover and approach them, so they or another threat that has not been identified can attack the officer.

From this position of cover, a police officer can control the threat environment and any suspects that were stopped. Cover should be maintained until backup arrives and the officers have determined that it is safe to approach and secure the suspect(s). The only exception to breaking cover without backup is when an officer is forced to do so or there is no backup available. In situations where backup is not available, the officer should move from positions of cover to cover, use concealment, and never place themselves in the open position, if at all possible.

While holding cover, an officer should not re-holster his sidearm and/or secure his long-arm immediately. Instead, the firearm should be positioned on the edge of cover in anticipation that the threat has not been fully stopped, or that there are additional threats that the officer has not stopped or identified. Depending upon the situation, the officer can use the controlling or glancing method of holding cover and monitor the threat environment.

Officers should also keep in mind that there might be innocent civilians in the immediate area that are in danger because the scene is not yet fully secure. If there are citizens in the threat environment and its surrounding area, the officer needs to control the movement and actions of those citizens to protect them. For example, if the shooting occurred in a residential or highly populated area, some citizens (out of curiosity or out of a civic need to help the officer in some way) may inadvertently expose themselves to the threat. In these situations, officers will need to issue verbal commands from their position of cover, instructing civilians to stay in a position of cover and not approach the scene because it is a dangerous setting for them.

Backup

Immediately following the shooting, the officer should also request backup. Backup is necessary to assist in taking control of the scene, to protect the public, attend to the injured, and to assist in crime scene preservation and the processing of evidence. As those officers involved in the shooting may also be in a heightened state of anxiety and experiencing both physical and psychological trauma from the shooting, they will be in no condition to deal with the scene, further requiring the need for backup officers.

When requesting backup, the officer must also request that supervisory personnel also arrive to take command of the scene. Supervisory personnel must be present to ensure that all policies and procedures are being followed and that the scene is preserved. Supervisory personnel can attend to the officers at the scene, deal with the media, and coordinate the preservation and collection of evidence, to name of few of the activities that they will be charged with in a police shooting.

Securing the Suspect(s)

Another key responsibility is to secure the suspect(s) by handcuffing them. A common misperception is that since the suspect has been shot and is perhaps semi-conscious or unconscious, they are no longer a threat, and for that reason they do not have to be handcuffed. Officers should keep in mind, however, that the suspect may not have a life-threatening wound, or they may regain consciousness at the scene or on the way to the hospital. As a consequence, officers may have to use some level of force to control the suspect's actions, including handcuffing them to prevent their escape and possibly injuring others.

Handcuffing the suspect may require giving up cover. Under the contact/cover principle, the contact officer should approach the suspect (using all available forms of cover and concealment, if possible, including their police car if necessary) and handcuff them. This individual should be the backup officer who was requested by the initial responding officer. The cover officer, meanwhile, can "cover" or protect that officer that broke cover to approach and secure the suspect.

The reason why the backup officer should approach is threefold. First, the initial cover officer must keep a weapon on the suspect. Because they are already in a position of cover, they are most likely the best suited to provide cover. Next, the initial officer may not have the physical capacity to handcuff a suspect because of the physiological effects the officer is experiencing from the shooting. The officer may also have injuries that prevent them from securing the suspect(s). Last, the officer involved in the shooting may be experiencing a variety of emotional reactions as a result of the shooting. In some cases, they may not be capable of securing a suspect because of these emotions. In other cases, the officer may be experiencing a sense of anger or rage where they may vent this anger against the suspect and use more force than necessary to secure the suspect. This could later result in a use of force complaint and lawsuit against that officer and the police agency.

First Aid

A fundamental duty of all police officers is to preserve and protect life. Because of this, officers must also immediately notify dispatch that EMS/ medical personnel are needed at the scene to provide medical attention for all individuals who were injured. Besides the physical injuries, EMS personnel can also provide emotional support for those who are experiencing psychological trauma from the shooting.

Once the scene has been cleared or determined safe and all suspects are secured, first aid must be given to all individuals requiring medical attention, regardless if they are suspects or innocents. Providing first aid must be based on the principles of triage, where the most severely injured receive medical attention before those who have less life threatening injuries, regardless of their status as a suspect or an innocent civilian. In some situations this may mean that the suspect receives medical attention first over innocent civilians. Providing first aid to the suspect may be a difficult concept to grasp. Keep in mind, however, that even though the suspect a few minutes ago engaged in a deadly force attack against the officer or a civilian, they are no longer a threat. That threat has been stopped. Now, they are a human being that is in need of medical attention.

Crime Scene Processing

Once the area has been determined safe, the area must be treated as a crime scene where officers must engage in those activities associated with evidence collection and preservation. Collected evidence will assist in building a case that deadly force was necessary and justified in stopping the suspect(s). The collected evidence will also prove to the public that the shooting conformed to departmental guidelines and all applicable laws regarding the use of force.

While specific guidelines vary among agencies regarding the collection and preservation of evidence, the goal of preserving the scene is to prove beyond a reasonable doubt that the person that was stopped was committing a crime that required the application of deadly force. Consequently, all evidence must be collected to prove that point. Depending upon departmental policies and procedures, some of the basic (and minimal) responsibilities include establishing and securing the crime scene perimeter, and securing any weapons that were used by the suspect(s) in the shooting. Once the scene is secure and a perimeter has been established, then other officers and evidence technicians can fully process the scene. Having other officers (perhaps from other agencies) process the scene will also reduce any issues or concerns that evidence was tampered with or altered by those directly involved in the shooting.

What Happens During a Shooting?

Officers must keep in mind that a shooting can be considered a traumatic event, as this type of incident may be considered a random, sudden, and arbitrary event, where the individuals involved (directly or indirectly) may experience various forms or levels of traumatic reactions to the event (Yeager & Roberts, 2003). Individuals involved in these situations may be facing a personal crisis as their usual coping mechanisms fail and they are suffering from some type of distress and functional impairment. In short, a situation like this could be thought of as a turning point in one's life (Yeager & Roberts, 2003). Sudden events that fall outside the normal range of ordinary human experiences can inflict severe psychological trauma or stress, and can overwhelm the coping skills of a person. These events are known as critical incidents (Kureczka, 1996).

There are three general stages that a police officer goes through after a shooting incident. According to Williams (1999), they include the exhilaration, remorse and the rationalization/acceptance stage. The exhilaration stage, which occurs immediately after the shooting and may last minutes or hours in length, can be characterized by the officer being grateful that they are alive and that they won the gunfight. The next stage is the remorse stage where the officer may experience some guilt associated with their actions and the feelings of exhilaration they experienced after the shooting. This stage may last for days, weeks, or forever. In the rationalization/acceptance stage, meanwhile, the officer takes a "me or them" position. This stage serves to rationalize their actions. And, it assists them in accepting that their actions were necessary and justifiable. This stage may continue throughout the remainder of the officer's life.

The above stages suggest that there are several physiological and psychological responses that occur during a shooting. These physiological and psychological responses, however, are not consistent from one person to another. Instead, as Peace and Porter (2004) point out, traumatic experiences are "subjective, and based on an individual's response to the event" (p. 1143). Some of the more common responses to a traumatic event include dissociative responses and problems in fully recalling the details of the event.

Acute Traumatic Dissociative Responses

Dissociation refers to an experience where a person's normal awareness is somehow altered from their normal state of being. According to Marmar, et al. (1996), dissociation occurs at the time of the event or when the person is trying to recall the event and their memory, identity, or perception of the environment is temporarily disrupted. This can be attributed to the fact that a person who experiences a traumatic event compartmentalizes or stores certain components or elements of the experience as isolated fragments rather than an integrated whole in their mind.

This dissociation or splitting of the experience is a coping tool. It protects the individual from "a full conscious appreciation of terror, helplessness, but at the cost of long-term difficulties in the integration and mastery of the event" (Marmar, 1996, p. 94). Some of these dissociative responses, according to Griffen, et al. (1997) may include the: 1) inability to recall important information that is not explained by normal forgetfulness (dissociative amnesia); 2) confusion about one's identity and assuming of a new identity (dissociative identity disorder); 3) persistent or recurrent feelings of detachment (depersonalization disorder); or, 4) sudden and unexpected travel (ex: the person states that they watching the shooting from above) accompanied by confusion and amnesia (dissociative fugue).

Dissociative responses are common in shootings. In one study of 115 officers involved in shootings, 90% reported experiencing a dissociative response, while 19% reported some form of memory impairment regarding details of the incident. The researchers from this study concluded that dissociative responses appear to be a normal mental state in shooting incidents. Because of dissociation, the authors questioned the ability of officers to give a full detailed account of the incident (Rivard, et al., 2002). However, peritraumatic dissociation (dissociation during an event) also varies among individuals. For example, a study involving approximately 200 emergency service personnel concluded that "rescue workers who are shy, inhibited, uncertain about their identity, or reluctant to take leadership roles, who have global cognitive styles, who believe their fate is determined by factors beyond their control, and who cope with critical incident trauma by emotional suppression and wishful thinking are at a higher risk for acute dissociative responses to trauma and subsequent posttraumatic stress disorder" (Marmar et, al, 1996, p. 94).

Perhaps one of the most common types of dissociative responses in a shooting is perceptual distortion. Research on police-related shootings has found that some police officers will experience perceptual distortions that can affect vision, hearing, balance, motor skills, time sense, and attentiveness (Rivard, et al. 2002). Research by Honig and Sultan (2004) on officer-involved shootings, for example, found the following perceptual disturbances:

- Sounds are quieter
- Tunnel vision
- Increased attention to detail
- Slowing of time
- Memory loss for certain parts of the incident
- Speeding up of time
- Louder sounds

Research by Klinger (2001) that examined the thoughts, feelings and perceptual distortions of 113 officers involved in shootings found that officers will experience a wide variety of thoughts and feelings during a gunfight, that also change over the course of the gunfight. The majority of the officers experienced fear and at least two types of perceptual distortions that included:

- 82% experienced diminished sound
- 56% experienced a heightened sense of visual detail
- 56% experienced slow motion during the shooting
- 51% experienced tunnel vision
- 23% experienced fast motion during the shooting

Klinger (2001) also found that visual distortions occur with officers before and during the firing of their weapon. He also found that officers experienced auditory exclusion or "blunting" just before the event, and a greater amount of auditory blunting when they fired their weapons. In the context of an officer's ability to recall how many rounds they fired, the majority of officers could recall the number of rounds they fired. However, it was also discovered that as the number of rounds fired increased, the ability of the officer(s) to accurately recall the number of rounds fired decreased.

Memory Recall Issues

There are several explanations on why an individual may not be able to fully recall a traumatic event. The traumatic memory argument proposes that a traumatic event triggers dissociation as a defensive coping mechanism where a person can only recall fragments of the event (Peace & Porter, 2004). Another explanation is based on how individuals process information in high-stress situations. In normal situations, individuals use a rational model for processing information, which relies upon conscious, analytical and deliberate cognitive processes. In a high stress situation, however, individuals engage in experiential thinking that is characterized by rapid and automatic responses, which in turn results in fragmented memories, instead of an integrated or holistic understanding of the event (Artwhol, 2001).

Amnesia may be another explanation. Scrivener and Safer (1988) report that individuals who suffer from psychological trauma may be unable to recall information because they may be suffering from retrograde and anterretrogade amnesia. Stedman's Medical Dictionary (2001) defines retrograde amnesia as "amnesia in reference to events that occurred before the trauma or disease that caused the condition" (p. 858). Anterretrograde amnesia meanwhile is the inability to remember ongoing events after the traumatic incident (Scrivener and Safer, 1988). Grossman and Siddle (1998) write that officers involved in shootings will experience critical incident amnesia. Although not a recognized condition in the fields of medicine and psychology, the term critical incident amnesia is useful in understanding that officers (as well as victims and witnesses to a traumatic event) may have memory recall problems because of the traumatic experience.

Aiding in Recall

While an officer may not be able to fully recall the details of an event immediately after it, some practices have been found to aid individuals in recalling the details of traumatic events. Some specific memory recall aids include allowing for sleep, the use of time in assisting in recall, using post event information as a recall aid, and having agencies use different types of interviewing techniques to assist the officer in recalling details of the event.

Sleep

Sleep has been identified as one way to assist police officers in recalling details of a traumatic event. Grossman and Siddle (1998) write that sleep serves to assist police officers in reconstructing the event. In order to reconstruct the event, the authors propose a series of interviews or steps to assist the officer in cognitively reconstructing the event, with sleep playing a major role in memory reconstruction and recall. Through the sleep process, the brain may be able to process and update information or data that has been stored. In order to ensure that this information is processed into the brain's long term memory, Grossman and Siddle recommend that the following steps be followed:

- An initial post-incident interview that is conducted as soon as possible after the event
- Within 24 hours of the officer's first sleep period, the officer(s) should be interviewed again
- A group interview/debrief following the completion of the individual interviews
- A second group interview conducted 2 to 3 days after the event

Time

Combined with sleep, time has also been found to assist in memory recall. Studies have found that trauma victims were able to recall details of the event months later, and that traumatic memories were more constant over time than positive memories. Furthermore, vividness/clarity, details and the individual's overall quality of memory remained high over time, with little increases in errors in recalling details of the event (Peace & Porter, 2004). In another study involving 90 individuals who watched a videotape of a burglary and violent shooting, their recall of the event improved over time, where they were able to recall more details at each of the four successive recall trials, up to two days after viewing the event. This phenomenon is referred to as hypermnesia, where a person has increased recall levels when they are exposed to repeated attempts to recall information (Scrivner & Safer, 1988).

Post Event Information (PEI)

If the incident involved multiple police officers, Post Event Information (PEI) may also be used to assist officers in recalling details of the event. The PEI process occurs when individuals who experienced the same event discuss that event. Through these conversations with others who experienced the same event, additional information can be recalled by the participants. While effective in assisting in recall, there may be some concerns with this process. Some research suggests that PEI discussions could actually lead to memory conformity issues. That is, a person's recall of an event could be influenced and altered through their discussions with other individuals involved in that particular event, where they essentially learn new material and do not recall information directly from the event. For example, in a study conducted by Gabbert et al. (2003), the researchers found that 71% of the individuals who discussed the events in a group setting prior to recalling the event alone, mistakenly recalled events. The authors concluded that normative and informational influences were factors. Normative influences basically mean that an individual may alter their recall of the event based on their need for social approval. Informational influences, meanwhile, are based on the fact that an individual may alter their recall of the event because they want to be more accurate.

Interviewing Techniques

Different types of interviewing techniques may also be used. A police officer may be interviewed using cognitive interview techniques where they are asked to recreate their experiences. They may be asked to recall the event from various starting points; they may be asked to recall the event from a different perspective (i.e. an observer to the event) to further enhance their recall; or they may be asked to close their eyes and use imagery to recall the event (Fisher, et al, 2000). Research has also found that allowing persons to freely report their account of the incident results in greater accuracy of recall. In the context of recalling the details of a shooting, this means that officers should be allowed to freely recall the event, without the interviewers using structured questions which, in turn, would structure the officer's responses (Koriat & Goldsmith, 1996).

Coping with Shooting-Related Stress

As discussed earlier in this chapter, a shooting will affect those officers involved in it in different ways and with varying levels of intensity. However, as pointed out by Yeager & Roberts (2003), "some stressors [like a police shooting] are so severe that almost everyone is susceptible to the overwhelming effects of the experience" (p. 9). While officers may be affected differently, a major point to consider is the simple fact that all officers involved in the shooting will experience some degree of stress. As pointed out by Waters (2002), survivors may experience "shock, disbelief, confusion, physical pain, shaking, crying, anger and guilt on the very first day" (p. 61). In other cases, officers may also experience resentment, denial, poor concentration and sleep problems. Individuals involved in the event may also have their sense of trust and security in persons destroyed (Yeager & Roberts, 2003).

Some research has been conducted on police officers' responses to traumatic events. Klinger's (2001) study on police shootings found that the five most reported common thoughts and feelings experienced at any point after the shooting included recurrent thoughts of the incident (83%), feelings of anxiety (40%), fear of legal and administrative problems (34%), elation (29%) and sadness (26%). The three most common physical responses following a shooting included trouble sleeping (48%), fatigue (46%), and crying (24%).

Additionally, a ten-year study by Honig and Sultan (2004) that interviewed 982 deputies 3-5 days after their involvement in a shooting found the following stressors:

- Approximately 50% of the deputies reported experiencing flashbacks, intrusive recollections and nightmares
- Approximately 50% reported that they experienced a sense of vulnerability or a heightened sense of danger
- 42% reported fears about future situations
- 40% reported feelings of rage or anger after the incident
- More than 33% reported increased startle responses, problems in concentrating and physical distress

These and other thoughts and psychological reactions require inter-vention by trained counselors or psychologists to assist the officer in coping with the after-effects of the shooting. Without adequate intervention, police officers may develop both short and long-term problems associated with the critical incident. Two of the more common disorders associated with a traumatic event include Acute Stress Disorder (ASD) and Post Traumatic Stress Disorder (PTSD).

Acute Stress Disorder

Acute Stress Disorder (ASD) can affect all individuals. According to the Diagnostic and Statistical Manual of Mental Disorders (DSM-IV-TR) (American Psychiatric Association, 2000), ASD occurs when a person is exposed to an extreme traumatic event accompanied by fear, horror, or helplessness. ASD's are stress reactions that occur from a period of two days to four weeks after the critical incident (Harvey & Bryant, 2002). An ASD diagnosis requires that the person experiences at least three dissociative symptoms: experiences significant anxiety, has a recurrent experience of the trauma, and experiences increased arousal within one month after exposure to the traumatic event.

Existing research provides an understanding of the nature and extent of ASD. One study, conducted on children who were injured by firearms, concluded that they were 18.6 times more likely to develop ASD, compared to youth who were not (Harmin, et al., 2004). Individuals who show symptoms of ASD have also been found to have a higher probability of experiencing symptoms associated with Post Traumatic Stress Disorder (PTSD) (Bryant & Harvey, 2003). For example, disaster workers who developed Acute Stress Disorder after dealing with a plane crash were 7.33 times more likely to develop PTSD (Fullerton, et al., 2004).

Post Traumatic Stress Disorder (PTSD)

One of the major concerns with an officer-involved shooting is Post-Traumatic Stress Disorder (PTSD). PTSD is a set of psychological symptoms that develop over time after a traumatic event. According to the American Psychiatric Association (2000), conditions that must be met for PTSD include: a) the source of stress must be an extremely traumatic event; (b) the situation must involve death or the realistic threat of death or serious personal injury; (c) it must be direct or must involve a family member or close associate; and, (d) the person's symptoms must include "intense fear, helplessness, or horror." The impact of the experience must also lead to marked impairment in important areas of functioning (including social relationships and occupational performance).

Halligan et al. (2003) writes that PTSD is:

> Characterized by recurrent, intrusive memories of a highly distressing traumatic event. These recollections tend to be vividly sensory, are experienced as relatively uncontrollable, and evoke extreme distress. The individual may lose the capacity to distinguish the memory from current perceptions, and the event is re-experienced as a flashback. Unwanted memories may be uncontrollably triggered by a variety of trauma related cues. The accompanying fear and distress are sufficient to stimulate substantial efforts (both overt and covert) to avoid recalling the event (p. 419).

The diagnostic criteria for PTSD is that it must occur at least one month post-trauma (Harvey & Bryant, 2002). PTSD may be acute, with symptoms lasting less than 3 months. It may also be chronic with symptoms lasting more than 3 months. And, it may be delayed onset, where symptoms appear at least six months (or more) after the initial traumatic stressor (Yeager and Roberts, 2003). A person experiencing PTSD may have this condition the rest of their life, suffering from recurring episodes that could be triggered by a variety of cues from the person's environment. A person may show or experience chronic symptoms of PTSD from memory flashbacks and even certain sounds and smells months or years after the traumatic event occurred (Waters, 2002).

Psychological and physical symptoms may also vary among individuals. They may include avoiding thoughts and emotions related to the event. Others may use drugs and alcohol to assist them in avoiding the memories of the incident. Physical symptoms may include headaches, chest pains, gastrointestinal problems and other problems that may shorten the life of the person. Officers experiencing PTSD may have problems in their personal lives including marital problems and/or the inability to maintain personal relationships (Waters, 2002). PTSD can be a stand-alone disorder or it can occur in conjunction (i.e. co- morbidity) with other psychological disorders, including depression (O'Donnell, et al, 2004).

Not all officers involved in a shooting will experience PTSD. A variety of factors may contribute to PTSD. For example, life experiences and individual psychological differences among individuals may affect the later development of posttraumatic stress symptoms (Berg, et al, 2005). Other factors may include their history of trauma or stress, their family history involving psychological disorders, and any personality disorders the person may have (Marshall, et al, 1999).

IACP Protocols

The International Association of Chiefs of Police, Psychological Services Section, has created guidelines for police agencies to follow when they have officers involved in a shooting. While many of these procedures specifically deal with administrative issues, many of them also deal with the psychological well-being of the officer, ensuring that the police agency does not do anything to further increase their stress levels. Box 15-1 provides an overview of some of the IACP's protocol recommendations.

BOX 15-1
IACP AGENCY PROTOCOL RECOMMENDATIONS

- Immediately after the incident, provide both physical and emotional first aid to officers involved
- Allow an officer recovery time before interviewing them
- Explain to the officer what administrative procedures will be followed over the course of the next few days to reduce their anxiety levels
- Provide the officer with literature on the physical and psychological responses to a traumatic event
- If a police officer's firearm is taken as evidence, replace it as soon as possible or let them know when the weapon will be returned to them (this reduces anxiety that they did something wrong)
- Give the officers some administrative leave so they can emotionally recover
- Expedite all investigations
- Show personal concern for the officer
- Give the officer the option to talk with others who have had similar experiences (peer support)
- Have the officer attend a post-shooting meeting with a mental health professional within one week of the event

(Adapted from the IACP's Officer Involved Shooting Guidelines, 2004)

Crisis Intervention Techniques

Because a police shooting is a traumatic event, immediate crisis intervention is needed to make sure that more serious symptoms do not emerge later in the officer's career and personal life (Waters, 2002). This is particularly important when considering the fact that a traumatic event can affect individuals differently. Some officers may experience psychological trauma and distress to a great degree. Others, meanwhile, may experience minimal or no psychological trauma because predisposing factors are minimal. Some of these predisposing factors may include genetic and health variables, prior life experiences and other trauma's that a person has experienced that may actually serve to reduce the psychological trauma associated with the specific event at hand (Waters, 2002).

Usually one of the first forms of crisis intervention by police agencies is Critical Incident Stress Debriefing (CISD). CISD is a group counseling technique that is conducted immediately after a traumatic event. The primary goal of CISD is to assist individuals in coping with and understanding their emotional reactions to the critical incident (Buck, 1995). The goal is to reduce the degree or the nature and extent of the psychological trauma by having individuals share their personal thoughts and feelings about the event with others who may have the same thoughts, emotions and feelings (Yandrick, 2003). Through this debriefing, individuals are provided problem solving skills and they gain an understanding that the emotions and reactions to the event are normal, as others that experienced the same incident have the same or similar emotions and trauma (Buck, 2004).

These debriefings may be voluntary or mandatory. In some situations a police officer may be resistant to attend a voluntary critical incident debriefing. For example, in one study of officers involved in shootings, 60% of the officers reported that they would not have attended a debriefing if it were voluntary. However, 100% of the 982 officers in this study reported that the debriefing was valuable (Honig & Sultan, 2004). If anything, officers should attend not only for their own well-being, but for the well-being of their fellow officers who need emotional support from their friends and peers.

CISD is usually designed to be a one-time intervention technique with no follow-up with those that experienced the traumatic event. However, CISD may not be the end of crisis intervention. In addition to debriefing, police officers as well as their families (it is a traumatic event for the family too) may seek the assistance of psychologists, counselors and other individuals who specialize in crisis situations at a later time.

To address coping and psychological issues after the initial CISD, some agencies may have a comprehensive Critical Incident Stress Management (CISM) program. The goal of these programs is to assist the officer and perhaps their family in preventing acute as well as chronic traumatic stress reactions from becoming stress disorders (Yaeger and Roberts, 2003).

An example of a CISM program is the FBI's multistage Critical Incident Stress Management (CISM) program, which assists employees and their families in dealing with the emotional trauma associated with a critical incident. This comprehensive program begins with initial defusing where the CISM team will spend 30-40 minutes with the individual alone or in small groups to normalize them. The next stage involves critical incident stress debriefing that is conducted 24 to 72 hours after the event. Other components of this program also include peer and one-on-one support, family assistance, managerial support, referrals and follow up services as needed, and post critical incident seminars where small groups of participants, in a group setting, can confidentially share their experiences (McNally & Solomon, 1999).

Counseling

As shown in Box 15-1, IACP guidelines recommend that officers attend a post-shooting intervention meeting with a mental health professional. Depending upon departmental policies and procedures, these confidential counseling sessions could be mandatory or voluntary. Mandatory post shooting interventions may reduce the stigma of seeking help from a mental health professional, while voluntary post-shooting intervention meetings may make an officer feel that they are more in control over what happens to them. Regardless of if the meetings are mandatory or voluntary, the primary purpose behind them is to ensure that the officer is coping well with the incident, and that they are properly dealing with any issues or problems that they may be experiencing. These programs also provide support and encouragement through what is referred to as the person's normalization process.

Depending upon the situation and departmental policy, individuals may also be referred to additional counseling and peer support programs to further assist them in coping with the shooting (IACP Model Guidelines, 2004). In addition to counseling for those individuals directly involved in the scene, police departments may also have counseling available for family members. This is based on concerns that the shooting may also be traumatic for family members. It may challenge their coping skills on a variety of issues, ranging from a loved one being exposed to a deadly force assault, to issues related to the officer shooting and killing another human being.

In some situations, critical incident debriefing and other forms of counseling for the employee may be looked upon with skepticism or contempt. Perhaps this is because of the bravado associated with police work and the belief in some agencies that part of being a police officer is to conceal their emotions, since revealing their true feelings may make them appear to be "weak." The reader should keep in mind, however, that police officers are first and foremost human beings that have a variety of emotional responses to various situations. This means that regardless of if a person is a rookie or a seasoned veteran, any traumatic event, including an officer-involved shooting, WILL have some type of psychological impact.

Fitness for Duty Evaluations

Independent of counseling, a police department may also require a Fitness For Duty (FFD) evaluation after a shooting. The purpose behind a FFD evaluation is to ensure that the officer can perform their job in a safe and effective manner, and that they do not have a psychological problem or symptoms of a psychological disorder. Unlike a counseling program that may be voluntary, FFD evaluations are usually mandatory. Based on the FFD examination that may encompass interviews, psychological tests, and a review of the officer's work performance, a psychologist can determine that the officer is: 1) fit for duty; 2) unfit for duty, where the officer can be placed on administrative or sick leave until determined fit; or a 3) provisional FFD, where the officer can continue working as long as they complete the treatment(s) determined by the psychologist (Fisher, 2001).

Post-Shooting Legal Procedures

Even though officers involved in a shooting may have acted in a completely legal, ethical, and tactical manner, there are some administrative issues that need to be addressed. Administratively, a thorough investigation must be carried out to verify that the officer-involved shooting was legal and followed all departmental policies and procedures. A complete and thorough investigation will also be demanded by the public to make sure that the agency and the officer(s) acted appropriately in the shooting. A thorough investigation will also serve as a liability shield if the agency or officer is exposed to a civil suit regarding their actions in the shooting.

These investigations (which could be quite lengthy) may make officers involved in the shooting feel uncomfortable, making them think that they did something wrong, which in turn may increase their stress levels related to the shooting and its aftermath. While many agencies do have progressive policies to reduce the concerns among officers involved in a shooting, it is a simple fact that an administrative investigation will be carried out to ensure that officers acted within all applicable laws, policies, and procedures. Since the shooting is considered to be a crime scene, those officers involved in the shooting (directly or indirectly) are also witnesses to the event. Depending upon departmental policy, they may be required to participate in a variety of interviews. The officers will also be required to write detailed reports of the event describing their actions during the shooting.

Legal Representation

The previous section shows that officers involved in a shooting (directly and indirectly) will have experienced a variety of psychological responses to the traumatic event. Based on the previous points, officers need to exercise caution before making immediate verbal and written statements. Officers may have difficulty in fully reconstructing the event due to issues related to dissociation, recall, and the fact that they may not have had adequate time to psychologically and physiologically recover from the shooting. At the same time, their statements may later be used in both criminal and civil court actions. Because of these issues, police officers should immediately retain an attorney to represent them. This legal counsel can be retained on the officer's personal initiative and expense, or legal counsel can be provided to the officer through an employee organization or union, if applicable.

Reports

Only after consulting with counsel should reports be written and submitted to the agency. Within these reports, officers will need to fully document the sequence of events and all relevant facts to articulate that they had probable cause for the shooting based on law, policy, training, and their experience as a police officer.

Departmental policies and procedures will dictate exact report writing procedures. These reports will begin with the rough draft, which will serve as a framework or foundation on which the officer will build additional details, additions, or addenda. These rough draft reports, if immediately requested, should clearly state that the report is a draft copy only and that certain details of the event may change, based on the officer's increased recall of specific details of the incident.

Officers must maintain a high degree of ethical conduct when writing their report and include only that information that they know is true and factual, based on what they saw, did, or experienced during the event. Only that information to which the officer has personal knowledge should be included in the report. For example, if multiple officers were involved in a shooting, only those details that the officer has specific knowledge of should be included. While there may be conflicting information on certain points when comparing their reports against one another, it must be remembered that each individual officer may have seen specific details that others did not because they were at a different perspective or angle. At the same time, dissociative responses experienced by the officer may also result in them not being able to recall certain details that others could recall. For example, one officer may recall that the suspect's gun was in his right hand while another report may state it was in their left. While the two reports may contradict one another regarding this detail, the two reports also show and confirm that both officers saw the suspect holding a handgun. This fact is much more important than what hand the gun was held in.

Evidentiary Issues

In addition to interviews and reports, police officers may also have their firearms taken as evidence. Firearms will be collected for their forensic evidentiary value, so the agency can verify that the officer's weapon was used in the shooting. In situations involving multiple officers at the shooting, ballistics evidence will also be necessary to determine which officer's projectile(s) hit the suspect (and where they hit), serving to build a forensic analysis of the event. For those rounds that missed the suspect, if applicable, the event can also be mapped regarding the relative positioning of the officers at the shooting. For many police officers, having their weapon taken from them implies that they are guilty or they did something wrong. This issue or concern, however, should not be considered. Weapons are only taken for their evidentiary value. To avoid any stress associated with an officer having their firearm taken as evidence, many police agencies delay taking the firearm into custody or they immediately replace it with another.

Testifying in Court

Police officers will also be required to testify in court regarding the shooting. If not in court, they may be required to testify in front of a Grand Jury (if applicable in that particular state), or provide testimony to a Special Prosecutor, if one is assigned, to investigate the shooting. In these situations, the officer himself may be on trial. In other situations the suspect (or other officers) may be on trial. Regardless of who is on trial and if the trial is criminal or civil, there are some key considerations when testifying in court.

The key to testifying in any situation is preparation. First, officers must be professionally dressed and groomed when they are present in the courtroom in order to project a professional and positive image of themselves to those in attendance. Officers should also have their own attorney with them. If the officer is facing the potential for some type of legal action, they must make sure that their legal counsel is properly briefed and prepared for the case. The officer also needs to make sure that the prosecutor is fully briefed and prepared so they can successfully prosecute the suspect(s) involved in the shooting.

When testifying, officers will need to know the law, policies and procedures, and the details and facts of the incident. This means that the officer must have a full and thorough understanding of federal and state laws related to the use of force. They must also be able to apply these laws to the shooting. Officers will also need to know those limitations and guidelines that departmental policies and procedures place on the use of deadly force. In addition to laws, policies and procedures, the officer must also review their report and field notes regarding the incident. This will ensure that they know the facts of the situation and that they can clearly articulate and explain the shooting in great detail to establish that probable cause did exist to use deadly force.

Besides knowing the law, policies, procedures, and the details of the event itself, the training and experience of the officer may come into question. In this context, officers must be prepared to prove that they had the requisite training in the use of force. This will require the officer to have an in-depth knowledge of all of the training they have received regarding the use of force. It will also require that the officer provides evidence of other forms of advanced training, their qualifications, and how their police experience proves that they were competent and acted in an appropriate manner in the shooting.

Criminal and Civil Liability Issues

Police officers, because of their actions in a shooting, can face criminal and civil sanctions. At the state level, a police officer may be criminally charged for such crimes as assault, manslaughter and murder. At the federal level, meanwhile, a police officer could be charged in the federal courts Under Title 18 Section 241 which states that police officers can be charged with conspiracy to deprive another person of their civil rights. Officers can also be charged under Section 242 of Title 18, which prohibits a person acting under color of law from violating another's civil rights (Driscoll, 2004).

Officers and their agency, although they have not been found criminally responsible for their actions, or have been cleared regarding any criminal activity, may also be later be involved in a civil lawsuit related to the deadly force action(s) taken. These civil lawsuits can be filed by the person(s) injured in the shooting, their estate if the individual died as a result of the shooting, and by civilians who might have been injured as a result of the officer's actions before, during, or after the event. They can also be filed against the officer and/or the agency. Civil lawsuits, depending upon the issue, can also be filed in both the federal and state courts.

The Rights of Police Officers

To provide some protection for police officers in investigations, police officers have certain rights in post-shooing investigations. In particular, these include Garrity and Weingarten Rights, which are granted to them through U.S. Supreme Court decisions. In addition to these rights that exist at the federal level, police officers may also possess certain rights as determined by the state they reside in, civil service regulations, collective bargaining agreements, and relevant case law that governs the rights of police officers in investigatory situations. In order to protect themselves against any unforeseen actions (legal or administrative), officers should always invoke those rights they do possess during investigatory interviews.

Garrity Rights

Garrity Rights evolved out of the Supreme Court decision *Garrity v. New Jersey* (1967) and other relevant court cases, including *Gardner v. Broderick* (1968). Based on these (and other) decisions, statements required through departmental rules and regulations that are made by a police officer in an administrative investigation cannot be later used against them in a criminal proceeding. Collectively, these rights are referred to as Garrity Rights.

The Garrity case dealt with a chief of police (Garrity), one of his officers, and a court clerk who were fixing drunk driving charges for a fee and reducing them to less serious motor vehicle violations. In a subsequent investigation by the district attorney, the suspects were told that if they refused to answer the questions (invoking their Fifth Amendment right against self-incrimination and the right to remain silent) they would be terminated. The officers answered the questions and were later terminated and convicted of conspiracy to obstruct justice, based in part on their testimonies. The U.S. Supreme Court found that the suspects were coerced into giving their testimony because they were faced with a choice between self-incrimination (which is protected under the Fifth Amendment) and losing their jobs. The Court also decided that their statements were involuntarily made and prohibited under the Fourteenth Amendment from being used in a criminal proceeding (Driscoll, 2004). Later, in the Supreme Court decision in *Gardner v. Broderick* (1968), which involved a police officer who invoked his 5th Amendment Rights at a Grand Jury regarding an investigation of police corruption and bribery and was dismissed for doing so, the Supreme Court found that dismissing a police officer for asserting their Fifth Amendment rights against self-incrimination was unconstitutional.

Garrity Rights are also considered to be a type of use immunity. Use immunity protects a police officer from any derivative use of their testimony or statements to be later used in a criminal trial. While the use immunity label has been interpreted differently by the courts, it does not completely bar the officer from being criminally charged. Instead, use immunity prohibits information given by the officer to be later used in a criminal trial (Bloch, 1992), or to use that information obtained from the compelled testimony to "seek out other information that would incriminate the defendant or other parties" (Herzig, 1993, p. 462). The key concept behind these rights is the fact that a police administrator or prosecutor can require a person to respond to questions and testify, under the penalty of dismissal or some other job action. However, these statements and/or testimony cannot be later used by the police and prosecutor as evidence to later criminally charge that person in a criminal trial. Instead, a completely independent investigation of the officer's actions must be conducted (Clymer, 2001).

> **Miranda vs. Garrity**
> **What's the Difference?**
>
> While Miranda and Garrity both deal with a person's Fifth Amendment rights, they are distinctly different. Miranda deals with voluntary statements, while Garrity deals with compelled statements. If, for example, an officer is Mirandized and then voluntarily provides statements to the investigator, they can be used against them in a criminal proceeding. This is not the case when an officer invokes their Garrity rights. Statements made under Garrity cannot be used against the officer in a criminal proceeding.

Under the Gardner and Garrity decisions, the following four elements apply to police officers regarding investigatory interviews:

1. If a law enforcement officer is not provided with immunity, any statement given under the threat of adverse personnel action is unconstitutionally coerced (Garrity holding)
2. If a law enforcement officer is not provided with immunity, the taking or threatening to take any adverse personnel action in response to the assertion of the privilege against self-incrimination has an unconstitutional chilling effect upon the privilege (Gardner holding)
3. If a law enforcement officer is granted immunity but nonetheless refuses to answer questions specifically, directly, and narrowly related to official duties, the officer may be dismissed (Gardner); and
4. If a law enforcement officer is granted immunity and answers questions specifically, directly, and narrowly related to their official duties, the officer may be dismissed if the answers provide cause for dismissal (Gardner, 1987, p. 472).

Courts in several jurisdictions require that the police officer be warned that their statements can later be used in a job action, including dismissal. To ensure that the officer understands this fact, often the courts will require that a tripartite warning be issued that includes the following:

1. That the officer can possibly be terminated for their statements;
2. Statements given cannot be used in a criminal proceeding; and,
3. Questions will be specifically related to the officer's performance of their official duties (Bloch, 1992).

Officers should also complete and sign a Garrity Statement. An example of a Garrity statement is shown in Box 15-2.

BOX 15-2
GARRITY RIGHTS STATEMENT

TO:
FROM:
DATE:
SUBJECT:

Constitutional Protection Statement:

"On _____(date) _____(time) at _____(place) I was ordered to submit this report (give this statement) by _____(name & rank). I submit this report (give this statement) at his order as a condition of my employment. In view of possible job forfeiture, I have no alternative but to abide by this order."

"It is my belief and understanding that the department requires this report (statement) solely and exclusively for internal purposes and will not release it to any other agency. It is my further belief that this report (statement) will not and cannot be used against me in any subsequent proceedings. I authorize release of this report to my attorney or designated union representative."

"I retain the right to amend or change this statement upon reflection to correct any unintended mistake without subjecting myself to a charge of untruthfulness."

"For any and all other purposes, I hereby reserve my constitutional right to remain silent under the FIFTH and FOURTEENTH AMENDMENTS to the UNITED STATES CONSTITUTION and any other rights PRESCRIBED by law. Further, I rely specifically upon the protection afforded me under the doctrines set forth in Garrity v. New Jersey, 385 U.S. 493 (1967), and Spevack v. Klien, 385 U.S. 551 (1956), should this report (statement) be used for any other purpose of whatsoever kind or description."

Weingarten Rights

The U.S. Supreme Court decision in *NLRB v. J. Weingarten, Inc.* (1975) found that union members have the right to have a union representative present at any investigatory interview, upon the employee's request, where the employee reasonably believes that the outcome of the information gathered at that interview could result in discipline against them. This is based on the fact that one of the roles of union is the mutual aid and protection of its members. Therefore, a union member can have another person present to assist and protect them to some degree from the actions of management. Under the Weingarten decision, the Supreme Court set forth some limitations on employer-based investigations that include the following:

- An employee seeking to invoke their rights to union representation must request representation. It is not automatic.
- The right is limited to those cases where the employee reasonably believes that disciplinary action will result as a consequence of that meeting.
- The exercise of the employee's right cannot interfere with the employer's legitimate choice to hold the meeting or interview.
- Employers do not have a duty to bargain with the union representative. The union representative is present at the meeting to clarify facts or provide information to the employer on additional employees who possess information about the issue at hand.

The employer, meanwhile, has some options regarding an employee invoking their Weingarten Rights. These options include: 1) granting the employee's request for representation and continuing on with the interview; 2) stopping the interview and imposing discipline; 3) stopping the interview and conducting their own investigation of the issue without input from the person being investigated; and, 4) offering the employee the option of continuing on with the interview unaccompanied by a representative or not having the interview at all (Blake & Knox, 2001).

Because an employee could receive some form of discipline related to their actions in the shooting, the employee should invoke their Weingarten Rights. Combined with Garrity, the addition of Weingarten Rights simply means that an officer can have their union representative or another person of their choosing with them at the investigatory meeting(s). This union steward cannot bargain or serve as a spokesperson. Instead, their role is to simply clarify issues and provide information on other employees who may have knowledge of the issue (Johnson, 2005).

Conclusion

A police-related shooting is a serious event for the officers involved, their families and significant others. First and foremost, for the safety of the officer(s) involved in the shooting, sound police tactics must be followed. Officers must hold cover and call for immediate backup. The suspect(s) must also be properly secured. In an administrative context, supervisors must immediately be requested at the scene, first aid must be given to all the injured based on the severity of their injuries, and the scene must be secured and treated as a crime scene.

Besides procedural and administrative concerns related to a police shooting, police officers who are directly and indirectly involved in the shooting will also encounter a variety of emotional and/or psychological stressors. They may include issues related to memory recall, Acute Stress Disorder (ASD), and Post Traumatic Stress Disorder (PTSD). To address and prevent these concerns, police agencies have a variety of intervention techniques. They include Critical Incident Stress Debriefing (CISD) and Critical Incident Stress Management (CISM) programs.

It is also important for officers to properly document the sequence of events in the shooting after consulting with counsel. These reports, in addition to their testimony, must be accurate, true, and establish the fact that probable cause existed, based on law, policy and the officers' training and experience. This chapter has also provided an overview of those rights police officers have in investigations related to the shooting. Under the Garrity decision, while an officer is required to provide information for the investigation, that information cannot be used later in criminal proceedings. Other rights that police officers may have come from their Weingarten Rights, relevant state laws, legal decisions, civil service regulations and their collective bargaining agreements.

REFERENCES

American Psychiatric Association (2000). <u>Diagnostic and statistical manual of mental disorders, text revision (4th ed.)</u>. Washington DC: APA.

Artwhol, A. (October, 2002). Perceptual and memory distortion during officer-involved shootings. <u>FBI law enforcement bulletin, 71</u>(10), 18-24.

Berg, J.S.; Greiger, T.A. & J.L. Spira. (January, 2005). Psychiatric symptoms and cognitive appraisal following the near sinking of a research submarine. <u>Military medicine,</u> 170(1), 44-47.

Bland, T.S. & Knox, D.P. (January, 2001). The non-union employee's right to a representative. <u>Federal lawyer, 48,</u> 34-37.

Bloch, K.E. (19920. Police officers accused of a crime: Prosecutorial and Fifth Amendment risks posed by police-elicited "use immunized" statements. <u>University of Illinois law review,</u> 625-689.

Bryant, R.A. & Harvey, A.G. (April, 2003). Gender differences in the relationship between acute stress disorder and posttraumatic stress disorder following motor vehicle accidents. <u>Australian and New Zealand journal of psychiatry, 37</u>(2), 226-229.

Buck, W.T. (October, 1995). Coping with crisis. <u>Risk management, 42</u>(10), 58-63.

Clymer, S.D. (November, 2001). Compelled statements from police officers and Garrity immunity. <u>New York University law review, 76,</u> 1309-1382.

Driscoll, D.W. (2004). Garrity v. New Jersey and its progeny: How lower courts are weakening the strong constitutional protections afforded police officers. <u>Buffalo public interest law journal, 22,</u> 101-144.

Fisher, G.L. (2001). Psychological fitness-for-duty examinations: Practical considerations for public safety departments. <u>Illinois law enforcement executive forum, 1,</u> 77-92.

Fisher, R.P.; Falkner, M.R.; & M. Trevisan. (April, 2000). Adapting the cognitive interview to enhance long-term (35 years) recall of physical activities. <u>Journal of applied psychology, 85</u>(2), 180-189.

Fullerton, C.S.; Ursano, R.J., & L. Wang. (August, 2004). Acute stress disorder, posttraumatic stress disorder and depression in disaster or rescue workers. American journal of psychiatry, 161(8), 1370-1376.

Gabbert, F.; Memon, A. and K. Allen. (April, 2003). Memory conformity: Can eyewitnesses influence each other's memories of an event? Applied cognitive psychology, 17, 533-543.

Gardner v. Broderick (392 U.S. 293, 278 (1968)).

Griffin, M.G.; Resick, P.A.; and, M.B. Mechanic (1997). Objective assessment of peritraumatic dissociation: Psychophysiological indicators. American journal of psychiatry, 154(8), 1081-1088.

Grossman, D. & Sidle, B.K. (1998). Critical incident amnesia: The psychological basis and implications of memory loss during extreme survival stress situations. Millstadt IL: PPCT Management Systems, Inc.

Halligan, S.L.; Michael, T.; Clark, D.M.; & A. Ehlers (2003). Posttraumatic stress disorder following assault: The role of cognitive processing, trauma memory, and appraisals. Journal of consulting and clinical psychology, 71(3), 419-431.

Harmain, V.; Jonker, B.; and L. Scahill (October-December, 2004). Acute stress disorder symptoms in gunshot injured youth. Journal of child and adolescent psychiatric nursing, 17(4), 161-172.

Herzig, A.M. (Fall, 1993). To serve and yet to be protected: The unconstitutional use of coerced statements in subsequent criminal proceedings against law enforcement officers. William and Mary law review, 35, 401-443.

Honig, A.L.; & Sultan, S.E. (December, 2004). Reactions and resilience under fire: What an officer can expect. The police chief, 71(12), 54-61.

Johnson, B.R. (2005). Principles of security management. Upper Saddle River, NJ: Prentice Hall.

Klinger, D. (2001). Police responses to officer-involved shootings. National Institute of Justice. Washington, D.C.: U.S. Department of Justice.

Koriat, A. & Goldsmith, M. (1996). Monitoring and control processes in the strategic regulation of memory accuracy. Psychological review, 103(3), 490-517

Kureczka, A.W. (March, 1996). Critical incident stress in law enforcement. FBI law enforcement bulletin, 65, 10-16.

Marmar, C.R.; Weiss, D.S.; Metzler, T.J. & K. Delucchi (July, 1996). Characteristics of emergency services personnel related to peritraumatic dissociation during critical incident exposure. American journal of psychiatry, 153(7), 94-102.

Marshall, R.D.; Spitzer, R.; & M.R. Liebovwitz (November 1999). Review and critique of the new DSM-IV diagnosis of acute stress disorder. American journal of psychiatry, 156(11), 1677-1685.

McNally, V.J. & Solomon, R.M. (Fall, 199). The FBI's critical incident stress management program. FBI law enforcement bulletin, 68(2), 20-26.

NLRB v. Weingarten, Inc., 420 U.S. 251 (1975).

O'Donnell, M.L.; Creamer, K. & P. Pattison (August, 2004). Posttraumatic stress disorder and depression following trauma: Understanding co morbidity. American journal of Psychiatry, 161(8), 1390-1396.

Officer-Involved Shooting Guidelines, Ratified by the IACP Psychological Services Section, Los Angeles, California, 2004.

Ostmann, L.L. (Fall, 2001). Union rights, no dues: In re Epilepsy Foundation and NLRB's extension of Weingarten Rights to nonunion employees. Saint Louis law journal, 45, 1309-1347.

Peace, K.A. & porter, S. (June, 2004). A longitudinal investigation of the reliability of memories for trauma and other emotional experiences. Applied cognitive psychology, 18, 1143-1159.

Rivard, J.M.; Dietz, P. Martell, D.; and M. Widawski (September, 2002). Acute dissociative responses in law enforcement officers involved in critical shooting incidents: The clinical and forensic implications. Journal of forensic science, 47(5), 1093.

Scrivner, E. & Safer, M.A. (1988). Eyewitnesses show hypermnesia for details about a violent event. Journal of applied psychology, 73(3), 371-377.

Snow, T.A. (Spring, 2001). Labor and employment - Epilepsy Foundation of Northeast Ohio: The National Labor Relations Board once again extends Weingarten representational right to non-union employees. University of Memphis law review, 31, 743-756.

Swanson, C.R.; Territo, L.; & R.W. Taylor (2005). Police Administration (6th ed.). Upper Saddle River, NJ: Prentice Hall.

The American Heritage Stedman's Medical Dictionary (2002). Boston: Houghton Mifflin.

Waters, J.A. (March, 2002). Moving forward from September 11: A stress/crisis/trauma response model. Brief treatment and crisis intervention, 2(1), 55-74.

Williams, G.T. (October, 1999). Reluctance to use deadly force. FBI law enforcement bulletin, 68(10), 1-5.

Yandrick, R.M. (June, 2003). Traumatic event debriefings getting second thoughts. HR Magazine, 48(6), 32.

Yeager, K.R. & Roberts, A.R. (March 1, 2003). Differentiating among stress, acute stress disorder, crisis episodes, trauma, and PTSD: Paradigm and treatment goals. Brief treatment and crisis intervention, 3(1), 3-25.

Introduction

C arrying a firearm off-duty is not a right per se. Instead, it is a privilege that police officers enjoy because of their job, those laws that allow them to carry off-duty, and because their police agency has allowed them to carry off-duty. With off-duty carry there comes a great deal of personal and professional responsibility. Personally, an officer will need to be fully prepared to address a potentially hostile situation off-duty. Professionally, they will need to conduct themselves as on-duty police officers, conforming to all moral, legal and tactical guidelines related to the use of force.

This chapter will provide the reader with an overview of the issues and concerns related to off-duty carry. Included in this chapter is a discussion of departmental regulations that may limit off-duty carry and perspectives on off-duty carry. This chapter will also provide a comprehensive plan for off-duty carry, including training-related issues and how to respond to off-duty incidents. Other topics include issues related to family members and significant others, off-duty "nevers," selecting an off-duty firearm, and home storage considerations. A review of the Law Enforcement Safety Act of 2004 and issues related to civil and criminal liability will also be reviewed.

Departmental Regulations & Off-Duty Carry

Regardless of the fact that state and federal laws allow police officers to carry off-duty, departmental policies and procedures supercede these laws. Policies and procedures, depending upon the agency, can exist on a continuum ranging from prohibiting off-duty carry, to restricted and unrestricted carry policies. Some agencies, for example, may completely prohibit the carrying of firearms off duty out of concern for their officers, the fear of litigation, or because they do not want their officers intervening in situations where they lack an arsenal of equipment and readily available backup. Another prohibition-based policy would be when an agency allows an officer to carry as a citizen only. In theses situations officers must abide by and follow those laws that regulate civilian concealed carry only and in no way represent themselves as a police officer in a violent confrontation.

Other agencies may have restrictive policies that specifically outline when and where firearms can be carried. As an example, a police agency could restrict off-duty carry within their geographical jurisdiction only. Restrictive policies may also prohibit carrying firearms in bars, nightclubs and stadiums. Other policies may prohibit the carrying of firearms if an officer is consuming alcoholic beverages, has a blood alcohol level (or is intoxicated), or is using prescribed or over-the-counter medications. Other restrictive off-duty carry policies may require the officer to seek written permission for each occasion they wish to carry off-duty.

On the other end of the continuum, agencies may have unrestricted policies for carrying off-duty firearms. They can range from an "always on duty/always armed" policy that requires police officers to carry their firearms with them at all times off-duty so they can respond to incidents, if necessary (Beyer, 2005). Unrestricted policies may also contain statements encouraging officers to act professionally and in accordance with existing state laws, emphasizing the responsibilities associated with off-duty carry.

Concealed Carry - Two Perspectives

The following is a discussion of some issues to consider regarding the option to carry or not carry.

The Carry Option

In some situations, a police officer may carry a firearm off-duty based on their personal beliefs that they are a police officer 24 hours a day, 7 days a week. Regardless of their off-duty status, they believe that their role is to protect society and individuals at all times. Others may take the perspective that state laws as well as departmental policies and procedures grant them the right or privilege to carry a firearm because of their status as a police officer. In other situations, the organizational culture of the agency may advocate carrying off-duty, as peers and friends in the agency may encourage off-duty carry.

The carry perspective may also be based on the officer safety issues. If a police officer works in a smaller agency, perhaps many members of the community know where the officer lives and his daily habits. Out of concern that they might be identified and confronted, an officer may carry for their protection and the protection of family and friends. Other reasons may also lead to a decision to carry. If, for example, an officer is currently or has been involved in high-risk undercover operations, or was involved in criminal cases that put his life in danger of retaliation for his actions, carrying off-duty may be a prudent decision. Likewise, if an officer's friends or family were threatened by people they arrested, carrying off-duty may be considered to be necessary to protect himself and/or others.

The Non-Carry Option

The main themes of the non-carry perspective address liability, safety, and the fact the police are citizens too. Individuals who hold this perspective may take the position that "off-duty is off-duty." The non-carry perspective takes the position that it is better to be a trained observer and a good witness to the incident instead of directly confronting the suspect. In the non-carry perspective, the officer may still act. Their actions however, will be to observe, call 911, and be a good witness.

Officer safety and the safety of others may be an issue in deciding not to carry. Police officers in off-duty situations will not enjoy having immediate backup and a wide array of personal defense tools (e.g. OC spray, baton) with them as if they would when they were on duty. Because they may not be properly equipped to handle the situation as if they were on duty, they could be at a tactical disadvantage that could result in the officer and other innocents' safety being compromised because of their actions. At the same time, if an officer did intervene off-duty and was injured, concerns related to sick time and medical leave, workman's compensation, and long-term disability could arise, based on the fact that the officer was perhaps not officially on-duty.

Engaging a threat off-duty, especially in gunfight, could also endanger individuals with the off-duty officer. Combined with the fact that an officer may be concerned with both the threat and those with him, they may not be fully attentive to the threat and instead, be more concerned about the safety of their loved ones. This could increase the odds of being injured or killed. At the same time, the off-duty officer may be exposing innocent civilians in their immediate vicinity to a greater risk of injury because of their actions. Combined with the issue that citizens and other police officers (on and off duty) may not be able to readily determine if the off-duty officer is a threat, the off-duty officer acting in good faith to protect himself or the public could wind up being the victim.

309

Last, is the position that police are citizens too. Some officers may take the position that other professions are not on-duty at all times. Therefore, they should have the same benefits as other occupations, and enjoy that time they have off. Carrying off-duty could alter or infringe upon the officer's lifestyle, requiring them to change certain activities (i.e. consuming alcohol, frequenting nightclubs, etc.), while also impinging upon other personal life choices including their dress or appearance. Not only could carrying off-duty impact the officer, but it could also impact family and friends. Significant others, friends and family members may feel uncomfortable socializing with a person who is armed.

Developing a Comprehensive Plan for Off-Duty Carry

An off-duty officer may simply think that all they need to carry off-duty is their firearm and nothing else. This thought is wrong. One of the reasons why an officer is carrying their firearm is in anticipation that a criminal event could occur, where they need to intervene to stop and control the threat. Off-duty carry requires a comprehensive plan of action. This comprehensive plan begins with developing a tactical mindset, wearing appropriate off-duty clothing, and selecting proper equipment for off-duty carry and use.

Tactical Mindset & Awareness

Besides dress, appearance, and attitude, an off-duty officer needs to ensure that they are tactically aware of their surroundings when carrying off-duty. While on-duty, police officers must be cautious and aware of their surroundings. This same concept applies when carrying off-duty. A police officer should know their surroundings, know where available cover and concealment exists, and be able to identify emerging threats so they can respond in an appropriate manner.

Off-Duty Carry Checklist
✓ Tactical Mindset
✓ Wear appropriate clothing
✓ Firearm is properly secured in a holster
✓ Extra Ammunition
✓ Portable Communication Device (Cell Phone or Radio)
✓ Handcuffs/Restraints
✓ Photo ID & Badge
✓ No Alcohol Use/Consumption

They may also want to consider other factors, including their relative positioning so they can monitor their threat environment, and perhaps engage in avoidance strategies, avoiding those known high risk locations to prevent themselves from getting into an incident that requires them to use their police powers. A tactical mindset also includes understanding strategies to avoid a confrontation; escaping or evading a confrontation; and, controlling the confrontation, if necessary. A tactical mindset also requires that off-duty officers should also exercise caution in revealing their profession to individuals that they do not know.

Tactical awareness also deals with the officer's off-duty dress and appearance. While many off-duty officers are quite adept at concealing their firearm, they may not be good at concealing the fact that they are police officers. An effective off-duty carry will succeed in both concealment of the firearm and concealment of the off-duty officer's profession. In order to achieve total concealment, the key is that a police officer should be "sterile" in appearance. The off-duty officer should appear as an "invisible person" in public. They should do nothing to stand out in the crowd. The officer should be a non-distinct person that can be easily overlooked by threat(s).

This concept of an invisible person requires that the off-duty officer does not do anything purposefully or inadvertently to advertise that they are a police officer. For example, an off-duty officer should not wear shirts or hats that advertise their profession or relationship to the police profession (i.e. charity-related shirts that list police departments as sponsors). Other dress-related identifiers may include the off-duty officer inadvertently exposing his/her badge in their wallet, wearing police-related jewelry or in the worst case, wearing police equipment off-duty such as boots or an old jacket with the patches removed. These and others identifiers may inadvertently advertise their profession, possibly putting themselves, their friends and loved ones in danger.

In other instances, an off-duty officer may be identified or targeted not because of their dress, but through other identifiers. For example, window decals of police professional associations on their vehicle(s) and a police hat in the back window are visible signs that the occupant is a police officer, or is associated with the law enforcement profession. Other indicators may include equipment that is in plain view in their vehicle and union membership badges attached to their license plates. In some states, there are also vanity license plates that police officers can purchase that have a police logo on them. These plates may serve to alert would-be attackers of the off-duty officer's profession.

Appropriate Clothing

A fundamental goal of concealed carry is that a person must appear unarmed. To ensure that the firearm is properly concealed, the off-duty officer must consider the concept: depth of concealment. Depth of concealment deals with properly concealing the weapon, striking that balance between making sure that the weapon is fully concealed, yet readily accessible, if necessary. Ensuring depth of concealment requires that the officer chooses and wears appropriate clothing that conceals the firearm, while allowing them to readily draw the firearm, if necessary.

At times depth of concealment is difficult to achieve. While a firearm could be concealed by clothing, it may not be invisible because the profile of the holster and/or firearm can be seen through the clothing, or there may be a bulge, contour, or outline. If the firearm is worn on the belt in a holster, for example, the off-duty officer will need to wear a jacket, sport coat, or a baggy or loose fitting shirt that is not tucked in the waistband to conceal the firearm and holster. The same issues apply to pants. If the officer is wearing an ankle holster, they will need to make sure that the pant leg is not too tight which, in turn, would impede drawing the firearm. The selection of proper clothing should also be based on various shooting positions. For example, the officer should make sure that the firearm could be readily drawn while sitting, standing and prone, without clothing obstructing the draw. Proper depth of concealment also needs to be considered from various positions to ensure that the firearm is always concealed from direct and indirect observation.

Holsters

When considering the fact that a significant number of police officers are killed with their own weapon that was taken away from them (Brown & Langan, 2001), a properly secured firearm is very important. Like on-duty, one of the safest and most secure places for an off-duty firearm is in a holster that has some level of retention. These off-duty holsters must be high quality and strong enough to prevent a suspect from literally tearing the holster apart to get at the firearm. It must also be properly secured to the body to prevent the holster and handgun from being stripped away, requiring the off-duty officer to have a sturdy belt with a buckle to keep the holster in place. Furthermore, an off-duty holster should be able to be operated with one hand only when drawing and re-holstering.

The type of holster may depend on the type of clothing that the person will be wearing when carrying. Choosing an off-duty holster may also depend upon one's gender, those activities they will be engaging in while carrying, and climate or season. It may also depend upon policy, particularly if the agency has any departmentally approved off-duty holsters that an officer can chose from. Because of these and other factors, a variety of holsters may be needed to properly carry off-duty. Some of the more common types include the belt, paddle, ankle, shoulder, and inside the waist holsters.

Belt-Styled Holsters

Perhaps one of the best types of off-duty holsters is that which the officer is used to while on duty - carrying the firearm on their waist in a belt holster located on the strong side of their body. There are several holster manufacturers that make the same style holster with the same retention device for off-duty or undercover use, where it is secured to the body by a sturdy belt that passes through the holster. By using the same holster in the same position on the body when off-duty, there is already a great deal of muscle memory present, which could serve to speed up the officer's draw in a high-stress situation, in comparison to other holster positions on the body. If not the same exact holster, there are many other types of through-the-belt holsters made by various manufacturers. Depending upon need, belt holsters can be strong or weak side draw, and can be constructed of leather, nylon, or other synthetic materials.

Paddle Holsters

Paddle holsters, by their design, are worn over the belt. They are not fully secured to the belt. Instead, there is a paddle-shaped piece of leather or plastic that the user slides down on the inside of the pant waist, while the holster then rests on the outside of the pant. Some paddle holster designs also have a plastic or metal clip attached to the back of the holster that snaps over the belt to prevent the holster from readily being taken away, while keeping the holster in place. Because a paddle holster usually does not have the belt pass through the holster itself, it may not be as secure as a traditional holster that is fully secured by a sturdy belt. Paddle holsters can also be worn on different locations on the waist. For example, they can be worn adjacent to the kidney on the strong or weak side which adds some versatility in comparison to other holster systems.

Ankle Holsters

Ankle holsters, as the name implies, permit the firearm to be carried on the user's ankle. Ankle holsters may be used when a person is not wearing a jacket or when they cannot properly conceal a firearm on their waist because of their dress. A basic ankle holster system is essentially a holster with a strap that the user wraps and secures around one of their ankles. With an ankle holster system, the user can carry on the strong or weak side, and on the inside or outside of the ankle. One of the drawbacks associated with the ankle holster is that an officer will have to squat or kneel down to draw their firearm. Squatting down in a gunfight could place the officer's head in the direct line of fire, since their head is now at waist level. Drawing from the ankle could also lead to a balance displacement issue. The draw could also be slower because of additional movements associated with the ankle draw, in comparison to a traditional belt holster draw.

Shoulder Holsters

Shoulder holsters are often used in undercover work or in those situations where the police officer is wearing some type of jacket to conceal the firearm and extra ammunition. A shoulder holster system carries the pistol in a yoke-style system on the support side. The pistol is in a holster that is located and attached to a shoulder harness that drapes over the top of the shoulder and is then suspended under the armpit. Spare ammunition, meanwhile, is located in the strong side armpit with a similar harness that wraps around the top of the shoulder and is attached to an ammunition pouch. To prevent the shoulder harness from moving around, there is usually an adjustable belt-style or elastic strap that is attached to the holster and magazine pouch that goes around the user's back. In other designs, the holster and or/ ammunition pouch may also have an elastic sling or belt that is attached to the holster and magazine pouch, which is then attached to the user's belt to further prevent the system from moving. These straps also facilitate a faster draw of the firearm and spare ammunition.

Shoulder holsters may not be the most tactically sound method of carry. A shoulder holster requires a shooter to draw the firearm across their body. In comparison to a belt holster, which allows the shooter to punch the firearm out, there is an additional movement with the shoulder holster, where the shooter must cross their body when drawing, and then sweep the firearm outward toward the threat. This may be a different movement from which the officer is accustomed to. Because of the extra movement(s), it may be a slower draw than having the firearm positioned elsewhere on the body, such as in a traditional strong side belt holster. Usually, shoulder holsters have the spare magazine located in the strong side armpit. During a magazine change, again the shooter must bring their support arm across their body to obtain a fresh magazine, perhaps slowing down their magazine change in the process.

Inside the Waist Systems

Inside the waist carry is when the off-duty officer carries the firearm between the body and the inside of the pant waist. There are a variety of products designed for inside the waist carry. They may include holsters that clip or attach to the inner waist band or belt. In other cases, some firearms are manufactured with a metal belt-style clip that is attached to the firearm's grip that clips onto the waistband or belt. Other after-market devices include grips that have metal or plastic clips built in so the firearm can be carried in the waistband without the need for a holster. By the very nature of the design of these devices, only a small amount of the firearm's grip will be exposed, making this type of carry system better concealed in comparison to other carry devices. Because these systems can be attached anywhere on the waist, they can be positioned on the back (i.e. a kidney carry), the front, and on the strong or weak side of the body. Like other different carry techniques, officers must practice their draw from their chosen carry position to become proficient. Depending upon their design, some of the inside the waist carry systems provide no level of security because they may lack a retention device that exists on other off-duty carry alternatives.

Other Carry Devices

Depending upon a variety of issues including the type of clothing the officer is wearing and their gender, a holster system may not be the most appropriate method of carry. Instead, an officer may have to carry the firearm in some type of system that is not directly secured to the body. For example, off-duty female officers, because of their dress, may have to carry the firearm in their purse. In other instances, off-duty officers may have to carry their firearm in a waist pack. One concern with carry systems that are not directly attached to the body is that the firearm (and carry device) could be easily taken away from the officer. Both the waist pack and purse, for example, are not as secure as a belt holster. A purse could be stripped from a person before they could get the gun drawn. A waist pack, although it has a belt system, is not as secure as a holster on a sturdy belt, and again it could be stripped away from the user. While there are some concerns associated with these types of holsters, many of these issues can be remedied through proper training.

Unsafe Carry Methods

In many off-duty carry situations, firearms are carried in an unsafe manner. An off-duty police officer may carry the firearm in their pocket or in the waistband of their pant, using their belt to secure the firearm against their body. This is not tactically sound. First, the firearm will not be in the same position all the time, as it "floats" somewhere on the officer's body. This will lead to problems in locating the firearm in a high stress situation, where the speed of the draw will be impaired or slowed down to the point that the officer has lost the element of surprise and they are now over the suspect's reaction time. Other unsafe carries may include carrying the firearm in the front or back pocket of the pant, in a jacket pocket, or in the user's sock. These carry methods do not secure the firearm, the draw may be impeded, and the firearm could easily be taken away.

Extra & Appropriate Ammunition

Like on duty, a police officer should carry some extra fully-loaded magazines with them when off-duty. These extra magazines should be stored in a magazine pouch that is readily accessible. The selection of proper ammunition is also necessary. In some cases, a police officer may be frugal when selecting their off-duty ammunition, as their agency may not provide for or pay for off-duty ammunition. Cost should not be a factor when selecting ammunition: quality should be. Off-duty ammunition should have the appropriate quality, accuracy, penetration and expansion to ensure terminal performance.

In some cases, the police department will specify what type of ammunition can be carried (i.e. the same ammunition as the duty weapon). In other cases, officers may be required to submit in writing what type of ammunition they will be carrying for evaluation and approval from the agency. The agency may also evaluate the performance of the off-duty ammunition prior to approval. Officers may also be required to qualify with their off-duty ammunition in order to demonstrate proficiency with that specific type of ammunition with their off-duty firearm.

Communication Devices

Off-duty officers will also need to have some type of reliable portable communication device with them to contact 911 and/or call for backup. These portable communication devices could include their police radios if they are issued to them, or at a minimum, it may be a cell phone.

Restraints

Off-duty officers should also have some departmentally approved restraint device with them. Restraint devices are needed because once the incident is over, the off-duty officer may have to physically restrain the suspect by handcuffing them or using some other departmentally approved device, such as plastic flex cuffs.

Photo ID and Badge

The last thing an off-duty officer wants is confusion by other police officers and citizens regarding their identity as a police officer. In order to reduce any confusion that could arise in an off-duty situation, police officers should always have their badge and photo identification card with them to verify their identity. Photo ID's and badges could be concealed and attached to the officer's belt, they could be worn concealed around the neck on a chain, or they could be carried in the officer's wallet or purse. Regardless of where they are carried, they must be readily available and accessible. Officers may also consider carrying their identification and badge on their support side so they can use their support hand to readily display their photo ID and badge, while keeping their gun hand free to use.

Training Issues

Off-duty issues and tactics are often dramatically different from those encountered on-duty. If an officer is not trained in off-duty tactics and confrontations, their repertoire of knowledge and experience will be sparse, perhaps leading to improper decisions that could put their life and the lives of others in greater danger than if they did not decide to engage the threat(s). To

Training Tip: Establish a quarterly or seasonal off-duty qualification course, requiring officers to wear normal street clothes for that season. Training in different types of clothes according to season will better prepare officers for off-duty force incidents they may encounter.

prevent this from occurring, police agencies should have a comprehensive training program for off-duty carry.

Training programs should include decision-making skills that consider the totality of the circumstances, with an emphasis on civilian and officer safety. Some decision-making skills related to engaging a threat off-duty as pointed by Pinizzotto and Davis (1992), who critiqued a police officer who was killed off-duty (when he failed to realize that there were three armed robbers, instead of only one) include: "would it have been wrong for an officer to act as witness in this case?" Might it have been more prudent to take note of the description of the robbers and only act when the robbers started to flee the scene? Wasn't the situation exacerbated by innocent lives placed in jeopardy unnecessarily by the officer and taking aggressive action in a crowded bar?" (p. 38). In addition to effective decision making skills, officers should also be trained in the agency's policies and procedures regarding off-duty carry. Officers should also be trained in what to expect in a situation in the context of how they could be treated as a suspect until their identity is verified. They should also know the criminal and civil consequences of carrying off-duty.

Besides training in decision-making and policies and procedures, the fundamentals associated with actual carry and use must also be considered. Primarily, officers should qualify with their off-duty firearm. Depending upon departmental policy, some agencies may not require officers to qualify with the off-duty firearm if it is not their duty gun. It is important, however, that an officer qualifies with their off-duty firearm and the agency's firearms staff records their performance. Even if the agency does not have a policy, having a record of qualification could serve as a liability reduction tool if the officer should ever get in a situation where they used their firearm. The qualification record will serve as evidence that the officer was at least qualified on their off-duty weapon.

Too often an officer will qualify with the firearm without wearing appropriate off-duty clothing. It is critical that the officer trains and qualifies in their off-duty clothing. In warmer months, they should qualify in light clothing. In the cooler months, the officer should qualify wearing a sweater, jacket or heavy winter coat and gloves. Training in off-duty clothing will let the officer realize how their performance could be affected by the holster system, and how the depth of concealment could impede their draw and subsequent performance. Through this type of training, however, the officer can overcome these barriers and become proficient.

Officers should also qualify and train with those holsters they will be using off-duty. Proper training will create muscle memory and economy of motion during a confrontation. If the firearm is secured on the ankle, for example, officers will need to be properly trained in lifting the pant leg and drawing the firearm from a squatting or kneeling position. Likewise, if a shoulder system is used, they must practice cross drawing the firearm and conducting magazine changes. Off-duty carry may also require training in multi-use techniques. For example, officers should be trained in how to properly move their clothing out of the way, draw their firearm, display their ID and badge, and issue verbal commands.

What to Do in a Situation

Off-duty officers generally have two options when dealing with an off-duty incident. First, they can avoid a direct confrontation, use their observational skills, and call 911 for an on-duty officer to deal with the situation. If the situation requires immediate intervention and control, however, the off-duty officer may become an active participant in the incident with the intent of de-escalating and controlling the situation.

One primary issue in a off-duty situation is the safety of the officer, their friends and family, and innocent civilians that are in the vicinity of the event. Before engaging in any activity, the officer must consider all alternatives to ensure the safety of everyone, with the needs of the innocent civilians as a top priority. If an officer decides to engage a threat and it is safe to do so, they must get all innocents out of harm's way.

When a situation does arise, and when tactically acceptable before, during, or after the situation is under control, the off-duty officer must call 911 for uniformed police assistance. If the off-duty officer is alone and they cannot personally request 911 assistance, they may have to tell others in the area that they are an off-duty police officer and they need police assistance immediately. Because the scene may not be fully secure, the off-duty officer should also warn and verbally instruct civilians in the area to stay back and out of the way, while clearly stating that they are an off-duty officer.

Off-duty officers should also keep in mind that they may need to engage in calming activities with civilians in the immediate area, assuring them first that they are an off-duty police officer, they are safe, and that uniformed police are on the way. An officer should also keep in mind that they will have limited control over how strangers or civilians will react and respond to their actions. Because the situation may prohibit the officer from immediately displaying their badge and photo identification card to the public to confirm their identity, civilians could respond in an aggressive manner toward the off-duty officer. Citizens could also report to the police (via 911) that there is a person/suspect/criminal with a gun, which is actually the off-duty officer.

When uniformed police do arrive, the off-duty officer is no longer in charge of the scene. This means that the off-duty officer must follow all verbal commands (even if they do not make sense to them) and comply with the responding officer's orders, not questioning any of their orders or actions. Uniformed on-duty officers from that specific jurisdiction are in charge, and the off-duty officer must fully cooperate with these officers to assist them in de-escalating and gaining control of the situation.

Because the off-duty officer's status is unknown, when uniformed officers arrive, the off-duty officer must also make sure that they clearly identify themselves as off-duty officers and show their ID and badge. If the off-duty officer is using cover (which he should be doing) when the police arrive, he should keep his hands in plain view, outside of cover and not engage in any action(s) that could be perceived as threatening. If they still have their firearm pointed toward the threat, or are in possession of the firearm in a holster or near them, it will also mean that the off-duty officer will most likely be told to slide or move the firearm away from himself.

At a minimum, the off-duty officer should be expected to be treated as a felon where responding officers will engage in a high risk felony stop, ordering the off-duty officer to follow their commands, leading up to being handcuffed. Even if the off-duty officer has proper identification and a badge, they will most likely be treated as a suspect, detained and even handcuffed during the incident. This will be necessary for the safety of officers at the scene until the identity of the off-duty officer is confirmed, most likely by contacting the off-duty officer's police agency.

Following the event, the off-duty officer will be questioned or interviewed by police officers in that jurisdiction where the incident occurred. Off-duty officers may also be required to write an incident report and they may be subjected to follow-up interviews and additional reports, if necessary. After the incident, the officer should immediately notify his own agency of the incident. Because the officer was acting under color of law and had police authority to intervene in the situation, their employer will need to ensure that they acted in a tactical, legal and ethical manner.

They may also want to make sure that the officer followed all agency policies and procedures during the incident. This will result in writing additional reports to their agency and perhaps an internal investigation of the officer's actions prior to and during the event that led to the use of force.

Family Members and Significant Others

If an officer opts to carry off-duty, another consideration is the concern for family members and significant others who may be with them when a situation occurs. Off-duty police officers need to understand that they must properly train their spouse, children and/or significant others in how to respond in the event of a violent confrontation. In order to prepare these individuals for a violent confrontation, they must be trained to act tactically. Some of the issues that need to be considered at a minimum include: 1) doing exactly what they are told to do; 2) walk on the officer's non-gun side; 3) use cover and concealment; and, 4) learn how to communicate with 911 and other officers.

Doing Exactly What They are Told to Do

Officers should train significant others not to question them when they are told to do something. At the same time, these individuals should be briefed in tactical communication techniques. They may include hand and body signs or other non-verbal cues that will serve to alert them to clear away from the officer and seek cover and/or concealment, and contact 911, making sure that dispatch is informed that an off-duty is officer involved in the force-related situation.

Walking on the Officer's Non-gun Side

In a high stress incident, a normal but dangerous reaction by those with an off-duty officer will be to perhaps crowd against and even grab the off-duty officer for protection. If the officer is grabbed on his gun side, however, it will impair his ability to draw and confront the suspect, slowing down their reaction time tremendously. To prevent the possibility of this occurring, individuals accompanying the officer should always walk on the officer's non-gun side.

321

Using Cover and Concealment

Civilians should also be taught how to seek and use cover and concealment. These individuals must also be taught to hold cover, regardless of if their significant other is injured. They should also be taught to wait behind cover or concealment until the scene is secured and determined safe by responding officers.

Communication with 911 and other Officers

Significant others also need to be properly trained in how to use whatever communication device is being carried by the off-duty officer (or themselves) and how to calmly notify 911 of the situation, with particular emphasis that there is an off-duty officer involved. Significant others should be taught how to "script" the 911 call, providing the location and specific details of the event. Significant others must also be taught how to provide an accurate, detailed and thorough description of the officer and suspect(s) so the police can differentiate friend from foe. These individuals should also be trained in how to approach and communicate with other officers who arrive at the scene, with an emphasis that there is an armed off-duty officer involved.

Off-Duty "Nevers"

Common sense must prevail when an officer decides to carry off-duty. At times, however, common sense involving off-duty carry is not that common and officers forget some issues and concerns that may be readily apparent to others. Some of the common sense "nevers" related to off-duty carry include not carrying for show, not consuming alcohol, not giving up immediate control of the fireman, and not allowing one's emotions to get the best of them.

Carrying for "Show"

Off-duty firearms should never be carried for the sheer glamour of carrying a firearm. A firearm is a tool. It is not jewelry. It serves a specific purpose and that purpose is not for show or prestige. It is to stop and control a threat that the officer has reason to believe (based on the totality of circumstances), can cause death or great bodily harm. It is not a toy for display and for others to fondle and look at. The firearm is to be carried concealed and it should never be displayed for show or to impress others.

Alcohol Use and Firearms

Some department policies prohibit an officer from carrying off-duty when they have a blood alcohol level or are legally impaired or intoxicated. For those agencies that do not have policies, a reasonable and prudent police officer should never carry while consuming alcohol or when they have a blood alcohol level. As already pointed out in the chapter on Safety, alcohol and firearms do not mix. Alcohol slows down one's reaction time and impairs effective decision-making. Not only could alcohol put the off-duty officer in danger, but because of the effects of alcohol, innocent civilians and loved ones could also be placed in greater danger of injury or death.

Consider the following examples involving alcohol and off-duty firearms. In one case, a police officer left her purse with her duty gun in it on the floor of a bar. When she made it to the next bar with her friends, she realized her mistake. Immediately she returned to the first bar, where she was met by the local police, who had responded to the bar when a waitress opened the off-duty officer's purse to look for her driver's license and found her pistol. The officer was legally intoxicated and police seized her weapon because of her condition. Later this officer was suspended for three days for her actions and ordered to attend mandatory firearms training related to off-duty use. In another case, the off-duty officer was removed from a bar because he was intoxicated and belligerent toward some of the patrons. Angered that the bouncers had removed him, he went back to his vehicle, retrieved his off-duty firearm and badge and confronted the bouncers with his badge and firearm in plain view. The bouncers, upon seeing his pistol immediately called the police. The police arrived and subsequently arrested the off-duty officer.

Never Give Up Immediate Control of the Off-Duty Firearm

Off-duty firearms must be under control of the owner at all times. If an off-duty firearm is kept in a moving vehicle, for example, a host of issues could arise from that poor decision. Imagine, for example, that the vehicle is loaned to a significant other or friend, and they get stopped for a motor vehicle violation. Unbeknownst to this person, a pistol is in the glove box. The responding officer asks for registration and proof of insurance, whereas the driver of the vehicle opens the glove box, exposing the firearm. Not only could this end tragically, but at a minimum the driver could be placed in a felony stop situation where they are now confronted by an officer with a firearm aimed at them. They could be arrested, and the officer could later be disciplined for their negligent behavior associated with their firearm. In other instances related to storing firearms in a vehicle, the vehicle could also be stolen where the officer's duty or off-duty weapon could be subsequently used in a variety of crimes. This again could cause problems for the both the officer and their agency.

In other situations, off-duty officers may temporarily give up immediate control of their firearm. Temporarily giving up a firearm could include having a significant other "hold" the firearm for them. For example, an officer going out with friends may decide to leave his firearm at a friend's house because they will be consuming alcoholic beverages. While a prudent decision not to carry while consuming alcoholic beverages, leaving a firearm at a friend's house unattended could lead to serious consequences. A more effective decision would be to carefully plan one's outings in advance to determine if they should carry off-duty. Other poor examples of not controlling the possession of the firearm may include having a friend or significant other physically carry the firearm for them or "hide" the firearm while attending a barbecue or house party. At a minimum, the officer could forget to retrieve his firearm. Temporarily giving up immediate control of a firearm is not tactically acceptable.

Never Let Your Emotions Get the Best of You

On and off-duty, a police officer should never let their emotions get the best of them. Individuals may be faced with off-duty situations where they lack authority and the powers of arrest. Yet, because they have their gun and badge with them (and they may be impaired by alcohol) they may identify themselves as a police officer and perhaps display their firearm. Not only could this lead to disciplinary action against the officer and perhaps criminal charges (such as assault), it also casts a poor image of policing in general. In other situations, off-duty officers may put themselves and others in greater danger because of their ego. If an officer forces a confrontation that could have been avoided or resolved through less action, the end result could be the possibility of a loved one being killed or severely injured. The officer could also face criminal and/or civil liability for his actions.

Selecting the Off-Duty Weapon

Selection of the off-duty weapon is also an issue. In some situations the police agency will determine what is an acceptable off-duty firearm. They may specify an appropriate make, model and/or caliber, or provide officers with a list of accepted off-duty firearms that they can choose from. Other agencies may actually provide an off-duty and/or backup firearm, while others may restrict the off-duty weapon to the duty weapon or a smaller variant of the same caliber firearm. Other agencies may be more liberal, allowing officers to carry any weapon of their choice while off-duty.

One key consideration of any off-duty weapon is that it must have the ability to rapidly incapacitate or stop an offender, and it must be able to be concealed. It must also be a well-constructed, high quality firearm. The National Institute of Justice on a regular basis conducts evaluations of commonly used firearms and sets forth certain requirements that must be met to be suitable for police use. These reports are readily available at the ncjrs.org website. These requirements provide information on what issues a person should consider when choosing an off-duty weapon. The specific criteria used to evaluate firearms are shown in Box 16-1.

The NIJ recommends that compliance with all the requirements of their standard is preferred. If the firearm that the officer is interested in carrying is not reviewed by the NIJ, it should be reviewed by the agency's firearms staff and/or armorer to ensure that if meet NIJ standards.

Firearms Finishes

Another important issue is selecting the type of finish for the off-duty firearm. The finish serves two distinct purposes. First, finishes are designed to protect the metal components on the firearm. They also serve a cosmetic purpose, giving the firearm some degree of aesthetic appeal. While a person may consider the looks of the finish as important, the durability of the finish should always be a top priority when selecting the off-duty weapon, because it will be exposed to a variety of environmental contaminants — especially rust. Some of the more common finishes for firearms include: nitro-carbonized, blued, stainless steel, parkerized, and stainless steel.

BOX 16-1
NIJ SELECTION REQUIREMENTS FOR
SEMIAUTOMATIC HANDGUNS

CRITERIA	REQUIREMENTS
Visual Inspection	• In the single action mode (if the pistol has a "single action" mode), the hammer will have sufficient over-travel to ensure achievement of the full cocked position
	• There will be no loose chips, shavings, or filings in the pistol
	• The pistol will have no chips, scratches, or burrs. There will be no sharp edges or corners that could cut the shooter's hand while firing or during manual cycling of the pistol
Functional Requirements	• Action - The slide will operate smoothly without binding or sticking when operated by hand or during firing tests
	• Ejection - the ejection mechanism shall eject cases without a hang-up and without hitting the shooter during the ejection test or the firing tests
	• Trigger - The single action trigger pull force will not be less than 3 lbf or more than 8 lbf when tested
	• The double action trigger pull force will be no more than 18lbf when tested
	• For a pistol employing a striker fire mechanism, trigger pull force will not be less than 5 lbf nor more that 15lbf when tested
	• Hammer - when tested, the hammer will operate smoothly without binding and will not release under an applied load of 10 lbf (plus or minus 1/4 lbf)
	• Safety Features - The pistol will have one or more design features to prevent inadvertent firing. Active (user activated) safety devices, if provided, will be designed so that the pistol can be made fire-ready by releasing the safety(s) with the shooting hand. The pistol will not fire when tested with the safety feature(s) engaged.
	• Magazine - The magazine will have a capacity of six rounds, minimum, and will be capable of being released without removing the shooting hand from the pistol.

CRITERIA	REQUIREMENTS
Model Qualification Firing Requirement	The pistol will fire 600 rounds of commercial ammunition with no structural or mechanical failures and no more than 5 malfunctions. Of those five allowable malfunctions, no more than three will be firing malfunctions (failure to feed, fire, or eject a round) not attributable to faulty ammunition.
Drop Safety Requirement	This pistol is dropped from a height of four feet onto a 1- inch thick rubber mat. If the weapon discharges, it is not suitable for use. The positions are: • Normal firing position • Upside down, barrel horizontal • On the grip, barrel vertical • On muzzle, barrel vertical • On left side, barrel horizontal • On right side, barrel horizontal • On the rearmost point of that device
Drop Function Requirement	After completing the drop safety test, the pistol will fire 20 rounds with no more than 3 malfunctions.

Source: Equipment performance report: 1999 autoloading pistols. Washington, D.C. National Institute of Justice.

Nitro-Carbonizing

Nitro-carbonized finishes are a relatively new method of protecting metals from oxidation. With a nitro-carbonized finish, carbon and nitrogen are infused into steel through a pressurized gas treatment process. This process impregnates the surface of the object with nitrogen which forms nitrides and carbides with iron and other alloys that exist, forming a thin oxide finish on the surface areas of the firearm. Unlike other types of finishes, with the nitro-carbonized processes, the finish penetrates and is diffused into the metal, forming a very hard, wear resistant finish. Perhaps one of the most common nitro-carbonized finishes is associated with Glock firearms that use the proprietary Tenifer name to coat their weapons. This type of finish requires very little maintenance.

Bluing

In effect, bluing is rust. It is controlled rusting that is enhanced by selenium. The purpose of bluing is not to completely prevent rust. Instead, bluing slows the oxidation process down. Bluing is simply an oxide coating that is applied to metals at relatively high temperatures (300 degrees and above). While there are many different types of bluing, "hot bluing" methods rely upon immersing the metals into a molten salt bath, giving the metal a deep blue/black luster. Modern, or "hot bluing" became popular after World War II. It is the standard bluing method used today. This method of bluing replaced some of the more complicated and expensive forms of earlier bluing processes that included cold bluing, case hardening (that gave the metal the look as if it was burnt, consisting of many shades of blue), and carbonia bluing which used a gas furnace to place almost a gloss black finish on steel.

Depending upon the type and quality of bluing, these finishes can be quite attractive, but perhaps not functional. Blued firearms, while they may look good, are difficult to maintain in comparison to other types of finishes. The key to maintaining a blued firearm is to prevent it from getting moisture on it as well as other corrosive elements, including salt. Any type of bluing rusts quickly when exposed to salts and moisture and when not properly maintained and stored. In fact, even when a blued firearm is thought to be properly maintained and stored, there may still be some corrosion concerns because of humidity and dust that settles on the bluing. Dust may serve as a sponge, absorbing the humidity in the air, causing rust spots on the firearm. If not rust spots, a film of rust could develop on the surface of blued firearms. This can often be seen with firearms that have been stored for a period of time. If a person were to wipe the blued portion of the firearm, they would see some rust on their rag they used to wipe the gun down with. Blued finishes can be so fragile, for example, that even carrying the firearm in a leather holster for a long period of time could result in corrosion problems, due to the level of moisture and salts the leather holster has absorbed.

Parkerizing

Parkerizing is more durable than bluing. A parkerized finish can best be described as a greenish-gray colored treatment. The process of parker-ization is achieved by dipping metal into phosphoric acid. Often these finishes are seen on military firearms. Like bluing, this finish will not prevent rust. It will only inhibit it to a certain degree. This type of finish will require more maintenance than finishes such as the nitro-carbonized and firearms manufactured from stainless steel.

Stainless Steel

Unlike the other finishes that are basically some type of coating, stainless steel finishes are the result of the base metal that is used to construct the firearm. Stainless steel is simply steel that contains chromium (more than 16% in total content) that makes it resistant to corrosion. The chromium content of the steel forms a thin layer of chromium oxide on the surface of the steel when exposed to oxygen. Even if this thin layer should be scuffed or scratched, a new layer of chromium dioxide quickly forms again on the surface, protecting the steel underneath. The name "stainless" steel, however, may be misleading. While it is quite resistant to staining and corrosion, it is not "stainproof." Depending upon what the steel is exposed to, it will still oxidize and stain. This degree of corroision, however, will be much less, requiring less effort to maintain the finish in comparison to other types of finishes.

The Law Enforcement Safety Act of 2004

On July 22nd, 2004, President George Bush signed into law the Law Enforcement Safety Act of 2004 (H.R. 218). This Act allows both retired and active duty police officers the right to carry a concealed firearm nationwide (see Box 16-2). Prior to this Act, some states offered reciprocity to police officers from other states to carry, while others did not. The primary purpose of this Act was to standardize requirements across the states and to provide police officers the same rights as citizens in those states to carry concealed firearms (Ferrell, 2004).

At a minimum, qualified active and retired police officers that fall under the Act are required to carry a departmental identification card. Active law enforcement officers must carry an identification card issued by their agency indicating that they are an active or qualified law enforcement officer. Retired officers, meanwhile, must have a photo identification card that indicates that they are a retired law enforcement officer and within one year of the date of issue of the card, they were tested or otherwise found by the agency to meet the standards established by the agency for training and qualification for active law enforcement officers to carry a firearm of the same type concealed. If retired officers do not have this type of identification card, they must have a photo identification card from their agency that indicates that they are a retired officer and certification from the state that they reside in, and that the individual has, within the past 365 days, been tested or otherwise been found by the state to meet the standards established by the state for training and qualification for active law enforcement officers to carry a firearm of the same type.

At first glance, this Act may appear to provide active and retired police officers with broad powers of concealed carry in other states. Even though federal law may allow active and retired police officers to carry a firearm concealed in another state, agency policies and procedures supercede federal law. As a result, agency policies and procedures may prohibit concealed carry in another state for both retirees and active officers, or restrict what types of firearms may be carried off-duty. Also, this Act does not supercede or limit the laws of any State. Therefore, retired or active officers may not have powers of arrest in other states unless they are specifically granted those powers or authority by the state (Ferrell, 2004). Additionally, these individuals may not be able to carry their firearms on private property if the owners prohibit or restrict concealed carry. Certain local government and state properties may also place restrictions or prohibitions on concealed carry by police officers.

Home Storage Considerations

The vast majority of adults will agree that firearms can cause injury and death and they should be properly stored. Nevertheless, approximately 30,000 individuals per year die from firearms-related injuries (Wiebe, 2003). Additionally, statistics on firearms-related injuries of children aged 14 or less who were admitted to hospitals from 1993-2000 show that an average of 4.9 per 100,000 children are shot per year. Of those shot, 90% of the cases involved an unintentional injury inflicted by themselves, a friend, relative, or another person (Eber, et al., 2004). To prevent firearms-related deaths and injuries, all firearms must be properly stored and secured in the home.

In some instances, police officers may disregard or forget the dangers associated with firearms. Police officers, because of their training and experience in firearms handling, may have unrealistic expectations that others will have the same level of safety and respect for firearms. For example, in a study of 207 police officers from a large police agency in the southern United States, the majority of police officers stored their weapons unlocked (59%) and loaded (68%). Their main rationale for not properly securing and unloading their firearms was the need to protect themselves or their family (Coyne-Beasley, 2001). Studies of storage practices of the general public, meanwhile, have found lower reported rates of storing firearms loaded and unlocked. For instance, in one study of over 1500 households in the U.S., 21.5% of the respondents stored firearms loaded and unlocked (Stennies, et. al, 1999). Another large study found that 43% of homes with children present reported that they had at least one unlocked firearm (Schuster, et al, 2000).

BOX 16-2
H.R. 218
THE LAW ENFORCEMENT OFFICERS SAFETY ACT OF 2004

Under Section 926B of the Act a qualified law enforcement officer must meet the following criteria:

- Is authorized by law to engage in or supervise the prevention detection investigation or prosecution of or the incarceration of any person for any violation of law and has statutory powers of arrest;
- Is authorized by the agency to carry a firearm;
- Is not the subject of any disciplinary action by the agency;
- Meets standards if any established by the agency which require the employee to regularly qualify in the use of a firearm;
- Is not under the influence of alcohol or other intoxicating or hallucinatory drug or substance; and
- Is not prohibited by federal law from receiving a firearm.

Qualified retired police officers meanwhile must meet the following criteria for concealed carry under Section 926C.

- Retired or in good standing from service as a public agency as a law enforcement officer other than for reasons of mental instability;
- Before such retirement was authorized by law to engage in or supervise the prevention detection investigation or prosecution of or the incarceration of any person for any violation of law and had the statutory powers of arrest;
- Before such retirement was regularly employed as a law enforcement officer for an aggregate of 15 years or more; or
- Retired from service with such agency after completing any applicable probationary period of such service due to a service-connected disability as determined by such agency;
- Has a nonforfeitable right to benefits under the retirement plan of the agency;
- During the most recent 12 month period has met at the expense of the individual the State's standards for training and qualification for active law enforcement officers to carry firearms;
- Is not under the influence of alcohol of another intoxicating or hallucinatory drug or substance; and
- Is not prohibited by Federal law from receiving a firearm.

Some officers may keep unsecured and loaded weapons in the home based on the rationale that if they need a firearm, they need it immediately. They may also justify unsecured, loaded firearms because they live alone, or they have no children, so they do not have to worry about firearm's safety. While an officer may live alone, they also need to consider the fact that there may be at-risk groups visiting their home. These visitors may include friends, children, family members, and elderly relatives who may be lacking their full mental capabilities. For those unwanted visitors - the criminal, the unsecured firearm has now become a crime gun that can be used in a variety of firearms-related crimes. In other instances, a police officer may keep a loaded firearm that is not properly secured under the premise that family members are taught not to handle the firearm or they are properly trained in safe handling of weapons. This position could be fatal as an officer may underestimate a child's understanding of, and curiosity levels related to, firearms. Because of the risk of a firearms-related accident, a common sense approach is that the officer must make sure that their firearm is properly secured at all times.

There are several different types of storage and security devices available. Some are designed to simply store the firearm. Others are designed to prevent the firearm from being loaded and/or fired. Some of the more common safety devices are shown in Box 16-3.

Officers need to determine the level of security needed, based on their particular needs and preference. One key point is the fact that a weapon should never be left unsecured and unattended, especially if it is loaded. The best level of security for a firearm will include locking mechanisms combined with a secure storage system. For example, a firearm may be secured with trigger lock and then placed in a lock box or cabinet to prevent it from being used. Relying upon the disassembly of the firearm without any other locking device is not recommended. Components can readily be re-assembled, leading to tragic consequences.

Ammunition and firearms-related accessories should also be properly secured and stored. Like firearms themselves, children may be quite curious about ammunition and firearms-related components, including magazines. Ammunition and magazines should also be stored separate from the firearm to prevent the two components from being combined together to cause a tragedy.

In some situations, some police departments may have specific policies and procedures related to the safe storage of firearms and ammunition. In one local sheriff's department, for example, if a deputy takes the duty weapon home, it must be secured with a trigger lock that is issued to the deputy. If an accident should occur with this firearm because it was not properly secured, the deputy can then face disciplinary actions. Other policies, meanwhile, may require that the firearm be secured in some particular way, while others may provide recommendations on the safe storage of firearms in the home. Other agencies may simply rely upon common sense that their officers are properly securing their firearms when off-duty.

	BOX 16-3 **FIREARMS STORAGE AND SECURITY DEVICES**	
Type	**Description**	**Drawbacks**
Trigger Locks	Prevent access to and prevent the trigger from being pulled to the rear. They Are usually 2 piece devices that fit around and through the trigger guard.	Does not prohibit unsafe handling of the firearm Does not deter theft
Cable Locks	Are designed to be placed through the action and chamber or magazine well of the firearm. They prevent ammunition from being loaded into the firearm and the action from being locked	Does not prohibit unsafe handling of the firearm Does not deter theft
Safes	Are storage devices. They prohibit access to firearms unless the user has a key and/or combination. Depending upon construction, they are difficult to break into.	May be quite large and expensive Does not physically prevent the firearm from being used.
Lock Boxes	Are storage devices. They are basically a box with some type of locking system that delays access to the firearm. They can be key, combination, or push-button style. Some can be mounted to wall studs or other areas, preventing them from readily being carried away.	Do not physically prevent the firearm from being used If not anchored, can be carried away because of their size
Cabinets	Are usually decorative storage devices that are designed for the display of firearms. Depending upon construction, they have glass doors or panes and may have a key locking mechanism.	Is a storage device that has minimal security Do not physically prevent the firearm from being used
Disassembly of Firearms	Is simply taking a firearm apart to prevent it from being used. In some cases, components are separated and placed in different locations	IS NOT a locking or storage method IS NOT a recommended permanent security /storage technique Components can readily be carried away and perhaps reassembled

333

Civil & Criminal Liability

Agencies and officers must realize that inappropriate off-duty actions can make them targets for a civil lawsuit in both the state and federal courts. Various standards exist to determine the relationship between the officer's off-duty actions and their relationship with official police powers or acting under color of law, or the fact that their actions were associated with using the state's power behind their actions (Libby, 1992; Miller, 1997). Civil lawsuits may not be limited solely to inappropriate actions. Even if an officer acted in a completely appropriate manner, they could still become the target of a civil lawsuit for their actions if the plaintiff perceived that they were somehow wronged by the officer's actions.

If an off-duty officer uses or stores their firearm in an inappropriate way they can also be criminally charged. Officers should keep in mind that they can face criminal charges ranging from brandishing a firearm to assault and homicide if they use their off-duty firearms in an inappropriate manner. Many municipalities and states have enacted access prevention laws that are designed to keep firearms out the hands of unauthorized users, especially children. These laws require that gun owners keep their firearms secured. Violations of these laws can result in misdemeanor or felony convictions against the legal owner (McClurg, 1999). Combined with criminal charges, officers can also face disciplinary measures for their off-duty actions involving the use of a firearm, up to and including dismissal from their agency.

Conclusion

There are many issues that need to be considered with off-duty carry. As pointed out in this chapter, police officers should never carry a firearm for show or prestige, and alcohol should never be consumed when carrying off-duty. Officers must also maintain immediate control of their firearms at all times and never let their emotions get the best of them in an off-duty (as well as an on-duty) situation. If departmental policies and procedures allow for off-duty carry, police officers must always balance their decision to carry with the safety of the public, their friends, and family. Other issues may be related to the officer's lifestyle choices and their personal beliefs or philosophy toward off-duty carry.

If the decision to carry off-duty is made, officers also need to develop a comprehensive plan for off-duty carry. This plan should include developing an appropriate mindset for off-duty carry, selecting proper clothing, and choosing the right type of holster. Besides carrying the firearm itself, officers will also need to carry extra ammunition, a communication device, restraints, their badge, and their photo identification card. Off-duty carry will also require proper training in decision making and tactics and how to properly respond to a situation. Other issues include training others in how to properly respond and act in situations, properly selecting the off-duty weapon, safely storing and securing the firearm in the home, and recognizing that officers can be held civilly and criminally responsible for their off-duty actions.

REFERENCES

Beyer, W.C. (Winter/Spring, 2005). Police shootings under the Fourth Amendment. Richmond journal of law and public interest, 1-57.

Brown, J.M. & Langan, P.A. (2001). Police and homicide: Justifiable homicide by police, police officers murdered by felons. Washington, D.C. U.S. Department of Justice.

Coyne-Beasley, T.; Johnson, R.M.; Charles, L.E. & V.J. Schoenbach. (August, 2001). American journal of preventive medicine, 21(2), 118-123.

Eber, G.B.; Annest, J.L.; Mercy, J.A. & G.W. Ryan (June, 2004). Nonfatal and fatal firearm-related injuries among children aged 14 years and younger: United States, 1993-2000. Pediatrics, 113(6), 1686-1692.

Equipment performance report: 1999 autoloading pistols. Washington, D.C. National Institute of Justice.

Ferrell, C.E. (October, 2004). Law enforcement safety act of 2004. The police chief, 71(10).

H.R. 218: The Law Enforcement Officers Safety Act of 2004.

Libby, S. (Summer, 1992). When off-duty state officials act under color of state law for the purposed of section 1983. Memphis state university law review, 22, 725-754.

McClurg, A.J. (1999). Child access prevention laws: A common sense approach to gun control. Saint Louis University public law review, 18, 47-78.

Miller, D.S. (Spring, 1997). Off duty, off the wall, but not off the hook: Section 1983 liability for the private misconduct of police officials. Akron law review, 30, 325-392.

Pinizzotto, A.J. & Davis, E.F. (September, 1992). Killed in the line of duty: A study of selected felonious killings of law enforcement officers. Washington, D.C.: U.S. Department of Justice.

Schuster, M.A.; Franke, T.M.; Bastian, A.M.; Sor, S.; & N. Halfon. (April, 2000). Firearm storage patterns in US homes with children. <u>American journal of public health, 90</u>(4), 588-594.

Stennies, G.; Ikeda, R.; Leadbetter, S.; Houston, B. & J. Sacks. (June, 1999). Firearm storage practices and children in the home, United States, 1994. <u>Archives of pediatrics and adolescent medicine, 153</u>(6), 586-590.

Wiebe, D.J. (2003). Homicide and suicide risks associated with firearms in the home: A national case-control study. <u>Annals of emergency medicine, 41</u>, 771-782.

Introduction

B allistics (in the context of physics) is "the science of the motion of a projectile during its travel through the barrel of a firearm, during its subsequent trajectory though the air, and during its final complication motion after striking the target" (Swan & Swan, 1984, p. 347). To a novice, the flight or travel of a bullet may appear to be simple. The bullet flies straight and strikes a target. This, however, is not necessarily the case. As this chapter will point out, several variables affect the flight and terminal performance of a bullet.

To gain a comprehensive understanding of the study of ballistics, this chapter will first provide the reader with an overview of the basics of interior ballistics. Next, it will review the principles of external ballistics. Last, this chapter will provide the reader with an understanding of terminal ballistics - what the bullet does to an object upon impact. This section of the chapter will also include a review of wound ballistics - a subsection of terminal ballistics that studies the "interaction of penetrating projectiles with living body tissues" (Fackler, 1998, p. 17).

Interior Ballistics

Interior ballistics investigates what happens within the firearm before the bullet exits the barrel. Interior ballistics begins with primer ignition. As pointed out in the Nomenclature chapter, primers are located in the primer pocket of the cartridge case. When struck by the firing pin or striker mechanism, the priming compound detonates and sends a flame through the flash hole at the base of the cartridge case, and ignites the powder grains located inside the cartridge case. Primers are classified as an initiating explosive; they are used to ignite the gunpowder contained in the cartridge case. Primers are very sensitive to heat and shock, and when detonated, they explode instead of burn (Saferstein, 1990).

The powder or propellant ignited by the primer does not explode. It burns rapidly, creating an expanding gas that builds up pressure on the base of the bullet, subsequently pushing and accelerating the bullet down and out of the barrel. This propellant is not a solid mass. It is composed of several pellets (or grains) that, depending upon their size and shape, will influence its burn rate and the production of gas and pressure inside the barrel of the firearm. These chamber pressures can reach 40 to 50 thousand pounds per square inch or higher. These pellets or grains of powder in handgun (and rifle) ammunition are known as degressive propellants. With a degressive propellant, the powder burns on its surface, inward (consider, for example, how tobacco burns in a cigarette), producing gas and heat in the process (Introduction to Naval Weapons Engineering, 1998). The size, design, and amount of propellant not only influences the burn rate of the powder, but it also influences how rapidly the gasses develop, and the amount of gas that is actually created. For example, as more powder burns, more gas pressure builds up, increasing the rate of acceleration (Firearms tutorial, 2005). When the burning powder reaches a maximum pressure in the barrel, the movement of the bullet down the barrel will actually reduce the amount of gas pressure due to the increased volume of space in the barrel (Introduction to Naval, 1998).

The copper jacket of the bullet, meanwhile, digs or cuts into the rifling as it travels down the barrel, creating a gas seal that prevents the escape of gas in front of the bullet. These lands and grooves (the rifling) also serve to put a spin on the bullet as it travels down the barrel. Depending upon the firearm, the nature and extent of rifling varies. Differences are based on the size of the bullet, the length of the barrel, and the amount of powder in the cartridge case. For example, one firearm may have a 1 in 12 twist, meaning that for every 12 inches of barrel, the bullet will complete one full rotation or turn, while another may have a 1 in 7 twist. A 1 in 7 twist, for example, will generate a faster spin rate on the bullet. Rifling can also be left or right handed, depending upon manufacturer and design.

Exterior Ballistics

Exterior ballistics investigates what a bullet does once it leaves the barrel of the firearm. Its primary focus is on factors that affect the flight of the bullet as it travels downrange. Some of the main issues associated with exterior ballistics include muzzle velocity, kinetic energy, and trajectory.

Muzzle Velocity

The speed or velocity of the bullet leaving the barrel is known as the muzzle velocity (Firearms tutorial, 2005). It is measured in feet per second (fps) or meters per second (mps). For example, a .40 caliber handgun round has a muzzle velocity of approximately 950 fps. Muzzle velocity depends upon a variety of issues related to internal ballistics including the powder, barrel length, caliber, and the mass of the bullet. One of the main benefits of increased velocity (to a certain point) is that it improves the effective range of the bullet (A short course in muzzle velocity, 2005). However, velocity is not constant. The bullet actually experiences negative acceleration (or deceleration) as it travels downrange toward the target because of the effects of drag on the bullet. In fact, the faster a bullet flies, the more drag there is on the bullet due to air friction. Consider, for example, a bullet that is traveling at supersonic speeds. When the bullet reaches supersonic speeds (approximately 760 mph), the drag actually increases on the bullet, decelerating it faster than if the bullet was traveling at a subsonic rate. This is because air molecules "pile up" in front of the bullet and cannot get out of the way fast enough, slowing the bullet in its flight (Hall, 2000). This phenomenon will be discussed in greater detail later on in this chapter.

Kinetic Energy

The bullet also possesses a certain amount of energy when it exits the barrel. This is known as the bullet's kinetic energy (KE), which is basically a measure of energy in motion. KE is calculated based on the weight of the bullet (in pounds [7000 grains = 1 pound]), and its velocity squared, divided by $450,400[1]$, which is the constant for converting weight into grains (Hall, 2000; Walker, 2004).

The equation for Kinetic Energy is:

Kinetic Energy = $\dfrac{W * V^2}{450,400}$ or $KE = (v^2 / 450400) * m$

Below is an example of calculating the KE of a 180-grain (m) bullet traveling at a muzzle velocity of 1200 feet per second:

---

[1] Other physics textbooks and/or authors use 450,435 as the constant.

$$KE = (v^2 / 450400) * m$$
$$KE = (1200^2 / 450400) * 180$$
$$KE = (1440000 / 450400) * 180$$
$$KE = 3.197158 * 180$$
$$KE = 575.488 \text{ foot-pounds}$$

KE is expressed in foot pounds of energy, which is the amount of force required to lift one pound of weight one foot above the ground. In the above example, the bullet has approximately 575 ft lbs. of energy which is equivalent to the energy needed to raise 575 pounds a distance of one foot.

Kinetic energy should not be thought of as the actual force or impact on a target. It deals with the quantity of energy transferred to the target and not with the rate of energy transfer. In addition, the actual work done by kinetic energy depends upon the projectile's mass, construction and velocity (Shooting holes in wounding theories, 2005). The KE of an object provides an understanding of how hard an object strikes. In other words, kinetic energy tells a person how much energy is transferred to the target, but it does not tell how this energy is used against the target. Additionally, kinetic energy only considers the foot-pounds of energy at the muzzle. It does not take into account factors related to the ballistic coefficient, such as air friction and the impact of the bullet against the mass of air molecules as it travels downrange (Hall, 2000). Also, it does not take into consideration the total energy required to overcome inertia and the resistance of the object in the context of getting it to initially move.

Bullet Trajectory

As pointed out earlier, when the bullet leaves the barrel, it is spin stabilized in flight by the rifling (the lands and grooves) that is longi-tudinally cut in the barrel of the firearm (Peters, et al., 1996; Seabourn & Peters, 1996). Even though it is spin stabilized, the path or trajectory of the bullet is not straight and level as it travels downrange. Instead, it has a curved trajectory as shown in Figure 17-1. As this section will show, there are several variables that affect the flight of a projectile.

Immediately upon exit from the barrel, the bullet is traveling below the bore of the barrel. This is because the line of the center of the bore is actually located beneath the sights of the firearm (also known as the line of sight [LOS]), where by its design, the bore of the firearm is actually angled slightly upward so the bullet will hit where the sights are aligned (A short course, 2005). The amount of this negative bullet path is equal to the height of the firearm's sights (Sierra Rifle, 1995). As the bullet travels downrange, its flight is parabolic where it forms an arch in flight. Because of this arch, the bullet may actually cross the line of sight at two different locations, depending upon the distance it travels.

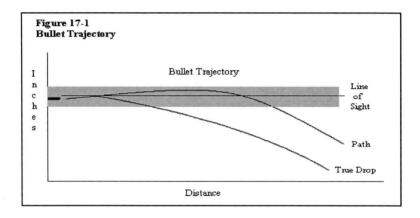

Figure 17-1
Bullet Trajectory

Due to of a variety of factors including distance, loss of velocity, and gravitational effects, the bullet will eventually drop. The dropping of the bullet is referred to as the back curve (A short course, 2005) and its flight is influenced by numerous factors, including the rifling that helps the bullet travel further than the bullet's true drop.

In comparison to the bullet path, there is the true drop of the bullet. The true drop of the bullet reflects the gravitational effects on the bullet without the impact of rifling. To understand the true drop, imagine taking a bullet of the same weight of the bullet that is chambered in the firearm and hold it at the same height as the muzzle, which is horizontal to the ground. At the same time the bullet is fired, drop the other bullet. Because each bullet is the same weight and at the same height, both bullets will hit the ground at the same time, regardless of the fact that the fired bullet has traveled a certain distance.

The Ballistic Coefficient

The bullet's trajectory is also determined by the ballistic coefficient (BC). The BC is a numerical value related to the effect of air drag (or coefficient of drag) on the flight of the bullet. The BC can be thought of as the ability of the bullet to overcome air resistance in flight. In other words, it predicts the bullet's flight or trajectory. The BC is based on the ratio of velocity retardation or slowing on account of air drag (referred to as the coefficient of drag) for a particular bullet compared against a reference bullet, known as the Standard Bullet.

The equation for determining the ballistic coefficient is:

$$\text{Ballistic Coefficient} = \frac{\text{Deceleration of Standard Bullet}}{\text{Deceleration of Actual Bullet}}$$

If the bullet slows the same as the Standard Bullet, it would have BC of 1.0. If it has a BC less than 1.0, it means that the bullet does not perform as well as the standard bullet. For example, a bullet that has a ballistic coefficient of .765 has less velocity erosion or drag than a bullet that has a BC of .50. In some cases, however, bullets may have a higher BC than 1.0 (Sierra Rifle, 1995). As shown below, several variables can affect the BC.

- Sectional Density & the Ballistic Coefficient

One factor that has an influence on the bullet's BC is its sectional density (SD). The SD is a measure of the mass of the bullet in pounds or grams. The equation for determining the sectional density is the weight of the bullet (in pounds [7,000 grains = 1 pound]) divided by the square of its diameter in inches (Hatcher, 1966) :

$$\text{Sectional Density} = \frac{\text{Weight in pounds}}{\text{Diameter in inches}^2}$$

As shown in the above equation, velocity is not an issue with SD. The SD does not change with increased velocities. However, SD will change based on its size or caliber. When the diameter of a bullet is small, its volume and mass is also small, resulting in a smaller sectional density. Smaller sectional densities, meanwhile, also have a lower BC value than larger calibers (Sierra Rifle, 1995). Bullets with a greater sectional density also are heavier objects and usually have a high initial velocity and more inertia, meaning that they will resist slowing better than lighter objects. This will result in the bullet having a greater velocity upon impact even after losing some of its velocity in its flight. However, even if a bullet has a greater mass, depending upon it shape, it may be heavier and less streamlined, resulting in a lower BC (Sierra Rifle, 1995).

- Bullet Shape & the BC

The BC will also change based on the bullet's shape. For example, a 180-grain .30-06 spitzer-style (i.e., pointed) bullet has a much higher BC than a 180-grain .30-06 round-nosed bullet because of its shape, even though their sectional densities remain the same. This can be attributed in part to the level of drag or resistance on the bullet. A blunt-nosed bullet (such as a wad cutter or hollow point), for example, can have the same SD as the most streamlined bullet of that same weight and caliber. However, the more streamlined a bullet is, the less drag there is on the bullet as it flies. Less drag, in turn, allows the bullet to maintain a greater velocity as it travels. This subsequently gives the bullet greater long-term performance in the context of its flight path (Sierra Rifle, 1995).

- Other Variables that affect the BC

Other variables that affect the ballistic coefficient (and its subsequent aerodynamic abilities) include what the bullet is traveling through (e.g. air or tissue), the velocity of the bullet (the faster the bullet the more resistance), and the spin or rotation of the bullet (Firearms tutorial, 2005). Bullet trajectory is also influenced by temperature (i.e. high temperatures decrease air density), barometric pressure, humidity, and altitude. Horizontal winds, such as a tailwind, crosswind and headwind, in addition to vertical winds, will also affect the bullet's trajectory (Sierra Rifle, 1995).

Rotational Forces Affecting Bullet Flight

Exterior ballistics also investigates the rotational forces affecting the flight of the bullet. Even though the bullet is spin stabilized from the rifling, and it is spinning on its axis once it leaves the barrel, the bullet is not flying perfectly straight. Rather, the bullet follows a non-circular path (i.e. epicyclical or oval flight path) and deviates as a result of various "aerodynamic forces and movements acting on the projectile" (Seabourn & Peters, 1996, p. S24). These rotational forces are commonly referred to as bullet yaw, precession and nutation. Eventually, the bullet may "go to sleep" or it dampens (i.e., straightens itself out) at a certain range, depending upon the bullet's ballistic qualities.

According to Swan and Swan (1984), yaw is when a bullet deviates from its straight line of flight. This deviation is the result of many factors. One cause of bullet yaw is from the gasses exiting the barrel. Immediately after the bullet exits the barrel, gasses rush by, around, and in front of the bullet, destabilizing its flight. These expanding gasses (actually an air/gas column) exert lateral (sideways) forces on the bullet, causing temporary yawing as much as 25 to 30 degrees from the bullet's straight path. Eventually the bullet will begin to stabilize on account of the rifling from the barrel (Silvia, 1999). Later on in the bullet's flight, meanwhile, yaw may also occur because of the bullet losing velocity (i.e. velocity decay) (Seabourn & Peters, 1996). Bullet yaw can also be seen in wound patterns. In some instances, the bullet does not enter the object nose-first. Instead, it may hit the target sideways, leaving a keyhole or oval-shaped entrance wound instead of a nice, clean circle (Bartlett, 2003).

In addition to the bullet yawing, the rotational forces of precession and nutation also exist. With yaw, the nose of the bullet is deviating upwards and/or downwards from its straight line of flight. While the nose of the bullet is deviating from a straight line of flight, it is also precessing (revolving like a top that has knocked on its side), causing the bullet to rotate in a cone-like or cork screw-styled path if the bullet was to be viewed in flight from its side. At the same time, the bullet is also nutating. If the flight of the bullet was to be viewed from its rear as it was traveling forward, its path would not be perfectly straight. Rather, as the bullet travels downrange, its path would be rosette-shaped, where the bullet is actually flying in small circles around its center of gravity (Bartlett, 2003; Sierra Rifle, 1995).

Terminal Ballistics

Terminal ballistics examines what the bullet does when it hits the target. For the purpose of this chapter, terminal ballistics addresses what the bullet does when it strikes the human body. According to Patrick (1989), there are four components of projectile wounding that should be considered in the context of terminal ballistics. They include: 1) penetration; 2) permanent cavity; 3) temporary cavity; and, 4) fragmentation. It is important that the effects of these projectiles on the human body be understood. The investigation of the effects of projectiles and/or bullets on the human body is also known as wound ballistics.

One example of what a projectile does in the context of wounding is explained by Swift and Rutty (2004). They state that the:

> ....projectile causes soft tissue damage through crushing, creating a temporary cavity that contains hot gases. The tissue is compressed

346

radially from the center of the cavity and, depending upon its elastic properties, results in tears to structures (as seen with injuries to solid abdominal viscera). The recoil of the tissues, together with the dissipation of the gases, causes the soft tissue to collapse inward on itself, the resultant defect being the permanent cavity (p. 108)

Figure 17-2 provides an illustration of a bullet/projectile striking human tissue. First, the bullet strikes and enters the human target (penetration). Upon penetration, the bullet stretches and crushes tissue, creating a temporary and permanent cavity. Depending upon the characteristics of the bullet and what the bullet struck, fragmentation may also occur.

In front of the bullet is a sonic pressure wave. This wave may cause some injury to blood vessels due to the fact that when sound waves encounter tissue with a greater density, the sound waves may be reflected back in the form of tension waves which could subsequently injure blood vessels (Sonden, et al., 2002). However, the sonic pressure wave will cause minimal injury to tissues. For example, sonic waves are used in some medical applications, including the crushing of kidney stones. In these applications there is very little if no damage to surrounding tissue (Silvia, 1999).

Penetration

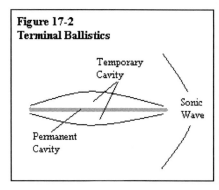

Figure 17-2
Terminal Ballistics

Temporary Cavity

Sonic Wave

Permanent Cavity

Penetration deals with the tissue that the projectile passes through, disrupts and/or destroys (Patrick, 1989). After the bullet breaks through the skin barrier, one way to visualize what the bullet does is to think of it as a drill bit. Because the bullet is spin stabilized in flight, upon impact, it is still spinning based on its rate of twist. Because it spins (and perhaps expands if it is a hollow point), the bullet drills, crushes, and cuts through tissue in is path. Eventually, the bullet loses energy and stops because of its shape, the displacement of energy to the target, and from the friction of the medium that it is passing through (Spinks, 2005).

Depending upon the angle of the bullet when it strikes the human body, the entry wound may be small and circular or asymmetric and irregularly shaped, often having an ellipsoid or egg shape to it (Korac, et al.,

2001c). The penetrating bullet will also leave a small abrasion ring on the skin, caused by friction when the bullet struck the skin (Russell & Noguchi, 1999). In other instances where the skin is directly exposed to the impact of the bullet (i.e. no clothing or other obstructions block the bullet), there will be a gray or white ring around the wound entrance. This is known as the bullet wipe and it can be attributed to bullet lubricant, soot from the burning powder, and barrel residue that is wiped off the bullet before it enters the body (Bailey, 2005). In other instances where the firearm is discharged at a close range, there may also be a soot ring on clothing or other barriers (Lepik & Vasiliev, 2005).

Factors Affecting Penetration

How deep the bullet penetrates and what is does in the body is dependent upon a variety of factors. Three specific variables that affect penetration (exclusive of bullet design, size and type) include the bullet's momentum (how hard it is to stop), its sectional density (how effectively it penetrates) and its kinetic energy (how hard it hits the object in foot pounds of energy).

Momentum

Momentum is the tendency of an object to stay in motion. It is the ability of a body to maintain its state of motion. It can also be thought of as how hard it is to stop an object in motion. Momentum depends upon two things: mass and velocity, and the product of these two quantities. The equation for momentum is:

$$Momentum = Mass * Velocity$$

Momentum is expressed in slug-feet per second. The physical weight of one slug of mass equals 32.174 pounds, where one slug of mass will accelerate one foot per second when acted on by one pound of force. At the same time, one grain (or 1/7000 of a pound) weighs 1/225218 of a slug (Hall, 2000).

To calculate the momentum of a bullet, the weight of the bullet must be converted from grains into pounds and then divided by 7,000 (7,000 grains equals one pound). After determining its weight (in pounds) it must also be divided by the force of gravity (32.174). This number is then multiplied by the speed of the projectile to determine its momentum (Hall, 2000).

The following is an example of calculating the momentum of a 180 grain bullet with a velocity of 1200 fps:

The calculation is:

Mass = 180/7000 = .0257lbs
Then .0257/32.174 = .0007987 slug
Next: .0007987 * 1200 = .958 slug/fps momentum

Momentum is important in the context of penetration. A bullet that has a greater proportion of its momentum from its mass will change its velocity (negative acceleration) at a slower rate than bullets that are lighter but have a greater velocity. This means that two bullets having equal momentum but unequal mass will result in the bullet with the greater proportion of its momentum from its mass penetrating deeper into the object. This also means that a bullet's momentum that is derived by increasing its mass will result in a greater gain in penetration than by simply increasing the bullet's velocity (this is true because the tissue's resistance is increased by the square of the velocity) (Shooting holes, 2005). A bullet with greater momentum will also take longer to stop because it has a greater level of impulse or drive than bullets that have a lower mass. As a bullet's velocity increases, for example, its resistant force does not equally increase. Instead, its resistant force increases exponentially. For example, if velocity doubles, the resistant force increases by four; if velocity increases fourfold, resistance forces increase 16 fold. This means that when a high velocity bullet strikes tissue, it will slow or decelerate faster than a slower moving projectile. The slower projectile, however, will have a higher slug value than the faster moving projectile (Walker, 2004)

Sectional Density

Penetration also relies upon the sectional density of the bullet. As a general rule, bullets with a greater sectional density tend to penetrate deeper (Fackler, 1994). As pointed out in the section on momentum, the denser the object (i.e. more mass), the more the momentum is conserved in that object, thus allowing it to penetrate deeper. Also, the less the amount of frontal surface area (per unit of its mass) that is presented to the target, the less the target's matter (relative to the penetrating object's mass) will be displaced by the passage of the object through the target. This is because there is a lower level of resistance on the frontal area of the projectile. For example, if the mass of a bullet is increased without changing its external dimensions, it will weigh more per unit of cross sectional area. Its sectional density will be increased, and it will penetrate further with any given applied force (Walker, 2004).

To illustrate the above point, the sectional density of a baseball versus a bullet can be analyzed in the context of penetration. A baseball that weighs 5 ounces and travels 90 feet per second has more kinetic energy than a bullet. However, the baseball has a lower sectional density because its mass is spread out over such a large area. Because of this, its momentum is easy to stop, and there is subsequently no penetration. On the other hand, a bullet has a greater mass or sectional density in comparison to the baseball. Because of the greater sectional density, and the fact that it is striking a smaller area on the target in comparison to the baseball, it will penetrate the object. Another example of sectional density and penetration is to compare the penetration performance of an arrow against a bullet when shooting them into a bucket of sand. If a person would discharge a .40 caliber bullet into a bucket of sand, the bullet would be stopped by the sand. The arrow, meanwhile, will penetrate all the way through the sand (and perhaps the bucket) because it has a higher sectional density and greater momentum, penetrating deeper because its momentum is preserved.

Kinetic Energy

In many instances, individuals believe that the bullet's kinetic energy (that is measured in foot-pounds) has "knock down power" against the suspect. That is, when the bullet hits the subject, the foot-pounds of energy that the bullet has will basically knock the person down. Even though it is popular in the movies to have people virtually flying through the air when they are shot, kinetic energy is not imparted to the threat in this manner. Being knocked down solely by the force of the bullet is false. Handgun bullets do not impart any type of knock down power per se. Nor do rifle rounds. In fact, being struck by a bullet is often compared to being struck by a fast ball or being stung by a bee.

In the context of penetration, however, kinetic energy is important in how the energy of the bullet is dissipated or transferred to the body. When the kinetic energy of the bullet is transferred to the body upon impact and penetration, it causes the lateral movement of material (i.e. tissue) away from the line of penetration. At different velocities, the medium (i.e., tissue) does not absorb momentum equally. Instead, there is a curve of resistance. In the context of water, for example, slower moving bullets may just pass through the water barrier. Higher velocity bullets, however, may fragment because the water gets "harder" (i.e. greater resistance) because the medium cannot move out of the way fast enough from the fast moving bullet. Therefore, the water "piles up" in front of the bullet, reducing momentum, where the energy from the bullet is released faster into the medium (Hall, 2000). For example, if a bullet has twice the energy of another bullet, then approximately twice the medium or material is moved away. Therefore, the volume of displacement is the product of kinetic energy and momentum (Walker, 2004). Consider, for example, passing one's hand through a bathtub of water. If one's hand is slowly stroked through the tub of water, there is less resistance. On the other hand, if one were to rapidly draw their hand through the tub of water, there would be a greater degree of the water's resistance against the hand.

Figure 17-3 provides an example of how kinetic energy can affect bullet penetration and how a cavity is created based on the shape and velocity of a bullet. It also shows the penetration of a .223 caliber bullet, which is a high velocity bullet. This bullet penetrates deep into the body, creating a large permanent cavity. This bullet has also fragmented because it could

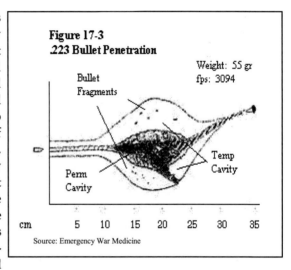

Figure 17-3
.223 Bullet Penetration

Weight: 55 gr
fps: 3094

Bullet Fragments

Temp Cavity

Perm Cavity

cm   5   10   15   20   25   30   35

Source: Emergency War Medicine

not maintain its form due to the fast negative acceleration and increased resistance against the nose of the bullet, causing it to break up.

Other Factors & Penetration

Penetration also depends upon what the bullet is passing through. One strong barrier that the bullet must pass through is the human skin that ranges from 1 to 4 millimeters in thickness. The skin is quite durable and it stretches, making it difficult to penetrate because of its tensile strength and elasticity. This means that upon impact the bullet must first stretch, crush, and then rupture the skin before it can penetrate into the underlying tissue (Jussila, et. al, 2005). In fact, some researchers point out that because of the resistance and elasticity of the skin, it is equivalent to about 4 inches of tissue (Fackler, 1987a). Other barriers or intervening obstacles, as pointed out by out by Pinziotto et al. (2004), may include building materials (drywall and wood), windshield glass, metal and clothing, leading some ballistics experts to propose that even though factory tests of ammunition reveal that bullets have enough penetration depth, the penetration value of many handgun rounds may be overestimated. (Patrick, 1989).

The Temporary Cavity

Immediately upon entry into the body, the bullet/projectile causes cavitation from the stretching and tissue crush that occurs. Cavitation is the displacement of tissue (either temporary or permanent) that results in a cavity forming along the bullet/projectile track. The temporary cavity can be compared to a wake produced by a boat. The boat (the projectile), cuts through the water, and produces a wake (the temporary cavity) in its path, where the water eventually returns to a normal resting state.

The temporary cavity is the result of the kinetic energy from the projectile that forces tissue forward and laterally away from the bullet/projectile. Within a few milliseconds after penetration, the cavity begins to collapse, reform, and then collapse again until all of the energy from the bullet/projectile has dissipated (Swan & Swan, 1984). The temporary cavity is the result of the wound channel (i.e. the permanent cavity) rapidly expanding. This temporary cavity then collapses in pulsations when the pressure from the penetrating bullet subsides (Jussila, 2005). The creation of a cavity is also based on the elasticity of the surrounding tissue, and the construction and material of the bullet (Oehmichen, et. al, 2004). Depending upon the velocity and kinetic energy of the bullet/projectile, the temporary cavity can be several times larger than the diameter of the projectile.

The Permanent Cavity

The permanent cavity is created by tissue crush. It is the volume of space that was once occupied by tissue that has been destroyed by the passage of the projectile. It is the hole left by the passage of the projectile/bullet where the once-living viable tissue in the permanent cavity is now composed of necrotic (dead) tissue and clot (Bowler & Rossiter, 1997).

The creation of the permanent cavity is a function of penetration and the diameter of the frontal area of the projectile. In addition to the frontal diameter of the bullet, the permanent cavity can be created by other forces. First, gyroscopically stabilized bullets will eventually become unstable in tissue (Clemens, et al, 1996), where they may yaw or tumble (yaw angles over 90 degrees) (Silvia, 1999; Peters, et al., 1996). This yawing and tumbling, in turn could create larger permanent wound channels. The size of the permanent cavity can also increase in size due to bullet deformation (flattening or mushrooming, for example, increases the diameter of the bullet) or through bullet fragmentation (which may cause multiple perforations or holes in adjacent tissue (Silvia, 1999)). The permanent cavity can also be increased in size by using hollow point bullets that, through their design, expand upon penetration, creating larger wound channels in the process.

Fragmentation

Another wounding mechanism is fragmentation. Bullet fragmentation does not really occur with handgun rounds for several reasons (unless the bullet hits bone, etc.). First, handgun rounds travel at a relatively slow speed (1000-1200 fps or less). Because of the relatively low velocity, the negative acceleration imparted against the bullet upon impact is not strong enough to cause fragmentation. In fact, if the bullet did fragment, it would actually break up too fast, and not penetrate deep enough to hit and damage vital organs (Patrick, 1989). Second (and related to the first point), based on construction, a handgun's round needs to maintain its sectional density (i.e. mass) to ensure adequate penetration. This means that bullets should not break up upon penetration. Instead, a well-designed bullet should maintain the vast majority of its mass (95% or more) to ensure that it will penetrate deep enough into the human body to cause sufficient damage to stop the threat. To illustrate this point, several bullet manufacturers now have developed bullets where the lead core of the bullet is chemically bonded to the jacket to prevent separation and fragmentation. These are called bonded bullets. By bonding the core to the jacket, expansion of the bullet may be better controlled, and fragmentation can be prevented, which enhances weight retention. This, in turn, promotes effective bullet penetration.

This is not to say that all bullets will not fragment. Fragmentation occurs with rifle rounds because of their design and ballistic properties. Since a rifle bullet is traveling faster than handgun rounds (3000 fps, for example), it may not hold together (because of rapid deceleration) when striking and penetrating tissue, creating what is often referred to as a "lead snowstorm," where upon examination of the wound by an x-ray, lead fragments are sprayed throughout the wound region (Kaplan, et al., 1998). This resulting fragmentation, in turn, could cause massive tissue disruption and injury (Fackler, 1987b). Fragmentation may also occur because the bullet hit an interposed object (something between the shooter and threat) before striking the body, causing the bullet to fragment before entry, which would be evidenced by multiple entrance wounds (Karger & Rand, 1998).

Mechanics of Projectile Wounding

While the mechanics of projectile wounding may appear to be simple, it is important for the reader to gain an understanding of how bullets cause trauma to the human body. As pointed out in the introduction to this chapter, the study of the interaction of projectiles with the human body is known as wound ballistics. As this section will show, there are a variety of factors that influence the wounding potential of bullets to the point where some researchers have concluded that "every bullet's path is a unique event" (Korac, et al., 2001b, p. 1068). Nevertheless, some general themes can be extracted from the wound ballistics literature regarding the mechanics of projectile wounding.

When a bullet strikes and penetrates the human body, there are two types of injuries: crush and stretch. The tissue that is destroyed as a result of the projectile is commonly referred to as the tissue crush, which causes the permanent cavity or wound channel. The tissue that stretches and then goes back to its original position, forming the temporary cavity, is called the tissue stretch. In the context of handgun wounding, it is the creation of the permanent cavity, or wound channel, that causes the most damage to the human body. Thus, the wound produced by a projectile depends upon the amount of tissue crush (Fackler, 1987b). This wound cavity depends upon several factors, including bullet design, size, velocity, expansion and the bullet's path.

Bullet Design & Type

What a bullet does in the human body in the context of creating a wound channel varies considerably based on the bullet's design (Korac, et al., 2001b). The key to effective wounding is to have a bullet that can penetrate deep enough into the human body to cause damage to vital organs, while having controlled expansion. For example, if a bullet expands too much, it may penetrate less, so expansion and penetration need to be balanced through proper bullet design and construction. In fact, even if a hollow point is used, it may not fully expand because it may become plugged with barrier materials. These barrier materials may include clothing, drywall, wood and even bone. Hollow point bullets, in comparison to more streamlined bullets, may decelerate faster, causing a larger permanent cavity early upon entry in comparison to an ogival-nosed, streamlined bullet. The ogival shaped bullet, meanwhile, creates a smaller permanent cavity upon entry. Because of its yaw and tumbling effects, however, it may produce a larger permanent cavity deeper within the bullet track (Celen, et al. 1996).

Of course, the caliber of the projectile is a large determinant of wounding potential. One of the keys to projectile wounding is to have the bullet cut large wound channels in the body. Thus, the larger the hole left by the bullet, the more wounding potential. Consider, for example, a .40 caliber bullet. This will leave a "hole" in the threat less than one-half of an inch. When considering the fact that tissue is elastic in nature, the actual wound channel may be much smaller and susceptible to sealing itself to a certain degree, preventing the loss of large amounts of blood. In comparison to the .40 caliber bullet is a 12 gauge shotgun round. A shotgun round loaded with shot that is fired at close distances will create massive tissue and bone loss, as well as the disruption of blood vessels (depending upon the size of the shot and pellet spread). If the wad from the shotgun shell, meanwhile, is deposited in the wound, this will also lead to additional wounding (Ordog, et al., 1988).

Velocity & Wounding

The speed (velocity) of the bullet also affects wounding potential (Russell & Noguchi, 1999). The medical field classifies firearm trauma into the categories of low and high velocity. Low velocity wounds are inflicted by projectiles with velocities less than 2000 feet per second, while high velocity wounds are classified as projectiles traveling faster than 2000 feet per second (Bartlett, 2003). Low velocity wounds generally cause a smaller amount of trauma, and the wounds are localized to the path of the bullet. On the other hand, with a high velocity bullet, wounds may be spread throughout the entire wound region. For example, lead may eject from the open base of the jacketed bullet traveling over 800 meters per second (Marraccini, 2001). These "baby bullets" could cause additional trauma by striking arteries and/or damaging organs. In fact, if the bullet is traveling faster than 2000 feet/second, the cavity, as a result of fragmentation, could be as large as 40 times the diameter of the bullet (Sabin, et al., 1998).

Controlled Expansion

The above points illustrate that in the context of wounding, the correct sized bullet with the right velocity is important in order to achieve maximum penetration and wounding. Combined with penetration, an effective handgun round should also expand. Because of the need for effective penetration and controlled expansion in order to create deep and large wound channels, hollow point bullets are regularly used in law enforcement. Many hollow point bullets, based on the manufacturer's design, actually have two chambers, consisting of front and rear compartments that are separated by a divider which is actually part of the jacket. These are known as partition bullets. Upon impact, the front chamber of the bullet (basically the nose of the bullet) expands to its base, producing a petal-like pattern, while the second compartment of the bullet does not expand at all. By having the second chamber (i.e. the rear of the bullet) maintain its mass and shape, it serves to assist the front compartment in fully expanding, because it maintains the bullet's mass and momentum to help "push" the bullet into and through tissue.

This penetration and expansion, however, should not be at the cost of controlling the firearm. A police officer should be issued a firearm that has the ability to create "big holes" in the threat. Having a large caliber firearm, however, could result in the officer not having the ability to deliver controlled and accurate fire at the threat, leading to poor shot placement. Therefore, the key is to have a firearm that can be used to deliver controlled and accurate fire at a threat to create large wound channels. These goals are achieved by having relatively small caliber firearms (i.e. .40 caliber) that have the right combination of bullet mass and velocity to ensure penetration. Combined with these factors, the use of hollow point bullets will cause a much larger wound channel, and hopefully, sufficient wounding.

The Bullet Path

Another important variable in projectile wounding is where the bullet strikes the human target. Where the bullet strikes and subsequently penetrates the body is often referred to as the bullet path. As pointed out earlier, the primary wounding mechanism is the creation of the permanent cavity. Subsequently, once a hollow point bullet penetrates and enters the body, it begins to expand, increasing in size approximately 50-90%. As it "mushrooms," it cuts a larger diameter wound channel, destroying all tissue in its path. Eventually the bullet slows or decelerates. And, it may tumble because it no longer is stabilized through the rifling from the barrel of the firearm (Jussila, 2005). This tumbling may also cause a larger permanent wound channel.

The bullet's path through the body must strike vital areas to be most effective. For this reason, the key behind incapacitation or stopping a suspect is bullet placement (Pinizzoto, et al, 2004) or the bullet's interaction with tissue, regardless of the speed of the projectile (Bowyer & Rossiter, 1997). For example, a bullet injury to the vena cava - one of the body's main veins (about 1 inch in diameter), located deep inside the abdomen and chest - may create a high-pressure, high volume hemorrhage leading to death. If the bullet struck the brain, meanwhile, bone fragments and injuries as a result of the temporary cavity (not to mention the permanent cavity) could cause additional "neuronal and axonal degeneration" (Facchin & Zanotti, 1998, p. 230). Transection injuries (i.e. across various organs), meanwhile, may cause more damage than localized injuries (Kuehne, et al, 1999), and if the bullet does not follow a straight path because it ricochets off of bone or tumbles, it may cause more internal injuries than following a straight path. The bullet/projectile may also create secondary missiles. Secondary missiles are dense objects that absorb the kinetic energy of the bullet/projectile and convert themselves into additional missiles. These missiles could include objects off of clothing (i.e. pieces of zipper, pins, and buttons) or parts from the human body such as bone and teeth (Swan & Swan, 1984).

The nature and extent of these injuries are also related to the characteristics of the tissue around the bullet path in relation to their elasticity and density (Korac, et. al, 2001c). Every organ has a specific gravity, which is the density of the organ's tissue in relation to the density of water at 4 degrees (Bruice, 2004). Because of the differences in the specific gravity in various tissues, some organs are more resistant to damage than others. For example, the lung has a low specific gravity (0.2 - 0.5) while skeletal muscle has a specific gravity of 1.02 -1.04 (Marraccini, 2001). As a rule of thumb, the higher the specific gravity (i.e. the denser the object), the greater the damage. Other solid organs such as the liver are not resistant to stretch, while additional organs such as the skin, lungs, muscles and bowels are resistant to stretch cavitation and are considered to be good shock absorbers (Fackler, 1987).

Conversely, the greater the elasticity, the less the damage there is from the bullet. For example, a bullet wound to the lung may create a bullet track; an injury to the liver or brain may not have a bullet track, but a greater degree of destruction because these two organs have a lower elasticity value than the lungs (George & Goodman, 1992). Thus, a major gunshot wound to the liver causes "exanguinating haemorrhage" (Marr, et al., 2000, p. 87) because of its high specific gravity and low elasticity.

Other Wounding Mechanisms

There are other wounding mechanisms besides the wound channel itself. The nature of the wound is also dependent on what the bullet does once it enters the human body. Other wounding mechanisms may include bullet yaw and tumbling in tissue (where the bullet may actually end up base first instead of nose first in a person), and bullet deformation, such as mushrooming, which could cause a larger wound channel and bullet fragmentation (Silvia, 1999).

Soft tissues in the human body can also be damaged or destroyed through fragmentation. According to Patrick (1989), fragmentation can consist of pieces of the actual projectile, or they may be secondary missiles such as bone that may damage tissues and blood vessels outside of the permanent cavity. However, "....Fragmentation is not necessarily present in every projectile wound. It may, or may not occur and can be considered [only] a secondary effect" (p. 3). For example, when the projectile strikes bone, pieces (or spicules) of bone may become secondary missiles and wounding mechanisms (Amato, et al. 1989). In other cases and depending upon the distance of the muzzle from the threat, tissue can also be damaged from the powder blast from the muzzle of the firearm if it is in contact with tissue or if it is close enough for gasses to force or expand the tissue (Fackler, 1998). These are referred to as contact wounds, and depending upon their location on the human body, they can cause serious, life threatening wounds, or even death (White, 1989; Karger, et al., 2002).

Besides the permanent cavity, the creation of a temporary cavity could have some wounding potential. The temporary cavity is composed of zones of contusion (bruising) and concussion, which may contain some devitalized tissue and bruising (Bowler & Rossiter, 1997). According to Peters and Seabourn (1996), under some conditions (as with elongated rifle bullets) a temporary cavity may have some wounding potential as it can cause prompt damage in the immediate area of the projectile because of stretching and shearing of the tissue. It can also cause tensile damage to tissue when the Maximum Temporary Cavity (MTC) is stretched to greater strains than the tissue's critical strain. There can be some damage to surrounding tissue because of compression. Nevertheless, the temporary cavity does not always cause a lot of tissue damage because skeletal muscle is tolerant of low-energy transfer (Bowler & Rossiter, 1997).

The reader must also keep in mind that the human body is very durable. In some cases, such as gunshot wounds to the abdominal area, many victims can be dealt with non-surgically (Demetriades, et al, 1997). Even if the bullet should penetrate organs, it is not a guarantee that the suspect will be immediately incapacitated. Medical journals have reported cases where some gunshot wounds to the kidney do not even need surgical exploration or repair if there are no signs of continued bleeding (Velmahos, et al., 1998). Other research has also found that, depending upon the degree of damage to the liver as the result of a gunshot, some patients may be managed without operation (Parks, et al., 1999).

Terminal Ballistics & Incapacitation Effects

The primary goal behind shooting the threat is to make sure that it is rapidly incapacitated. Incapacitation is defined by Pollack & Rothchild (2004) as "a rapid and ensuing inability to perform complex and longer lasting movements independent of consciousness or intention" (p.212). Several variables can affect incapacitation. If, for example, a suspect is on drugs, is psychotic, has a strong will to fight, or has a high tolerance for blood loss, they may be less likely to be readily incapacitated by gunshot wound(s). Terminal performance of the bullet could also be affected by heavy clothing and items in a suspect's pockets that could plug a hollow point bullet and limit its expansion. Other obstacles that could impede the terminal performance of the bullet could include: windshield glass, automotive sheet metal, and tissue and bone debris from an offender's arm that slows the bullet before it can penetrate the suspect's torso (Dodson, 2001).

According to Newgard (1992), "the only method of reliably stopping a human with a handgun is to decrease the functioning capability of the central nervous system (CNS), and specifically, the brain and cervical spinal cord" (p.14). This can be accomplished two ways: 1) direct trauma to the CNS tissue, and/or 2) through the lack of oxygen to the brain as a result of the loss of blood pressure and/or bleeding. In the field of firearms, these forms of incapacitation are commonly referred to as Type I and II forms of incapacitation. Combined with these two types is a third form of incapacitation, referred to as Psychological Incapacitation. These forms of incapacitation will be discussed in the following sections.

359

Type I Incapacitation

The key behind a Type I incapacitation is that there is instantaneous or immediate incapacitation and/or death. Immediate incapacitation does not mean death. It means that the suspect can no longer engage in various physiological or motor activities such as walking. Immediate incapacitation only occurs when the threat is struck in the Central Nervous System - specifically the brain or upper spinal cord (Pinizzotto, et al, 2004). In the context of a shot to the brain, the resulting injuries will include destruction and damage to cerebral tissue, blood loss, and poten-

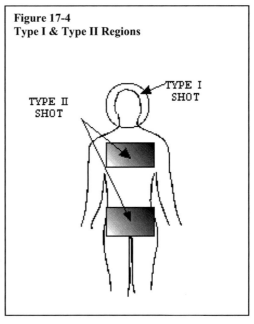

Figure 17-4
Type I & Type II Regions

tial damage to the ventricular system, which is the fluid conducting system in the brain that is filled with cerebrospinal fluid that bathes the brain and spinal cord (Erdogan, 2004). In only very rare or lucky circumstances, according to one medical researcher, could a person actually have the ability to act after being shot in this region (Karger, 1995). This is based on the fact that the CNS is the main processing center for all of the nerves in the human body. Because the CNS is damaged or destroyed, it cannot send motor commands to the skeletal, cardiac, and smooth muscles. Hence, at a minimum, the suspect will not be able to think and move. Type I shots are not caliber dependent. Even a small caliber firearm that creates a small permanent cavity or wound channel in the CNS can cause immediate incapacitation.

While the Type I shot will ensure immediate incapacitation, one of the main issues with these shots is related to the ability of the officer to hit the threat in this region. In comparison to the torso, the head and the spinal column are relatively small targets. Considering this point, and based on the fact that many shots fired by police officers do not even hit the threat (see Chapter 1) due to the stress of the situation and the distance between the threat and officer, an officer may not be able to effectively deliver a

Type I shot. In some instances, however, Type I shots are used in law enforcement applications. Snipers who are better trained, have more time for effective shot placement, and have better weapons (i.e. rifles with scopes) possess a greater chance of employing a Type I shot. Hence, one of the areas where snipers are trained to shoot is in the orbital region (eyes and nose) of the threat's head to ensure penetration of the brain stem, causing immediate incapacitation and/or death.

Type II Incapacitation

The next best alternative is a Type II form of incapacitation. The key behind a Type II form of incapacitation is blood loss. More specifically, a human being must lose enough blood so their central nervous system no longer functions (Silvia, 1999), where it eventually shuts downs and the threat dies from the loss of blood and oxygen. This blood loss must be massive (i.e. from the heart or major blood vessels) (Pollack & Rothchild, 2004) causing hemorrhagic shock (Hardaway, 2000), severe hypotension (extremely low blood pressure) or respiratory failure (Facchin & Zanotti, 1998). A person may also die from hypoxia which is the lack of oxygen in tissue. Besides the direct wounding effects, mortality is also related to the physical condition of the threat. For example, the suspect's age could affect their mortality rate, as older individuals may be more fragile to some types of injuries in comparison to younger, more physically fit persons (Facchin & Zanotti, 1998)

With a type II incapacitation, the threat is not immediately stopped. With the Type II shot, a police officer can only hope for rapid — not immediate — incapacitation, or at the least, delayed incapacitation where the threat slowly bleeds to death (Polllack & Rothchild, 2004). Even if the thoracic artery (the largest artery in the human body) is completely severed from a handgun round, it would take approximately 4.6 seconds for a human being to lose 20% of their blood volume, which would then begin to impair their central nervous system (Newgard, 1992). To further illustrate this point, one study found that damage to the vena cava (the largest vein going to the heart) by penetrating injuries caused less trauma than blunt force injuries (Kuehne's et al., 1999). Thus, a hard blow may cause more trauma than a penetrating bullet!

In order to ensure rapid incapacitation with a Type II shot, the large blood-bearing organs, arteries and veins must be struck. The majority of vital organs (i.e. heart and lungs), as well as the large arteries and veins (as shown in Figure 17-4) are located at armpit-height and are deep within the body. To hit these major blood bearing areas, bullets need to reach a depth in the human body where major blood vessels, including the aorta and vena cava can be struck, causing severe blood loss (Silvia, 1999). Silvia (1999) writes that the "major blood vessels are in the ero abdominal or retro thoracic cavities of the body at an average depth of 15 centimeters" (p. 73). Effective penetration of these areas requires that the bullet pass through them. As pointed out by Patrick (1989), this may mean that a bullet may have to penetrate 10-12 inches to hit a vital organ if it first passes through the suspect's arm, or it will have to penetrate at least 7 inches in a slender adult to strike major blood vessels in the back of the abdominal cavity. Because of these issues, Patrick (1989) recommends that a bullet should have the capacity to penetrate at least 12 inches of tissue, with a preferable penetration value of 18 inches.

Besides the major blood-bearing organs, arteries and veins at armpit height, another region where an effective Type II shot can be placed is the pelvic girdle. The pelvic girdle, also known as the hip girdle, is composed of those bones that make up the pelvis. Within the pelvic region, there are several blood-bearing vascular structures, including the femoral artery. Besides blood-bearing vascular structures, the pelvic girdle also supports or holds organs including the bladder and reproductive organs (Gray, 1977). A well-placed shot in this region can also result in damage to those bones that make up the hip. Because the hips support the spine and the weight of one's body, a well-placed shot that causes severe bone damage would also result in the suspect dropping to the ground, limiting their movement and ability to fight back. If the damage were severe enough, this would also physically incapacitate the suspect in the process.

Because a type II wound requires adequate penetration, it is caliber-dependent. That is, a large caliber bullet is needed to ensure rapid blood loss. To further ensure rapid blood loss, multiple wound channels should also be created, based on the principle of fluid dynamics. Basically, the principle of fluid dynamics states that the larger the volume of the tube or hole, combined with the number of holes, the greater the flow of fluid will be out of the pipe. Applying this principle to wounding, the more holes that are placed in the threat, the greater the likelihood of increased blood loss and the faster the incapacitation.

Psychological Incapacitation

In other instances, the threat may become incapacitated, not from the direct effects of the bullet's performance, but from the degree of psychological distress they experience as a result of being shot. This potential wounding mechanism is known as psychological incapacitation. Psychological incapacitation is the offender's mental state, and it is a factor to consider in addition to the terminal performance of the bullet and the body's physiological responses to being shot (Dodson, 2001). It is a response to pain or other stimulus, such as the sight of blood. For example, a person who is shot in the extremities (arm or leg) and voluntarily gives up is most likely surrendering due to psychological incapacitation (Dodson, 2001). This psychological incapacitation may be attributed to the many fear responses that humans possess including freezing, flight, fright, and faint responses. Some individuals, for example, may have what is known as a Blood Injection Injury (BII) phobias, where they may experience faintness at the sight of blood (Bracha, 2004). Others, meanwhile, may experience freezing, which is actually a defensive survival technique among many species of animals, including humans (Azevedo, et al., 2005). Another fear reaction, however, is to become aggressive toward the perceived threat. In combination with the fact that the wound is a Type II and they are not immediately incapacitated, it could take a long period of time for sufficient blood loss to occur to incapacitate an individual, especially if they have the psychological drive or survival mindset to fight back and win, even when facing a critical injury. Therefore, psychological incapacitation is not a guarantee. It is erratic in nature, affecting individuals differently (Marshall & Sanow, 2001). Some may panic and surrender immediately, while others may become more aggressive. Psychological Incapacitation is not caliber dependent.

Conclusion

This chapter has provided the reader with a review of the physics of ballistics, which is the scientific study of the motion of a projectile in flight. The study of ballistics can be divided into interior, exterior, and terminal ballistics. Interior ballistics examines what happens within the firearm, before the bullet exits the barrel. Exterior ballistics, meanwhile, investigates what the bullet does after it leaves the barrel of the firearm. Some issues to consider with exterior ballistics include the muzzle velocity, kinetic energy, trajectory, and the ballistic coefficient. Last is terminal ballistics, which investigates what the bullet does when it hits the target in the context of projectile wounding. The four main components of projectile wounding include 1) penetration; 2) the permanent cavity; 3) the temporary cavity; and, 4) fragmentation. Fragmentation does not reliably occur with a handgun round because of bullet design and the fact that it is a low velocity projectile.

This chapter also provided an overview of the mechanics of projectile wounding. The primary wounding mechanism of a bullet is the destruction of tissue which is crushed in the bullet's path as it penetrates, creating a permanent cavity or wound channel. In order to create a permanent cavity that penetrates deep enough into the human body, the bullet must be properly designed and have an appropriate mass and velocity. If the bullet is a hollow point, meanwhile, it must have controlled expansion as it penetrates, cuts, and destroys tissue.

This chapter has also pointed out the two ways to stop a threat through Type I and Type II shots. Type I shots occur when the threat is shot in the Central Nervous System (CNS). A well placed shot to the CNS causes immediate incapacitation, where the threat will no longer be able to function because of the loss of brain activity. With Type II shots, however, incapacitation is not immediate. These types of shots rely upon rapid or delayed forms of incapacitation that can be attributed to blood loss. They are dependent upon shot placement to vital organs, veins, and arteries that are located at armpit height/center mass, or in the pelvic girdle. Type II forms of incapacitation may also rely upon the creation of multiple wound channels to ensure rapid blood loss. Additionally, there is psychological incapacitation which relies upon how the threat reacts to being shot. This reaction, depending upon a variety of factors, could be positive in nature where they surrender out of the fear of being shot; or, it could be negative in nature, where the threat could become more aggressive in their actions toward the officer(s).

REFERENCES

A short course in exterior ballistics (2005). Retrieved from www.steyrscout. org/extbal.htm. Last visited: January 7th, 2006.

Amato, J.J., Syracuse, D., P.R. Seaver & N. Rich. (May, 1989). Bone as secondary missile: An experimental study in the fragmenting of bone by high-velocity missiles. Journal of trauma, 29(5), 609-612.

Azevedo, T.M., Volchan, E., Imbiriba, L.A., Rodrigues, E.C., Oliveira, J.M., Oliveira, L.F., Lutterbach, L.G. & C.D. Vargas. (May, 2005). A freezing like posture to pictures of mutilation. Psychophysiology, 42(3), 255-260.

Bailey, J.A. (July/August, 2005). Analyses of bullet wipe patterns on cloth targets. Journal of forensic identification, 55(4), 448-460.

Bartlett, C.S. (March, 2003). Clinical update: Gunshot wound ballistics. Clinical orthopedics and related research, 408, 28-57.

Bowyer, G.W. & Rossiter, N.D. (November, 1997). Management of gunshot wounds to the limbs. Journal of bone and joint surgery, 79(6), 1031-1036.

Bracha, H.S. (September, 2004). Freeze, flight, fright, faint: Adaptationist perspectives on the acute stress response spectrum. CNS spectrums, 9 (9), 679-685.

Bruice, P. (2004). Organic chemistry (4th ed.). Upper Saddle River, NJ: Prentice Hall.

Celens, E., Pirlot, M. & A. Chabotier. (1996). Terminal effects of bullets based on firing results in gelatin medium and in numerical modeling. Journal of trauma, 40(3), S27-S30.

Demetriades, D., Velmahos, G., Cornwell, E., Berne, T.V., Cobere, S., Paradeep, S.B., Belzberg, H. & J. Asensio. (February, 1997). Selective nonoperative management of gunshot wounds to the Anterior Abdomen. Archives of surgery, 132(2), 178-183.

Dodson, S. (April, 2001). Reality of the street? A practical analysis of offender gunshot wound reaction for law enforcement. Tactical briefs: Firearms tactical institute, 1-9.

Emergency War Surgery (2nd. ed). U.S. Army. Washington, D.C.

Erdogan, E., Izci, Y., Gonul, E., & E. Timurkaynak (2004). Ventricular injury following cranial gunshot wounds: Clinical study. Military medicine, 169(9), 691-695.

Fackler, M.L. (February, 1998). Civilian gunshot wounds and ballistics: Dispelling the myths. Emergency medicine clinics of North America, 16 (1), 17-28.

Fackler, M. L., (1994).: FBI 1993 wound ballistics seminar: Efficacy of heavier bullets affirmed. Wound Ballistics Review, 1(4): 8-9.

Fackler, M.L. (1987a). Bullet performance misconceptions. International defense review, 3, 369-370.

Fackler, M.L. (July, 1987b). What's wrong with the wound ballistics literature, and why. CA: Presidio of San Francisco, Letterman Army Institute of Research, Division of Military trauma Research, Institute Report No. 239.

Firearms tutorial: The Internet pathology laboratory for medical education. (2005). Retrieved from www-medlib.med.utah.edu/WebPath/webpath. html. Last visited: 1/07/06.

George, P.Y. & Goodman, P. (November, 1992). Radiographic appearance of bullet tracks in the ling. American journal of roentgenology, 159(5), 967-970.

Gray, H. (1977). Gray's anatomy. Random House.

Hall, J.N. (2000). Kinetic pulse: A study in bullet impact. Retrieved from www.kineticpulse.us/math/kp.html. Last visited: January 6, 2006.

Hardaway, R.M. (March, 2000). Traumatic shock alias post-trauma critical illness. The American surgeon, 66(3), 284-290.

Hatcher, J.S. (1966). Hatcher's notebook. Harrisburg, PA: Stackpole books.

Introduction to Naval weapons engineering, ES310 (1998). Weapons and Systems Engineering Department: Annapolis: United States Naval Academy. Retrieved from www.fas.org. Last visited: 1/6/2006.

Jussila, J. (May, 2005). Measurement of kinetic energy dissipation with gelatine fissure formation with special reference to gelatine validation. Forensic science international, 150(1), 53-62.

Jussila, J., Leppaniemi, A., Paronen, M., & E. Kulomaki. (May, 2005). Ballistic skin stimulant. Forensic science international, 150(1), 63-72.

Kaplan, J., Klose, R., Fossum, R. & V. DiMaio (December, 1998). Centerfire frangible ammunition: Wounding potential and other forensic concerns, American journal of forensic medicine and pathology, 19(4), 299-302.

Karger, B. (1995). Penetrating gunshots to the head and lack of immediate incapacitation. Review of case reports. International journal of legal medicine, 108(3), 117-126.

Karger, B. & Rand, S. (March, 1998). Multiple entrance wounds from one bullet due to the use of a silencer. American journal of forensic medicine & pathology, 19(1), 30-33.

Karger, B., Billeb, E., Koops, E., & B. Brinkmann (2002). Autopsy features for relevant discrimination between suicidal and homicidal gunshot injuries. International journal of legal medicine, 116, 273-278.

Korac, Z., Kelenc, D., Mikulic, D., Vukovic, D. & J. Nancevic. (December, 2001b). Terminal ballistics of the Russian AK 74 assault rifle: Two wounded patients and experimental findings. Military medicine, 166 (12), 1065-1068.

Korac, Z., Kelenc, D., Baskot, A., Mikulic, D. & J. Hancevic (2001c). Substitute ellipse of the permanent cavity in gelatin blocks and debridement of gun shot wounds. Military medicine, 166(8), 689-694.

Kuehne, J., Frankhouse, J., Modrall, G., Golshani, S., Aziz, I., Demetriades, D. & A.E. Yellin. (October, 1999). Determinants of survival after inferior vena cava trauma. The American surgeon, 65(10), 976-981.

Lepik, D. & Vasiliev, V. (2005). Comparison of injuries cause by the pistols Tokarev, Makarov and Glock 19 at firing distances of 10, 15 and 25 cm. Forensic science international, 151, 1-10.

Marr, J.D.F., Krige, J.E.J., & T. Terblanche (2000). Analysis of 153 gunshot wounds to the liver. British journal of surgery, 87, 1030-1034.

Marraccini, J.V., Lentz, K., & M.D. McKenney (April, 2001). Blood pressure effects of thorasic gunshot wounds: The role of bullet image diameter. The American surgeon, 67(4), 354-356.

Marshall, E. & Sanow, E.J. (2001), Stopping power: A practical analysis of the latest handgun ammunition. Boulder CO: Paladin Press.

Newgard, K. (1992). The physiological effects of handgun bullets: The mechanisms of wounding and incapacitation. Wound ballistics review, 1(3), 12-17.

Oehmichen, M., Meissner, C., Konig, H.G. & H.B. Gehl. (2004). Gunshot injuries to the head and brain caused by low-velocity handguns and rifles. Forensic science international, 146, 111-120.

Ordog, G.J., Wasserberger, J.A. & S. Balasubramaniam (May, 1988). Shotgun wound ballistics. Journal of trauma, 28(5), 624-631.

Patrick, U.W. (July, 14, 1989). Handgun wounding factors and effectiveness. Washington, D.C.: U.S. Department of Justice, Federal Bureau of Investigation.

Parks, R.W., Chrysos, E. & T. Diamond. (1999). Management of liver trauma. British journal of surgery, 86, 1121-1135.

Peters, C.E., Sebourn, C.L. & H.L. Crowder (1996). Wound ballistics of unstable projectiles: Part I: Projectile yaw and growth and retardation. Journal of trauma, injury, infection and critical care, 40(3), S10-S15.

Pinizzotto, A., Kern, H.A. & E.F. Davis. (October, 2004). One-shot drops. FBI law enforcement bulletin, 73(10), 14-23.

Pollack, S. & Rothchild, M.A. (September, 2004). Gunshot injuries as a topic of medicolegal research in the German-speaking countries from the beginning of the 20th century up to the present time. Forensic science international, 144(2-3), 201-211.

Russell, M.A. & Noguchi, T.T. (September, 1999). Gunshot wounds and ballistics: Forensic concerns. Topics in emergency medicine, 21(3), 1-10.

Sabin, S.L., Lee, D. & G. Har-El. (October, 1998). Low velocity gunshot injuries to the temporal bone. Journal of Laryngology and Otology, 122, 929-933.

Saferstein, R. (1990). Criminalistics (4th ed). Englewood Cliffs, New Jersey: Prentice Hall.

Sebourn, C.L. & Peters, C.E. (1996). Flight dynamics of spin-stabilized projectiles and the relationship to would ballistics. Journal of trauma, 40(3), S22-S25.

Shooting holes in wounding theories: The mechanics of terminal ballistics (2005). Retrieved from: www.rathcoombe.net/sci-tech/ballistics/myths.html. Last visited: January 6th, 2006.

Sierra Rifle Reloading Manual, (4th ed.). (1995). Sierra Bullets, L.P.

Silvia, A.J. (May, 1999). Mechanisms of injury in gunshot wounds: Myths and reality. Critical care nursing quarterly, 22(1), 69-74.

Sonden. A., Svensson, Bengt., Roman, N., Brismar., Palmblad., & B.T. Kjellstrom (2002). Mechanisms of shock wave induced endothelial cell injury. Lasers in surgery and medicine, 31, 233-241.

Spinks, J.L. (2005). Understanding arrow penetration. Retrieved from www.alaskafrontierarchery.com. Last visited: October 25, 2005.

Swan, K.G. & Swan, R.C. (1984). Man's best friend or man? The physiologist, 27(5), 347-349.

Swift, B., & Rutty, G.N. (January, 2004). The exploding bullet. Journal of clinical pathology, 57(1), 108.

Velmahos, G.C., Dematriades, E.E., Cornwell, H., Belzberg, J.M., Asenio, J., & T.V. Berne (1998). Selective management of renal gunshot wounds. British journal of surgery, 85, 1121-1124.

Walker, J.S. (2004). Physics (2nd ed.). (2004). Upper Saddle River, NJ: Prentice Hall.

White, K.M. (March, 1989). Injuring mechanisms of gunshot wounds. Critical care nursing clinics of North America, 1(1), 97-103.

Introduction

T arget analysis is the practice of studying shot groups to evaluate and diagnose any issues related to the fundamentals of marksmanship. The underlying goal of target analysis is to improve one's shooting performance through a critical analysis of their shot placement on the target. As this chapter will show, in the vast majority of cases, poor shot placement is not the fault of the gun (i.e. "my sights are off"). Instead, it is the fault of the user because s/he disrupted the sight picture and subsequent aim before the trigger released and the bullet exited the barrel of the firearm.

This chapter will assist the shooter in diagnosing some of the common problems related to shot placement. While there are several variables that can be attributed to the misalignment of the sights and subsequent poor shot placement, the common denominator of all the problems boils down to the fact that the shooter has failed to apply some of the basics of marksmanship. Through the analysis of shot patterns, specifically through the use of the "shot clock," and by following the recommended methods to correct these problems, this chapter will assist individuals in becoming more proficient in their shooting.

Performance vs. Outcome

One common problem that shooters have is that they are often overly concerned about shot placement to the point where the majority of their attention is no longer focused on the fundamentals of shooting (their performance). Instead, they are focused on the impacts or holes on the target (the outcome). Consider, for example, the fact that in many cases, as soon as the round leaves the barrel, the shooter immediately "eye sprints" to see where the round hit the target. If "eye sprinting" is not the problem, the shooter may fail to rapidly recover their sights back on the target (i.e. sight picture) or not have an effective follow through. These and other problems, especially trigger control, can be attributed to placing too much emphasis on the outcome and not enough attention on performance.

371

What a shooter may fail to recognize, however, is that their outcome is inexplicably tied to their preceding performance. As a consequence, concentrating solely on outcome is contradictory to being an effective shooter. Rather, what a shooter should be concerned about is how their style or performance leads to the positive outcome - a tight group of shots. This same concept can be applied to professional football players, particularly running backs. While their emphasis is scoring touchdowns (outcomes), they cannot achieve this outcome without using the proper techniques of the game (i.e. performance). Performing well by applying the basics of marksmanship before, during, and immediately after the shot will result in positive outcomes.

Target Analysis Techniques

One of the keys behind effective shot placement is to make sure that the basics of marksmanship are followed before, during, and after every shot. These basics include:

- Stance
- Grip
- Sight Alignment
- Trigger Control
- Follow Through
- Breathing

Figure 18-1 shows a simulated target that is divided into 8 different zones. These zones correspond to the common problems experienced with shot placement for right-handed shooters. For left-handed shooter's meanwhile, the left-handed version is the mirror image of Figure 18-1. For example, zone B should be switched with zone H; zone C with zone G; and, zone D with zone F. The key to using this chart is that the shooter must examine a series of shots that have been fired.

Target analysis is easy to do. First, the shooter should establish a center mass sight picture, aiming for the bull's eye, and then fire a series of shots (four or more) to establish a shot pattern or group. This shot pattern should then be used to diagnose any potential problems that the shooter may have, depending upon where the group is located on the target. After diagnosing the problem, the shooter must then correct that specific problem by following the prescribed methods of correction as listed in the following pages.

The shooter should not try any other techniques to correct their problem(s). For example, if rounds are impacting the target low-left (in the "F" zone) and the shooter is right handed, s/he may think that the best way to fix their problem is to adjust their sight picture to the high-right (e.g. "Kentucky wind-age"). While this may "fix" their immediate problem (shot place-ment), it will not correct the shooter's inherent problem, which is poor trigger control. In fact, this method of correction could lead to additional problems. Changing the sight picture to compensate for "jerking" the trigger, and then eventually mastering the trigger pull will subsequently result in the shooter placing their shot groups high and right. For this reason, the key is to keep the sights exactly where the shooter wants the rounds to impact, and then fix the identified problem in a correct manner.

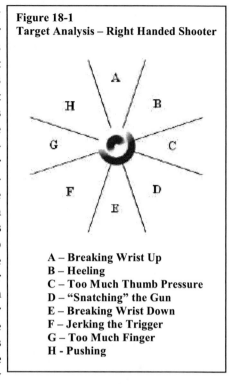

Figure 18-1
Target Analysis – Right Handed Shooter

A – Breaking Wrist Up
B – Heeling
C – Too Much Thumb Pressure
D – "Snatching" the Gun
E – Breaking Wrist Down
F – Jerking the Trigger
G – Too Much Finger
H - Pushing

One of the most common problems related to poor shot placement is anticipation of the recoil. In the majority of cases involving poor shot placement, the shooter is anticipating the release of the trigger and the subsequent recoil of the weapon. Because of this anticipation, just before the trigger releases and the bullet leaves the barrel, the shooter inadvertently (or unconsciously) changes their trigger pull in the context of speed, consistency, and equal pressure on the trigger face. In order to avoid this problem, shooters should make sure that the trigger releases with no disruption to the sights. The shooter should also remember to work with the recoil—not against it. Perhaps a natural reaction to the recoil (or some degree of force against the hand and body) is to fight against it. Fighting against the recoil, however, will lead to a variety of problems. As an alternative, by working with the recoil, and not fighting against it (in addition to following the basic firearm's fundamentals), a natural shooting rhythm will develop, which will result in a faster recovery back to the weapon's sights and target.

In the majority of cases involving poor shot placement, the actions taken by the shooter are not conscious. Instead, they are often unconscious that become habitual in nature. Because these problems may become habituated over time through poor practice, it is important to detect the problems early on in order to prevent the development of muscle memory and reflexive bad habits in shooting. Detecting these problems, however, will require a high degree of concentration and commitment to excellence in shooting.

There are several techniques that can be used to detect shot placement problems. One of the most common methods is to use dummy rounds. By inserting dummy rounds into the cartridge chamber or magazine of a firearm, the shooter will be able to see how their point of aim becomes disrupted without the effects of the weapon's recoil (which often serves to mask the shooter's unintentional movements). With jerking the trigger, for example, which is one of the most common problems for a shooter, s/he will be able to see their front sight dip to the low left (if the person is a right-handed shooter) and physically feel themselves force the muzzle downward. While the dummy round technique is perhaps the simplest and least expensive method to detect problems, depending upon the technologies that are available, shooters can also have their shots diagnosed through computerized range training systems such as Range 2000® and FATS® which both have the capacity to track a shooter's point of aim and trigger pull before, during, and after the round is fired.

Listed below are the diagnostic criteria to pinpoint flaws in a shooter's technique, based on the location of a group of shots on the target for a right-handed shooter.

Zone A: (12 O'Clock Position)

Shots placed in the A Zone (or 12 o'clock position) are characterized by the following problem(s):

- *Breaking the Wrist Up/Anticipating*

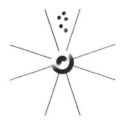

Breaking the wrist up is caused when the shooter anticipates the gun going off and its subsequent recoil. As the name suggests, this problem occurs when the shooter breaks their wrist upward just before the release of the trigger. This problem can be avoided by making sure that the wrist stays locked throughout the course of fire.

- *Tensing up of the Body/Anticipating*

  In other cases, a shooter may be relaxed just before the guns fires. However, as they anticipate the gun firing, part of or their entire body to some degree will tense up, causing the muscles in these areas (such as in the legs, shoulders, and arms) to seize up. As the body tenses up, meanwhile, sight alignment (as well as other fundamentals) may slightly change, where the shots may strike above the intended point of aim. This can be avoided by making sure that the body does not tense up prior to, during, and between shots that are fired.

- *"Riding the Recoil"*

  "Riding the Recoil" is also related to anticipating the trigger releasing and the gun discharging. What inadvertently happens in these cases is that the shooter is actually using their shoulder and arm muscles to lift the firearm in anticipation of the recoil, just before the weapon discharges. Lifting the arms subsequently results in a high 12 o'clock shot placement. In order to prevent this from happening, the shooter should keep the strong-arm wrist locked forward and not use the arm and shoulder muscles to lift the gun. Additionally, the body should naturally "flow" with the recoil of the firearm, letting the gun operate on its own in the context of its recoil, establishing a natural rhythm with the recoil of the firearm.

Zone B: (2 O'Clock Position)

Shots placed in the B Zone (or 2 o'clock position) are characterized by the following problem(s):

- *Heeling/Anticipating the Recoil*

  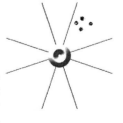

  Heeling occurs when the shooter applies pressure to the base and rear of the grip, with the heel part of the palm of their hand, just before the weapon fires. In effect, the shooter pushes the base of the firearm's grip with the heel of their palm to "fight the recoil," often because they inadvertently increase their grip strength. To avoid this problem, shooters must keep the same consistent grip strength throughout their course of fire. The shooter cannot increase their grip strength just prior to or during the course of fire.

Often heeling is the result of jerking the trigger. In an effort to control or compensate for the jerking problem, for example, the shooter may increase their grip strength in order prevent the gun and sights from dipping low-left. This action of heeling the firearm, however, then causes the rounds to hit at the 2 o'clock zone, instead.

- *Slack Wrist*

  The diagnosis of a slack wrist is simply a situation where the shooter's strong-arm wrist is too relaxed when the trigger releases and the bullet travels down the barrel. Relaxing the strong hand wrist (and not using the support hand properly) before the trigger releases will result in the round impacting the target in this region. By not supporting the weapon properly, it will essentially jump and/or rotate in the shooter's hands, where the rounds will impact the target in the 2 o'clock region. This problem can be avoided by making sure that the strong-arm wrist is locked forward. Additionally, the support arm/hand must be pulling straight back, toward the shooter, to make sure that there is even rearward pressure to further stabilize the wrist and firearm.

Zone C: (3 O'Clock Position)

Shots placed in the C Zone (or 3 o'clock position) are characterized by the following problem(s):

- *Thumbing/Too Much Thumb Pressure*

  If the strong and support hand thumbs are exerting pressure on the frame or slide of the firearm, this increased pressure against the left side of the firearm will force the front sight out of alignment and to the right, just before the trigger releases and the bullet leaves the barrel.
  To prevent this from occurring, the thumbs should be relaxed,

stacked on top of one another, and point forward and toward the threat throughout the course of fire.

Zone D: (4 O'Clock Position)

Shots placed in the D Zone (or 4 o'clock position) are characterized by the following problems:

- *Tightening the Grip while Pulling up on the Trigger*

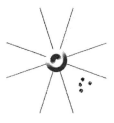

  This flaw is the result of the shooter increasing their grip strength and pulling upward, instead of straight back on the face of the trigger. The increase in grip strength disrupts and moves the front sight to the right. Pulling the trigger upward instead of straight to the rear, meanwhile, forces the front sight to dip or drop downward. The combination of these two actions will cause the rounds to impact low and right. To prevent this, the grip and grip strength must stay consistent throughout the course of fire and the trigger must be pulled straight to the rear, every time.

- *Snatching the Gun/Trigger*

  "Snatching the gun" occurs when the shooter aggressively grabs or squeezes the grip of the firearm with their entire hand (an example of this type of movement is when a person aggressively grabs an object off of a table, using their hand and forearm muscles to complete the task). In combination with this sudden, aggressive movement, the shooter may apply more pressure to the right side of the face of the trigger (the outside of the trigger), causing the front sight to become disrupted to the low-right, just prior to the trigger releasing and the round leaving the barrel. In order to prevent this from occurring, the shooter must properly grip the weapon and make sure that the trigger pull is smooth, consistent, and even. The shooter must also make sure that their grip strength stays consistent and does not change throughout the course of fire. The shooter must also make sure that their finger pressure is centered on the face of trigger and it is pulling straight to the rear.

Zone E: (6 O'Clock Position)

Shots placed in the E Zone (or 6 o'clock position) are characterized by the following problems:

- *Breaking the Wrist Downward*

    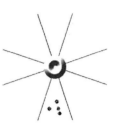

    Breaking the wrist downward occurs when the shooter breaks the wrist in a downward motion just before the trigger is released. It is the result of the shooter anticipating the weapon firing and the subsequent recoil. Because of this forward action, the wrist moves slightly downward, where the front sight dips and the rounds strike below their intended point of aim. Breaking the wrist downward can also be the result of relaxing the wrist just before the weapon fires. To prevent this from occurring, the wrist should be solidly locked throughout the course of fire.

Zone F: (8 O'Clock Position)

Shots placed in the F Zone (or 8 o'clock position), strike the target low and left and are characterized by the following problem(s):

- *Squeezing the Finger Tips*

    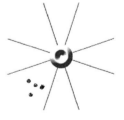

    This problem occurs when the shooter tenses up their finger tips just before the trigger releases in anticipation of the recoil. As the finger tips tense up, the resulting pressure on the side of the grip forces the front sight down and to the left, where the rounds subsequently impact the target low and left of the intended point of aim. This problem is usually found closer to the 8 o'clock position. To avoid this problem, the shooter should concentrate on maintaining the same grip strength in the context of how hard their fingers are gripping the firearm.

- *Jerking the* trigger

  Usually a problem related to jerking the trigger is located in the 7 o'clock area. Jerking can be attributed to the lack of strength, concentration, and anticipating the firearm's recoil. This is one of the most common problems encountered in shooting. Jerking occurs when the shooter aggressively pulls the trigger to the rear. Combined with this sudden, aggressive movement, the shooter applies more pressure to the left side of the trigger face, causing the front sight to become disrupted, and dip to the low and left. This uneven pressure, meanwhile, is often concentrated at the bottom left of the trigger face, further causing the front sights to inadvertently drop to the low-left. Like snatching, jerking is also attributed to the hand and forearm muscles tensing up just before the trigger releases. The key behind effective trigger control is that the shooter must build up positive pressure evenly on the face of the trigger. This pressure must also be consistent (not "jerky") until the trigger releases and the bullet leaves the barrel.

Zone G: (9 O'Clock Position)

Shots placed in the G Zone (or 9 o'clock position) are characterized by the following problem(s):

- *Too Much Finger on the Trigger*

  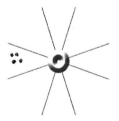

  Too much pressure on the left side of the trigger face when pulling the trigger to the rear will result in the front sight moving to the left just before the trigger releases. With this type of problem, the shooter must be aware that when pulling the trigger to the rear, there may be a natural tendency for the finger to curl or "hinge" to the left as it closes. Because of the natural tendency for it to curl and not pull straight to the rear, the shooter may inadvertently place too much trigger pressure on the left (or inside) side of the trigger face. This unequal pressure (more on the left than right side) will result in the front sight and muzzle of the firearm moving to the left and the rounds hitting in the "G" Zone. In order to prevent this from occurring, the shooter must concentrate on their trigger pull, making sure that their trigger finger is properly placed on the face of the trigger. They must also make sure that it is pulled straight to the rear.

Zone H: (10 O'Clock Position)

Shots placed in the H Zone (or 10 o'clock position) are characterized by the following problem(s):

- *Pushing/ Anticipating the Recoil*

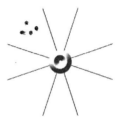

  Pushing occurs when the shooter tenses up just prior to the round being fired. In effect, the shooter is fighting against the natural recoil of the gun where they "push" the entire gun forward just before the trigger releases. By doing so, they push the firearm forward, causing the front sight to move high-left. Often, pushing the firearm can be seen when the shooter locks their elbow out just before the trigger releases. The key to avoiding this problem is to simply accept that fact that there will be some recoil that pushes against the shooter. The shooter should, therefore, work with the recoil and not push against it by consciously pushing against the gun or inadvertently tensing the body up which could also serve to "push" the gun forward just before it discharges.

- *Relaxing the Strong Arm Elbow*

  If the shooter should fail to lock out the strong-arm elbow or prematurely relax it just before the shot is released or fired, the point of impact may also be high left. By relaxing the elbow, the right arm will naturally "hinge" to the left. As it hinges to the left, the front sight and muzzle will also naturally move slightly upward and to the left. In order to prevent this from occurring, the strong-arm elbow should remain locked throughout the course of fire.

Other Common Shot Problems

No Groups

A "no group" pattern looks like a person took a handful of projectiles and threw them at the target. The shot pattern basically looks like a "splatter" of bullets. When a shooter has a "no group" pattern on their target, this indicates that the shooter may have a variety of problems. These problems could be as simple as failing to focus on sight alignment and establishing the sight picture. It could also be more complex, where the shooter has a variety of issues that confound effective shot placement.

In order to diagnose the specific problem with these types of groups, the shooter should first concentrate on sight alignment. After sight alignment is mastered, the shooter should then concentrate on their sight picture. Following these two procedures, a distinct pattern of shots should emerge, where the shooter can then diagnose any other issues (if any) that exist, and correct those identified problems.

Vertical Groups

Often referred to as a "zipper" or "buttons" because of the bullet group's vertical pattern, this problem can be attributed to the lack of strength, an unstable stance, and breathing incorrectly. These problems could exist separately or in combination with one another.

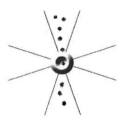

- *Lack of Strength*

    The shooter must have enough strength to hold the firearm in a stable, level manner. If, for example, a shooter has weak shoulder muscles, they will not be able to hold their arms and firearm up, especially when firing multiple shots, or shooting for long periods of time. This lack of strength may not necessarily cause the misalignment of the front sight. It will, however, cause a misalignment of the sight picture, where some or all of rounds that are fired will impact above and below their intended point of aim due to the repositioning of the front sight on the target or the front sight "floating" too much on the target.

- *Unstable Stance*

  Another problem related to vertical groups is an unstable stance, where the shooter may be rocking forward and backwards while shooting. Because of this forward and backward motion, the sight picture will be disrupted to the point where rounds may impact above or below the intended point of aim. This problem can also be attributed to changing one's stance during the course of fire.

- *Incorrect Breathing*

  Another explanation for vertical groups is incorrect breathing. If a person is breathing from their chest and not their abdomen, the rising chest wall could disrupt the sight picture to the point where there is a vertical shot pattern.

Horizontal Groups

Horizontal groups are often the result of an unstable stance where the shooter has too much lateral or side-to-side movement during the course of fire. This poor side-to-side stance causes the body to sway, which is reflected on the target by a horizontal shot pattern. Horizontal groups can also be attributed to lack of strength and the inability to maintain a strong, aggressive stance.

Overholding

Overholding occurs when the shooter waits too long to release the trigger because they are waiting for or trying to set up the "perfect shot." What actually happens when they wait for the "perfect shot," however, is that they may become fatigued from holding the firearm too long. They may also lose their ability to focus on the front sight, perhaps from the lack of oxygen. Overholding could also lead to hand tremors and the loss of fine motor skills. Shot patterns associated with overholding vary from person to person, depending upon the specific problems they have created. Overholding can be preventing by first recognizing that all shooters will have an arch of movement that could interfere with their "perfect shot."

With this in mind, what the shooter should strive for is the best possible shot, in light of their arch of movement.

Lack of Rhythm

All shooters develop a natural rhythm or a recurring pattern of activities when they shoot. This natural rhythm incorporates all of the fundamentals of shooting, the number of shots that are fired in a certain amount of time, the use of their trigger reset, getting the sights back on target (recovering), and the amount of time the shooter holds their sights on the target before releasing the trigger.

To address this issue, it should first be recognized that each shooter has a different style and rhythm that is unique to them. With this in mind, every shooter should make sure that they develop their own rhythm that adheres to the fundamentals of shooting, which is also maintained throughout the course of fire. A shooter's rhythm should also be smooth and fast. Consider for example, a shooter that has a good, smooth rhythm throughout the majority of their course of fire. Near the end of the sequence of fire, however, the shooter becomes anxious or lazy, breaking their smooth rhythm. Most likely this will be displayed on the target though an inconsistent shot pattern, where the last shot is not grouped with the previous shots.

Loss of Concentration

If a shooter should fail to concentrate on all of the basics they will become sloppy. Consider, for example, a person who is required to shoot a certain amount of rounds to qualify. Perhaps on the last round, they lose their mental concentration and simply "crank a round off" to get the task over with, in part because they are over-anxious. Regardless of the reasons why they have lost their concentration, shooters must train themselves to be continually conscious of their activities. This concentration must be maintained throughout the course of fire in order to deliver a flawless series of shots on the target.

Laziness

Laziness can be attributed to a shooter who is not committed to excellence, but mediocrity. Laziness is simply an attitudinal problem, where, mentally, the shooter does not care to strive for perfection. Instead, he or she simply hopes for the "good" shot. The lazy shooter accepts the minor problems that they have with the fundamentals of shooting and does little, if anything, to address their problems or engage in any remedial activities that would improve their performance. For example, a lazy shooter may consider a great performance as simply when all of their rounds impact within the scoring ring, regardless of where the groups were placed or how large their shot pattern was. Laziness should not be tolerated when shooting.

Conclusion

This chapter has provided the reader with an overview of some of the common problems associated with poor shot placement. Effective shot placement begins with an emphasis on the fundamentals of shooting. The lack of concentration on these skills, in combination with not developing the skills related to shooting, will result in unintended results and less-than-perfect outcomes. This will be readily shown on the target in the context of poor shot groups.

One way to diagnose specific problems related to the fundamentals of shooting, based on shot placement, is through the use of the "shot clock." By dividing the target into specific zones, a shooter will be able to determine why their shots hit in that particular zone, based on the specific problem(s) s/he has in the context of shooting fundamentals. As this chapter has pointed out, in the majority of cases, poor shot placement can often be attributed to the shooter anticipating the trigger releasing (and the bullet leaving the barrel). Because of this anticipation, they engage in a variety of actions that result in the front sight of the firearm becoming disrupted. Usually the issue is trigger control, which is one of the more common problems when shooting. If not trigger control, poor shot placement could also be attributed to anticipating the recoil of the firearm, where the shooter may engage in various unconscious actions including heeling and pushing.

In order to avoid these and other problems, shooters must always be fully concentrated on the fundamentals of shooting. In addition to concentrating on the fundamentals, shooters must also be aware that overholding, the lack of rhythm and concentration, and laziness are additional factors that contribute to poor shot placement. Through a commitment to training and concentrating on the basics, in conjunction with practice, the front sight of the firearm will no longer become disrupted. This, in turn, will result in consistently placed shot groups on the target within the intended point of aim.

392